T0228682

Cloud Computing:
Theory and Applications

Cloud Computing:
Theory and Applications

Edited by
Amanda Wegener

WILLFORD PRESS

www.willfordpress.com

Published by Willford Press,
118-35 Queens Blvd., Suite 400,
Forest Hills, NY 11375, USA

ISBN: 978-1-68285-596-6

Cataloging-in-Publication Data

Cloud computing : theory and applications / edited by Amanda Wegener.
    p. cm.
Includes bibliographical references and index.
ISBN 978-1-68285-596-6
1. Cloud computing. 2. Web services. 3. Electronic data processing--Distributed processing.
I. Wegener, Amanda.
QA76.585 .C56 2019
004.678 2--dc23

For information on all Willford Press publications
visit our website at www.willfordpress.com

Contents

Permissions

List of Contributors

Index

Preface

This book aims to highlight the current researches and provides a platform to further the scope of innovations in this area. This book is a product of the combined efforts of many researchers and scientists, after going through thorough studies and analysis from different parts of the world. The objective of this book is to provide the readers with the latest information of the field.

Cloud computing allows the storage of data over the internet. The user can access this data easily and swiftly from remote areas, through a number of different devices. Cloud computing is especially important for data exchange, retrieval and storage in organizational set-ups and frameworks. Cloud computing falls under the domain of information technology. Some of its significant aspects include utility computing, hardware virtualization, autonomic computing and service-oriented architecture, among many others. In recent years, there has been rapid progress in this field and its applications are finding their way across multiple industries. This book presents detailed information about the key concepts and theories of cloud computing. It also discusses the varying nature of the applications of this technology. The objective of this book is to give a general view of the diverse areas of this field. It is designed to serve as an ideal reference text for students and researchers alike.

I would like to express my sincere thanks to the authors for their dedicated efforts in the completion of this book. I acknowledge the efforts of the publisher for providing constant support. Lastly, I would like to thank my family for their support in all academic endeavors.

Editor

Fast methods for designing circulant network topology with high connectivity and survivability

Rui Lu

Abstract

This paper proposes two fast methods to design network topologies with high connectivity and survivability based on circulant graph theory. The first method, namely, the Combination Method (CM), investigates the average distances of circulant graphs with different combinations of chordal jumps, and tries to locate the optimal one among them. For this purpose, empirical formulas are proposed to describe the fluctuation features of average distances on curved surfaces. Furthermore, an enhanced Local Search Method (LSM) is proposed to find the local minimum points in troughs of the surfaces. The second method, namely, the Spider Web Method (SWM), is based on a bionic concept deriving from observation of the spider web, which is a classical example of network connectivity and survivability in natural world. The relation between CM and SWM in certain situations is also discussed. Finally, the connectivity and survivability of the topologies designed by CM and SWM are verified via simulated experiments involving vertex destruction.

Keywords: Network, Topology design, Circulant graph, Average distance, Local search method

Introduction

Topology design plays an important role in network planning. Various topologies have been studied and analyzed for different networks [1–3]. A circulant graph outperforms other topologies owing to its low message delay, high connectivity, and strong survivability [4–8]. Therefore, it has been widely employed in many technical fields such as telecommunication networks, computer networks, parallel processing systems, and social networks [9–12].

The connectivity and survivability of circulant graph networks can be evaluated by several metrics, such as average distance and connectivity ratio [2, 12–15]. The average distance is preferred as the prime optimization objective for it effectively represents network connectivity. In general, the smaller the average distance is, the shorter the delay is. Although network with complete graph topology has the minimum average distance of 1, the demand of a huge number of nodes and link resources usually render it impractical in projects.

Therefore, the performance of circulant graphs with limited resources is a major focus of network planning. Lower bounds and heuristic algorithms locating the minimum average distance of a circulant graph have been proposed [2, 6, 15]. Furthermore, the average distance of a recursive circulant graph, i.e., a special type of circulant graph, has also been investigated [16]. However, the optimal jump sequence of a circulant graph can be determined only when its degree is 4.

In this paper, we propose two fast methods to construct network topology with small average distance and high connectivity ratio based on circulant graph theory and bionics. Furthermore, we verify the effectiveness of the proposed methods by simulated experiments.

The remainder of this paper is organized as follows: In section Definitions of chordal ring, average distance and connectivity ratio, the concepts of circulant graphs and evaluation metrics are introduced. In section The Combination Method for topology design, we propose a Combination Method (CM) that develops formulas and algorithms to construct a circulant graph with a relatively minimum average distance, based on the features and characteristics of the average distance fluctuation

Correspondence: lurui@cert.org.cn
National Computer Network Emergency Response Technical Team/
Coordination Center of China, Beijing, China

curves. A Local Search Method (LSM) is also developed to optimize the search for the jump sequence with the minimum average distance. In section The Spider Web Method for topology design, we propose a more intuitive design method, namely, the Spider Web Method (SWM). This method is typically effective when the degree of each node is 4. In section Survivability experiments, survivavility experiments are implemented to verify the survivability of topologies designed by CM and SWM. Different nodes and links are destroyed enumerately, and the worst connectivity ratios of the networks are recorded and compared. Finally, research results in this paper are summarized and concluded.

Definitions of chordal ring, average distance and connectivity ratio

Circulant graph and chordal ring

A circulant graph is a special case of a Cayley graph. Suppose that $G(V, E)$ ($V = \{v_1, v_2, ...,v_m\}$, $E = \{e_1, e_2, ..., e_n\}$) is a graph with m vertices and n edges. The circulant graph can be defined as follows [2, 13]:

Definition 1: $G(V, E)$ is a simple graph with m vertices and n edges. There are integers $w_1, w_2, ..., w_j$ ($w_1 < w_2 < ... < w_j < (m + 1)/2$) that represent a jump sequence. Two vertices v_k and v_l of V are connected if and only if $(k + w_i)$ mod $m = l$, or $(k - w_i)$ mod $m = l$. This graph is defined as a circulant graph. A circulant graph with j jumps is usually denoted by CG(m; $w_1, w_2, ..., w_j$) or CG(m; W) with jump sequence $W = \{w_1, w_2, ..., w_j\}$, and $|W| = j$.

This definition does not guarantee that a circulant graph is connected. For example, CG(8; 1, 2) is a connected circulant graph, but CG(8; 2, 4) is not connected. Boesch and Tindell [5] found that a circulant graph is connected if and only if the greatest common divisor gcd($m, w_1, w_2, ...,w_j$) is equal to 1. Such a graph is always known as a connected circulant graph. Furthermore, it has been proved that every connected circulant graph has a Hamiltonian cycle [17]. In particular, a complete graph can always be considered as a combination of all CG(m; w_i) ($1 \le i \le \lfloor m/2 \rfloor$), which are considered as basic parts, as shown in Fig. 1.

In addition, the chordal ring network is introduced. There are two definitions for a chordal ring [13].

Definition 2: If a circulant graph CG(m, W) has w_1 equal to 1, it is known as a chordal ring. The edges with $w_i \ne w_1$ ($2 \le i \le j$) are denoted by chords of length w_i.

Definition 3: $G(V, E)$ is a simple graph with m vertices and n edges. Vertices $v_1, v_2, ...,v_m$ in V are connected in sequence into a Hamiltonian cycle. There are integers $w_1, w_2, ..., w_j$ ($w_1 < w_2 < ... < w_j < (m + 1)/2$). Two vertices v_k and v_l of V are connected if and only if k and l are odd numbers, and $(k + w_i)$ mod $m = l$. This graph is defined as a chordal ring. A circulant graph with j chords is usually denoted by CR(m, w_1, w_2, ..., w_j) or CR(m, W).

In this work, we consider the former definition of a chordal ring, i.e., Definition 2. From this definition, it can be deduced that a chordal ring is a special case of a connected circulant graph.

Average distance

The average distance $\bar{D}$ is defined as the average length of the shortest paths between any two nodes in the network [2]. It is illustrated on the basis of bi-directed graphs, which are essentially undirected graphs with edges represented by bi-directed arrows instead of full lines [18]. $\bar{D}$ can be expressed as

$$\bar{D} = \frac{\sum_{v_i \in V} \sum_{v_j \in V, v_j \ne v_i} D_{ij}}{m(m-1)} \qquad (1)$$

D_{ij} is the shortest path distance between vertices v_i and v_j. In general, the shortest path distance can be expressed as

$$D_{ij} = \min \sum_{e_{ij} \in E} c_{ij} x_{ij}$$

$$s.t. \quad \sum_{j:e_{ij} \in E} x_{ij} - \sum_{j:e_{ji} \in E} x_{ji}$$
$$= \begin{cases} 1, & i = s, \\ -1, & i = t, \quad x_{ij} \ge 0 \quad (2) \\ 0, & i \ne s, t. \end{cases}$$

In the definition of D_{ij}, x_{ij} denotes whether there is an edge e_{ij} from v_i to v_j on the path from v_s to v_t, and c_{ij} denotes the cost of edge e_{ij}. They can be expressed as follows:

$$x_{ij} = \begin{cases} 1 & e_{ij} \text{ is on the path from } v_s \text{ to } v_t \\ 0 & e_{ij} \text{ is not on the path from } v_s \text{ to } v_t \end{cases} \quad (3)$$

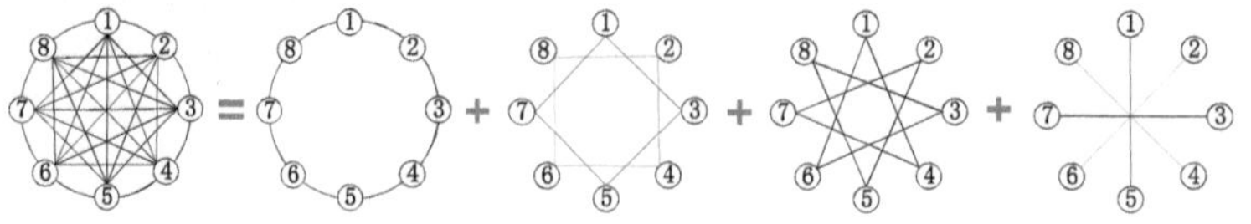

Fig. 1 Decomposition of a complete graph

$$c_{ij} = \begin{cases} 1 & \textit{If there is an edge between } v_i \textit{ and } v_j \\ +\infty & \textit{If there is no edge between } v_i \textit{ and } v_j \end{cases} \quad (4)$$

According to the isomorphism of a circulant graph, $\bar{D}$ can be simplified as [19–23]

$$\bar{D} = \frac{\sum_{v_j \in V, v_j \neq v_1} D_{1j}}{m-1} \quad (5)$$

A typical lower bound for the average distance is the Moore bound [2]. However, the Moore bound is attainable only for some special topologies [2, 6].

A circulant graph with a jump relatively prime with m is isomorphic to a chordal ring. Therefore, its average distance is equal to that of the corresponding chordal ring. In most cases, the optimal distance of a chordal ring is equal to that of a circulant with the same m. The smallest m that does not fit this rule is 450, according to the exhaustive research of Fiol [24, 25].

According to the definition of a circulant graph, there are $C(\lfloor m/2 \rfloor, j)$ circulant graphs with different W for certain m and j. Correspondingly, the number of chordal rings for the same m and j is $C(\lfloor m/2 \rfloor - 1, j - 1)$, which is $j/\lfloor m/2 \rfloor$ the number of circulants on the same scale.

Connectivity ratio

Connectivity ratio is defined as the ratio of the number of reachable node pairs to the total number of node pairs in the network, and it can be calculated as

$$C = \frac{\sum_{i \in V} \sum_{j \in V, j \neq i} l_{ij}}{m(m-1)}, \text{ subject to}$$

$$l_{ij} = \begin{cases} 1 & \textit{there is a path from } v_i \textit{ to } v_j; \\ 0 & \textit{there is no path from } v_i \textit{ to } v_j. \end{cases} \quad (6)$$

The maximum network connectivity ratio for a network with q node failures can be expressed as

$$C_{q,\max} = \frac{(m-q)(m-q-1)}{m(m-1)} \quad (7)$$

Assuming that the probability of q node failures is p_q, we propose the probability weighted connectivity, calculated as $\bar{C} = \sum_{q=1}^{m} p_q C_q$

$\bar{C}$ is more suitable for measuring network survivability in the event of a disaster that may take a heavy toll.

The Combination Method for topology design

Average distance of chordal ring

In this section, the average distance of a chordal ring is calculated in an enumerated manner, and some

characteristics are deduced. The number of edges in a chordal ring $CR(m, W)$ is given by

$$n = \begin{cases} jm & w_j \neq \dfrac{m}{2} \\ \left(j - \dfrac{1}{2}\right)m & w_j = \dfrac{m}{2} \end{cases} \quad \left(1 \leq j \leq \dfrac{m}{2}\right) \quad (8)$$

The average distance of chordal rings for $j = 1$ and 2 has already been investigated; however, the average distance of more general chordal rings is still being studied. All these chordal rings are discussed stepwise:

① If $j = 1$, n is equal to m ($m \geq 3$) and the chordal ring is a Hamiltonian cycle. The average distance of the Hamiltonian cycle can be deduced from the following proposition:

Proposition 1: $G(V, E)$ is a Hamiltonian cycle, $|V| = m$ ($m \geq 3$), $|E| = n$ ($n = m$). If m is odd, its average distance is $(m + 1)/4$; if m is even, its average distance is $(1/4)[1/(m - 1) + m + 1]$.

② If $j = 2$, the average distance of the chordal rings can be expressed as a function $\bar{D} = f(m, w_1, w_2)$ with $w_1 = 1$. However, this function becomes too complex to be expressed analytically. We draw a curve that connects discrete average distance points that vary with w_2, as shown in Fig. 2. This figure shows 3 features of the average distance that varies with w_2-jump:

First, there are several local minimum values scattered in the troughs among several local peak values. The values of the local minimum average distances do not differ significantly and are very close to the values of the global minimum points among them. All of them contribute to the flat envelope at the bottom of the curve.

Second, there are local maximum average distance points near $(2/k)w_{\max}$, $[4/(2k + 1)]w_{\max}$ ($k \geq 2$), where $w_{max} = \lfloor m/2 \rfloor$. The values of the peaks are approximately linearly proportional to their positions when k is small. Specifically, the average distance is nearly $(2/k)\bar{D}_{\max}$ at points $w_2 = (2/k)w_{\max}$. Further, $\bar{D}_{\max}$ is the average distance when $w_2 = w_{\max}$. However, if k is large, the peaks cannot be resolved and is no longer linearly proportional to its position. The peaks can clearly be observed along the red and green lines in Fig. 2.

The tendency of the optimal average distances varying with m is presented in Fig. 3. Although it has been proved that the average distance does not increase monotonically with m [24], it approximately has a relation with m. From Fig. 3, the global minimum average distance in our topology with $n = 2m$ is nearly proportional to $\sqrt[2]{m}$. The relation between $\bar{D}_{\min}$ and m can be represented approximately as

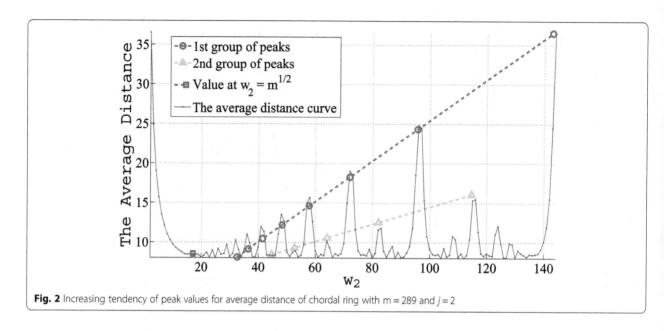

Fig. 2 Increasing tendency of peak values for average distance of chordal ring with $m = 289$ and $j = 2$

$$\bar{D}_{\min} \approx 0.47\left(\sqrt[2]{m} - \sqrt[2]{5}\right) + 1 \quad (9)$$

③ If $2 < j \leq \lfloor m/2 \rfloor$, the average distance of the chordal ring can be expressed as a function as follows:

$$\bar{D} = f\left(m, w_1, \dots, w_i, \dots, w_j\right) \quad \begin{pmatrix} w_1 = 1 \\ 2 < w_i \leq \left\lfloor \dfrac{m}{2} \right\rfloor, 2 \leq i \leq j \\ w_i < w_k, i < k \leq j \end{pmatrix}$$

$$(10)$$

There are $C(\lfloor m/2 \rfloor - 1, j - 1)$ choices for $W = \{w_1, w_2, \dots, w_j\}$. Figure 4 shows an example of $\bar{D}$ varying with w_2 and w_3 ($w_1 = 1$). Even though the curved surface is rough, the envelope of the local minimum points is on a relatively flat surface. In Fig. 11, several peak sequences can be found radiating with increasing peak values from positions where w_2 and w_3 are small. They are local maximum points at (w_2, w_3), with w_3 near $(2/k)w_{\max}$ or $[4/(2k + 1)]w_{\max}$ and w_2 near $(2/s)w_3$ or $[4/(2s + 1)]w_3$ ($k \geq 2$, $s \geq 2$).

Empirical formulas of the minimum average distance values are also studied by a curve fitting method.

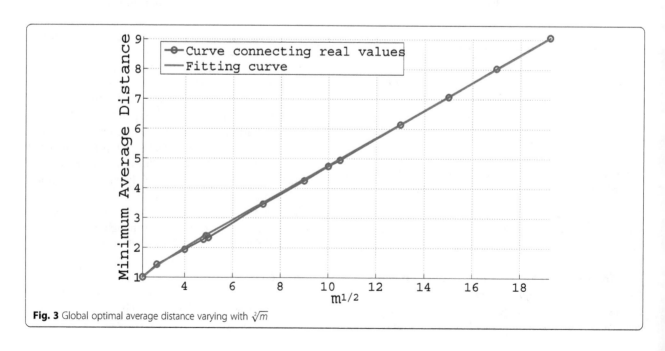

Fig. 3 Global optimal average distance varying with $\sqrt[2]{m}$

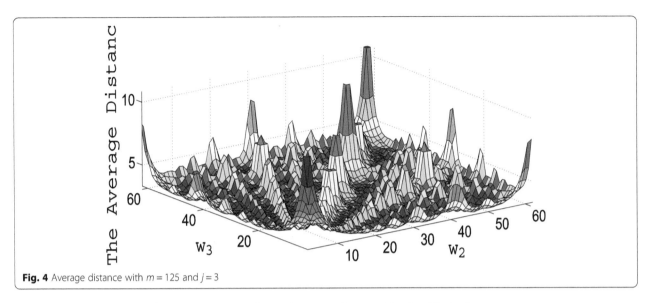

Fig. 4 Average distance with $m = 125$ and $j = 3$

The shortest average distance varying with j and m can be approximately expressed as

$$\bar{D}_{min}(j, m) \approx \begin{cases} \dfrac{j}{4}\left[0.94 + \dfrac{4j-5}{m}\right]\left[m^{\frac{1}{j}} - (2j+1)^{\frac{1}{j}}\right] + 1 & 2 \leq j < \left\lfloor\dfrac{m}{2}\right\rfloor \\ 1 & j \geq \left\lfloor\dfrac{m}{2}\right\rfloor \end{cases}$$

$$(11)$$

To verify the effectiveness of the formula, we compare the real $\bar{D}_{min}$ selected in enumerated manner according to the definition of average distance, with that calculated using formula (11). The result is presented in Fig. 5. According to the empirical formula described above, $\bar{D}_{min}$ is approximately proportional to $j\,m^{1/j}$.

The Combination Method

The idea of Combination Method is to select the optimal combination of chordal jumps by avoiding the peaks on the curved surface of the average distance. The formula for different number of jumps (j) is proposed as follows.

① If $j = 2$, the average distance curve has a rough surface which does not vary monotonous with w_2 and is hard for choosing the optimal w_2-jump. However, if the peak positions can be avoided, some local minimum points are still locatable. In this work, two peak avoidance methods are developed: The first method is Global Peak Avoidance (GPA). As shown by the pink marker in Fig. 6, there is a relatively slow varying region that has very small average distance values. Although the values may

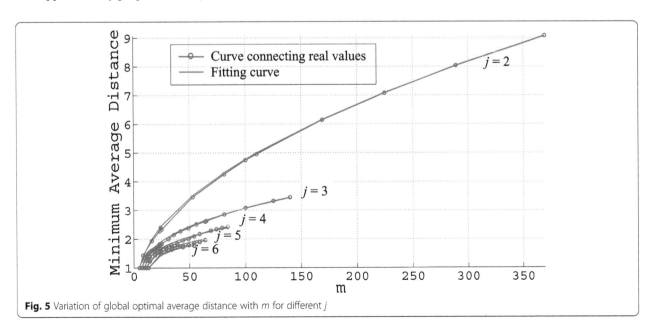

Fig. 5 Variation of global optimal average distance with m for different j

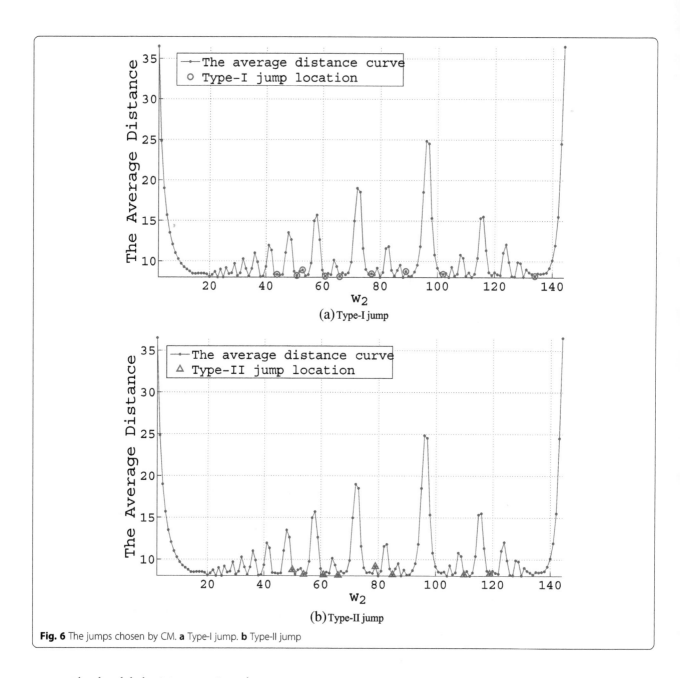

Fig. 6 The jumps chosen by CM. **a** Type-I jump. **b** Type-II jump

not be the global minimum points, they are very close to the optimal ones. We can quantitatively locate w_2-jump in this region as

$$w_2 = \left\lfloor \sqrt[2]{m} \right\rfloor \qquad (12)$$

For example, for $m = 289$, $w_2 = 17$, and the corresponding $\bar{D}_{sel} = 8.5$. This is very close to the minimum average distance of 8.0278.

The second method is Local Peak Avoidance (LPA). This method derives from the motivation to select jump sequence W in the trough between peaks near the positions of $(2/k)w_{\max}$, $[4/(2k+1)]w_{\max}$.

$$w_2 = \left\lfloor (2/k)w_{\max} \pm \beta \right\rfloor, \quad \beta = \sqrt[2]{\left[\frac{2}{k} - \frac{2}{k+1}\right]m} \quad (13)$$

$$w_2 = \left\lfloor [4/(2k+1)]w_{\max} \pm \gamma \right\rfloor, \qquad (14)$$

$$\gamma = \sqrt[2]{\left[\frac{4}{2k+1} - \frac{2}{k+1}\right]\left(\frac{m}{2}\right)}$$

The former w_2 is termed as Type-I jump, whereas the latter is termed as Type-II jump.

A simulation is implemented to verify these formulas. The chordal ring with $m = 289$ is still

Table 1 An instance of jump sequence selection

(a) Type-I

k_2	Col.	2		3		4	
k_3							
2	(w_2,w_3)	—	—	—	—	—	—
	D_{sel}	—	—	—	—	—	—
	(w_2,w_3)	—	(48,55)	(40,55)	(32,55)	(30,55)	(24,55)
	D_{sel}	—	3.3871	3.7419	3.4516	3.5161	3.6129
3	(w_2,w_3)	—	(39,45)	(33,45)	(26,45)	(25,45)	(19,45)
	D_{sel}	—	4.0645	3.6613	3.6452	3.5161	3.3871
	(w_2,w_3)	—	(31,36)	(27,36)	(20,36)	(20,36)	(15,36)
	D_{sel}	—	3.5323	3.8226	3.6613	3.6613	3.5806
4	(w_2,w_3)	—	(29,34)	(26,34)	(19,34)	(19,34)	(14,34)
	D_{sel}	—	3.8871	3.3387	3.7581	3.7581	3.3871
	(w_2,w_3)	—	(22,27)	(21,27)	(15,27)	(15,27)	(11,27)
	D_{sel}	—	3.6290	3.4194	3.8871	3.8871	3.4355

(b) Type-II

k_2	Col.	2		3		4	
k_3							
2	(w_2,w_3)	—	(51,52)	(41,52)	(36,52)	(31,52)	(28,52)
	D_{sel}	—	4.5645	3.9677	4.1774	4.1290	3.5161
	(w_2,w_3)	—	(41,46)	(33,46)	(29,46)	(26,46)	(22,46)
	D_{sel}	—	3.9516	3.9839	3.4194	3.6452	3.8710
3	(w_2,w_3)	—	(33,37)	(27,37)	(23,37)	(21,37)	(18,37)
	D_{sel}	—	3.4677	3.4194	3.4194	3.4032	4.5161
	(w_2,w_3)	(30,33)	(26,33)	(22,33)	(18,33)	(17,33)	(14,33)
	D_{sel}	5.1290	3.6935	3.5968	3.5484	4.0323	3.4032
4	(w_2,w_3)	—	(25,29)	(20,29)	(17,29)	(16,29)	(13,29)
	D_{sel}	—	3.5645	3.6129	3.3710	3.5484	3.7419
	(w_2,w_3)	(23,25)	(19,25)	(16,25)	(14,25)	(13,25)	(10,25)
	D_{sel}	4.5968	3.5323	3.5484	3.7097	4.5968	3.4677

—: Denotes that W is out of the range of definition

considered as an instance. For Type-I jump, select $k = \{2, 3, 4, 5, 6\}$, and calculate w_2 that complies with the Type-I jump formula (13). After the removal of w_2 from the range of $(1, w_{\max})$, the results are obtained as shown in Fig. 6 (a).

Similarly, for the Type-II jump, select $k = \{2, 3, 4, 5\}$, and calculate w_2 that complies with the Type-II jump formula (14). The results are shown in Fig. 6 (b). The mean value of the average distance of the Type-I jump location $\bar{D}_{sel-Type-I}$ is 8.3927, and that of the Type-II jump location $\bar{D}_{sel-Type-II}$ is 8.3733. They are also very close to the optimal average distance of 8.0278.

② If $j = 3$, troughs with relatively small values on the average distance surface can also be found.

Similarly, this can be accomplished by avoiding local peaks. We select two types of $W = (1, w_2, \ldots, w_i, \ldots, w_j)$ $(2 \le i < j)$. For the Type-I jump sequence,

Table 2 Local search algorithm

Step 1: Calculate the set of jump sequence points surrounding W, which can be denoted by $W' = \{w_1', w_2', \ldots, w_j'\}$, with $w_i' \in (w_i - a, w_i + a)$. Calculate $\bar{D}_{center} = f(m, W)$

Step 2: Calculate all $\bar{D}_{neigh} = f(m, W')$, and determine the W'_{neigh_min} that corresponds to the minimum $\bar{D}_{neigh}$ within the neighborhood. The minimum $\bar{D}_{neigh}$ is denoted by $\bar{D}_{neigh\ min}$.

Step 3: If $\bar{D}_{neigh\ min} < \bar{D}_{center}$, set $W = W'_{neigh\_min}$, $\bar{D}_{center} = \bar{D}_{neigh\ min}$, and goto Step 1. Otherwise, output W'_{neigh_min}.

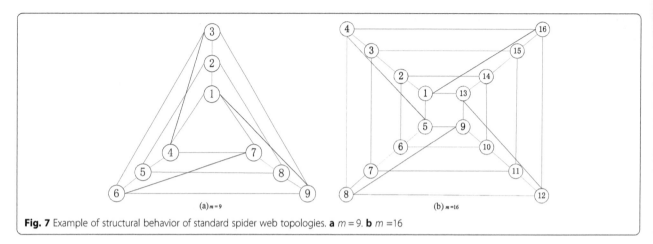

Fig. 7 Example of structural behavior of standard spider web topologies. **a** $m = 9$. **b** $m = 16$

$$w_j = \left\lfloor (2/k_j) w_{\max} \pm \beta_j \right\rfloor, \quad \beta_j = \sqrt[2]{\left[\frac{2}{k_j} - \frac{2}{k_j + 1}\right] m}$$

$$(15)$$

$$w_i = \left\lfloor (2/k_i) w_{i+1} \pm \beta_i \right\rfloor, \quad \beta_i = \sqrt[2]{\left[\frac{2}{k_i} - \frac{2}{k_i + 1}\right] (2w_{i+1})}$$

$$(16)$$

For the Type-II jump sequence,

$$w_j = \left\lfloor [4/(2k_j + 1)] w_{\max} \pm \gamma_j \right\rfloor,$$

$$\gamma_j = \sqrt[2]{\left[\frac{4}{2k_j + 1} - \frac{2}{k_j + 1}\right] \left(\frac{m}{2}\right)}$$

$$(17)$$

$$w_i = \left\lfloor [4/(2k_i + 1)] w_{i+1} \pm \gamma_i \right\rfloor,$$

$$\gamma_i = \sqrt[2]{\left[\frac{4}{2k_i + 1} - \frac{2}{k_i + 1}\right] w_{i+1}}$$

$$(18)$$

When $m = 125$ and $j = 3$, the average distances of the selected W according to the above formulas, are listed in Table 1. From the experiments, the mean values of the average distances selected by the Type-I and Type-II peak avoidance methods are 3.6252 and 3.8170, respectively. They are very close to the optimal average distance of 3.3226.

The Local Search Method for further optimization

In this section, Adaptive algorithm is devloped to minimize the average distance, based on the conclusions made above.

In general, An adaptive algorithm is divided into two steps: configuration of the initial parameters and iteration of the objective function. In this context, the parameter is

the jump sequence $W = \{w_1, w_2, ..., w_j\}$ with a fixed number of vertices m and j jumps. The objective function is the average distance $\bar{D} = f(m, w_1, ..., w_i, ..., w_j)$ in equation (12). The algorithm is described as follows.

① Initial value for iteration

The initial W can be configured by the peak avoidance method mentioned above. Using these methods, W with a relatively small average distance can be achieved.

The initial step for iteration can be configured as α.

② Optimization by local search method

A local search method is an algorithm that searches for the local minimum average distance of a chordal ring. The details of the algorithm are presented in Table 2.

This local search process starts from different initial W in parallel; all these local optimal results are compared, and the minimum one which is closest to the global optimal point is chosen. The chordal ring

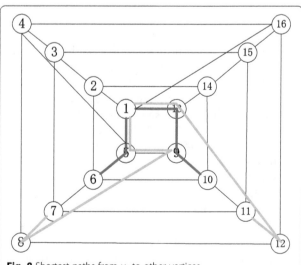

Fig. 8 Shortest paths from v_1 to other vertices

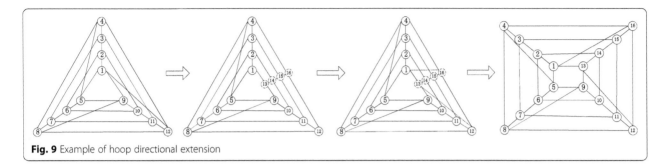

Fig. 9 Example of hoop directional extension

with $m = 289$ and $j = 2$ is considered as an instance. $w_2 = 79$ is an initial jump according to the peak avoidance method. After one iteration of the local search algorithm, $w_2 = 80$, and the corresponding $\bar{D}_{center} = 8.0278$, which is equal to the global optimal average distance.

The Spider Web Method for topology design

The spider web method is proposed based on the bionic phenomenon of robust nets weaved by spiders.

Design method description

For a graph with $m = k^2$ ($k \geq 3$), where the degree of each vertex is 4, we can construct our robust topology as follows:

① Divide m vertices into k groups with each group containing k vertices. The groups are numbered from 1 to k. The vertices in group i ($1 \leq i \leq k$) are denoted by $V_i = (v_{k+i}, v_{2k+i}, \ldots, v_{jk+i}, \ldots, v_{(k-1)k+i})$ ($0 \leq j \leq k-1$).

② Connect the vertices in each group into a ring.

③ For every j, connect vertices v_{jk+i} in all groups from V_1 to V_k into a line.

④ For every j, connect vertices v_{jk+k} and $v_{[(j+1)\%k]\cdot k+1}$ with an edge.

An example of this structural behavior of spider web topologies with 9 and 16 vertices is shown in Fig. 7.

There are three types of edges in this figure. The edges in red are generated in step 2 to construct rings; thus, they are termed as hoop directional edges. The edges in blue are generated in step 3 to construct lines; thus, they are termed as radial directional edges. The edges in black are generated in step 4 to connect two vertices on neighboring radial directional lines and rings with the largest difference in group indices; they are termed as bevel edges. Because these topologies are very similar to a spider web when the number of nodes is large, we refer to them as standard spider web topologies.

In addition, an obvious conclusion is that the average distance of a standard spider web topology where the number of vertices is $m = k^2$ is given by $\bar{D} = k/2 = \sqrt[2]{m}/2$.

Proof:

We assume that k is even. A path length is a combination of three parts: hoop sub-path, radial sub-path, and bevel sub-path. First, the distance from vertex v_1 to the other vertices is considered. For vertices with smaller indices on a radial directional line, the shortest path can go along the cycle first, and then, move up along the radial direction line to the destination vertex, as shown by the red path in Fig. 8. For vertices with larger indices on a radial directional line, the shortest path can go along the cycle first, and then move along a bevel edge and down the radial direction line to the destination vertex, as shown by the blue path in Fig. 8.

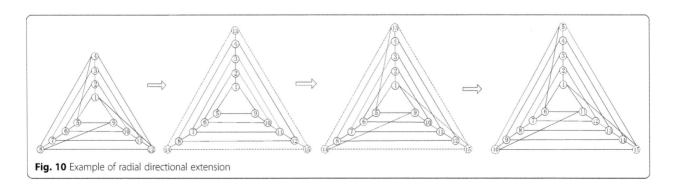

Fig. 10 Example of radial directional extension

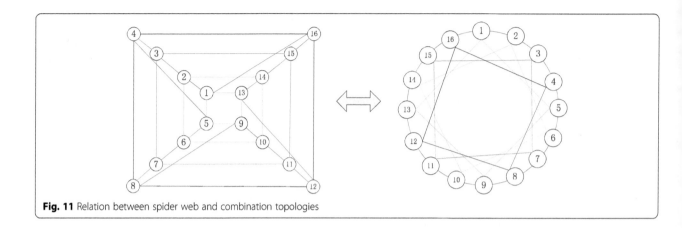

Fig. 11 Relation between spider web and combination topologies

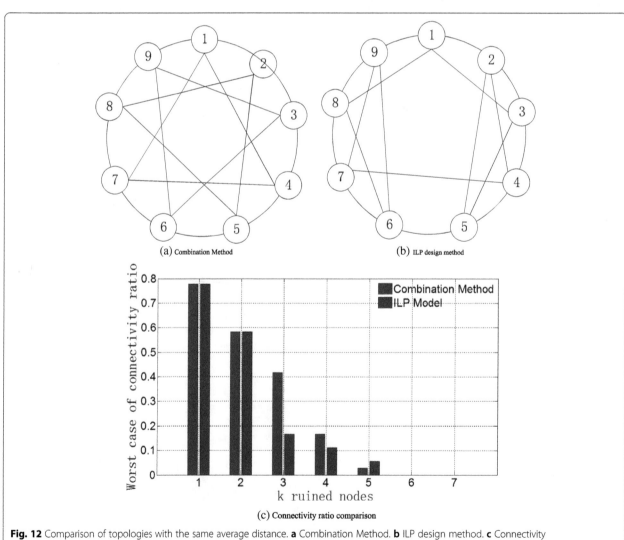

Fig. 12 Comparison of topologies with the same average distance. **a** Combination Method. **b** ILP design method. **c** Connectivity ratio comparison

The sum of the shortest paths from v_1 to other vertices can be written as

$$L = \left[\frac{k}{2}\left(\sum_{i=0}^{\frac{k}{2}}i + \sum_{i=2}^{\frac{k}{2}}i + 2\cdot\sum_{i=1}^{\frac{k}{2}}i\right) + 2\cdot k\sum_{i=1}^{\frac{k}{2}-1}i\right]$$
$$= \frac{k}{2}\left(k^2-1\right)$$

Because every vertex in the spider web is equally important, the average distance can be written as

$$\bar{D} = \frac{mL}{m(m-1)} = \frac{k}{2} = \sqrt[2]{m}\,\frac{-}{2}$$

Similarly, when k is odd, we can come to the same conclusion.

Therefore, the average distance of a standard spider web is $\sqrt[2]{m}/2$.

Extension of spider web topologies

Spider web topologies can be extended in a very intuitive manner. There are two main directions for the extension of spider web topologies: hoop directional extension and radial directional extension.

For hoop directional extension, one vertex is added to each vertex group and is connected into the corresponding ring between the vertices with the maximum and minimum indices in the group. Then, the new vertices are connected into a radial directional line. Finally, bevel edges are added before and after the new radial directional line. A topology extended from 12 vertices to 16 vertices is shown as an example in Fig. 9.

For radial directional extension, s vertices are added to the graph, and they are connected into a new ring. Each radial directional line is extended to connect a vertex on the new ring. The bevel edges start from the new vertex and extend to the vertex with the minimum index on the neighboring radial directional line. A topology extended from 12 vertices to 15 vertices is shown as an example in Fig. 10.

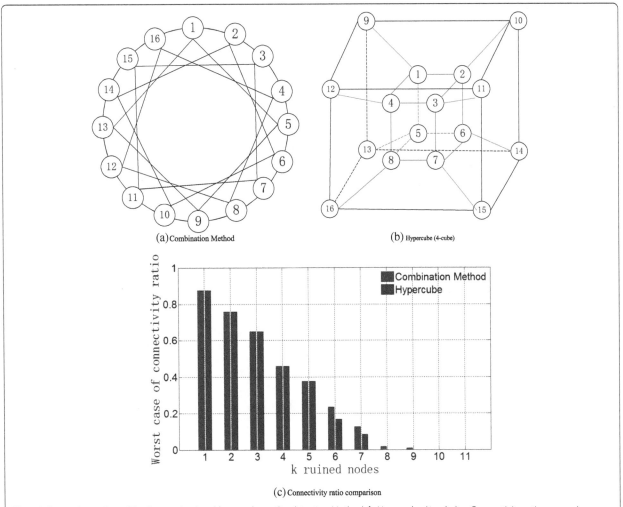

(a) Combination Method

(b) Hypercube (4-cube)

(c) Connectivity ratio comparison

Fig. 13 Comparison of combination method and hypercube. **a** Combination Method. **b** Hypercube (4-cube). **c** Connectivity ratio comparison

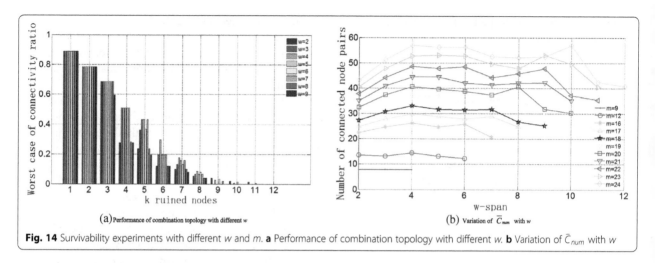

Fig. 14 Survivability experiments with different w and m. **a** Performance of combination topology with different w. **b** Variation of $\bar{C}_{num}$ with w

By these extension methods, spider web topologies can be conveniently transformed without complex reconstruction.

Relation with the combination method

The standard spider web topology is identical to the combination method with $m = k^2$ ($k \geq 3$) and $w = k$. Their connection matrices have the same eigenvalues. This relation can be seen intuitively in Fig. 11. In conclusion, the spider web topology is a special case of the topology constructed using the combination method, but it is more intuitive.

Survivability experiments

To evaluate the survivability of topologies, we design an survivability experiment. It is implemented by the targeted nodes attack. For a topology with m nodes and n links, we destroy k out of m nodes in an enumerated manner. Then, we select the worst case of the connectivity ratio among all the attack results as the metric for comparison with other topologies.

For topologies with different design methods, the worst-case connectivity ratio is used to verify the effectiveness of the combination method. Figures 12 and 13 show comparisons of these topologies.

From Fig. 12, we can see that a topology designed using the combination method performs better than a topology designed using an integer linear programming (ILP) model with the equal degree and node connection constraints. From Fig. 13, we can see that the combination method is slightly better than the hypercube when k is large.

For all topologies constructed using the combination method with the same m and n, the worst-case connectivity ratio is used to verify the effectiveness of w selection.

Figure 14 (a) shows the connectivity ratio of a designed topology with $m = 18$ nodes. The connectivity

ratio decreases more slowly when $w = 4$. In particular, when 5 nodes fail, the connectivity ratio is nearly 0.3, which is much higher than that for other w. Figure 14 (b) shows the variation of $\bar{C}_{num}$ with w for different m. In this simulation, p_q is set to $1/m$. All these curves have higher points at $w = 4$ or 5. This verifies the selection of

$$w_{sel} = \left\lfloor \sqrt[2]{m} \right\rfloor$$

in formula (12).

Conclusion

We proposed two quick methods to construct topologies with small average distance and high connectivity: CM and SWM. CM can be divided into two special methods according to different empirical formulas, namely, the Global Peak Avoidance method and the Local Peak Avoidance method. Further, CM can be enhanced by a local search method. SWM is essentially a special case of CM; it is a more intuitive and expandable approach. Experimental results showed that the topologies designed by CM and SWM perform well in terms of network connectivity and survivability.

Competing interests
The author declared that they have no competing interests.

Authors' contributions
Author LR proposed the idea of this paper, carefully designed two methods and the experiments. Author LR also drafted and revised the manuscript. The author read and approved the final manuscript.

Acknowledgement
The author thanks Professor Xiaoping Zheng and Dr. Qingshan Li in Tsinghua University who carefully revised this paper for grammar and spelling. The author also thanks Mrs. Cuilan Du in CNCERT who provides facility for this study.

References
1.   Dégila JR, Sanso B (2004) A survey of topologies and performance measures for large-scale networks[J]. Commun Surv Tutorials, IEEE 6(4):18–31

2. Kotsis G (1992) Interconnection topologies and routing for parallel processing systems[M]. ACPC-Austrian Center for Parallel Computation
3. Nemhauser GL, Kan AR, Todd M (1989) Handbooks in operations research and management science[J]. Optimization 1:1–78
4. Van Doorn EA (1986) Connectivity of circulant digraphs[J]. J Graph Theory 10(1):9–14
5. Boesch F, Tindell R (1984) Circulants and their connectivities[J]. J Graph Theory 8(4):487–499
6. Boesch FT, Wang JF (1985) Reliable circulant networks with minimum transmission delay[J]. Circuits Syst, IEEE Trans 32(12):1286–1291
7. Li Q, Li Q (1998) Reliability analysis of circulant graphs[J]. Networks 31(2):61–65
8. Penso LD, Rautenbach D, Szwarcfiter JL (2011) Connectivity and diameter in distance graphs[J]. Networks 57(4):310–315
9. Banerjee S, Jain V, Shah S (1999) Regular multihop logical topologies for lightwave networks[J]. Commun Surv, IEEE 2(1):2–18
10. Mohan Reddy E, Reddy E (1996) A dynamically reconfigurable WDM LAN based on reconfigurable circulant graph[C]//Military Communications Conference, 1996. MILCOM'96, Conference Proceedings, IEEE. IEEE 1996(3):786–790
11. Arden BW, Lee H (1981) Analysis of chordal ring network[J]. Comp, IEEE Trans 100(4):291–295
12. Marklof J, Strömbergsson A (2013) Diameters of random circulant graphs[J]. Combinatorica 33(4):429–466
13. Bujnowski S, Dubalski B, Zabłudowski A (2003) Analysis of chordal rings[J]. Mathematical Techniques and Problems in Telecommunications. Centro International de Matematica, Tomar, pp 257–279
14. Morillo P, Comellas F, Fiol M A. The optimization of chordal ring networks[J]. Commun Technol 1987: 295-299
15. Toueg S, Steiglitz K (1979) The design of small-diameter networks by local search[J]. IEEE Trans Comput 7:537–542
16. Park J H, Chwa K Y. Recursive circulant: A new topology for multicomputer networks[C]//Parallel Architectures, Algorithms and Networks, 1994.(ISPAN), International Symposium on. IEEE, 1994: 73-80
17. Chen CC, Quimpo NF (1981) On strongly hamiltonian abelian group graphs[M]//Combinatorial mathematics VIII. Springer, Berlin Heidelberg, pp 23–34
18. Lupparelli M, Marchetti GM, Bergsma WP (2009) Parameterizations and Fitting of Bi-directed Graph Models to Categorical Data[J]. Scand J Stat 36(3):559–576
19. Ádám A (1967) Research problem 2-10[J]. J Combin Theory 2(393):217
20. Alspach B, Parsons TD (1979) Isomorphism of circulant graphs and digraphs[J]. Discret Math 25(2):97–108
21. Muzychuk M (1997) On Ádám's conjecture for circulant graphs[J]. Discret Math 176(1):285–298
22. Xu MY (1998) Automorphism groups and isomorphisms of Cayley digraphs[J]. Discret Math 182(1):309–319
23. Dobson E (2008) On isomorphisms of circulant digraphs of bounded degree[J]. Discret Math 308(24):6047–6055
24. Bermond JC, Comellas F, Hsu DF (1995) Distributed loop computer-networks: a survey[J]. J Parallel Distrib Comput 24(1):2–10
25. Fiol MA, Yebra JLA, Alegre I et al (1987) Discrete optimization problem in local networks and data alignment[J]. IEEE Trans Comput 6:702–713

2

Can functional characteristics usefully define the cloud computing landscape and is the current reference model correct?

Neil Caithness* ⓘD, Michel Drescher and David Wallom

Abstract

The NIST definition of cloud computing has been accepted by the majority of the community as the best available description to fully capture the variety of factors which determine how different stakeholders create, use or interact with cloud computing. With the breadth of the cloud computing landscape there is a need being expressed from within different cloud activities to consider how it may be best segmented so that the diversity might be more easily understood by the different stakeholders. The NIST definition considers four different deployment models (Private, Public, Hybrid, Community Cloud), three different service models (IaaS, PaaS, SaaS), and a number of characteristics (five in the final published version, but 13 in previous unpublished drafts). Exploring the definition further, this study aims to answer two questions: first, how can we use the affinity that different activities have with the definition's characteristics and second, how well does the definition describe the whole cloud ecosystem? We find that utilising a quantitative methodology shows a clustering of different cloud projects and activities that are technically aligned and therefore likely to benefit from interactions and shared learning, and that the final (short-list) definition is more robust than the draft (long-list) definition. Finally, we present a segmentation of the cloud landscape that we believe can best support a sharing of learning between projects in individual clusters.

Keywords: Cloud computing, Cloud ecosystem, NIST definition of cloud computing

Introduction

Since the emergence of cloud computing as a distinct paradigm within distributed computing, and as an important emerging market for ICT based services, there have been a number of efforts to support and encourage the adoption of cloud computing, as well as to foster a more geographically diverse cloud computing provider community. This has resulted in a large number of research and innovation projects receiving European Commission (EC) support over the past five years through the FP7 and H2020 programmes.

As part of the methodology to ensure success of supported projects there have been regular funder led attempts to bring projects together to share learning. Using the domain description as the key differentiator it was thought that synergistic clusters of projects similar enough to share learning on both technical and social best practices would naturally emerge. Unfortunately, this has resulted in only limited appeal, as it has been unclear to participants exactly how the clusters are to be useful or effective as they are only superficially similar but differ widely in the cloud technologies and techniques in use.

Parallel to this European experience, in the US attempts to characterise the diverse landscape of cloud computing began at the National Institute of Standards and Technology (NIST). After years of development and 15 drafts, the final version of the cloud computing definition was published in September 2011 [5]. We describe this reference model more fully below but here we highlight a key feature—the model defines a limited set of functional characteristics that can be used to derive a quantitative description of the emerging cloud computing landscape. At a time when a large number of EC supported projects are maturing, we take the opportunity to make a quantitative assessment of their affinity to these functional characteristics and to derive a robust quantitative description of

*Correspondence: neil.caithness@oerc.ox.ac.uk
Oxford e-Research Centre, University of Oxford, 7 Keble Road, OX1 3QG
Oxford, UK

the cloud landscape. We identify clusters of projects that fully segment the landscape and provide a rational basis for enhancing shared learning.

Finally, appreciating the diversity of cloud computing activities is crucial to the process of deriving consistent and useful standards for cloud adoption and interoperability. We present a segmentation of the landscape of cloud computing that we believe can best inform this process.

ISO published cloud standards

The International Standards Organization and the International Electrotechnical Commission, together with the International Telecommunication Union, have recently released a new International Standard for cloud computing, *ISO/IEC 17788, Cloud computing–Overview and Vocabulary* and *ISO/IEC 17789, Cloud computing–Reference architecture*. These new standards provide definitions of common cloud computing terms, including those for cloud service categories such as Software as a Service (SaaS), Platform as a Service (PaaS), and Infrastructure as a Service (IaaS). They also specify the terminology for cloud deployment models such as "public" and "private" cloud. Crucially, both new standards draw on previous developments by NIST, including *SP 800-145* [5] which has provided the primary dataset for this study. In light of these evolving developments we regard our present study as a timely appraisal of the foundational work.

Defining a methodology

Cloud computing resides in a complicated ecosystem of stakeholders with differing requirements and expectations. Even with a broad consensus that cloud computing is a general term describing anything that delivers hosted services over the Internet, interpretations of this vary widely and the field is subject to excessive hyperbole. Consequently, there is great latitude for interpretation on what exactly constitutes cloud computing and there are many approaches that might be adopted to gain insight into this dynamic and difficult to grasp ecosystem.

We require our approach to produce repeatable, insightful, and accurate information on the landscape and its segmentation. We therefore require the method to be evidence based rather than merely prescriptive. To this end, we define a methodology as follows:

1. Adopt the NIST characteristics of cloud computing as variables against which to make quantitative assessments.
2. Engage with project participants in the quantitative self-assessment of affinity to the characteristic variables.
3. Apply repeatable unsupervised machine learning techniques to these data as evidence-based

characterisation of the total cloud computing landscape.
4. Test for the robustness of the landscape as defined by the NIST characteristics.
5. Derive a clustering of cases (projects) along the complex dimensions of cloud computing and thereby facilitate the experience of shared learning.
6. Derive a segmentation of the landscape with respect to interactions among the variables (characteristics) to inform the process of standards development.

NIST defining characteristics of the cloud

The NIST model is the most commonly cited third party definition of cloud computing. As previously noted this definition took significant time and number of iterations before final publication, indicative of the difficulties associated with reaching a consensus on which even a restricted set of experts in the field could agree.

By consensus agreement [5, p.2]

Cloud computing is a model for enabling ubiquitous, convenient, on-demand network access to a shared pool of configurable computing resources (...) that can be rapidly provisioned and released with minimal management effort or service provider interaction.

The NIST model intends to capture this complexity in simple, understandable characteristics. The model is composed of five essential characteristics, three service models, and four deployment models. In earlier drafts of the definition NIST included a further eight common characteristics. These were dropped in the final published version. At the time of writing the earlier draft had been replaced in all on-line references that we could find. However, we were able to collect self-assessment data on the full set of 13 characteristics. We present analyses of both the NIST long- and short-lists.

Here we provide short explanations of each of the 13 characteristics:

Essential characteristics (1-5)

(Note that these descriptions of the five essentials are intended to be similar, but not necessarily identical to the NIST published descriptions. This was due to the need for brevity to give projects with which we engaged succinct and easy to understand and rate definitions.)

1 On-demand self-service

Consumers can log on to a website or use web services to access additional computing resources on demand, whenever they want, without human interference in the process.

2 Broad network access

Because they are web-based, you can access cloud-computing services from any internet-connected device.

With a web browser on a desktop machine, or even a thin client computer terminal, you can do any computing that the cloud resources provide.

3 Resource pooling
In multi-tenanted computing clouds the customers share a pool of computing resources with other customers, and these resources, which can be dynamically reallocated, may be hosted anywhere.

4 Rapid elasticity
Cloud computing enables computing resources or user accounts to be rapidly and elastically provisioned or released so that customers can scale their systems up and down at any time according to changing requirements.

5 Measured service
Cloud computing providers automatically monitor and record the resources used by customers or currently assigned to customers, which makes possible the pay-per-use billing model that is fundamental to the cloud-computing model.

Common characteristics (6-13)
6 Massive Scale
A cloud platform may, depending on the resources offered, provide individual users with access to large-scale or even massive-scale computing.

7 Homogeneity
In many situations, it is advantageous to both customers and providers to have essentially homogeneous systems at their disposal. Where requirements are particularly difficult or unusual, a cloud platform may be built out of non-homogeneous systems and components.

8 Virtualisation
Virtualisation of machines as software systems massively increases the scale of cloud resources that can be made available. Virtualisation is not an essential characteristic but it is becoming the only way that scale demands can be met by providers; customers generally don't care either way as the virtualisation is entirely transparent.

9 Low cost Software
If increased scale reduces per-unit, or per-use cost, then cloud-computing offers a drive towards lower- cost software. It is important to note that this may not be the case across all sectors and activities.

10 Resilient computing
In some sectors, continuous availability of computing with zero-downtime is crucial to the sectors requirements, for example, emergency and financial systems. In these sectors, requirements for resilient, rather than just fail-safe computing will be the norm.

11 Geographic distribution
Some sectors have legal requirements that physical data stores are in particular geographical jurisdictions. This places certain restrictions on providers favouring a cloud-anywhere model. More commonly, the user is not concerned about location per se.

12 Service orientation
The design of the services that run and operate on the cloud frameworks are normally operated as services such they can take advantage of other factors that give resilience. This includes the ability to scale different components within the system depending on their load and capability.

13 Advanced security
There may be the capability to perform both system and network level security within the cloud system.

Data collection by quantitative self-assessment
Our final sample used in this analysis includes as many of the projects funded under the EC FP7-ICT-2013-10 calls 5, 7, 8 and 10 from which we were able gather data. We approached authoritative project representatives and asked them to self-asses their project's affinity to the 13 characteristics based on the descriptions given above on an ordinal scale from 0-9, with 0 indicating no affinity (the project is indifferent to considerations of this feature) and 9 indicating the strongest affinity (the project regards this feature to be crucially important).

We were able to compile responses from 37 projects (the SeaClouds project supplied two scorings independently from two different representatives). Table 1 gives a complete list of project names and self-assessed scores on the 13 variables.

Goals and techniques of analysis
Faced with a cases-by-variables data matrix (as in Table 1) the analyst seeks to summarise, simplify and explain. With high-dimensional data, there are a number of issues of interest:

- What are the relationships among the cases?
- What are the relationships among the variables?
- What insights may be gained from a summarized joint representation?
- Is the summary robust against possible variations and errors of case sampling?

Specifically for this analysis, the relationships among cases (cloud projects) lets us propose a clustering of

Table 1 Self-assessed scores of 38 cases (projects) on 13 variables

Project number	Project name	On demand self-service	Broad networked access	Resource pooling	Rapid elasticity	Measured service	Massive scale	Homogeneity	Virtualisation	Low cost software	Resilient computing	Geographic distribution	Service orientation	Advanced security
1	ARTIST	3	5	8	7	8	2	1	1	6	1	7	7	3
2	ASCETiC	7	2	5	7	9	7	3	5	7	8	7	6	2
3	BETaaS	7	8	6	7	6	4	3	4	2	7	6	7	5
4	BigFoot	9	4	9	9	1	9	1	9	1	6	4	4	1
5	BNCweb	7	4	4	3	2	4	5	3	5	2	1	7	2
6	Broker@Cloud	3	4	7	4	7	2	8	7	2	8	5	9	7
7	Catania Sci. Gateway	8	6	6	7	5	6	6	8	7	5	6	5	5
8	CELAR	8	4	7	9	5	2	4	7	5	9	6	7	3
9	CloudCatalyst	6	6	6	4	1	1	1	6	8	4	4	6	5
10	CloudLightning	9	7	8	7	6	9	5	5	6	5	5	5	3
11	CloudScale	9	9	6	9	6	9	3	6	7	1	1	9	1
12	CloudSpaces	9	9	9	9	9	9	7	9	9	9	7	9	9
13	CloudTeams	9	9	7	2	1	1	7	1	8	1	2	1	7
14	CloudWave	8	8	8	8	9	4	3	7	8	7	3	9	5
15	COMPOSE	7	4	6	7	6	2	4	7	7	6	2	9	4
16	DICE	2	2	7	8	8	6	2	6	8	9	7	6	6
17	Embassy Cloud	7	7	2	1	6	3	6	8	3	8	1	7	9
18	GEMMA	8	7	8	8	7	3	3	4	3	8	5	8	9
19	INPUT	7	5	5	8	6	4	2	8	2	5	8	5	2
20	IOStack	9	9	9	8	8	7	7	9	6	9	2	9	2
21	LEADS	9	8	2	4	3	7	7	8	8	8	5	9	3
22	Leicester	6	6	5	5	3	2	7	3	4	5	2	6	8
23	MCN	9	9	5	1	5	9	2	8	5	5	9	9	8
24	Mobizz	9	7	9	7	7	6	8	4	6	9	7	8	6
25	MODAClouds	8	4	5	9	9	9	1	1	8	8	8	9	1
26	OpenModeller	9	7	8	7	3	7	8	8	9	4	7	8	5
27	PaaSword	7	1	7	4	1	3	1	3	1	5	4	9	9
28	PANACEA	8	9	8	8	6	6	5	7	5	8	7	9	8
29	S-CASE	9	7	7	3	3	5	3	3	7	6	4	9	7
30	SeaClouds(1)	7	3	3	9	9	7	2	4	7	8	9	8	2
31	SeaClouds(2)	8	4	5	9	9	9	1	1	8	8	8	9	1
32	STORM CLOUDS	6	7	8	8	9	6	3	6	6	4	7	8	9
33	SUPERCLOUD	8	2	7	4	2	3	8	8	2	9	7	5	9
34	Texel	5	8	7	7	8	4	4	4	4	8	3	8	7
35	U-QASAR	5	7	6	7	7	2	2	5	4	4	4	7	6
36	Umea	5	3	3	2	2	2	4	6	4	3	3	7	7
37	Varberg	8	7	8	5	4	3	4	5	3	6	3	8	8
38	WeNMR	9	8	8	9	5	7	9	8	7	3	9	6	3

Scores are on an ordinal scale from 0–9, with 0 indicating no affinity and 9 indicating the strongest affinity. The first column shows the case number corresponding to the number used in the biplot and cluster diagrams projects that are technically aligned and therefore likely to benefit from interactions and shared learning. The relationships among variables (NIST characteristics) lets us present a segmentation of the cloud landscape that we believe can inform where different projects may find examples of best practice or technology choices suitable in those type of projects. The joint representation informs projects about their position in the landscape, and informs standards developers about the relevant cloud activities when considering the landscape characteristics. Finally, measuring robustness for different partitions of the variables (all 13 characteristics; 5 essentials; 8 common) lets us reach conclusions about which of these partitions may be more meaningful and in that sense better.

Dimension reduction

For any high-dimensional dataset, the statistical techniques of dimension reduction are indispensable to the aim of summarizing, simplifying and explaining meaning contained in the dataset. Here we give a brief description of the linear algebra exploited by the family of multivariate dimension-reduction methods that includes principal component analysis (PCA), log-ratio analysis (LRA), correspondence analysis (CA), and various forms of discriminant analysis. All of these methods are basic decompositions (or factorizations) of a target matrix into left- and right-vector matrices representing respectively the cases (rows) and the variables (columns) of the original data matrix.

What distinguishes the various methods is the form of normalization and differential weighting of points, chosen depending on the type of data, which is applied before the decomposition into left- and right singular vector matrices.

For ordinal survey data such as ours, CA is the appropriate method [3]. The normalization in CA is the matrix of standardized residuals $T = D_r^{-1/2}(P - rc^T)D_c^{-1/2}$, where $P = N/n$ is the so-called correspondence matrix with N being the original data matrix and n its grand total. Row and column marginal totals of P are r and c respectively, and D_r and D_c are the diagonal matrices of these. Singular value decomposition (SVD) provides the appropriate factorization of T, with convenient properties, such that $T = U\Gamma V^T$. The right singular vectors V, are the contribution coordinates of the variables. A further transformation involving a scaling factor D_q, such that $F = D_q^{-1/2}U\Gamma$ defines the principal coordinates of the cases.

Visualization and interpretation

The biplot [2, 3] is a joint display of the two sets of points in V and F which, with the above transformation, can often be achieved on a common scale thereby avoiding the need for arbitrary independent scaling to make the biplot legible. The dimensions (Dim 1, Dim 2, ... Dim N, i.e. the columns) of V and F are arranged in decreasing order of importance to the reduced-dimension solution. That means that a biplot of the first two dimensions is showing the most important relationships that can be represented on a planar 2-d plot. Cases are arranged in approximately Euclidean space so that proximity equates closely with similarity. Cases further from the origin have a stronger influence in the reduced-dimension solution; cases closer to the origin have a lesser influence. Variables are represented as vectors; the angular distance between vectors equates with correlation, and vector length again equates with relative contribution to the solution. One aspect of interpretation lies in identifying vectors with the same orientation, vectors at right angles, and vectors in opposing directions, and then identifying peripheral cases and how these are arranged with respect to the vectors. A second aspect of interpretation is to identify vectors aligned with the primary dominant dimension (Dim 1), and those aligned with the secondary dimension (Dim 2).

An important shortcoming of the biplot is that only two, or at most three, of the dimensions of the reduced-dimension solution can be visualised together. However, there may be more dimensions that are relevant for interpretation. The singular values of the SVD decomposition, in the description above, are the square roots of the eigenvalues; these indicate the relative importance of a dimension, i.e. its contribution to capturing information content in the analysis. When the eigenvalues are scaled so that their sum equals the number of variables, a conventional rule is to regard at least all those dimensions with eigenvalues>1 as relevant. This is the conventional Kaiser-Guttman stopping rule [4, 6]. Scree plots below show eigenvalues with the Kaiser-Guttman reference line.

Addressing this shortcoming, we develop additional analytic displays in the form of hierarchical dendrograms based on the cosine distances between vectors in any number of dimensions. The hierarchical ordering of nodes in the tree then indicates closeness of orientation in the n-dimensional equivalent biplot.

Robustness testing

The robustness of a particular solution to possible errors and variation in sampling can be assessed by the statistical technique of bootstrapping [1]. The technique involves resampling rows from the data table, with replacement, to construct a replicate dataset of the same size as the original. The analysis is then repeated on the replicate, and the whole process is repeated a large number of times (typically 1000).

Computation

All analysis was performed on a standard desktop computer using Matlab Version 9 (R2016a) and custom software we developed for CA and contribution biplots based on [3].

Results

We performed separate analyses on three partitions of the dataset in Table 1:

- 38-cases by 13-variables full dataset (NIST long-list).
- 38-cases by 5-variables essential characteristics (NIST short-list).
- 38-cases by 8-variables common characteristics (NIST residual-list).

We present results of these analyses in a series of biplots, scree plots and cluster trees as follows in Figs. 1, 2, 3, 4, 5, 6, 7, 8, 9 and 10. See the figure captions for detailed descriptions and interpretation.

Summary of results

NIST long-list

- Figure 1: broad and roughly even spread of cases and variables.
- Figure 2: there are at least four relevant dimensions.
- Figure 3: bootstrap values for all relationships are <50%, some ≪50%.

NIST short-list

- Figure 4: well-clustered cases associated across an even spread of variables.
- Figure 5: there are at least two relevant dimensions.
- Figure 6: bootstrap values for two distal nodes >50%, one internal node ≈50%.
- Figure 7: cluster tree of cases with broadly even bifurcations.

NIST residual-list

- Figure 8: broad and roughly even spread of cases and variables.
- Figure 9: there are at least three relevant dimensions.
- Figure 10: bootstrap values for all relationships are <50%.

Discussion and conclusions

The aims of this study were to characterise the abstract landscape of cloud computing, determine if that characterization is robust, and then to learn something from the landscape to the benefit cloud participants and stakeholders. The characteristics of the NIST definition of cloud computing provided the framework for a quantitative

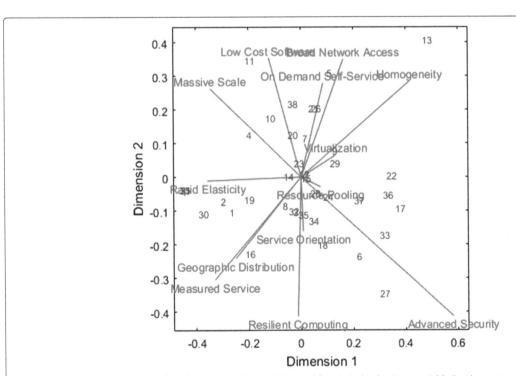

Fig. 1 2-dimensional biplot of the full 13-characteristic dataset. *Advanced Security* is the dominant variable (i.e. the vector with the greatest magnitude) of the solution driven largely by cases 27, 6 and 33. Diametrically opposed to *Advanced Security* is *Massive Scale* and *Low Cost Software*, driven largely by case 11. *Virtualisation*, *Resource Pooling* and *Service Orientation* contribute little to the solution. Other associations are evident, e.g. orthogonal to these are Measured Service and *Geographic Distribution* driven by case 16, and opposed to this is *Homogeneity* driven strongly by case 13

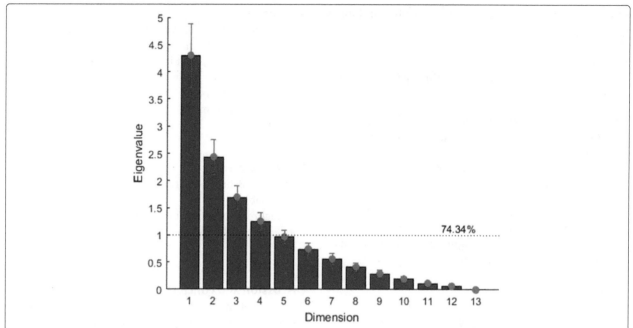

Fig. 2 Scree plot showing eigenvalues of the decomposition of the full 13-characteristic dataset. The *dotted line* shows the Kaiser-Guttman reference line for eigenvalues>1 indicating that at least four of the 13 dimensions are relevant. These account for 74.34% of the total variance in the 13-dimensional dataset. Error *bars* show standard errors for 1000 bootstrap replicates of the CA analysis

survey of participants. Standard multivariate dimension reduction techniques provided the definition of the landscape which we visualise in biplots and cluster trees.

The robustness analysis of three partitions of the dataset (NIST long-list, short-list and residual-list) is decisive: any

interpretations drawn from the cloud landscape depicted in the analyses of the long- and residual-lists are essentially meaningless if applied to the general cloud ecosystem that these sample projects were drawn from. Only the NIST short-list of 5 essential characteristics leads

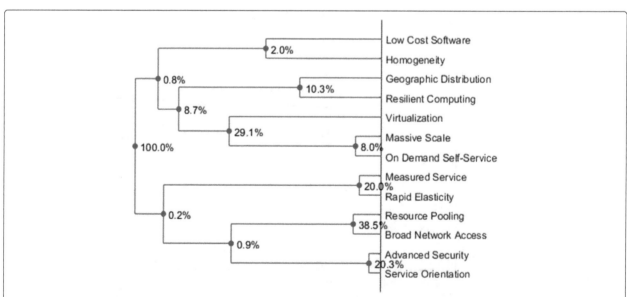

Fig. 3 Hierarchical dendrogram of variables in a 4-dimensional representation of the decomposition of the full 13-dimensional dataset. *Advanced Security* and *Massive Scale* are shown at opposite ends of the tree connected only by the deepest node, consistent with the view in the 2-d biplot. *Measured Service* and *Geographic Distribution*, shown very close together in 2-d, are in fact very distant when considering more relevant dimensions. Internal nodes are labelled with bootstrap percentages indicating the proportion of times in 1000 bootstrap replicates of the CA analysis that a node is observed. All values are <50%, with many values much smaller, indicating that this solution is not robust to bootstrap resampling. i.e. no grouping shown here is strongly supported by evidence

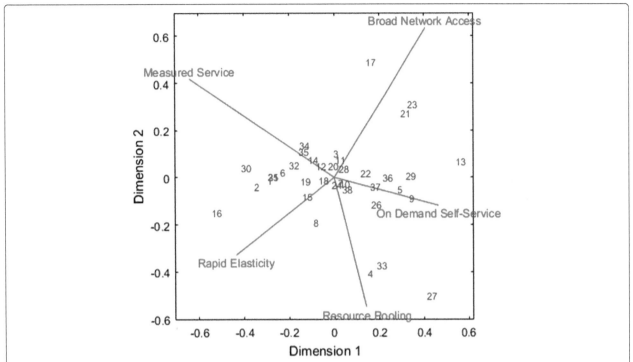

Fig. 4 2-dimensional biplot of the 5-dimensional partitioned dataset of the Essential Characteristics. Here *Measured Service* and *Broad Network Access* are slightly dominant in the solution, but perhaps insignificantly. *Broad Network Access* is driven largely by cases 17, 21 and 23, *Resource Pooling* by cases 27, 4 and 33, *Measured Service* and *Rapid Elasticity* jointly by a larger set of cases, in decreasing significance, 16, 2, 30, 1, 31, 25, 6 and 32. The cluster of cases 13, 29, 9, 5, 36, 37, 26 and 22, drives *On Demand Self Service*. The remaining cases close to the centre form a distinct cluster of similarity, but do not contribute significantly to the 2-d solution

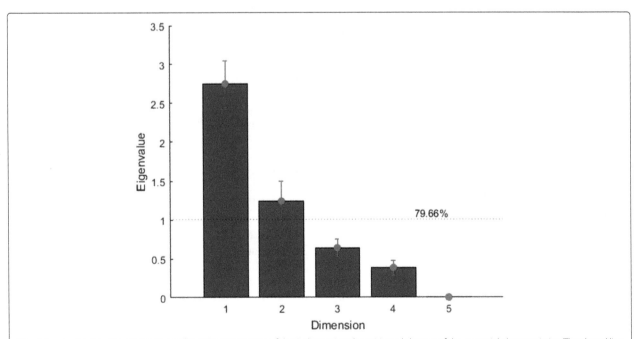

Fig. 5 Scree plot showing eigenvalues of the decomposition of the 5-dimensional partitioned dataset of the essential characteristics. The *dotted line* shows the Kaiser-Guttman reference line for eigenvalues>1, indicating that at least two of the five dimensions are relevant. These account for 79.66% of the total variance in the 5-dimensional dataset. Error *bars* show standard errors for 1000 bootstrap replicates of the CA analysis

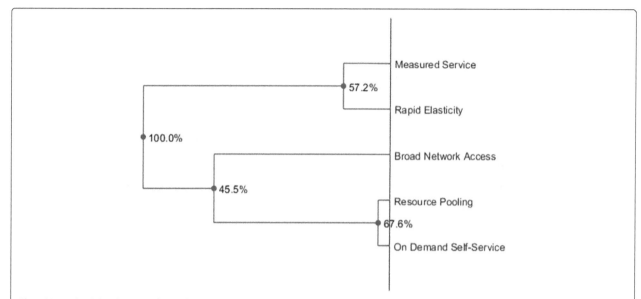

Fig. 6 Hierarchical dendrogram of variables in a 2-dimensional representation of the decomposition of the 5-dimensional partitioned dataset for the essential characteristics. Internal nodes are labelled with bootstrap percentages indicating the proportion of times in 1000 bootstrap replicates of the CA analysis that a node is observed. The two distal nodes with values >50% indicate that no other arrangement occurred more often in the bootstrap replicates, and that they are therefore strongly supported. The association of *Broad Network Access* with either distal node is then the only remaining degree of freedom, and occurs roughly half of the time with each (45.5% vs. 54.5%). Looking again at the biplot in Fig. 4 we see that this would result from only slight alterations to the angle of the vector towards either *On Demand Self-Service*, or towards *Measured Service*. Overall, this is a robust result and the two association of (i) *Resource Pooling* with *On Demand Self-Service*, and (ii) *Measured Service* with *Rapid Elasticity* are both stable and well supported by the evidence

to a stable and robust depiction of the landscape and general interpretations should be made only against this depiction.

Figure 4 (biplot) and Fig. 7 (cluster tree) provide the interpretive mechanisms. Five groups of projects labelled I-V in Fig. 7 are a useful focus for discussion, though clusters at any level of the tree are equally meaningful.

Cluster I
- 23 MCN
- 21 LEADS
- 17 Embassy Cloud

These are the primary drivers of *Broad Network Access*, which is also one of the two dominant features of the landscape.

Cluster II
- 13 CloudTeams
- 26 OpenModeller
- 37 Varberg
- 36 Umea
- 22 Leicester
- 29 S-CASE
- 9 CloudCatalyst
- 5 BNCweb

The primary drivers of *On Demand Self Service*, with CloudTeams being the most significant to this axis, and Leicester being the least.

Cluster III
- 27 PaaSword
- 33 SUPERCLOUD
- 4 BigFoot

The primary drivers of *Resource Pooling*, with PaaSword being the most significant.

Cluster IV
- 35 U-QASAR
- 34 Texel
- 19 INPUT
- 15 COMPOSE
- 18 GEMMA
- 14 CloudWave
- 12 CloudSpaces
- 8 CELAR
- 38 WeNMR
- 10 CloudLightning
- 24 Mobizz
- 7 Catania Sci. Gateway
- 28 PANACEA
- 20 IOStack

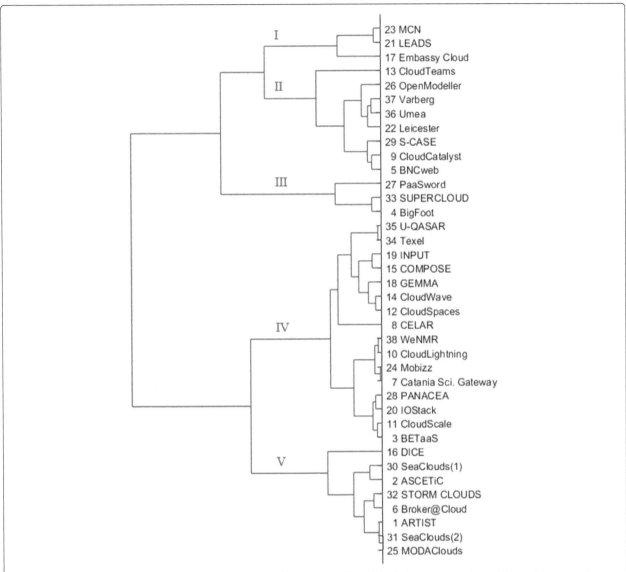

Fig. 7 Cluster tree of cases in the 2-dimensional representation of the decomposition of the 5-dimensional partitioned dataset for the essential characteristics. Ward's agglomerative hierarchical method was used to form the clusters. Numbered groups are referred to in the "Discussion" section

- 11 CloudScale
- 3 BETaaS

The large central cluster not distinguished by a tendency towards any of the NIST characteristics over any other.

Cluster V

- 16 DICE
- 30 SeaClouds(1)
- 2 ASCETiC
- 32 STORM CLOUDS
- 6 Broker@Cloud
- 1 ARTIST
- 31 SeaClouds(2)
- 25 MODAClouds

This cluster subtends the two remaining characteristics, *Measured Service* and *Rapid Elasticity*, with DICE being the most significant and leaning towards *Rapid Elasticity*. As a final observation we note that although *Measured Service* is one of the dominant features of the landscape, no projects identify significantly with this feature.

Finally, we suggest that this interpretation of project clusters can provide the basis for enhanced shared learning among projects that are technically aligned on the axes of cloud characteristics, and that the further development of standards for cloud implementation and adoption can benefit from this depiction of the landscape and the association shown between projects and characteristics.

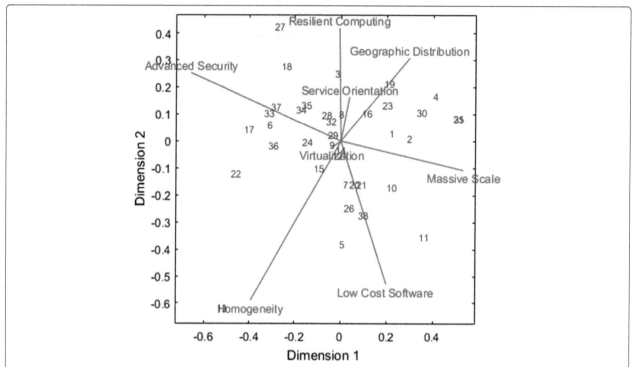

Fig. 8 2-dimensional biplot of the 8-dimensional partitioned dataset of the common characteristics. *Service Orientation* and *Virtualisation* appear almost insignificant to this solution. There is a roughly even spread of cases, though similar inferences could be made as illustrated in Fig. 1

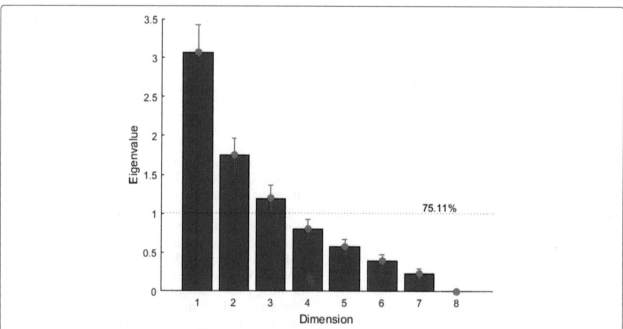

Fig. 9 Scree plot showing eigenvalues of the decomposition of the 8-dimensional partitioned dataset for the common characteristics. The *dotted line* shows the Kaiser-Guttman reference line for eigenvalues>1, indicating that at least three of the eight dimensions are relevant. These account for 75.11% of the total variance in the 8-dimensional dataset. Error *bars* show standard errors for 1000 bootstrap replicates of the CA analysis

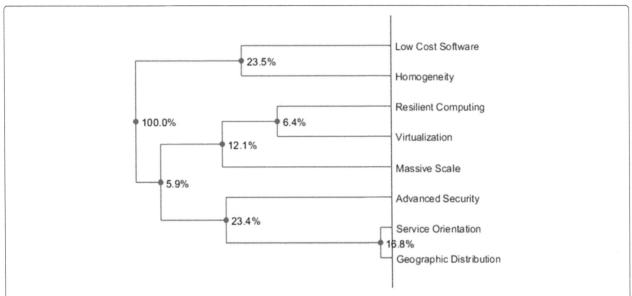

Fig. 10 Hierarchical dendrogram of variables in a 3-dimensional representation of the decomposition of the 8-dimensional partitioned dataset for the common characteristics. Internal nodes are labelled with bootstrap percentages indicating the proportion of times in 1000 bootstrap replicates of the CA analysis that a node is observed. All values are <50%, with a few values much smaller, indicating that this solution is not robust to bootstrap resampling. i.e. no grouping shown here is strongly supported by evidence

Responses to the methodology and future work

In this paper, we have presented a methodology for characterising the landscape of cloud computing based on the set of NIST defining features. The same methodology identifies the location of a project or cloud enterprise within the landscape. Taken together, the resulting biplot and the cluster tree offer rich interpretive tools in defining the current cloud computing landscape.

Presenting these results to partners in the supporting projects, and to the wider circle of EC-funded cloud related projects, participants accepted the methodology as sound and applicable, and they generally regarded the characterisation of the landscape as useful. However, several observations are noteworthy.

- In draft form, *SP 800-145* defines characteristics of cloud computing only, however, many more IT service characteristics are applicable that are not specific to cloud computing.
- Several of the characteristics in the draft form subsume important aspects under a single term that is too general to be meaningful, such as *Privacy* and *Data Protection* being subsumed under the term *Advanced Security*.
- Despite *SP 800-145* having been published over five years ago in 2011, participants disagree on interpretation of certain characteristics. *Measured Service*, for example, is frequently misinterpreted as describing the monitoring of a cloud service system.

Several avenues of future work have emerged from this activity.

- An automated web-hosted tool that allows the self-assessment of new cloud enterprises and shows their location within the existing landscape would be informative to new enterprises.
- Exploring the impact of reducing the set of characteristics from 13 to five may be instructive. For instance, does the larger set define a much finer grained landscape than the reduced set, or is the information content of the reduced set sufficient?
- Does expanding the set of characteristics to include more applicable IT service characteristics improve the resolution of the landscape, or does this perhaps significantly change the orientation of the existing characteristics?

Acknowledgements
The authors thank two anonymous reviewers for helpful comments and suggestions.

Funding
This work was supported by the EC Framework 7 CloudWatch project (EC grant no. 610994).

Authors' contributions
DW proposed a landscape segmentation analysis using the NIST model characteristics as variables for a quantitative study and drafted the descriptive definitions. MD wrote the first draft of the paper and interpreted appropriate segmentations of the cluster tree. NC devised the methodology, liaised with projects on data collection, implemented the software, performed all computation, and wrote subsequent drafts of the paper with significant

contributions from the co-authors. All authors read and approved the final manuscript.

Competing interests
The authors declare that they have no competing interests.

References
1. Efron B, Tibshirani RJ (1994) An Introduction to the Bootstrap. Chapman and Hall/CRC, New York
2. Greenacre M (2010) Biplots in Practice. BBVA Foundation, Madrid
3. Greenacre M (2013) Contribution biplots. J Comput Graph Stat 22:107–122
4. Jackson DA (1993) Stopping rules in principal components analysis: a comparison of heuristical and statistical approaches. Ecology 74(8):2204–2214
5. Mell P, Grance T (2011) The NIST definition of cloud computing. US National Institute of Standards and Technology. Available: http://dx.doi.org/10.6028/NIST.SP.800-145
6. Peres-Neto PR, Jackson DA, Somers KM (2005) How many principal components? Stopping rules for determining the number of non-trivial axes revisited. Comput Stat Data Anal 49(4):974–997

3

A risk assessment model for selecting cloud service providers

Erdal Cayirci[1], Alexandr Garaga[2,3], Anderson Santana de Oliveira[2*] and Yves Roudier[3]

Abstract

The Cloud Adoption Risk Assessment Model is designed to help cloud customers in assessing the risks that they face by selecting a specific cloud service provider. It evaluates background information obtained from cloud customers and cloud service providers to analyze various risk scenarios. This facilitates decision making an selecting the cloud service provider with the most preferable risk profile based on aggregated risks to security, privacy, and service delivery. Based on this model we developed a prototype using machine learning to automatically analyze the risks of representative cloud service providers from the Cloud Security Alliance Security, Trust & Assurance Registry.

Keywords: Risk assessment, Cloud computing, Security, Privacy

Abbreviations: A4Cloud, Accountability for cloud and other future internet services; CAIQ, Consensus assessment initiative questionnaire; CARAM, Cloud adoption risk assessment model; CCM, Cloud control matrix; CNIL, Commission nationale de l'informatique et des libertés; CSA, Cloud security alliance; CSC, Cloud service consumer; CSP, Cloud service provider; ENISA, European network and information security agency; IEC, International electrotechnical commission; ISACA, Information systems audit and control association; ISO, International organization for standardization; IT, Information technology; JRTM, Joint risk and trust model; NIST, National institute of standards and technology; SecLA, Cloud security level agreements; SMB, Small-medium business; STAR, Security, trust & assurance registry

Introduction

Moving business processes to the cloud is associated with a change in the risk landscape to an organization [1]. Cloud Security Alliance (CSA) [2] has found that insufficient due diligence was among the top threats in cloud computing in 2013. This threat is linked to the fact that organizations which strive to adopt cloud computing often do not understand well the resulting risks.

Regulations related to data protection, financial reporting, etc. put certain requirements that should be complied with even when outsourcing business processes to 3rd parties, like cloud service providers (CSPs). For example, EU Data Protection Directive, in particular Article 29 Data Protection Working Party [3] recommends that all data controllers (usually corporate cloud customers) perform an impact assessment of moving personal data of their clients to the cloud.

However, most of the cloud service customers (CSCs), especially Small-Medium Businesses (SMBs), may not have enough knowledge in performing such assessments at a good level, because they may not necessarily employ IT specialists and the lack of transparency is intrinsic to the operations of the CSPs. This makes difficult to choose an appropriate CSP based on CSC's security requirements, especially considering the abundance of similar cloud offerings [4].

This work proposes a methodology, cloud adoption risk assessment model (CARAM), to help in assessing the various risks to business, security and privacy that CSCs face when moving to the cloud by leveraging information from CSCs, CSPs and several public sources. CARAM consists of the following tools that complement the various recommendations from European Network and Information Security Agency (ENISA) [1], and Cloud

*Correspondence: anderson.santana.de.oliveira@sap.com
[2]SAP Labs France, Mougins, France
Full list of author information is available at the end of the article

Security Alliance (CSA) for a complete risk assessment framework:

- A questionnaire for CSCs
- A tool and an algorithm to classify the answers to Cloud Assessment Initiative Questionnaire (CAIQ) to discrete values
- A model that maps the answers to both questionnaires to risk values
- A multi-criteria decision approach with posterior articulation of CSC preferences for relative risk analysis, using a few parameters for security, privacy and quality of service, allowing to to quickly and reliably compare multiple CSPs

This paper extends our work in [5] with experimental results - we devised profiles representing realistic customer categories to classify providers according to the CSC needs. We also used a more precise risk scale for comparing CSPs, allowing one to visualize the differences in security practices of the most representative players in the cloud services landscape. Therefore the current version brings significative improvements with respect to the previous paper [5].

In Section "Related work" we elaborate on the literature related to the risk assessment for adoption of cloud computing: we focus on the work carried out by ENISA and CSA because CARAM is based on them; In Section "Risk levels computation" we introduce CARAM, and then a multi-criteria risk assessment approach with posterior articulation of the CSCs; In Section "Experimental results" we demonstrate experimental results from using CARAM on a case study; In Section "Limitations" we outline some limitations of the approach; We conclude our paper in Section "Conclusion".

Related work

Several large standardization bodies such as International Organization for Standardization (ISO), International Electrotechnical Commission (IEC) and National Institute of Standards and Technology (NIST) and Information Technology (IT) Governance Institute and the Information Systems Audit and Control Association (ISACA) published standards on IT risk management and risk assessment: ISO 31000 [6], ISO/IEC 31010 [7], ISO/IEC 27005 [8], NIST SP 800-30 [9], SP 800-37 [10] and COBIT [11]. All these standards are generic i.e. not specific to cloud deployments, and while possible to use them for evaluating different cloud solutions, it will require a considerable amount of effort and expert knowledge, which SMBs cannot always afford.

Some adaptations of these standards were developed specifically for cloud deployments. E.g. Microsoft proposed a Cloud Decision Framework [12] based on ISO 31000. It provides guidance for risk assessment to be performed by potential CSCs when choosing a cloud solution. The risk profiles of different cloud solutions are constructed based on a predefined set of risks from four categories: compliance, strategic, operational and market and finance. The authors suggest using CSA Cloud Control Matrix (CCM) [13] as guidance for evaluating mitigating controls. While this approach could be more practical than other generic risk assessment frameworks for evaluating different cloud solutions it is still quite abstract and largely rely on experts' opinions for estimating and evaluating the risks and mitigations. In contrast, we propose a concrete step by step approach to automate the estimation and evaluation of risks of adopting different cloud solutions. This could be more suitable for smaller organizations that lack sufficient resources for a full-scale risk assessment.

ENISA [1] provided recommendations and a framework for generic qualitative inductive risk assessment for cloud computing. Their recommendations include extensive lists of possible incident scenarios, assets and vulnerabilities in cloud computing deployments. It suggests estimating risk levels on the basis of likelihood of a risk scenario mapped against the estimated negative impact, which is the essence of the risk formulation by also many others in the literature [7, 11, 14, 15]. Although ENISA's recommendations are specific for cloud computing, it is a generic framework that does not provide an approach to map the specifics of CSPs and CSCs to the 35 risk scenarios listed in the report [1]. In Section "Risk levels computation" we describe how CARAM fine-tunes this approach to estimate risk values based on some known information about CSCs and CSPs.

Another qualitative inductive scheme was published by "The Commission nationale de l'informatique et des libertés" (CNIL) or in English: The French National Commission on Informatics and Liberty [16] more recently. CNIL's methodology is similar to the ENISA's framework with the following difference: it is a risk assessment focused on privacy risks in cloud computing. It also recommends measures to reduce the risks and assess the residual privacy risks after the application of these measures. However, it is still generic and does not account for specific requirements of CSPs or CSCs.

The CSA Cloud Assessment Initiative Questionnaire (CAIQ) [17] is a questionnaire prepared for CSPs to document the implemented security measures. It is based on the CSA Cloud Control Matrix (CCM) taxonomy of security controls [13] and is aimed to help CSCs understand the security coverage of specific cloud offerings in relation to popular security standards, control frameworks and regulations. The questionnaires answered by many CSPs are publicly available in the CSA Security, Trust and Assurance Registry (STAR) [4]. We propose a methodology that uses the data extracted from STAR to evaluate the implementation of various controls provided by cloud solutions (see Subsection "The vulnerability parameter for a CSP").

Luna et al. introduced in [18] Cloud Security Level Agreements (SecLA) and proposed a methodology to benchmark SecLA of CSPs with respect to CSCs' requirements [19]. Both CSP SecLA provisions and user requirements are expressed using a special data structure: Quantitative Policy Trees, allowing expressing controls with different granularity: CCM control areas, control groups, and controls (corresponding to CAIQ answers). The authors demonstrate their approach using data on several CSPs from STAR, by calculating security levels for respective controls and control groups. While similar in the intent CARAM is a model for risk assessment, while [19] proposes a ranking algorithm for matching CSC requirements vs. CSP provisions. In [19] CSCs need a certain level of security expertise to specify their requirements, while in CARAM this is not necessary: CSCs only need to specify acceptable risk levels for security, privacy and service categories, while still allowing a more fine grained specification. Another major difference is that [19] assumes the existence of a mapping from provisions to quantitative Local Security Levels to allow further analysis. Given a high number of potential CSPs and controls for each CSP creating this mapping would require significant manual work. In CARAM we propose a way to automatically construct such a mapping (see Subsection "The vulnerability parameter for a CSP").

Habib et al. proposed a multi-faceted Trust Management system architecture for a cloud computing marketplace [20]. The system evaluates the trustworthiness of CSPs in terms of different SLA attributes assessed using information collected from multiple sources. This is done by evaluating opinions related to SLA attributes and aggregating them into a trust score for a CSP. The authors mention CAIQ answers as a source of information, however they do not specify how exactly the CSP trust score is computed from the answers, especially considering that the answers are in free text form.

In [21], the EU funded project SECCRIT enumerated very relevant cloud risk scenarios systematically, in a similar fashion to what ENISA [1] did a few years earlier, but this time they evaluated the risk perception from the users point of view. They used a survey-based methodology to ask respondents to rank risks in a standard way - assessing probability and impact. CARAM is innovative when compared with this approach in two ways: it is using real information disclosed by cloud providers to estimate the likelihood of threats affecting the cloud would become concrete. Second, it allows the user of the methodology to focus on what they know best, their assets: the methodology only requires to assign priorities to assets in order to provide quantifiable risk information.

Other EU projects such as SPECS [22] and Escudo-Cloud [23] also looked at quantifying the capacity of a given cloud provider to satisfy security Servive Level Agreements (SLAs) using information published in the CSA STAR registry. It also has a focus on usability, but the endeavour is different in essence. Here we are assessing risk scenarios in an automated way, whereas in that work [23] does not provide an automated processing for the answers given by the CSPs to the CAIQ, making it difficult to compare more than three providers quickly.

Joint Risk and Trust Model (JRTM) [24] was developed by Accountability for Cloud and Other Future Internet Services Project (A4Cloud). JRTM is a quantitative risk assessment model that assesses the cloud service security and privacy risks for a specific CSP and CSC. It counts on a third party (i.e., a Trust as a Service Provider) to accumulate statistical data (i.e., evidence) on the trustworthiness of CSPs. These evidences include the number of security, privacy and service events that a CSP was subject to and the percentage of the events that the CSP recovered from before they become an incident (i.e., they impact on CSC). However, such detailed statistical data is not always available and even if available they will not be normally shared with (potential) CSCs—hence the need for a trusted third party. In this work, instead, we rely on public information already provided by CSPs regarding their implementation of various security controls for a qualitative risk assessment of their solutions. This can be considered as an extension of JRTM when statistical data is available or a substitution otherwise.

One of the main advantages of CARAM is that it is easy to make it evolve to cover further risk scenarios and to make it evolve if the security control frameworks evolve. As we will introduce in the next section, the risk level computation is parametrized by mappings between threats and security controls that help to mitigate them, making the approach relevant over time.

Risk levels computation

ENISA [1] identified 35 incident scenarios that fall in one of the following four categories: policy and organizational, technical, legal and the other scenarios not specific to cloud computing (see Table 1). The likelihood of each of these scenarios and their business impact are determined in consultation with an expert group. The scale of probability and impact has five discrete classes between very low and very high. For example, the probability and impact of Incident Scenario P1 in "Policy and Organizational Scenarios" category (i.e., lock-in) are given as HIGH and MEDIUM relatively.

ENISA also provides a list of 53 vulnerabilities (i.e., 31 cloud specific and 22 not cloud specific vulnerabilities, see Table 2) and 23 classes of CSC assets (see Table 3) that may be affected by the cloud adoption. Each of 35 incident

Table 1 ENISA's list of risk scenarios and their categories

Risk category	Risk name
Policy & Organizational	P1. Lock-in
	P2. Loss of governance
	P3. Compliance challenges
	P4. Loss of business reputation due to co-tenant activities
	P5. Cloud service termination or failure
	P6. Cloud provider acquisition
	P7. Supply chain failure
Technical	T1. Resource exhaustion (under or over provisioning)
	T2. Isolation failure
	T3. Cloud provider malicious insider - abuse of high privilege roles
	T4. Management interface compromise (manipulation, availability of infrastructure)
	T5. Intercepting data in transit
	T6. Data leakage on up/download, intra-cloud
	T7. Insecure or ineffective deletion of data
	T8. Distributed denial of service (DDoS)
	T9. Economic denial of service (EDOS)
	T10. Loss of encryption keys
	T11. Undertaking malicious probes or scans
	T12. Compromise service engine
	T13. Conflicts between customer hardening procedures and cloud environment
Legal	L1. Subpoena and e-discovery
	L2. Risk from changes of jurisdiction
	L3. Data protection risks
	L4. Licensing risks
Not Specific to the Cloud	N1. Network breaks
	N2. Network management (ie, network congestion / mis-connection / non-optimal use)
	N3. Modifying network traffic
	N4. Privilege escalation
	N5. Social engineering attacks (ie, impersonation)
	N6. Loss or compromise of operational logs
	N7. Loss or compromise of security logs (manipulation of forensic investigation)
	N8. Backups lost, stolen
	N9. Unauthorized access to premises (including physical access to machines and other facilities)
	N10. Theft of computer equipment
	N11. Natural disasters

Table 2 ENISA's list of vulnerabilities

Cloud specific vulnerabilities

- V1. Authentication Authorization Accounting (AAA) vulnerabilities
- V2. User provisioning vulnerabilities
- V3. User de-provisioning vulnerabilities
- V4. Remote access to management interface
- V5. Hypervisor vulnerabilities
- V6. Lack of resource isolation
- V7. Lack of reputational isolation
- V8. Communication encryption vulnerabilities
- V9. Lack of or weak encryption of archives and data in transit
- V10. Impossibility of processing data in encrypted form
- V11. Poor key management procedures
- V12. Key generation: low entropy for random number generation
- V13. Lack of standard technologies and solutions
- V14. No source escrow agreement
- V15. Inaccurate modelling of resource
- V16. No control on vulnerability assessment process
- V17. Possibility that internal (cloud) network probing will occur
- V18. Possibility that co-residence checks will be performed
- V19. Lack of forensic readiness
- V20. Sensitive media sanitization
- V21. Synchronizing responsibilities or contractual obligations external to cloud
- V22. Cross-cloud applications creating hidden dependency
- V23. SLA clauses with conflicting promises to different stakeholders
- V24. SLA clauses containing excessive business risk
- V25. Audit or certification not available to customers
- V26. Certification schemes not adapted to cloud infrastructures
- V27. Inadequate resource provisioning and investments in infrastructure
- V28. No policies for resource capping
- V29. Storage of data in multiple jurisdictions and lack of transparency about this
- V30. Lack of information on jurisdictions
- V31. Lack of completeness and transparency in terms of use

Vulnerabilities not specific to the cloud

- V32. Lack of security awareness
- V33. Lack of vetting processes
- V34. Unclear roles and responsibilities
- V35. Poor enforcement of role definitions
- V36. Need-to-know principle not applied
- V37. Inadequate physical security procedures
- V38. Misconfiguration
- V39. System or OS vulnerabilities
- V40. Untrusted software

Table 2 ENISA's list of vulnerabilities *(Continued)*

V41. Lack of, or a poor and untested, business continuity and disaster recovery plan

V42. Lack of, or incomplete or inaccurate, asset inventory

V43. Lack of, or poor or inadequate, asset classification

V44. Unclear asset ownership

V45. Poor identification of project requirements

V46. Poor provider selection

V47. Lack of supplier redundancy

V48. Application vulnerabilities or poor patch management

V49. Resource consumption vulnerabilities

V50. Breach of NDA by provider

V51. Liability from data loss

V52. Lack of policy or poor procedures for logs collection and retention

V53. Inadequate or misconfigured filtering resources

scenarios is related with a subset of vulnerabilities and assets. For example, the Incident Scenario P1 is related to Vulnerabilities V13 (lack of standard technologies and solutions), V31 (lack of completeness and transparency in terms of use), V46 (poor provider selection), V47 (lack

Table 3 ENISA's list of assets

A1. Company reputation

A2. Customer trust

A3. Employee loyalty and experience

A4. Intellectual property

A5. Personal sensitive data

A6. Personal data

A7. Personal data - critical

A8. HR data

A9. Service delivery - real time services

A10. Service delivery

A11. Access control / authentication / authorization (root/admin v others)

A12. Credentials

A13. User directory (data)

A14. Cloud service management interface

A15. Management interface APIs

A16. Network (connections, etc.)

A17. Physical hardware

A18. Physical buildings

A19. Cloud Provider Application (source code)

A20. Certification

A21. Operational logs (customer and cloud provider)

A22. Security logs

A23. Backup or archive data

of supplier redundancy) and Assets A1 (company reputation), A5 (personal sensitive data), A6 (personal data), A7 (personal data critical), A9 (service delivery - real time services), A10 (service delivery).

The likelihood and business impact values that are determined by the experts are converted to the risk levels for each incident scenario based on a risk matrix with a scale between 0 and 8 as shown in Fig. 1. Then, the risk levels are mapped to a qualitative scale as follows:

Low → 0-2
Medium → 3-5
High → 6-8

Hence, a CSC can assess the risk level related to an incident scenario qualitatively and understands what kind of vulnerabilities and assets are related to each scenario by examining [1]. These values represent educated guesses over a wide range of common cloud deployments and do not have a precise semantics. In practice, the risk levels are related to many factors such as the security controls that CSPs implement and the concerned assets of the specific users. Therefore, a generic value cannot be applied to all CSPs and CSCs. Although vulnerabilities and assets for each incident scenario are given by the ENISA framework, it does not describe how those values can be adapted for a specific CSP and CSC pair. CARAM fills this gap. For that, first the qualitative scale used by ENISA as probability and impact values are mapped to a quantitative scale as follows:

Very low → 1
Low → 2
Medium → 3
High → 4
Very high → 5

For example, probability P_1 and impact I_1 values for the first scenario (i.e., lock in) is HIGH and MEDIUM respectively. We map these values as follows: $P_1 = 4$ and $I_1 = 3$.

To compute the risk levels considering particular vulnerabilities and assets involved CARAM adjusts the values from ENISA, taken as a baseline, taking into account

Probability					
very high	4	5	6	7	8
high	3	4	5	6	7
medium	2	3	4	5	6
low	1	2	3	4	5
very low	0	1	2	3	4
	very low	low	medium	high	very high	**impact**

Fig. 1 ENISA definition of risk levels

additional information about the cloud service. For that, we use Eqs. 1 and 2:

$$\beta_i = P_i \times \nu_i \tag{1}$$

$$\delta_i = I_i \times \alpha_i \tag{2}$$

In Eq. 1, for the risk scenario i, β_i is the adjusted probability, ν_i is the vulnerability index of a given CSP, δ_i is the adjusted impact and α_i is the asset index for a given CSC. Here we assume that probability and impact of an incident are proportional to the number of non-addressed vulnerabilities by a CSP; and impact is proportional to the number of CSC assets related to a risk scenario.

Note that vulnerability index of a CSP is the same for all CSCs and the asset index of a CSC is the same for all CSPs. Vulnerability and asset indices are calculated as given in Eqs. 3 and 4 respectively, where $\nu_{ki} = 1$ if vulnerability k is in the list of vulnerabilities [1] for risk scenario i, and 0 otherwise. Similarly, $\alpha_{ki} = 1$ if asset k is in the list of assets [1] for risk scenario i. Please note again that there are 53 vulnerabilities (see Table 2) and 23 assets (see Table 3) listed in [1]. The vulnerability related parameter ϵ_k in Eq. 3 is derived from the answers to CAIQ, and elaborated on later in Subsection "The vulnerability parameter for a CSP". The asset related parameter γ_k in Eq. 4 is given value 0 if the CSC's answer to the question "Does the service that you seek will involve any asset of yours that fall in the same category as asset k?" is "No", and value 1 otherwise.

$$\nu_i = \frac{\sum_{k=1}^{53} \nu_{ki} \times \epsilon_k}{\sum_{k=1}^{53} \nu_{ki}} \tag{3}$$

$$\alpha_i = \frac{\sum_{k=1}^{53} \alpha_{ki} \times \gamma_k}{\sum_{k=1}^{53} \alpha_{ki}} \tag{4}$$

We would like to highlight that CARAM is independent from the number of incident scenarios and probability, impact, vulnerability and assets assigned to the incident scenarios. Moreover, it is possible to assign weight values for each of assets and vulnerabilities if some of them are assumed as of higher importance comparing to the others.

The vulnerability parameter for a CSP

We use CSPs' responses to CAIQ from [4] to assign a value to the vulnerability related parameter ϵ_k. Most of the entries in STAR are using the CAIQ v1.1 template [25] that provides 148 questions grouped into the control areas shown in Table 4 covering the state of implementation of security controls.

The v1.1 template accepts a free text answer in contrast to the newer v3.0.1 template where the CSPs are expected to choose their answers between "Yes", "No" and

Table 4 The control areas in CAIQ

Compliance (CO)	Operations Management (OP)
Data Governance (DG)	Risk Management (RI)
Facility Security (FS)	Release Management (RM)
Human Resources Security (HR)	Resiliency (RS)
Information Security (IS)	Security Architecture (SA)
Legal (LG)	

"Not applicable". This makes the answers unsuitable for automated analysis. We proposed a mechanism to map the answers given to the questions in CAIQ to one of the control implementation status categories in Table 5.

The category *Implemented* has a positive meaning (the control is in place), but the answer "Yes" to a CAIQ question does not always imply a more secure system. For example, the "Yes" answer to CAIQ Question RS06-01 *"Are any of your data centers located in places which have a high probability/occurrence of high-impact environmental risks (floods, tornadoes, earthquakes, hurricanes, etc.)?"* implies a negative outcome, which means the control is not implemented. In such cases we classify the "Yes" answer as *Not Implemented* and the "No" answer as *Implemented*.

We analyzed 44 out of 70 CSPs from the mentioned registry providing answers to about 200 questions each. To be included in the selection a provider had to fill in the CAIQ questionnaire in the format provided by CSA (to enable automated processing). The responses of some of the big CSPs (e.g. Amazon, HP, Microsoft, RedHat, or SAP[1]) who provided answers in other forms, though, were processed manually to ensure the consideration of the major players. Given the workload, we decided to automate the classification of the free text answers to CAIQ questions using the supervised machine learning algorithms (sequential minimal optimization and string vectorization) provided by the WEKA tool [26]. We created a training set from a random sampling of around 300 manually classified answers out of overall circa 9000 answers and used it to classify the other remaining answers. The 10-fold cross-validation provided an accuracy of around 84 % of correctly classified instances, which we consider enough for our purpose.

Table 5 The categorization of the answers given to the questions in CAIQ

Implemented	the control is in place
Conditionally implemented	the control can be implemented under some conditions
Not implemented	the control is not in place
Not applicable	the control is not applicable to the provided service

After classification of the answers to one of the categories in Table 5, the implementation value q_m is assigned for each of the controls identified by question m:

- *Implemented* $\rightarrow$ $q_m = 0$: the related vulnerabilities are mitigated
- *Not Applicable* $\rightarrow$ $q_m = 0$: these controls do not impact the risk value
- *No* $\rightarrow$ $q_m = 1$: the related vulnerabilities are not mitigated
- *Conditionally Implemented* $\rightarrow$ the CSC needs to clarify with the CSP if the control can be implemented. If yes, $q_m = 0$. Otherwise, $q_m = 1$.

When q_m is known for a CSP and a CSC, Eq. 5 gives the vulnerability related parameter ϵ_k for the CSP and the CSC. Please note that this value is for a specific CSP and CSC pair.

$$\epsilon_k = \frac{\sum_{m=1}^{n} r_{mk} \times q_m}{\sum_{m=1}^{n} r_{mk} \times b_m} \qquad (5)$$

In Eq. 5, n is the number of questions in CAIQ. r_{mk} is the mapping of the CAIQ questions to vulnerabilities: it is 1 if the control representing the question m mitigates the vulnerability k, and 0 otherwise (see Table 6 for an example mapping excerpt and Additional file 1 — Mapping CAIQ questions to vulnerabilities.xlsx for the full mapping).

Finally, $b_m = 0$ if the answer to the question m is "Not Applicable" and 1 otherwise. This allows discarding the unrelated questions to avoid wrongly penalizing the CSPs.

In Eq. 5 ϵ_k receives a minimum value 0 if all the controls related to the vulnerability k are implemented and hence the vulnerability does not impact negatively the risk

values. The more controls related to the vulnerability k are not implemented, the higher ϵ_k is. Its maximum value is 1, which means the CSP has no measures against the vulnerability k.

Relative risk assessment-based CSP selection

ENISA's risk assessment model is based on 35 incident scenarios. These numerous risks make it difficult for customers to meaningfully compare multiple providers. Therefore, we first reduce the number of criteria from these 35 incident scenarios to three categories of cloud risks: security, privacy and service [24]. For that, we compute the probability that a privacy (β_r), a security (β_s) and a service (β_e) incident can occur and the impact of a privacy (δ_r), a security (δ_s) and a service (δ_e) incident by applying Eqs. 6 to 11. In Eqs. 6 and 9, $r_i = 1$ if ENISA incident scenario i is related to privacy, and 0 otherwise (see Table 7 for an example mapping). ω_{ri} and α_{ri} are real numbers between 0 and 1. They are the weight factors for probability and impact respectively. The significance of every scenario may not be the same when calculating an aggregated value for privacy, security and service incidents. Moreover, the scenarios may need to be treated differently for each CSC especially when calculating the aggregated impact values. The weight factors are for making these adjustments. If the significance of each scenario is the same, then the weight factors can be assigned 1. Similar to r_i, s_i and e_i are the mapping values for security and service risks respectively (see Table 7). ω_{si} and α_{si} are the weight factors for security scenarios, and ω_{ei} and α_{ei} are the weight factors for service scenarios.

$$\beta_r = \frac{\sum_{i=1}^{35} \beta_i \times r_i \times \omega_{ri}}{\sum_{i=1}^{35} r_i \times \omega_{ri}} \qquad (6)$$

$$\beta_s = \frac{\sum_{i=1}^{35} \beta_i \times s_i \times \omega_{si}}{\sum_{i=1}^{35} s_i \times \omega_{si}} \qquad (7)$$

$$\beta_e = \frac{\sum_{i=1}^{35} \beta_i \times e_i \times \omega_{ei}}{\sum_{i=1}^{35} e_i \times \omega_{ei}} \qquad (8)$$

$$\delta_r = \frac{\sum_{i=1}^{35} \delta_i \times r_i \times \alpha_{ri}}{\sum_{i=1}^{35} r_i \times \alpha_{ri}} \qquad (9)$$

$$\delta_s = \frac{\sum_{i=1}^{35} \delta_i \times s_i \times \alpha_{si}}{\sum_{i=1}^{35} s_i \times \alpha_{si}} \qquad (10)$$

$$\delta_e = \frac{\sum_{i=1}^{35} \delta_i \times e_i \times \alpha_{ei}}{\sum_{i=1}^{35} e_i \times \alpha_{ei}} \qquad (11)$$

Table 6 Mapping r_{mk} of CAIQ questions to ENISA vulnerabilities (excerpt)

Control group	Vulnerabilities mitigated
Audit Planning CO-01	V02, V03, V13, V14, V16, V23, V25, V26, V27, V29, V33, V35, V50
Independent Audits CO-02	V02, V03, V13, V14, V16, V23, V25, V26, V27, V29, V33, V35, V50
Third Party Audits CO-03	V02, V03, V13, V14, V16, V23, V25, V26, V27, V29, V33, V35, V50
Contact/Authority Maintenance CO-04	V14, V21, V29, V30
Information System Regulatory Mapping CO-05	V07, V08, V09, V10
Intellectual Property CO-06	V34, V31, V35, V44
Intellectual Property CO-07	V34, V31, V35, V44
Intellectual Property CO-08	V34, V31, V35, V44

Table 7 Mapping (r_i, s_i, e_i) of ENISA risk scenarios to risk categories

Risk scenario i	Privacy r_i	Security s_i	Service e_i
P1	0	0	1
P2	1	0	0
P3	1	1	1
P4	0	1	0
P5	0	0	1
P6	1	1	1
P7	0	0	1
T1	0	0	1
T2	1	1	0
T3	1	1	1
T4	1	1	1
T5	1	1	0
T6	1	1	0
T7	1	1	0
T8	0	0	1
T9	0	0	1
T10	1	1	0
T11	1	1	0
T12	1	1	1
T13	0	1	0
L1	1	1	0
L2	1	0	0
L3	1	1	0
L4	0	0	1
N1	0	0	1
N2	0	0	1
N3	0	0	1
N4	1	1	1
N5	0	1	0
N6	0	1	1
N7	0	1	1
N8	1	1	1
N9	1	1	0
N10	1	1	1
N11	0	0	1

When probability (i.e., β) and impact (i.e., δ) values are calculated, they are mapped to the qualitative scale as follows:

$[0, 0.5) \rightarrow$ Negligible
$[0.5, 1) \rightarrow$ Extremely Low
$[1, 1.5) \rightarrow$ Very Low
$[1.5, 2) \rightarrow$ Low
$[2, 2.5) \rightarrow$ Below Average

$[2.5, 3) \rightarrow$ Above Average
$[3, 3.5) \rightarrow$ High
$[3.5, 4) \rightarrow$ Very High
$[4, 4.5) \rightarrow$ Extremely High
$[4.5, 5] \rightarrow$ Not Recommended

Please note that this is a higher resolution scale with 10 values comparing to ENISA's original five value qualitative scale. We need a higher resolution scale to differentiate CSPs because the adjusted probabilities of risk scenarios are mostly below the average for the CSPs that answer CAIQ. Those CSPs are clearly aware of the incident scenarios and implement at least a subset of the controls, which are subject in CAIQ. Finally, by using the matrix in Fig. 2—which is similar to but has a higher resolution than the matrix in Fig. 1—the risk values for privacy R_r, security R_s and service R_e are obtained. Please note that these values are calculated for each CSP-CSC pair. Although, the color codes in Fig. 2 are only for the three value qualitative scale (i.e., Low < Medium < High) as in the ENISA's assessment, the quantative scale for the overall risk assessment is also higher resolution (between 0 and 18 instead of 0 and 10) which is the result of selecting higher resolution scales for probability and impact.

At this stage, the CSC provides CARAM with the maximum acceptable levels of risks for privacy R_{rmax}, security R_{smax} and service R_{smax}. The CSC may also provide a set $U = \{p_1, \ldots, p_n\}$ of CSPs that should be excluded from the assessment due to reasons like business relations, politics, past experience, etc. When this information is available, CARAM creates a set F of feasible CSPs out of the set S of all the CSPs available for assessment (i.e. CSPs that have a completed CAIQ in STAR) such that $F \subset S$ using Eq. 12.

$$p_i \in F \iff (p_i \notin U) \wedge (R_{rmax} > R_{ri}) \wedge \\ (R_{smax} > R_{si}) \wedge (R_{emax} > R_{ei}) \quad (12)$$

where R_{ri}, R_{si} and R_{ei} are the privacy, security and service risks for the CSP p_i.

F can be an empty set, a set with only one element or multiple elements. If F is an empty set, there is no feasible solution for the CSC. If F has only one element, that is the only feasible solution for the CSC under the given constraints. In both of these cases, CARAM informs the CSC directly with the result. If F has multiple elements, all the dominating CSPs are removed from F resulting in the set F'. Here we define the dominating relation $\succ$: $CSP_1 \succ CSP_2 \iff R_{ri}, R_{si}$ and R_{ei} for CSP_1 are higher than those for CSP_2. If the resulting F' includes only one CSP, CARAM informs the CSC about the solution that fits the best to it. If there are multiple CSPs in F', the CSC is given the complete F' for the posterior articulation of the preferences.

Probability

9	10	11	12	13	14	15	16	17	18
8	9	10	11	12	13	14	15	16	17
7	8	9	10	11	12	13	14	15	16
6	7	8	9	10	11	12	13	14	15
5	6	7	8	9	10	11	12	13	14
4	5	6	7	8	9	10	11	12	13
3	4	5	6	7	8	9	10	11	12
2	3	4	5	6	7	8	9	10	11
1	2	3	4	5	6	7	8	9	10
0	1	2	3	4	5	6	7	8	9

Impact

Fig. 2 CARAM definition of risk levels

Experimental results

We prototyped CARAM and run experiments the data in STAR [4] during the course of 2015. In this section we present the results of these experiments (see Additional file 2 — CARAM Experiments.xlsx for the detailed data). Figures 3 and 4 illustrate the vulnerability index v_i and the adjusted probability β_i values for the 44 CSPs included in our analysis from STAR. These are calculated by the CARAM prototype as explained in Section "Risk levels computation".

The differences between the vulnerability indices and therefore the adjusted probabilities of various CSPs in STAR are in the order of magnitude. For example, the lowest vulnerability index is 0.011, which is the vulnerability index of a CSP called as Iguana (we call the CSPs in STAR database by using animal names to preserve their confidentiality). On the other hand, the vulnerability index

for the highest risk CSP (i.e., Gazelle) is 0.491. Although the vulnerability index of Gazelle is more than 44 times higher than the Iguana's, it is less than 0.5. This means that the probability value for the highest risk CSP in STAR will be reduced more than 50 %, and become "LOW" according to our higher resolution qualitative scale. This results from the fact that the CSPs from STAR declare to implement the majority of controls. That makes sense because the CSPs in STAR represent a subset of CSPs which are putting an effort to reduce their risk. Their submission of CAIQ is an indication for that.

Another interesting observation in Figs. 3 and 4 is about the differences among privacy, security and service vulnerability index and adjusted probability for each CSP. The differences among these three values are observable only for few CSPs. This is an indication that the CSPs in STAR do not focus on one of privacy, security or service, but

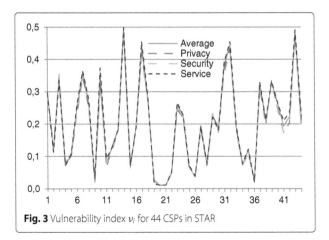

Fig. 3 Vulnerability index v_i for 44 CSPs in STAR

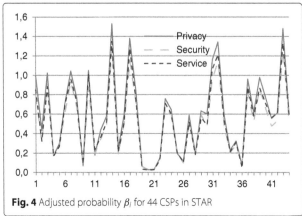

Fig. 4 Adjusted probability β_i for 44 CSPs in STAR

typically treat them equally. This is coupled with the fact that the categories of privacy, security and service risks are overlapping, and the number of risks in the privacy, security and service categories by our selection are almost the same: 19, 22 and 22 respectively (see Table 7).

For our experiments, we considered five types of CSCs based on the nature of their assets. We calculated the percentage of the risk incident scenarios that each asset is related to the ENISA risk assessment. We noticed that the following three assets are not related to any scenarios: $A15$ management interface APIs, $A18$ physical buildings, and $A19$ cloud provider application (source code). We call any asset related to at least 10 % of the incident scenarios as highly exposed asset. Some assets are service-related and some are data assets. Finally, data assets can be personal or not personal. Based on these, we use the following five types of CSCs in our experiments:

CSC_1 have all the assets in the ENISA's list.
CSC_2 have all highly exposed assets.
CSC_3 have all the data and service assets.
CSC_4 have only data assets.
CSC_5 have only personal data assets.

CARAM computes the privacy, security and service impact values adjusted for these five classes of CSCs as depicted in Fig. 5. As clearly shown, the privacy impact of risk scenarios is somewhat higher than the service and security impacts. This may be explained by the fact that most of the risks directly or indirectly may impact an asset related to privacy. Since the higher order CSCs (i.e., CSC_5 is the highest order and CSC_1 is the lowest order CSC) have only a subset of the assets owned by the lower order CSCs, their adjusted impact values are predictably lower.

In Figs. 6, 7 and 8 the risk levels for various CSC classes and three CSPs, which have the lowest, average and the highest adjusted probability, are illustrated. The darker

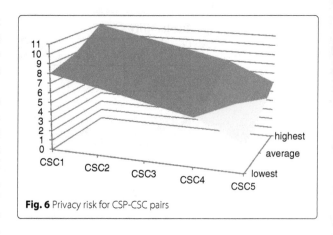

Fig. 6 Privacy risk for CSP-CSC pairs

part of the figures shows the CSC-CSP pairs with medium level of risk, and the lighter part shows the CSC-CSP pairs with low level of risk according to the ENISA's qualitative risk scale. The vertical axis of the figures gives the risk level according to the CARAM's higher resolution scale as in Fig. 2. We cannot observe any CSC class and CSP (the CSPs from STAR) pair that have high level of risk. This is as expected because all the CSPs in STAR apply at least half of the controls from the CSA CCM. The effects of measures are also assessed in the cloud risk assessment of CNIL [16]. Almost the same shift in risk levels is addressed in [16]. CARAM's difference from CNIL's risk assessment is that CARAM can take into account the effects of measures for specific CSC-CSP pairs. In Figs. 6, 7 and 8 it can be observed that privacy risk is higher than the security and the security risk is higher than the service risk. The privacy risk is low only for CSC_4 and CSC_5 when the CSPs with adjusted probability value below the average. For all the other types of CSC-CSP pairs, the privacy risk is medium.

Figures 7 and 8 indicate that the security and service risk levels for almost all the CSPs in STAR is low for CSC_3, CSC_4 and CSC_5. When the CSC uses cloud also for service assets (i.e., CSC_3) the security and service risks for CSPs with average or above adjusted probability becomes

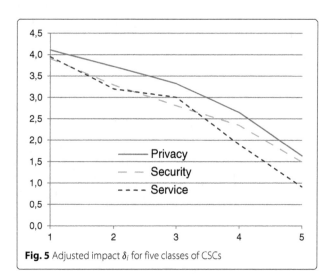

Fig. 5 Adjusted impact δ_i for five classes of CSCs

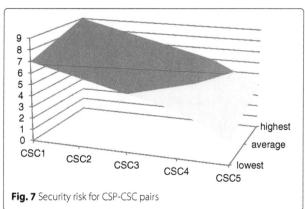

Fig. 7 Security risk for CSP-CSC pairs

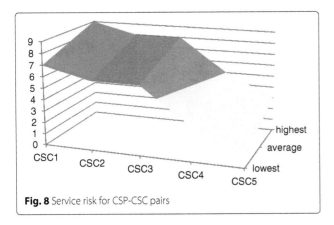

Fig. 8 Service risk for CSP-CSC pairs

medium. The security and service risks for CSC_1 and CSC_2 are always medium for the CSPs in STAR.

Limitations

There are a few limitations that may impact the accuracy of the results mainly stemming from the analyzed input data, some of which were also outlined in [5]:

- Vague formulation of the CAIQ answers provided by the analyzed CSPs: some CSPs avoid direct yes/no answers to the CAIQ questions and use generic wording instead;
- Possibility for deliberate misinformation in the CAIQ answers provided by the analyzed CSPs: CSA has a process of reporting misinformation in CSA STAR [4];
- Ineffective implementation of the security controls by the analyzed CSPs: only 3 of them have third party certification from CSA and CSA does not provide a detailed breakdown of scores for each control. To address this additional methods for evaluating control effectiveness are required, e.g. penetration testing or analysis of previous incidents (see [24, 27] for example approaches);
- In the CAIQ v1.1 [25] there is a misalignment between the description of the security controls and the actual questions that are querying their implementation; this seems to be addressed though by CSA in the newer version of CAIQ.

Notwithstanding, all results exposed in this paper are verifiable and reproducible. Variations can be introduced according to the interpretation of the cloud provider answers. We favoured an impartial, automated classification of the answers based on our training set. Smaller scale uses of CARAM can reach much better precision in the case of manual classification of the CSP answers to the CAIQ questionnaire - which is time consuming but doable and even advisable for some categories of CSCs. Such manual check of the CSPs security practices can

sometimes be done in coordination between CSP and CSC, what would lead to more transparency. As big cloud players are unlikely to invest in such reviews, CSCs can perhaps increase the pressure for (automated) continuous monitoring of security controls, which would provide more visibility to them on the security operations of the providers.

Conclusion

CARAM is a qualitative and relative risk assessment model for assisting CSCs to select a CSP that fits their risk profile the best. It is based on the existing frameworks such as ENISA, CAIQ and CNIL and complements them to provide the CSC with a practical tool. It is a risk assessment approach such that evaluation is carried out for a specific CSC, which means assessment for each CSP-CSC pair is for that pair and not generic. Moreover, the model can be easily adapted to assess further risks scenarios and/or security control frameworks, might they change in the future. These multiple features make CARAM unique with respect to the state of the art in risk assessment techniques and also among other works proposing cloud security metrics.

We have implemented a Proof-of-Concept prototype as part of the Data Protection Impact Assessment tool developed in A4Cloud project [28, 29]. The tool asks a (potential) CSC to select a CSP from a given list of around 50 providers, which answered to the CAIQ and evaluates a risk landscape of 35 risks from Table 1 grouped into 3 categories: service, security and privacy using the described methodology. Also the tool allows the CSCs to compare the risk profiles of any two providers, thus helping to select the most suitable CSP from the security point. We performed the analysis of the risk profiles for 44 CSPs from STAR and 5 imaginary classes of CSCs illustrating the coverage of security controls by the different CSPs.

Endnote

[1] The answers concerning the SAP HANA Enterprise Cloud were only available to customers on demand.

Additional files

Additional file 1: Mapping CAIQ questions to vulnerabilities. This file contains a table representing an example mapping r_{mk} of CAIQ questions to ENISA vulnerabilities (see Section The vulnerability parameter for a CSP). This is the full version of the mapping provided in Table 6. (XLSX 16.6 kb)

Additional file 2: CARAM Experiments. This file contains the simulation data (see Section Experimental results) including the risk values for several classes of CSCs for all the analyzed CSPs from STAR. (XLSX 331 kb)

Acknowledgements
This work was partly conducted during the EU-funded FP7 project titled as "Accountability for Cloud and Other Future Internet Services", A4Cloud (Grant No. 317550). We also acknowledge the FP7 EU-funded project Coco Cloud

"Confidential and compliant clouds" (Grant No. 610853) as it benefited from fruitful interactions with the project's team members.

Authors' contributions

EC drafted the model, conducted the experiments and drafted the manuscript. AG revised the model, performed a statistical analysis of the data from STAR, compiled the related work and drafted the manuscript. AS revised the model, implemented a proof of concept prototype and drafted the manuscript. YR revised the model and statistical analysis of the data from STAR and critically reviewed the manuscript. All authors read and approved the final manuscript.

Competing interests

The authors declare that they have no competing interests.

Author details

[1] Electrical and Computer Engineering Department, University of Stavanger, Stavanger, Norway. [2] SAP Labs France, Mougins, France. [3] Network Security Team, Eurecom, Biot, France.

References

1. Catteddu D, Hogben G (2009) Cloud Computing. Benefits, risks and recommendations for information security. Technical report. ENISA. http://www.enisa.europa.eu/activities/risk-management/files/deliverables/cloud-computing-risk-assessment/at_download/fullReport. Accessed 13 Aug 2015
2. The Notorious Nine Cloud Computing Top Threats in 2013 (2013). Technical report, Cloud Security Alliance. https://downloads. cloudsecurityalliance.org/initiatives/top_threats/The_Notorious_Nine_Cloud_Computing_Top_Threats_in_2013.pdf. Accessed 13 Aug 2015
3. Article 29 Data Protection Working Party, Opinion 05/2012 on Cloud Computing (2012). http://ec.europa.eu/justice/data-protection/article-29/documentation/opinion-recommendation/files/2012/wp196_en.pdf. Accessed 13 Aug 2015
4. Cloud Security Alliance, Security CSA Trust & Assurance Registry (STAR). https://cloudsecurityalliance.org/star/. Accessed 25 Jul 2014
5. Cayirci E, Garaga A, Santana A, Roudier Y (2014) A Cloud Adoption Risk Assessment Model. In: 2014 IEEE/ACM 7th International Conference on Utility and Cloud Computing. pp 908–913. doi:10.1109/UCC.2014.148. http://ieeexplore.ieee.org/lpdocs/epic03/wrapper.htm?arnumber=7027615. Accessed 13 Aug 2015
6. ISO 31000:2009. Risk management - Principles and guidelines (2009). Technical report, ISO/IEC. http://www.iso.org/iso/catalogue_detail?csnumber=43170. Accessed 13 Aug 2015
7. ISO 31010:2009. Risk management - Risk assessment techniques (2009). Technical report, ISO/IEC. http://www.iso.org/iso/catalogue_detail?csnumber=51073. Accessed 13 Aug 2015
8. ISO/IEC 27005:2011 Information technology - Security techniques - Information security risk management (2011). Technical report, ISO/IEC. http://www.iso.org/iso/catalogue_detail?csnumber=56742. Accessed 13 Aug 2015
9. NIST Special Publication 800-30 Revision 1: Guide for Conducting Risk Assessments (2012). Technical Report September, NIST. http://csrc.nist.gov/publications/nistpubs/800-30-rev1/sp800_30_r1.pdf. Accessed 13 Aug 2015
10. NIST Special Publication 800-37 Revision 1: Guide for Applying the Risk Management Framework to Federal Information Systems A Security Life Cycle Approach (2010). Technical report, NIST. doi:10.6028/NIST.SP.800-30r1. Accessed 13 Aug 2015
11. COBIT 5. A Business Framework for the Governance and Management of Enterprise IT (2012). Technical report, ISACA. http://www.isaca.org/cobit/pages/default.aspx. Accessed 13 Aug 2015
12. Stone G, Noel P (2013) Cloud Risk Decision Framework. Technical report. Microsoft. http://download.microsoft.com/documents/australia/enterprise/SMIC1545_PDF_v7_pdf.pdf. Accessed 13 Aug 2015
13. Cloud Security Alliance Cloud Control Matrix (CCM). https://cloudsecurityalliance.org/research/ccm/. Accessed 25 Jul 2014
14. Kaplan S, Garrick BJ, Kaplin S, Garrick GJ (1981) On the quantitative definition of risk. Risk Anal. 1(1):11–27. doi: 10.1111/j.1539-6924.1981.tb01350.x
15. Ezell BC, Bennett SP, von Winterfeldt D, Sokolowski J, Collins AJ (2010) Probabilistic Risk Analysis and Terrorism Risk. Risk Anal 30(4):575–589. doi:10.1111/j.1539-6924.2010.01401.x
16. Methodology for Privacy Risk Management; How to implement the Data Protection Act (2012). Technical report, CNIL. http://www.cnil.fr/fileadmin/documents/en/CNIL-ManagingPrivacyRisks-Methodology.pdf. Accessed 13 Aug 2015
17. Cloud Security Alliance Consensus Assessment Initiative Questionnaire (CAIQ). https://cloudsecurityalliance.org/research/cai/. Accessed 25 Jul 2014
18. Luna J, Ghani H, Vateva T, Suri N (2011) Quantitative Assessment of Cloud Security Agreements: A Case Study
19. Luna J, Langenberg R, Suri N (2012) Benchmarking cloud security level agreements using quantitative policy trees. In: Proceedings of the 2012 ACM Workshop on Cloud Computing Security Workshop - CCSW '12. ACM Press, New York. p 103. doi:10.1145/2381913.2381932. http://dl.acm.org/citation.cfm?doid=2381913.2381932. Accessed 13 Aug 2015
20. Habib SM, Ries S, Muhlhauser M (2011) Towards a Trust Management System for Cloud Computing. In: 2011 IEEE 10th International Conference on Trust, Security and Privacy in Computing and Communications. pp 933–939. doi:10.1109/TrustCom.2011.129. http://ieeexplore.ieee.org/lpdocs/epic03/wrapper.htm?arnumber=6120922. Accessed 13 Aug 2015
21. Busby J, Langer L, Schöller M, Shirazi N, Smith P (2013) SEcure Cloud computing for CRitical infrastructure IT Deliverable: 3.1 Methodology for Risk Assessment and Management. Technical report, SECCRIT Project. http://www.ait.ac.at/uploads/media/D3-1-Methodology-for-Risk-Assessment-and-Management.pdf. Accessed 13 Aug 2015
22. SPECS Secure Provisioning of Cloud Services Based on SLA Management. http://www.specs-project.eu/. Accessed 13 Aug 2015
23. Luna J, Taha A, Trapero R, Suri N (2015) Quantitative Reasoning About Cloud Security Using Service Level Agreements. IEEE Transactions on Cloud Computing PP(99):1–1. doi:10.1109/TCC.2015.2469659
24. Cayirci E (2013) A joint trust and risk model for MSaaS mashups. In: 2013 Winter Simulations Conference (WSC). pp 1347–1358. doi: 10.1109/WSC.2013.6721521. http://ieeexplore.ieee.org/lpdocs/epic03/wrapper.htm?arnumber=6721521. Accessed 13 Aug 2015
25. Cloud Security Alliance Consensus Assessments Initiative Questionnaire V1.1. https://cloudsecurityalliance.org/download/consensus-assessments-initiative-questionnaire-v1-1/ Accessed 25 Jul 2014
26. Machine Learning Group at the University of Waikato WEKA 3: Data Mining Software in Java. http://www.cs.waikato.ac.nz/ml/weka/. Accessed 25 Jul 2014
27. Habib SM, Varadharajan V, Muhlhauser M (2013) A Trust-Aware Framework for Evaluating Security Controls of Service Providers in Cloud Marketplaces. In: 2013 12th IEEE International Conference on Trust, Security and Privacy in Computing and Communications. pp 459–468. doi: 10.1109/TrustCom.2013.58. http://ieeexplore.ieee.org/lpdocs/epic03/wrapper.htm?arnumber=6680875. Accessed 13 Aug 2015
28. Cloud Accountability Project. http://www.a4cloud.eu/. Accessed 10 Aug 2015
29. Garaga A, Santana de Oliveira A, Cayirci E, Dalla Corte L, Leenes R, Mhungu R, Stefanatou D, Tetrimida K, Felici M, Alnemr R, Pearson S, Vranaki A (2014) D:C-6.2 Prototype for the data protection impact assessment tool. Technical report, A4Cloud Project. http://www.a4cloud.eu/sites/default/files/D36.2%20Prototype%20for%20the%20data%20protection%20impact%20assessment%20tool.pdf. Accessed 13 Aug 2015

4

MDA: message digest-based authentication for mobile cloud computing

Saurabh Dey[1*], Srinivas Sampalli[1] and Qiang Ye[2]

Abstract

The emerging area of mobile cloud computing will influence the future of varied applications, such as electronic commerce and health informatics. It is expected to rise in popularity over other models in cloud computing. This is facilitated by its simplicity, accessibility and ease of use. With mobile cloud computing, resource-constrained mobile devices could capitalize on the computation/storage resources of cloud servers via communication networks. Despite the advantage of this innovative computing model, mobile devices in mobile cloud computing are open to more security risks because they often have to access cloud servers through untrusted networks from different locations. Therefore, security is a critical problem to be tackled in mobile cloud computing. One of the most important aspects of mobile cloud computing security is to establish authenticated communication sessions between mobile devices and cloud servers. In this paper, we present a novel authentication scheme, Message Digest-based Authentication (MDA). Technically, MDA strategically incorporates hashing, in addition to traditional user ID and passwords, to achieve mutual authentication. The effectiveness of MDA is validated with Scyther, a widely-used security protocol analyzer. Our experimental results indicate that MDA is capable of withstanding a variety of different security attacks, such as man-in-the-middle, replay attacks, etc.

Keywords: Cloud computing, Security, Mobile devices, Authentication, Hashing

Introduction

The emergence of cloud computing has increased the productivity of a variety of different fields through three service models: SaaS (software as a service), IaaS (infrastructure as a service), and PaaS (platform as a service) [11, 30]. In traditional cloud computing, the following technologies have been used to provide varied services:

- Public Cloud: Public cloud does not require the initial investment and offers a plethora of services to the general mass. However, it does not provide a high level of security for the data, nor does it provide control over the cloud infrastructure [45].
- Private Cloud: Private cloud, as its name indicates, is contrary to public cloud. Private clouds are owned by specific business organizations and are mainly used for internal services. Private cloud can be considered as another form of a traditional server. It provides

customized security for data and more control over the cloud infrastructure [18, 45].

- Hybrid Cloud: Hybrid cloud is a combination of both private and public cloud, which is usually used by organizations to improve their resource performance. The organization places its non-important components on the public cloud and controls the computing environment through its private cloud [3].
- Virtualization: Virtualization is the core technology used in cloud computing environment. The cloud server provides the access to a pool of hardware, network and storage resources through virtualization [33]. A virtual platform is created to serve a client with customized configuration and requirements, and by initializing many virtual machines of this kind with limited number of actual physical resources, the cloud server is able to provide its services to multiple concurrent users.
- PaaS (platform as a service): Platform as a service allows product deployment on the cloud, which requires distributed resources [4]. A web-based product might require the access to various resources

*Correspondence: saurabh@cs.dal.ca
[1]Dalhousie University, Halifax, Canada
Full list of author information is available at the end of the article

or infrastructures that are distributed over multiple locations. In order to deploy these products, PaaS provides a platform that has the access to the cloud-based distributed resources.

- IaaS (infrastructure as a service): Using infrastructure as a service, any individual or organization can lease cloud resources to accomplish their tasks [39], such as utilizing storage servers (e.g. renting EMC2 data servers as a storage) provided by a cloud service provider.
- SaaS (software as a service): Software as a service is the most commonly used cloud service, where clients use open or proprietary cloud- based software, such as cloud based anti-virus and word processing software.
- In addition to SaaS, PaaS, and IaaS, cloud service providers offer network-as-a-service (NaaS) [34] by providing the access to virtualized network resources and desktop-as-a-service (DaaS) [15] considering the demand of the availability of desktop resources on mobile devices.

With the advancement of cloud services and mobile technology, it is possible to access and process a large volume of data at any time and from any location. In today's fast-paced environment, this mobility-based complex computing system acts as one of the key components for the growth of research, economy, and society. This combination of cloud infrastructure and mobile technology brings in a new computational model called mobile cloud computing. With mobile cloud computing, resource-constrained mobile devices could capitalize on the computation/storage resources of cloud servers via communication networks. All of the technologies mentioned previously can be used in a mobile cloud computing system.

Despite the advantages of ease of access and 24-7 availability, mobile cloud computing leads to unprecedented security vulnerabilities because data has to be transferred between mobile devices and cloud servers. Therefore, we focus on the security aspect of mobile cloud computing, although many existing studies have attempted to address the behaviour, quality of service, scalability, flexibility, and pricing problem of cloud computing systems [27, 29, 35]. Addressing the security/vulnerability problem in mobile cloud computing is critical to the success of this promising technology.

In this paper, we attempt to improve the security of mobile cloud computing by introducing a novel authentication scheme, Message Digest-based Authentication (MDA). Existing studies indicate that, in general, a mobile cloud computing system uses either user id and password based authentication [36], or USIM (universal subscriber identity module) based authentication [2]. Different from the existing schemes, MDA employs both hashing and

the traditional user id/password to arrive at an effective authentication mechanism. MDA ensures that mobile cloud computing is secured from any type of unauthorized access at the beginning of each communication session. This paper is an extension of the previously-published study [38]. As an improvement over the previous study, MDA employs the client registration expiry period and one-way mathematical hashing function to encrypt the user ID in order to make the authentication process more secure and more unpredictable.

The rest of the paper is organized as follows. "Related work" section describes the related work. The details of the proposed authentication scheme, MDA, are included in "MDA: message digest based authentication" section. The evaluation methodology and the in-depth security analysis are presented in "Evaluation methodology and Security analysis" sections respectively. Finally, "Conclusion" section concludes this paper.

Related work

It is important to address the security problems associated with cloud computing in general and mobile cloud computing in particular. Therefore, the related work is categorized into two themes according to the addressed problems. For both of these two themes, the security challenges are highlighted.

Cloud computing security

Popovic et al. describe a number of security issues related to cloud computing [32]. Their study identifies that remote location of resources and virtualization technologies make the cloud computing environment vulnerable to attacks. In cloud computing, all clients access a common resource location, which introduces security threat to the system. In addition, there is an integrity issue in cases of transfer, storage and retrieval. Furthermore, there is a no common standard to ensure data integrity. Different vendors follow different structures for data storage and access, as a result, clients cannot switch vendors easily and remain locked with one vendor. The other mentioned concern is the need for a common standard of encryption and decryption and client's control. Without proper encryption and security, a cloud environment becomes vulnerable, which introduces threat to attack during the transfer and store of sensitive data (identity or location of individual, race, health, union membership, sexual orientation, job performance, biometric, etc.).

Mathisen et al. explain the different policy issues related to cloud computing [30]. If employees of the cloud hosting company are careless and cannot be trusted, then it implies that there is an inherent vulnerability in the service offered. Similar to Popovic et al. this study also mentioned a potential major future concern with vendor lock-in [32]. Since there is no common standard for APIs (application programming interfaces), storage images and disaster recovery, portability from one vendor to another is an expensive operation. Other than these issues, software used in cloud computing is also an important part, which is vulnerable to external attacks. So by avoiding the use of only open source software in server virtualization, the vulnerability can be reduced.

Yandong et al. focus on different types of clouds viz, public, private and hybrid cloud, and the security issues associated with the public cloud [42]. Public cloud is accessible to a large majority of the general population without much restrictions. This, coupled with the fact that public cloud has plenty of user information, implies that the public cloud is susceptible to attacks.Furthermore, virtualization of the platform introduces security threats. Regulating administrator privileges is required for better authentication, security and privacy. If the virtualization platform is compromised, it implies that a majority of the virtual machines are under attack, which is a potential threat to data security.

To address the above mentioned issues, it is essential to have a standard cloud computing design and usage policy, employee trust, proprietary software for virtualization, and finally physical security of servers. However, data transmitted from a mobile device to a cloud server is still susceptible to several security issues, which will be addressed in the following sub-section.

Mobile cloud computing security

Increased use of mobile devices has meant that extensive research is being performed in the area of security in mobile cloud computing, particularly on authentication. Apart from policy and physical security, there are numerous security issues involved with data transmission and authentication, since mobile devices access cloud from different geographical locations, with different types of networks. The main focus of the study is to design a secure authentication scheme, which is a major component for a secure data transmission process.

Hong et al. describe the mobile cloud security issues related to malicious programs that are injected in a mobile cloud virtualization environment [21]. Virtual mobile instances running on cloud infrastructure are accessed using mobile devices to access resources such as, CPU, memory etc. The research involves usage of machine learning algorithm for detecting abnormal behaviour in the virtual mobile instances. This research is useful to secure the virtualization environment from malware. However, this research does not address issues related to authentication or integrity.

Jana et al. describe the various types of security threats that can appear in a mobile cloud computing environment [23]. Accessing enterprise data through mobile devices brings in privacy and security issues, e.g. locationservices

of a mobile device help an adversary to predict the user's behaviour and movement. They focus on various threats related to AAA (Authorization, Authentication, and Accounting), such as malicious insiders, sniffing, spoofing, identity theft etc. As a control measure they suggest digital signature as used in SAML (Security Assertion Markup Language), security gateways, SSL, encryption, hashing. With the help of fishbone analysis they present, security and privacy threats associated with a mobile cloud computing environment.

Yoo et al. highlight about a cellular automata (*CA*) based lightweight scheme, which is used for multi-user authentication in the cloud environment [44]. The authentication is performed using a one-time password (OTP). For a sender, *A*, the authentication server sends a seed value (*SeedA*) and a *CA* rule. The *CA* is encrypted with the public key of *A*. Though this approach is OTP based and secure, *SeedA* is sent from the authentication server to user *A* without encryption.

Revar et al. describe the usefulness of single sign-on in a mobile cloud computing environment [36]. Single sign-on (SSO) is used on the top layer of cloud. They verified the single sign-on authentication scheme on a Ubuntu server. In SSO, a single user name and password combination is used to access multiple cloud applications. This scheme does not address exactly how a mobile device or any cloud compatible device will access the cloud using SSO.

Ahmad et al. propose a security framework that is based on the subscriber identity module [2]. The authentication is done at boot-time, and is based on USIM response to a random challenge issued by the cloud authentication service. The cloud authentication service has a database to store a list of services, mapping of users and their related services, mapping of IMSIs (International Mobile Subscriber Identity). This scheme works only with mobile devices that support USIM, which is a drawback in case cloud users want to switch to mobile devices that do not support USIM, such as tablets or laptop computers.

MDA: message digest based authentication

In a mobile cloud computing environment, a mobile device has to be registered with a cloud server as a prerequisite process prior to avail any kinds of cloud services. The data transmission between the mobile device and the cloud server must be performed once the mobile device authenticates the cloud server and vice-versa. A strong authentication scheme ensures secure communication between two legitimate parties even if the communication channel experiences potential vulnerability. Since the mobile device lacks of computational capability, it is not suitable to employ complex operations in the mobile device for authentication process. In a mobile cloud computing environment, if a mobile device is registered with a particular cloud service provider, both mobile device and cloud server must authenticate each other in a uniform way in order to secure the communication with a single authentication scheme, which allows a mobile user to access the cloud server from different locations using different networks and different types of mobile devices. A single and secure authentication scheme will help in preventing third party from posing as a legitimate mobile device or as a legitimate cloud service provider. Therefore, we focus on the following research question (RQ).

RQ: Will the use of mathematical hashing, in addition to simple user ID and password authentication improve the security between the mobile device and the cloud server?

To address this research question, we hypothesize that:

H_a: In mobile cloud computing environment, the proposed authentication scheme introduces hashing based security, which reduces the vulnerability of the system to attacks. To determine the vulnerability of the system, we compute the vulnerability score, S_v, which is a measure of the number of attacks a scheme can prevent. The value of S_v lies between 0.0 and 1.0:

$$H_a : 0.0 <= S_v <= 1.0 \qquad (1)$$

A low score of S_v indicates that a scheme offers more security. The details of S_v calculation are discussed in "Evaluation methodology" section.

Ahmad et al. mentioned that IMSI can be used as a mode of authentication [2]. However, not every mobile device has the built-in IMSI chip. For example, many iPads and laptops are not equipped with IMSI chips. Therefore, an authentication scheme based on IMSI is not appropriate for mobile cloud computing. Different than IMSI-based approaches, the proposed scheme, MDA, does not require any additional hardware infrastructure. Thus, MDA is applicable to a variety of different mobile devices, including those that do not have IMSI chips. In addition, with MDA, even if the mobile device is stolen, the authentication information of the user can remain to be safe. Furthermore, when users change their registered mobile devices, they can still access the cloud using other mobile devices after a few encrypted files (such as hashed user and cloud certificates, and/or policies) are ported. MDA is composed of three phases: Registration, Authentication and Update. The details of these phases are presented as follows.

Registration phase

The registration process of a mobile device or mobile user to a cloud server is a one time process wherein the user ID and the password are setup and some encrypted files are exchanged. Figure 1 presents an overview of the registration process. Technically, registration (i.e. setting up an account) involves the exchange of user id, password and other unique information, such as credit card for accessing pay-per-use cloud services. We have considered

a standard mobile device and cloud server registration process that can be accomplished using any standard protocol, such as SSH (secure shell). Upon setting up the mobile user account with cloud server, the cloud server performs a series of operations. Algorithm 1 shows the detailed registration process adopted in our research.

Algorithm 1 Registration: mobile_with_cloud

Require:
    isAlive (*mobile, cloud*)
    hasNetworkAccess (*mobile*)

Ensure:
    Role_Mobile
    const *userID*
    var *password*
    $uid = $ **hash**(*userID*)
    $pwd = $ **hash**(*password*)
    $cloud \leftarrow$ **send**($uid \| pwd$)
    $T_k = uid \oplus pwd$

    Role_Cloud
    recv($uid \| pwd$)
    $T_k = uid \oplus pwd$
    $EXP = $ Registration expiry period for the client
    $\#CF \leftarrow$ **pointer**{**store**(uid, pwd, T_k)}
    $MD_{user} = $ **hash**(usage policy, user access level, user certificate)
    $MD_{cloud} = $ **hash**(user add policy, cloud resource restriction, cloud certificate)
    $MD = $ **hash**($MD_{cloud} \| MD_{user}$)
    $Temp = MD_{user} \| MD_{cloud} \| \#CF \| Pk_{pub\_cloud}$
    $msz = $ **encrypt**($Temp, T_k$)
    $mobile \leftarrow$ **send**(msz)

The two parties involved in the registration process are mobile device and the cloud server. Both the parties must be alive or be in the network to accomplish the registration process. During this phase, the mobile user's user ID and password are created to access the cloud server. Cloud Server stores *hash{userID}*, *hash{password}*, and user's mobile device information in big table for efficient lookup. It generates two hashed messages or message digests. The first, MD_{user}, which consists of user policy (cloud resource usage policy, and user access level), and User certificate. The second message digest is MD_{cloud}, and it consists of cloud policy (user add policy, cloud resource restriction/accessibility information), and Cloud certificate.

Upon generating both message digests, cloud server creates an encrypted message to transmit these information to the mobile device. The encrypted is message is: $E_{T_k}\{Pk_{pub\_cloud} \| MD_{user} \| MD_{cloud} \| \#CF\}$, where

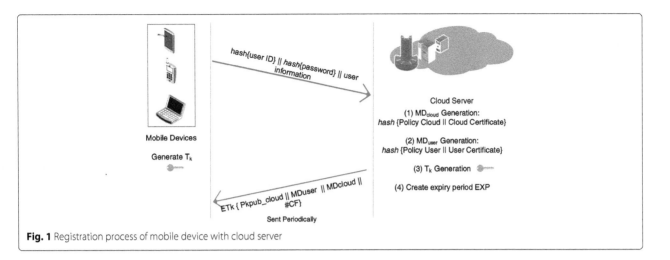

Fig. 1 Registration process of mobile device with cloud server

Pk_{pub_cloud} is the cloud's public key, MD_{user} and MD_{cloud} are the generated message digests, and $\#CF$ is the column reference, which refers to the cloud authentication database for that particular cloud user information. These information are sent from the cloud server to the mobile device after encrypting with key T_k that is generated in both the mobile device and cloud server by XOR-ing (Exclusive OR) hashed $userID$ and hashed $password$ (Eq. 2). In addition, the cloud server generates an expiry period for the client registration information, which triggers a periodic update to the authentication parameters and thereby reduces the vulnerability of the system.

$$T_k = hash\{userID\} \oplus hash\{password\} \qquad (2)$$

The proposed authentication scheme is applicable once the MD_{user}, MD_{cloud}, and $\#CF$ are transferred to the mobile device during the registration process.

Authentication phase
In our research, we have the following assumptions:

- The cloud user has two message digests MD_{user}, and MD_{cloud} in the mobile device.
- He/she knows his/her $userID$ and $password$ to access cloud services.

With these stated assumptions, we can proceed to describe our authentication scheme. At the beginning of each session, the mobile user or mobile device and the cloud server need to authenticate each other in order to start transferring actual data. The authentication process is divided into two steps: cloud authenticating mobile device and mobile device authenticating cloud. The details of these two steps are presented as follows.

Cloud authenticating mobile
The step of cloud authenticating mobile devices can be further split into two sub-steps. In the first sub-step, the

following operations are carried out. Specifically, when a mobile device wants to send an authentication request to the cloud server, it generates a key T_k, using hashed $userID$ and hashed $password$ (Eq. 2). The key T_k, works as the seed for the PRNG (pseudo random number generator) to generate an authentication key, $Auth\_Key_i$. This authentication key $Auth\_Key_i$ is required to encrypt the message digest MD, which is generated by hashing MD_{cloud} and MD_{user} (Eq. 3). The $Auth\_Key_i$ is the nth sequence of bits generated by PRNG that is specified by the state identifier SI. Key T_k is used to encrypt the state identifier SI, and the encrypted message digest $E_{Auth\_Key_i}\{MD\}$. Finally, the encrypted message, $E_{T_k}\{E_{Auth\_Key_i}\{MD\}\|SI\}$ is sent to the cloud server (Fig. 2) along with the column reference $\#CF$. Therefore, the message sent from mobile device to cloud server is $\#CF\|E_{T_k}\{E_{Auth\_Key_i}\{MD\}\|SI\}$

$$MD = hash\{MD_{cloud}\|MD_{user}\} \qquad (3)$$

Algorithm 2 summarizes the operations involved in the first sub-step. These operations are carried out at the mobile device before the authentication request is transmitted to the cloud server. A flow chart for these operations is included in Fig. 2.

In the second sub-step, the following operations are carried out. Upon receiving the authentication request message, the cloud server performs decryption operations. The cloud server searches the specific hashed $userID$ and hashed $password$ in the cloud authentication database based on the shared column reference $\#CF$ that is sent in plain text along with the encrypted message.

Once the hashed $userID$ and hashed $password$ are found, the cloud server checks the registration validity of the user using EXP, stored at the server. If the user registration is not expired, then T_k is generated (Eq. 2) by XOR operation. During this phase, the operations performed at the cloud server are shown in Fig. 3. The generated T_k at the cloud server decrypts the

Algorithm 2 Mobile_to_cloud_auth_req

Require:
  isAlive (*mobile, cloud*)
  hasNetworkAccess (*mobile*)
  isRegistered (*mobile, cloud*)
  uid = **hash**(*userID*)
  pwd = **hash**(*password*)
  cloud ← **send**(*uid*∥*pwd*)
  T_k = *uid* ⊕ *pwd*
Ensure:
  MD = **hash**(MD_{cloud}∥MD_{user})
  $Auth\_Key_i$ ← T_k **PRNG** *SI*
  Enc_1 = **encrypt**(*MD, Auth_Key_i*)
  Temp = Enc_1∥*SI*
  Enc_2 = **encrypt**(*Temp, T_k*)
  cloud ← **send**(Enc_2∥#*CF*)

Algorithm 3 Cloud_authenticating_mobile

Require:
  isAlive (*mobile, cloud*)
  hasNetworkAccess (*mobile*)
  isRegistered (*mobile, cloud*)
Ensure:
  cloud ← **recv**(Enc_2∥#*CF*)
  SearchEntity ← (*uid*∥*pwd*)
  search(*SearchEntity,* #*CF*)
  if *SearchEntity* == *found*
    if *EXP* == *expired*
      triggerUpdatePhase()
    else
      T_k = *uid* ⊕ *pwd*
      Temp = **decrypt**(Enc_2, T_k)
      Temp = Enc_1∥*SI*
      $Auth\_Key_i$ ← T_k **PRNG** *SI*
      MD = **decrypt**($Enc_1, Auth\_Key_i$)
      MD' = **hash**(MD_{cloud}∥MD_{user})
      if *MD* == *MD'*
        integrityCheck(*pass*)
        authentication(*pass*)
      else
        integrityCheck(*fail*)
        authentication(*fail*)
      endif
    endif
  else
    authentication(*fail*)
  endif

message $E_{T_k}\{E_{Auth\_Key_i}\{MD\}∥SI\}$ to obtain the state identifier (*SI*), and encrypted message digest $E_{Auth\_Key_i}\{MD\}$. In addition, the key T_k is used as the seed to the PRNG, and the retrieved *SI* is used to specify the nth sequence of bits obtained from PRNG as the authentication key, $Auth\_Key_i$. The authentication key, $Auth\_Key_i$ decrypts the encrypted message digests $E_{Auth\_Key_i}\{MD\}$ and obtains *MD*, which is then matched with the existing message digest stored at the cloud server. Both of the message digests will match only if the user is legitimate.

Algorithm 3 summarizes the operations involved in the second sub-step. These operations are performed at the

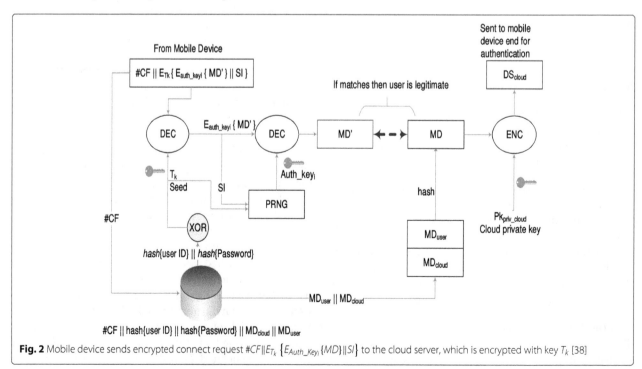

Fig. 2 Mobile device sends encrypted connect request #$CF∥E_{T_k}\{E_{Auth\_Key_i}\{MD\}∥SI\}$ to the cloud server, which is encrypted with key T_k [38]

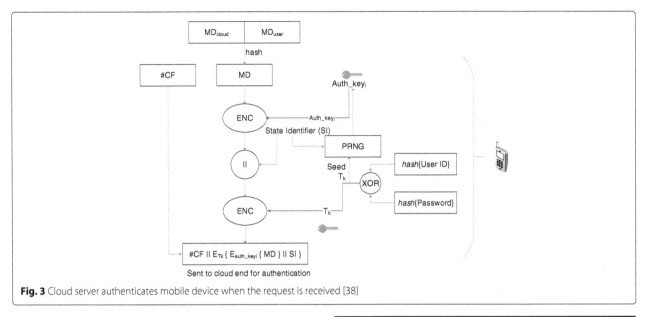

Fig. 3 Cloud server authenticates mobile device when the request is received [38]

cloud server once the authentication request is received. A flow chart for these operations is included in Fig. 3.

Mobile authenticating cloud

Once the mobile device is authenticated, the cloud server sends its digital signature, which consists of MD encrypted with cloud's private key Pk_{priv_cloud}, to the mobile device end. Algorithm 4 summarizes the operations performed at the cloud server during this phase, which includes the creation of digital signature DS and the transfer to mobile devices. A flow chart for these operations is included in Fig. 4.

Algorithm 4 Cloud_to_mobile_auth_req

Require:
  isAlive ($mobile, cloud$)
  hasNetworkAccess ($mobile$)
  isRegistered ($mobile, cloud$)
Ensure:
  $MD = \textbf{hash}(MD_{cloud}\|MD_{user})$
  $DS = \textbf{encrypt}(MD, Pk_{priv\_cloud})$
  $mobile \leftarrow \textbf{send}(DS)$

After receiving the digital signature DS, the mobile device decrypts it with cloud's public key Pk_{pub_cloud}, stored in the mobile device. If the decrypted MD matches with the message digest MD' stored in the mobile device, then it can be stated that the cloud server is legitimate. Algorithm 5 provides the operations that are performed by the mobile device after receiving cloud's digital signature DS.

On successful execution of the authentication process, both mobile device and cloud server establish a session for data transmission.

Algorithm 5 Mobile_authenticating_cloud

Require:
  isAlive ($mobile, cloud$)
  hasNetworkAccess ($mobile$)
  isRegistered ($mobile, cloud$)
  $uid = \textbf{hash}(userID)$
  $pwd = \textbf{hash}(password)$
  $T_k = uid \oplus pwd$

  $MD = MD_{user}\|MD_{cloud}$
  $msz \leftarrow \textbf{decrypt}((MD\|\#CF\|Pk_{pub\_cloud}), T_k)$
  $msz = MD\|\#CF\|Pk_{pub\_cloud}$
Ensure:
  $mobile \leftarrow \textbf{recv}(DS)$
  $MD' = \textbf{decrypt}(DS, Pk_{pub\_cloud})$
  if $MD == MD'$
      authentication($pass$)
      integrityCheck($pass$)
  else
      authentication($fail$)
      integrityCheck($fail$)
  endif

Update phase

The main purpose of the update phase is to modify the existing authentication entities to increase the degree of unpredictability in the authentication process. This phase is triggered due to reset of the expiry period EXP assigned to each registered mobile client. During the registration phase the cloud server generates an expiry period for each mobile client. This expiry period EXP is checked at the cloud server for each authentication request made by a mobile client. The assigned EXP for a mobile client is basically a real value that decrements over time and if it is reset

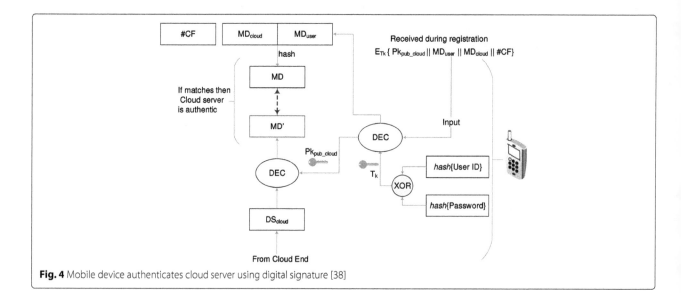

Fig. 4 Mobile device authenticates cloud server using digital signature [38]

or reaches zero then the client is considered as an unregistered client. Apart from assigning an expiry period for a registered client, the cloud server assigns the rate of decrement $rate_{EXP}$ for each expiry period associated with each client. Decrementing the value of EXP by $rate_{EXP}$ is activated by a trigger time tr_{EXP} that enables the decrement process. The cloud server assigns varied expiry periods EXP, rate of decrements $rate_{EXP}$, and trigger time tr_{EXP} for its registered clients, which introduces variability in the expiry period.

If the expiry indicates the registration is expired, then the cloud server sends a re-registration request to the mobile device. The re-registration phase is same as registration phase. However, it verifies the old password and prompts to enter a new password. These information is sent to the cloud server in the similar fashion as the registration phase performs. Upon receiving the re-registration request, the cloud server generates a fresh MD_{user}, and EXP for the client. Since, the password is changed, the new hashed *password* will be different than the old hashed *password* and thereby the generated T_k (Eq. 2) will be different.

Evaluation methodology

We evaluate the proposed scheme by security analysis. By computing the vulnerability score, S_v, we summarize the security offered by the scheme. The proposed scheme is coded using computer simulation environment [9]. We assume that the mobile device is already registered with the cloud server and obtained MD_{cloud}, MD_{user}, #CF, and Pk_{pub_cloud}. In addition, we assume that both the mobile device and the cloud server are running the proposed scheme. During the operation of the proposed scheme, when a registered mobile sends the

authentication request $\{E_{T_k}\{E_{Auth\_Key_i}\{MD\}\|SI\}\|#CF\}$ to the cloud server, or when the cloud server sends authentication response $Pk_{priv\_cloud}\{MD\}$ to the mobile device, it may get compromised by some adversary. The computer simulation provides a way of creating mobile-cloud computing environment, where the initiator is configured as mobile device and the responder is configured as cloud server.

Simulation environment

A research can be performed by performing different types of studies, such as surveys, field study, experiments, computer simulation etc. [9]. We have considered computer simulation to validate our proposed scheme. In one of our simulations, we used a protocol analyzer called *Scyther* [12] as part of the security analayis to launch attacks on the proposed authentication scheme. *Scyther* analyzes a protocol once it is written in *Scyther* coding format. It accepts a minimum of two roles, where one role represents an initiator or sender and the other role represents a receiver. It allows us to define what type of key is used in the protocol, such as symmetric key, or asymmetric key, in addition it allows us to define whether a parameter is constant or variable. Once the protocol is defined, we can configure the attack scenarios. It has many predefined attack scenarios, which are used to test whether a protocol lacks confidentiality and integrity.

Methodology

We compute a vulnerability score (S_v) and we perform a security analysis of the scheme to describe how secure it is. Let us consider N is the number of attacks that are launched on the proposed scheme and $N_{success}$ is the number of successful attacks that are recorded. Then, the likelihood of successful attacks on the scheme defines its vulnerability score (S_v) (Eq. 4). Lesser vulnerability score indicates that the proposed scheme can prevent more number of attacks. The value of S_v lies between 0.0 and 1.0 (Eq. 1)

$$S_v = \frac{N_{success}}{N} \tag{4}$$

We configured the ted setup and the protocol analyzer *Scyther* for validating the MDA scheme. *Scyther* is configured from the setting option to launch all types of attacks. We analyzed our scheme for 10 RUNs, where both the mobile client and the cloud server have run the scheme to exchange messages. In order to compromise the system, during the execution of each run, *Scyther* tried to launch different types of attacks considering hackers have initial knowledge of the system. We made various security claims, which are validated by running our proposed scheme using *Scyther*. We have recorded the number of attacks to obtain the S_v score.

MDA emulation

We have emulated the operations involved in MDA using Java program and validated it for man-in-the-middle attacks, and replay attacks. The proposed scheme MDA uses public key encryption in the registration process, symmetric encryption in authentication process and a standard hashing algorithm in generating the message digests. MDA does not have any specification for algorithms and therefore, any standard combinations of encryption algorithms and hashing algorithms could be used in the operations of MDA. In order to emulate the operations of MDA, we have used RSA (Rivest, Shamir, and Adelman) as the public key encryption algorithm,

SHA1 (Secure Hash Algorithm 1) as the hashing algorithm, and AES (Advanced Encryption Standard) as the symmetric key encryption algorithm. Instances of two user defined java classes (CloudServer and MobileClient) are used to run the operations of MDA.

In addition, we configured the emulated MDA setup with two man-in-the-middle objects. These objects are responsible for modifying the authentication request frames sent from a mobile client to the cloud server, and authentication response frames sent from the cloud server to a mobile device. Upon creation of the mobile device object, we perform the registration process by sending the registration request to the cloud server. The cloud server object uses SHA1 algorithm to generate the client and cloud message digests. RSA Keypair generation is performed at the cloud server and the Pk_{pub_cloud} is sent along with the MD_{user} and MD_{cloud}. Both entities, the mobile device and the cloud server use AES encryption with key T_k during the authentication process. The expiry period EXP is set by the cloudserver. For our experiment, we considered only a single client-server model and therefore, we set both tr_{EXP} and $rate_{EXP}$ as zero.

By invoking $run()$ method of authentication thread, 1000 authentication request frames are sent from the registered mobile device to the cloud server as shown in Fig. 5. The man-in-the-middle attack object is activated randomly, and it modified the request frames that are sent. Among 1000 frames, 256 frames are modified in transit. The cloud server running MDA scheme has rejected all the modified request frames. Only 744 non modified request frames are processed by the cloud server and 744 authentication response frames are generated and sent back to the mobile device as shown in Fig. 6. MDA is a mutual authentication scheme, therefore, the authentication response frames are authenticated by the mobile device. Further, the second man-in-the-middle object has

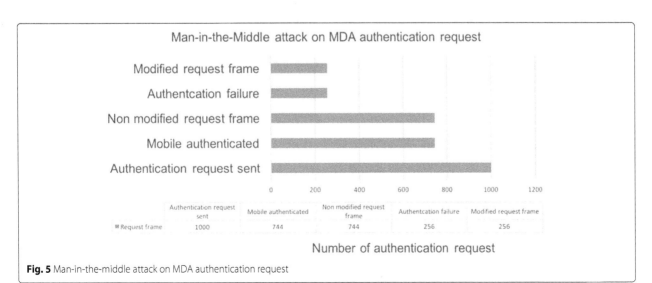

Fig. 5 Man-in-the-middle attack on MDA authentication request

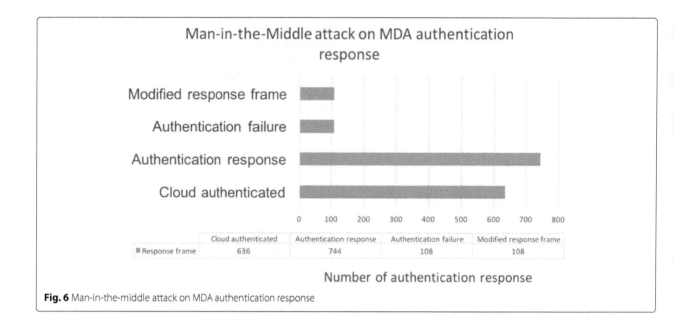

Fig. 6 Man-in-the-middle attack on MDA authentication response

launched random attacks on the response frames. Among 744 response frames, 108 are modified, which are later rejected by the mobile device. Only 636 non modified response frames are accepted. Less than 744 response frames are generated by the cloud server, if we use a non zero positive real value for $rate_{EXP}$, which resets the EXP before sending all the 1000 request frames. Although the request frames are non modified and received from registered mobile device, reset of EXP forces the cloud server to reject the authentication request. If EXP resets, a registration object is initialized to perform the re-registration.

With MDA emulation, we are able to validate the operations of the MDA scheme and exhibit that MDA can withstand man-in-the-middle attacks. However, our emulation has failed to establish that MDA can prevent replay attacks on request or response frames. The scheme does not have any timestamp component, which makes it difficult to identify if a valid request frame is sent from an adversary at later stage. Therefore, replay attacks could be launched on the request frames before EXP resets.

Security analysis

The highlight of our scheme is the authentication process. However, the authentication scheme depends on an initial registration phase, which must be reliable and secure in order to keep safe the information required during the authentication phase. We evaluate the vulnerability of the registration phase using *Scyther* and identified that in the absence of security, $hash\{userID\}$, $hash\{password\}$, MD_{user}, MD_{cloud} are falsified and man-in-the-middle attack can be launched. Therefore, in order to establish our approach as a standard authentication scheme in the mobile cloud computing environment, we perform the registration process in a secure manner by employing standard protocol, such as SSH (secure shell). Upon completion of the registration process with SSH, both parties (mobile and cloud server) obtain the necessary parameters for the authentication phase, which is performed using MDA.

To perform the security analysis of the authentication phase, we focus on evaluating the vulnerability of certain parameters such as, $hash\{userID\}$, $hash\{password\}$, MD_{user}, MD_{cloud}, which are used in our authentication scheme. If the vulnerability is high, i.e. these parameters are compromised at any level of communication between the mobile device and the cloud server during the authentication process, then we will fail to establish our hypothesis H_a. In addition, we need to check the aliveness and synchronization of the mobile device and the cloud server during the authentication. We use the security analyzer *Scyther* to check the vulnerability of each of these parameters.

Table 1 summarizes our claims and how secure the scheme is for each claim. In this section, we provide detailed security analysis of the claims that are validated using *Scyther*.

> **Claim 1:** $Auth\_Key_i$ remains secret throughout the authentication process.
> $Auth\_Key_i$ is used to encrypt and decrypt the message digest MD to provide multi layer security.
> A Mobile device sends the message digest MD to the cloud server by encrypting with $Auth\_Key_i$, which is a symmetric key. Both parties, the mobile device and the cloud server can independently generate the

Table 1 Security analysis of the proposed scheme using Scyther during authentication phase

Role	Sl.Num.	Claim	Status	Comment
Mobile	1	secret $Auth\_Key_i$	Ok	No Attacks
	2	secret SI	Ok	No Attacks
	3	secret $password$	Ok	No Attacks
	4	secret $userID$	Ok	No Attacks
	5	secret MD_{user}	Ok	No Attacks
	6	secret MD_{cloud}	Ok	No Attacks
	7	Alive	Ok	No Attacks
	8	Weakagree	Ok	No Attacks
	9	Niagree	Ok	No Attacks
	10	Nisynch	Ok	No Attacks
Cloud	1	secret $Auth\_Key_i$	Ok	No Attacks
	2	secret $password$	Ok	No Attacks
	3	secret $userID$	Ok	No Attacks
	4	secret SI	Ok	No Attacks
	5	Alive	Ok	No Attacks
	6	Weakagree	Ok	No Attacks
	7	Niagree	Ok	No Attacks
	8	Nisynch	Ok	No Attacks

$Auth\_Key_i$ using state identifier SI. Since $Auth\_Key_i$ is not exchanged between both the parties, it remains secret.

Claim 2: *State identifier SI is kept secret.*

SI is the state identifier for PRNG used to specify the nth sequence of PRNG as the desired pattern. The mobile device sends SI to the cloud server for specifying the nth sequence of PRNG to generate the $Auth\_Key_i$. SI is sent from mobile device to cloud server after encrypting with key T_k. The claim at the mobile end that SI being secret is validated using *Scyther*. On the other hand, the cloud server does not share or send SI, therefore, it is safe at the cloud end.

Claim 3: *password is secret.*

The safety of the *password* depends on the user. Typically no one shares their password, thereby keeping it safe. The password can be a 512 bit string, which is hashed and a copy of the user's *password* is stored at the cloud server during registration process. The mobile device does not send the *password* during authentication process, but it is used at both ends to generate the key T_k. Our *password* safety claim is validated by *Scyther*, but, in reality, it is dependent on the user.

Claim 4: *userID is safe.*

$userID$ is sent to the cloud server only during the registration process, which is required along with the *password* to generate T_k. The $userID$ is hashed and a

copy is stored at the cloud server during registration process. The mobile device does not send *userID* to the cloud server during authentication process. Therefore, *userID* remains safe. Our *userID* safety claim is validated by *Scyther*, but, in reality, it is dependent on the user.

Claim 5: *The scheme requires MD_{user} to be a secret.*

MD_{user} is the hashed information related to the user, which may contain policy information and unique information about the user. This information is generated at the cloud server end and sent to the mobile device after a successful registration process. The information is hashed and encrypted with $Auth\_key_i$ before transmitting from the user mobile device to the cloud end. *Scyther* validated our claim that MD_{user} is safe.

Claim 6: *The scheme requires MD_{cloud} is secret.*

MD_{cloud} is the hashed information related to the cloud server, which may contain the cloud server certificate or other policy related information. As with MD_{user}, this information is hashed and encrypted with $Auth\_key_i$ before transmitting from mobile device to the cloud server. As part of the authentication process, the combination of MD_{user} and MD_{cloud} is used at the cloud end to verify whether the mobile device is legitimate. In addition, the combination of MD_{user} and MD_{cloud} encrypted with Pk_{priv_cloud} is used as the cloud server digital signature to authenticate the cloud server by the mobile device. The protocol analyzer (*Scyther*) validated the claim that MD_{cloud} is safe.

Claim 7: *Mobile device and the cloud server remains alive during the execution of the protocol.*

The cloud server is said to be *alive* if it has been using the proposed scheme for the initial $(i-1)$ messages exchanged with the mobile device, when the latter sends the ith message. The protocol analyzer (*Scyther*) validates the *aliveness* claim.

Claim 8: *Guarantees Weakagree* [28].

Our proposed scheme guarantees that the mobile device is in *weakagreement* with the cloud server. Therefore, the mobile device is running the proposed scheme with the cloud server; likewise the cloud server is running the scheme with the mobile device. The communication is not affected by adversary during the operation of the proposed scheme. This claim is validated using the protocol analyzer (*Scyther*).

Claim 9: *Assures Niagree between the mobile device and the cloud server* [28].

Niagree or Non-injective agreement ensures that the mobile device and the cloud server agree upon some data exchange during running of the proposed scheme. During the operation of the proposed scheme, the mobile device can send data to the cloud server safely (and vice-versa). If *Niagree* fails, then we can conclude that there is a man-in-the-middle attack during the operation of the protocol. However, our claim is validated using protocol analyzer (*Scyther*). Claim 10: *Holds Nisynch during the authentication process* [20].

Nisynch or non-injective synchronization is valid if all actions before the claim are performed as per the proposed scheme description. *Nisynch* ensures that there is no synchronization problem between the mobile device and the cloud server during the authentication process. *Nisynch* is validated using the protocol analyzer, *Scyther*.

Our security analysis results are based on *Scyther* validation, which indicates that MDA supports all of the claims that we have made during the execution of the scheme for multiple runs. The claims are not compromised by any types of attacks during the authentication process. Therefore, the vulnerability score (S_v) obtained is 0.0 , which satisfies the condition of our alternative hypothesis (H_a).

Hashing is a mechanism that makes the proposed scheme secure, and implicitly provides a means for integrity check. Even if any adversary sniffs the message that is sent during the authentication process, it is not possible for the adversary to interpret the message digests, MD_{cloud} or MD_{user} . Furthermore, it is worth noting that MDA is completely based on a technique employing simple *userID, password*, and hashing. It does not include any of the system specific properties such as IMSI of mobile phone or MAC (media access control) address of a laptop, which makes the scheme applicable to any type of mobile device without any alteration.

Conclusion

The emergence of mobile cloud computing has transitioned modern computing into a new phase. Mobile devices and cloud resources, the key components of mobile cloud computing, have enabled people to access and utilize the cloud services irrespective of their geographical locations and medium of communications. Numerous fields, such as healthcare, transportation, and financial services, can significantly benefit from mobile cloud computing. Despite the advantages of this innovative computing model, mobile cloud computing could seriously suffer from security/privacy problems. In this paper, we propose a novel authentication scheme for mobile cloud computing, Message Digest-based Authentication (MDA). Technically, MDA is composed of three phases: registration, authentication, and update. With these phases, MDA utilizes hashing, in addition to traditional user id and password based authentication, to ensure confidentiality and integrity during the authentication process. Our analysis results indicate that MDA can survive a variety of different attacks, such as man-in-the-middle, replay attacks, etc.

Acknowledgements
Not applicable.

Authors' contributions
All sections of the paper are written by the author. All authors contributed in the manuscript. All authors read and approved the final manuscript.

Competing interests
The authors declare that they have no competing interests.

Author details
[1] Dalhousie University, Halifax, Canada. [2] University of Prince Edward Island, Charlottetown, Canada.

References
1. Abolfazli S, Sanaei Z, Shiraz M, Gani A (2012) MOMCC: Market-oriented architecture for Mobile Cloud Computing based on Service Oriented Architecture. In: 2012 1st IEEE International, Conference on Communications in China Workshops (ICCC). pp 8–13. doi:10.1109/ICCCW.2012.6316481
2. Ahmad Z, Mayes KE, Dong S, Markantonakis K (2011) Considerations for mobile authentication in the Cloud. Inf Secur Tech Rep 16(3–4):123–130. ISSN 13634127. doi:10.1016/j.istr.2011.09.009
3. Alizadeh M, Hassan WH (2013) Challenges and opportunities of Mobile Cloud Computing. In: 2013 9th International, Wireless Communications and Mobile Computing Conference (IWCMC). pp 660–666. doi:10.1109/IWCMC.2013.6583636
4. Alrokayan M, Buyya R (2013) A web portal for management of aneka-based multicloud environments. In: Proceedings of the Eleventh Australasian Symposium on Parallel and Distributed Computing - Volume 140. pp 49–56
5. Behl A, Behl K (2012) An analysis of cloud computing security issues. In: World Congress on, Information and Communication Technologies (WICT). pp 109–114. doi:10.1109/WICT.2012.6409059
6. Behl A (2011) Emerging security challenges in cloud computing: An insight to cloud security challenges and their mitigation. In: 2011 World Congress on Information and Communication Technologies. pp 217–222. doi:10.1109/WICT.2011.6141247
7. Benkhelifa E, Fernando DA (2014) On a Real World Implementation of Advanced Authentication Mechanism in a Multi-Tenant Cloud Service Delivery Platform. In: 5th International Conference on Information and Communication Systems (ICICS). pp 1–6
8. Bouayad A, Blilat A, El Houda Mejhed N, El Ghazi M (2012) Cloud computing : security challenges. Colloquium in Information Science and Technology (CIST)
9. Carpendale S, Kerren A, Stasko JT, Fekete J-D, North C (2008) Evaluating Information Visualizations. In: Information Visualization, volume 4950 of Lecture Notes in Computer Science, Springer, Berlin Heidelberg, ISBN 978-3-540-70955-8. pp 19–45. doi:10.1007/978-3-540-70956-5_2
10. Choudhury AJ, Kumar P, Sain M, Lim H, Jae-Lee H (2011) A Strong User Authentication Framework for Cloud Computing. In: 2011 IEEE Asia-Pacific Services, Computing Conference. pp 110–115. doi:10.1109/APSCC.2011.14
11. Chow R, Jakobsson M, Davis UC, Shi E (2010) Authentication in the Clouds: A Framework and its Application to Mobile Users. CCSW10, Chicago
12. Cremers C (2008) The Scyther Tool: Verification, Falsification, and Analysis of Security Protocols. In: Proceedings of the 20th International Conference on Computer Aided Verification, Princeton
13. Dash SK, Mohapatra S, Pattnaik PK (2010) A Survey on Applications of Wireless Sensor Network Using Cloud Computing. International Journal of Computer Science & Emerging Technologies 1(4):50–55

14. Dinh HT, Lee C, Niyato D, Wang P (2011) A Survey of, Mobile Cloud Computing : Architecture, Applications, and Approaches. Published online in Wiley Online Library. doi:10.1002/wcm.1203/abstract

15. Eaves A, Stockman M (2012) Desktop as a service proof of concept. In: Proceedings of the 13th annual conference on Information technology education - SIGITE '12. p 85. doi:10.1145/2380552.2380577

16. Ficco M, Rak M (2015) Stealthy denial of service strategy in cloud computing. IEEE Trans Cloud Comput 3(1):80–94. ISSN 2168-7161. doi:10.1109/TCC.2014.2325045

17. Guan L, Ke X, Song M, Song J (2011) A Survey of Research on Mobile Cloud Computing. In: 2011 10th IEEE/ACIS International Conference on Computer and Information Science. pp 387–392. doi:10.1109/ICIS.2011.67

18. Joshi JBD, Takabi H, Ahn G (2010) Security and Privacy Challenges in Cloud Computing Environments. Security & Privacy, IEEE 8:24–31

19. Hoang DB, Chen L (2010) Mobile Cloud for Assistive Healthcare (MoCAsH). In: 2010 IEEE Asia-Pacific Services Computing Conference. pp 325–332. doi:10.1109/APSCC.2010.102

20. Hollestelle G (2005) Systematic Analysis of Attacks on Security Protocols

21. Hong JW (2012) Monitoring and detecting abnormal behavior in mobile cloud infrastructure. In: 2012 IEEE Network Operations and Management Symposium. pp 1303–1310. doi:10.1109/NOMS.2012.6212067

22. Huang D, Zhou Z (2011) Secure data processing framework for mobile cloud computing. In: 2011 IEEE Conference on Computer Communications Workshops (INFOCOM WKSHPS). pp 614–618. doi:10.1109/INFCOMW.2011.5928886

23. Jana D, Bandyopadhyay D (2013) Efficient management of security and privacy issues in mobile cloud environment. Annual IEEE India Conference (INDICON), Mumbai, 2013:1–6. doi:10.1109/INDCON.2013.6726077

24. Konstantinou I, Floros E, Koziris N (2012) Public vs Private Cloud Usage Costs: The StratusLab Case. In: Proceedings of the 2Nd, International Workshop on Cloud Computing Platforms. pp 3:1–3:6. doi:10.1145/2168697.2168700

25. Kulkarni G, Gambhir J, Patil T, Dongare A (2012) A security aspects in cloud computing. In: 2012 IEEE International Conference on Computer Science and Automation Engineering. pp 547–550

26. Larosa YT, Chen J-L, Deng D-J, Chao H-C (2011) Mobile cloud computing service based on heterogeneous wireless and mobile P2P networks. In: 2011 7th International, Wireless Communications and Mobile Computing Conference. pp 661–665. doi:10.1109/IWCMC.2011.5982625

27. Lin J-W, Chen C-H, Chang JM (2013) Qos-aware data replication for data-intensive applications in cloud computing systems. IEEE Trans Cloud Comput 1(1):101–115. ISSN 2168-7161 doi:10.1109/TCC.2013.1

28. Lowe G (1997) A hierarchy of authentication specifications. In: Proceedings 10th, Computer Security Foundations Workshop. pp 31–43. doi:10.1109/CSFW.1997.596782

29. Malik SUR, Khan SU, Srinivasan SK (2013) Modeling and analysis of state-of-the-art vm-based cloud management platforms. IEEE Trans Cloud Comput 1(1):1–1. ISSN 2168-7161 doi:10.1109/TCC.2013.3

30. Mathisen E (2011) Security Challenges and Solutions in Cloud Computing, Vol. 5

31. Nkosi MT, Mekuria F (2010) Cloud Computing for Enhanced Mobile Health Applications. In: 2010 IEEE Second International, Conference on Cloud Computing Technology and Science. pp 629–633. doi:10.1109/CloudCom.2010.31

32. Popović K, Hocenski Z (2010) Cloud computing security issues and challenges, Vol. 2010. Opatija, Croatia

33. Qi H, Gani A (2012) Research on mobile cloud computing: Review, trend and perspectives. In: Second International, Conference on Digital Information and Communication Technology and it's Applications (DICTAP). pp 195–202. doi:10.1109/DICTAP.2012.6215350

34. Rangarajan S, Verma M, Kannan A, Sharma A, Schoen I (2012) V2c: A secure vehicle to cloud framework for virtualized and on-demand service provisioning. In: Proceedings of the International Conference on Advances in Computing, Communications and Informatics. pp 148–154. doi:10.1145/2345396.2345422

35. Ranjan R, Wang L, Zomaya AY, Georgakopoulos D, Sun X-H, Wang G (2012) Recent advances in autonomic provisioning of big data applications on clouds. IEEE Trans Cloud Comput 3(2):101–104. ISSN 2168-7161 doi:10.1109/TCC.2015.2437231

36. Revar AG, Bhavsar MD (2011) Securing user authentication using single sign-on in Cloud Computing. In: 2011 Nirma University International Conference on Engineering. pp 1–4. doi:10.1109/NUiConE.2011.6153227

37. Sampangi RV, Dey S, Urs SR, Sampalli S (2012) Iamkeys: Independent and adaptive management of keys for security in wireless body area networks. In: Advances in Computer Science and Information Technology, volume 86, Springer, Berlin Heidelberg. pp 482–494. ISBN 978-3-642-27316-2 doi:10.1007/978-3-642-27317-9_49

38. Dey S, Sampalli S, Ye Q (2013) Message Digest as Authentication Entity for Mobile Cloud Computing, 32nd IEEE International Performance Computing and Communications Conference (IPCCC 2013), San Diego

39. Shaikh FB, Haider S (2011) Security Threats in Cloud Computing. In: International Conference for Internet Technology and Secured Transactions (ICITST), (December). pp 11–14

40. Shiraz M, Gani A (2012) Mobile Cloud Computing : Critical Analysis of Application Deployment in Virtual Machines. Int Conf Inf Comput Netw (ICICN 2012) 27(Icicn):11–16

41. Wang S, Dey S (2013) Adaptive Mobile Cloud Computing to Enable Rich Mobile Multimedia Applications. IEEE Trans Multimed 15(4):870–883. ISSN 1520-9210 doi:10.1109/TMM.2013.2240674

42. Yandong Z, Yongsheng Z (2012) Cloud computing and cloud security challenges. In: Information Technology in Medicine … pp 1084–1088

43. Yang L, Cao J, Tang S, Li T, Chan ATS (2012) A Framework for Partitioning and Execution of Data Stream Applications in Mobile Cloud Computing. In: 2012 IEEE Fifth International Conference on Cloud Computing. pp 794–802. doi:10.1109/CLOUD.2012.97

44. Yoo K-Y (2012) A lightweight multi-user authentication scheme based on cellular automata in cloud environment, Vol. 1. doi: 10.1109/CloudNet.2012.6483680

45. Zhang Q, Cheng L, Boutaba R (2010) Cloud computing: state-of-the-art and research challenges. J Internet Serv Appl 1(1):7–18. ISSN 1867-4828 doi:10.1007/s13174-010-0007-6

46. Zhang X, Schiffman J, Gibbs S, Kunjithapatham A, Jeong S (2009) Securing elastic applications on mobile devices for cloud computing. In: Proceedings of the 2009 ACM workshop on, Cloud computing security - CCSW '09. p 127. doi:10.1145/1655008.1655026

47. Zhou F, Cheng F, Wei L, Fang Z (2011) Cloud Service Platform - Hospital Information Exchange (HIX). In: 2011 IEEE 8th International Conference on e-Business Engineering, (2009). pp 380–385. doi:10.1109/ICEBE.2011.35

5

Towards energy aware cloud computing application construction

Django Armstrong, Karim Djemame[*] (ID) and Richard Kavanagh

Abstract

The energy consumption of cloud computing continues to be an area of significant concern as data center growth continues to increase. This paper reports on an energy efficient interoperable cloud architecture realised as a cloud toolbox that focuses on reducing the energy consumption of cloud applications holistically across all deployment models. The architecture supports energy efficiency at service construction, deployment and operation. We discuss our practical experience during implementation of an architectural component, the Virtual Machine Image Constructor (VMIC), required to facilitate construction of energy aware cloud applications. We carry out a performance evaluation of the component on a cloud testbed. The results show the performance of Virtual Machine construction, primarily limited by available I/O, to be adequate for agile, energy aware software development. We conclude that the implementation of the VMIC is feasible, incurs minimal performance overhead comparatively to the time taken by other aspects of the cloud application construction life-cycle, and make recommendations on enhancing its performance.

Keywords: Cloud computing, Virtualization, Energy efficiency, Cloud engineering, Cloud architectures, Cloud interoperability, Performance evaluation

Introduction

Current trends in industry show continuous growth in the adoption and market value of cloud computing with many companies changing their business models and products to adapt to a service oriented outlook. Cloud computing as a leading ICT approach provides elastic and on-demand ICT infrastructures makes up a large proportion of the total ICT energy consumption. Predictions have been made on an unsustainable quadrupling in the energy consumption and carbon emissions of data centres used to operate cloud services by 2020 [1] with comparable emissions to the aeronautical industry. As energy efficiency is at the heart of governments/institutions for smart, sustainable and inclusive growth as part of a transition to a resource efficient economy, considering and improving the energy efficiency of cloud computing is therefore of paramount importance.

Research on energy efficiency in clouds has attracted considerable attention and has focused on many aspects including ICT equipment (servers, networks) as well as

software solutions running on top of ICT equipment (e.g. cloud management system domain for managing the cloud infrastructure), see [2] for a survey. This paper is concerned with the topical issue of energy efficiency in clouds and specifically focuses on the design and construction of cloud services through the implementation of tools within a reference energy-aware and self-adaptive architecture. Such architecture provides novel methods and tools to support software developers aiming at optimising energy efficiency and minimising the carbon footprint resulting from designing, developing, deploying and running software in clouds. Cloud services are made of several shared software components, which are utilised many times. These components can then be characterised, which allows the Software developers to relate service construction and energy use. This relationship will further depend on the deployment conditions and the correct operation of the service, which can be achieved by means of an adaptive environment.

Software developers need to construct and analyse their applications using a programming model as part of a Software as a Service (SaaS) cloud layer. Currently, they usually optimise code to achieve high performance but

---
*Correspondence: K.Djemame@leeds.ac.uk
School of Computing, University of Leeds, Leeds, UK

guidelines for energy optimisation are also valuable. Consider an application which is developed using a programming model and the resultant program is analysed for potential energy hotspots [3]. Methods from automatic complexity analysis and worst-case execution time analysis of the application can be extended and combined with energy models of the hardware, giving the developers an approximate energy profile for the program. This analysis provides feedback to the software developers thus enabling an adaptive software development methodology through monitoring (the code's performance), analysing (identifying energy hotspots), planning (potential changes to the code to improve its performance) and executing (recompiling the code enabling further monitoring).

Similarly for software developers evaluating different deployment scenarios for the applications will need various installation configurations. For example, a developer models via UML the different deployment scenarios they wish to evaluate for potential use in a production environment. After which, these models are translated into descriptions, e.g. XML that can be processed into deployable virtual format artefacts.

In both cases *image construction* is required prior to the application deployment scenario which is realised as a collection of Virtual Machines (VMs) containing application components. To the best of our knowledge, no current software solution provides capabilities to both generate base images that contain a functional operating system and install and configure a cloud application automatically. This therefore provides the opportunity to create multiple different configurations of an application, where these different deployment configurations can be exploited, by selecting the most appropriate configuration to serve the required system load while saving energy. For comparison, a tool such as Packer [4] can be used to create golden images for multiple platforms from a single source configuration but does not provide support for the automated installation of software into these images. Another example tool such as Vagrant [5] enables software development teams to create identical development environments but does not provide a mechanism to automate the deployment of software into these environments.

A Virtual Machine Image Constructor (VMIC) is therefore key to support adaptive software development processes in an energy-aware SaaS architecture. Such component implements the automation of image construction that would otherwise make the burden and cost too high of considering iteratively adapting an application to use less energy in the software development stage through incremental out-of-band (of normal application operation) test based deployment scenarios. In addition to this, the VMIC is considered as an important contribution from the perspective of Software Engineering filling the gap between generating base images in cloud computing

and automatic configuration of cloud applications. This component supports the energy efficiency goal within the cloud architecture by providing means of packaging cloud applications in a way that enables provider agnostic deployment, while maintaining energy awareness.

The paper's main contributions are:

1. The detailed architecture of a SaaS layer component that facilitates an energy aware and efficient cloud development methodology.
2. The results of a performance evaluation and feasibility study of the VMIC tool for the construction of cloud application components.
3. Our practical experience during implementation and recommendations on enhancing the performance of the tool.

The remainder of the paper is structured as follows: "Related work" section reviews the literature on energy-aware cloud computing. "Energy efficient cloud architecture" section describes the proposed architecture to support energy-awareness with emphasis on the importance of the SaaS layer for facilitating energy efficiency in cloud applications. "Cloud engineering" section explains our vision of a self-adaptive development life-cycle and how this can enable energy aware cloud application construction through our VMIC tool. "Experimental design" section presents the experimental design where we evaluate the performance of the VMIC tool, and "Results and recommendations" section discusses the results. Finally, "Conclusion" section provides a conclusion on this paper and discusses plans for future work.

Related work
Research effort has targeted energy efficiency support at various stages of the cloud service lifecycle. In the *service development stage*, *requirements elicitation* includes techniques for capturing, modelling and reasoning with energy requirements as well as product line oriented techniques to model and reason about system configuration [6, 7]. In terms of *software design* in relation to energy consumption, some research efforts relate energy awareness and optimization at the application and system level [8], focus on profiling the application's energy consumption at runtime to iteratively narrow down on energy hot spots [9], or considers cloud architecture patterns to achieve greener business processes [10]. Energy efficiency has also been the subject of investigation in *Software development*, e.g. by studying the energy consumption of the application prior to deployment [11]. In the service *deployment stage*, research effort has focused on *Service Level Agreement* (SLA) deployment strategies especially with regard to SLAs that are energy-aware, e.g. by implementing specific policies to save energy [12, 13], as well

as service deployment technologies which play a critical role in the management of the cloud infrastructure and thus have an effect on its overall energy consumption [14]. In the service *operation* stage, energy efficiency has been extensively studied and has focused for example on approaches towards energy management for distributed management of VMs in cloud infrastructures, where the goal is to improve the utilization of computing resources and reduce energy consumption under workload independent quality of service constraints [15].

Configuration management tools provide four core benefits to managing the cloud. These are i) the reproducibility and industrialization of software configuration, ii) the continuous vigilance over running systems with automated repairs and alert mechanisms, iii) enhanced control over and rationalisation of large scale deployments and iv) the ability to build up a knowledge base to document and trace the history of a system as it evolves. The most well know tools include CFEngine, Puppet and Chef.

CFEngine [16] provides automated configuration management for large networked systems and can be deployed to manage various infrastructure such as servers, desktops and mobile/embedded devices. It uses decentralised, autonomous software agents to monitor, repair and update individual machines. CFEngine central concept is the idea of convergence [17], where the final desired state of the system is described instead of the steps needed to get there. This enables CFEngine to run whatever the initial state of the system is with predictable end results. The downside of this approach is that only statistical compliance or best effort can be achieved with a given configuration policy, where by a system cannot be guaranteed to end up at a desired state but slowly converges at a rate defined by the ratio of environmental change to the rate at which CFEngine executes. Puppet [18] was forked from CFEngine and provides graph and model driven approaches to configuration management, through a simplified declarative domain specific language that was designed to be human readable.

Chef [19], a fork of Puppet, places emphasis on starting up services from newly provisioned clean systems, where the sequence and execution of configuration tasks is fixed and known by the user. This makes Chef particularly well suited to the paradigm of cloud computing where VM instances are short lived and new instances are spawned from a newly provisioned base image. Chef uses the analogy of cooking and creates "recipes" that are bundles of installation steps or scripts to be executed.

The Open Virtualization Format (OVF) is an open standard for defining, packaging and distributing virtual appliances that can run virtualized on a cloud [20]. Its use as part of a service descriptor to define the requirements of an applications is not new and has been implemented within the OPTIMIS Toolkit [21], where an OVF fragment resides in a non-standard XML based service manifest schema. One issue with this approach is the impact on interoperability with cloud providers that need to support this schema to enable application deployment. This compared to the solution that is presented in this paper where a pure OVF document is used, extended and implemented according to the capabilities of the OVF Specification version 1.1.1, makes our solution 100% compliant with cloud providers and technologies that already support OVF.

In this paper, the proposed software tool provides capabilities to both generate base images that contain a functional operating system and install and configure a cloud application automatically. This sits alongside previous work [14, 22] that allows for the contextualisation and recontextualisation of virtual machines, so that the environment can be reconfigured dynamically at runtime, leading to a dynamic reconfigurable environment. This is key to support: 1) adaptive software development processes in a cloud architecture, and 2) the energy efficiency goal within the architecture by providing means of packaging cloud applications in a way that enables provider agnostic deployment, while maintaining energy awareness.

Collectively the automated configuration and reconfiguration of cloud applications, along with enhanced energy awareness of the different deployment solutions gives rise to the possibility of performing energy saving techniques. These techniques can be quite expansive such as: consolidation [23], horizontal and vertical scaling and the usage of DVFS [24] and RAPL [25].

Energy efficient cloud architecture

To reduce the energy consumption of a cloud system, a reference architecture is needed to first enable energy awareness of all phases of an application's life-cycle and secondly provide actuators to reduce and optimizes energy efficiency. To this end we have realised such a reference architecture through the implementation of a toolbox, details of which can be found in [26]. To facilitate the reader's understanding of the research in this paper, Figs. 1, 2 and 3 provide an overview of the proposed architecture which includes the high-level interactions of all components, is separated into three distinct layers and follows the standard cloud deployment model.

In the SaaS layer, illustrated by Fig. 1, a set of components and tools interact to facilitate the modelling, design and construction of a cloud application. The components aid in evaluating energy consumption of a cloud application during its construction. A number of plug-ins are provided for a frontend *Integrated Development Environment* (IDE) as a means for developers to interact with components within this layer. The Requirements and Design Modelling Plug-in provides developers with tools to aid in is based on the energy aware modelling

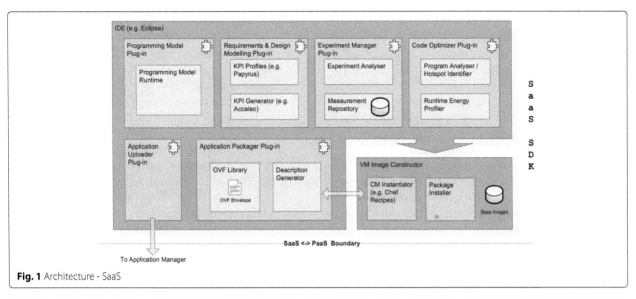

Fig. 1 Architecture - SaaS

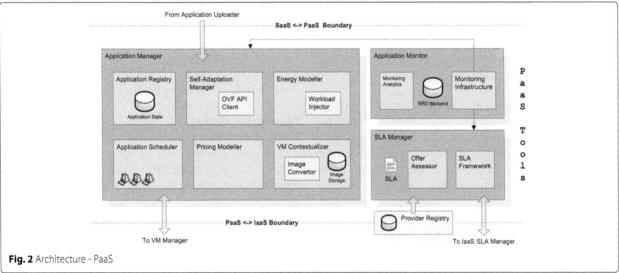

Fig. 2 Architecture - PaaS

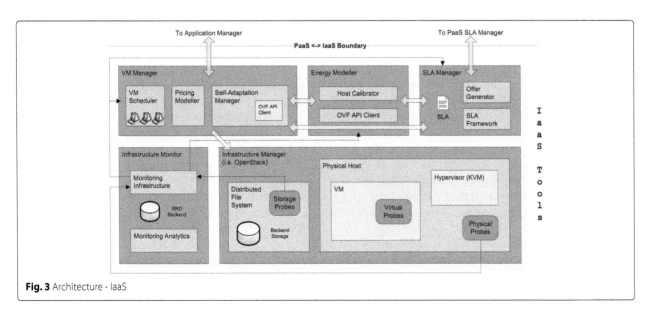

Fig. 3 Architecture - IaaS

of an application, while the Code Optimiser Plug-in provides offline functionality to profiler an application's energy consumption during development. The Programming Model Plug-in is based on COMPSs [27] and provides an interface to the developer to create applications that follow the energy aware programming model [28]. Finally the Deployment Experiment Manager Plug-in, helps to associate the outputs of the SaaS Modelling tools with the workloads and the energy-aware architecture.

A number of packaging components and tools are also made available to enable cloud provider agnostic deployment of the constructed cloud application, while also maintaining energy awareness. The Virtual Machine Image Constructor (VMIC) tool is responsible for fabricating the images and included software needed to deploy an application, which is in turn handled by the Application Uploader Plug-in, which uploads a packaged application created in the SaaS SDK layer to the Application Manager at the PaaS layer. The VM Image Constructor communicates with both the Programming Model Plug-in and Application Packager Plug-in for the installation of the programming model runtime and for packaging more traditional cloud applications into base images.

The PaaS layer, illustrated by Fig. 2, provides middleware functionality for a cloud application and facilitates the deployment and operation of the application as a whole. Components within this layer are responsible for selecting the most energy appropriate provider for a given set of energy requirements, stored as OVF properties, and tailoring the application to the selected provider's hardware environment. Application level monitoring is also accommodated for here, in addition to support for Service Level Agreement (SLA) negotiation.

In the IaaS layer, illustrated by Fig. 3, the admission, allocation and management of virtual resource are performed through the orchestration of a number of components. The Virtual Machine Manager (VMM) is responsible for managing the complete life cycle of the VMs that are deployed in a specific infrastructure provider. Energy consumption is monitored, estimated and optimized using translated PaaS level metrics. These metrics are gathered via a monitoring infrastructure and a number of software probes. The *Energy Awareness* provision is an important step in the architecture implementation plan as it concentrates on delivering energy awareness in all system components. Monitoring and metrics information is measured at IaaS level and propagated through the various layers of the cloud stack (PaaS, SaaS) via the use of a OVF document.

The *Cloud Stack Adaptation* with regard to energy efficiency focuses on the addition of capabilities required to achieve dynamic energy management per each of the cloud layers, in other words:

1. *Intra* layer adaptation: refers to local layer adaptation in isolation. It considers the extensions of the runtime environment in order to be able to orchestrate the invocation of different application components with advanced scheduling techniques that take into account energy efficiency parameters.
2. *Inter* layer adaptation: the aim is to achieve steering information among cloud layers for triggering other layers to adapt their energy mode, the focus being information sharing and decision making among SaaS, PaaS and IaaS layers.

The key research challenge is the ability to take adaptive actions based upon energy consumption, performance and cost factors within each layer of the architecture and examine the effect that these have upon the running applications. Self-adaptive cloud-based software applications can be realized via a MAPE (Monitor, Analyse, Plan and Execute) feedback control loop architecture [29]. The cloud stack adaptation is then tailored for the Self-Adaptation Manager that manages applications at runtime and maintains performance and energy efficiency at the PaaS (Fig. 2) and IaaS (Fig. 3) layers, respectively. This is the subject of continued work [30].

Cloud engineering

Cloud engineering plays an important role in the context of creating energy efficient application development. Automation of cloud engineering tasks such as out of band testing and automated deployment are also necessary to gain full benefits from a cloud provider. In this section we discuss the importance of a self-adaptive development life-cycle that considers application energy consumption while maintaining other more traditional quality aspects of software such as performance at an acceptable level.

Towards a self-adaptive development life-cycle

To enable energy awareness in cloud applications, a self-adaptive software development methodology that considers energy at each stage: requirements gathering, software construction and testing is a necessity. Self-adaptation in this context refers to the ability to provide feedback in the form of energy metrics that guide a developer within an iterative development process towards an optimal energy efficient software solution. For any such methodology to exist a number of tools must be available to reduce the burden of energy consumption optimization. This is where the SaaS layer components of the architecture presented in 'Energy efficient cloud architecture" section can reduce time-to-market of cloud applications through the automation of standard developer practices, enabling quicker feedback on energy efficiency and more development iterations. Some of the more time consuming and challenging aspects of developing a cloud Application are the construction of VM images and installation of software dependencies. This is where the work on the VMIC is positioned. This tool manages software dependency installation and creates cloud provider agnostic VM images in an automated fashion, reducing developer effort.

Cloud application construction - VMIC

Figure 4 shows the automated interaction between the VMIC and other components in the SaaS layer of the energy efficient architecture. The VM image construction process is coordinated by Eclipse Plug-ins which invokes the VMIC with an application description. This description is provided in the form of an industry standard OVF [20] document. The VMIC parses the application descriptor for details on what packages should be installed in each base image, where each image represents a packaged software component to form a cloud application.

The VMIC can operate in two modes, *offline* and *online*. The first phase of the VMIC automation process copies an appropriate base image such as a variant of Linux or Windows. After copying, depending on the nature of the packages to be installed, it either mounts the image using

qemu-nbd [31] (*offline* mode) or instantiates it remotely (*online* mode) using libvirt [32]. During *offline* mode packages are placed into the Web root of a pre-installed tomcat container and is primarily used by the Programming Model Plug-in. In *online* mode, a locally running Chef [19] configuration management server is used to issue Chef recipes to the base VM that contains configuration information, package repositories and packages to install. Finally after packages have been installed in the VM, the image is saved either by unmounting the image, as is the case with *offline* mode or by saving a snapshot of the base VM image to the local file system, as is the case in *online* mode. The image and its content can then be tested on a local infrastructure or passed to the PaaS layer for future deployment on an IaaS provider.

These two modes of operation cover the necessary features and functionality to enable support for both COMPSs [27] enabled applications (packaged as Java Tomcat Web Services) invoked via the Programming Model Plug-in and more generic cloud applications (such as a n-tier web application) invoked via the Application Packager Plug-in, while minimising the time to create an

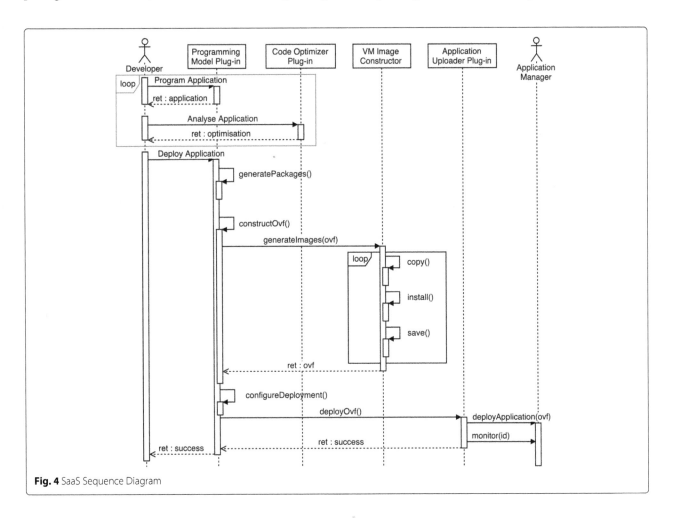

Fig. 4 SaaS Sequence Diagram

image. The remainder of this paper concentrates on the more flexible and challenging *online* mode.

Figure 5 illustrates the subcomponent that comprise to make up the VMIC in addition to showing interactions with external components and baseline technologies. The VMIC is comprised of two main Java packages one for each mode of operation and a Java library for parsing OVF. The process of constructing an image involves a number of different internal phases and coordination of baseline technologies within the VMIC. These phases are highlighted in order as follows:

1. **Initialise** - The OVF document passed to the VMIC is parsed for VM components attributes and their associated Chef *cookbooks* that contain *recipes* (instructions for installing software written in a domain specific language).
2. **Copy Image** - For every component and the given image type parsed from the OVF, the VMIC selects and copies an appropriate base image.
3. **Boot Image** - Using libvirt the baseline image selected is instantiated via a hypervisor such as KVM [33].

4. **Bootstrap Image** - Once the instantiated VM's operating system has initialised, the VMIC bootstraps a Chef Client either via Secure Shell (Linux) or Windows Remote Management, registering it with a local Chef server.
5. **Upload Cookbooks** - The VMIC downloads *cookbooks* from URLs parsed from the OVF that reside on a remote repository running on a Web server. These cookbooks are then uploaded to the local Chef Server.
6. **Deploy Cookbooks** - The VMIC associates the uploaded Chef cookbooks with the instantiated VM within the Chef Server and invokes the Chef Client to download and install the cookbooks.
7. **Clean Up** - After installation is complete, the VMIC shuts down the instantiated VM and deletes the uploaded *cookbooks*.

Experimental design

To evaluate the feasibility of the VMIC architecture and the construction phases as outlined previously, the following section discusses the experimental design to test the performance of the VMIC tool. "Cloud testbed"

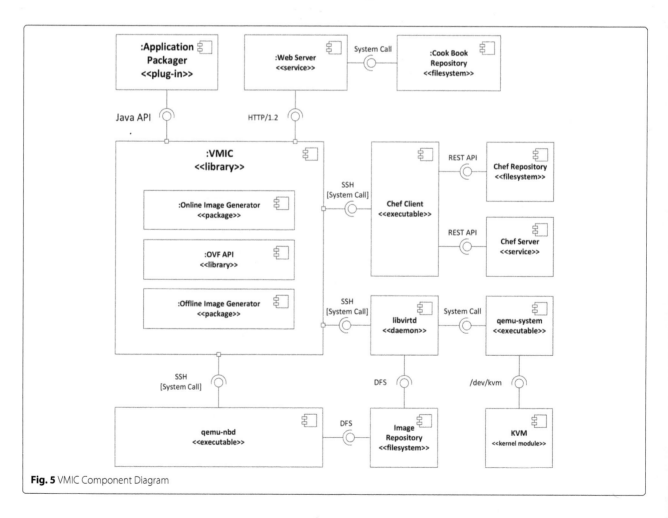

Fig. 5 VMIC Component Diagram

subsection discusses the cloud testbed used for the experimentation and the environment in which the VMIC was deployed. "Cloud application & experimental set-up" subsection describes the cloud application used to test the VMIC and the experimental set-up that includes a description of variables monitored.

Cloud testbed

The cloud testbed used in experimentation is located at the *Technische Universität Berlin* (see Fig. 6). The computing cluster consists of 200 commodity 1U nodes and 4 2U nodes used as a staging environment. Each of the 1U nodes is equipped with a quad-core Intel E3-1230 processor at 3.3 GHz, 16 GB of RAM, 1 TB of local hard disk capacity. The 2U nodes are equipped with 2 quad-core Intel E5620 processors at 2.66 GHz, 32 GB of RAM, 750 GB of local hard disk capacity. An 8 node Ceph cluster with a replica pool size of 2 and 16 TB of usable storage provided a Distributed File System (DFS). Additionally,

the cloud testbed deploys OpenStack [34] to manage virtual infrastructure and Zabbix [35] to store monitored data. The power measurements were taken with *Gembird EnerGenie Energy Meters* [36]. All experiments presented in this paper were performed on the 1U nodes.

Each node is connected to two different networks (See Fig. 7) and is able to transfer in duplex at full speed 1 Gbit/s. The first network is dedicated for infrastructure management via OpenStack, as well as regular data exchange between the nodes and VMs (both private and public subnets). The second network is available for storage area network usage only, with storage nodes accessible via the Ceph DFS. Access to the testbed is provided by VPN.

Figure 8 illustrates the deployment configuration of the VMIC in the context of the energy efficient cloud architecture (see "Energy efficient cloud architecture" section) as implemented by the ASCETiC project [37]. The ASCETiC components/tools were deployed by layer into three VMs:

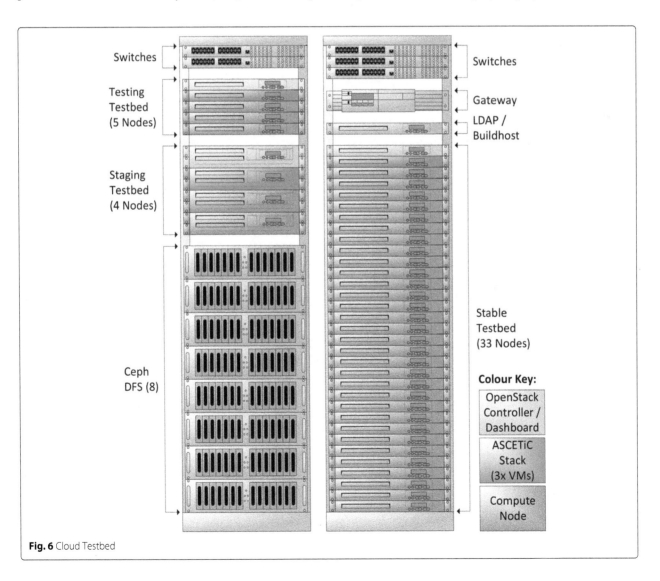

Fig. 6 Cloud Testbed

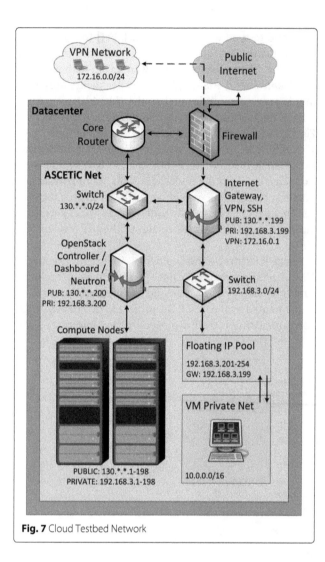

Fig. 7 Cloud Testbed Network

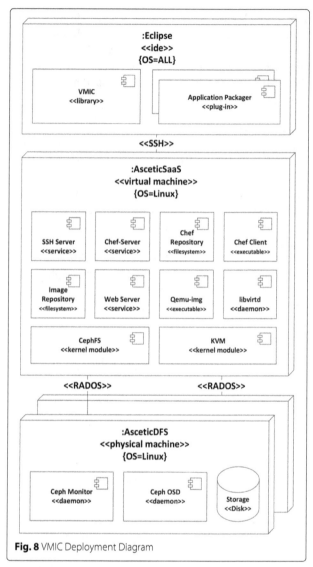

Fig. 8 VMIC Deployment Diagram

SaaS, PaaS and IaaS. The VMIC and its associated baseline technology dependencies were installed within the SaaS VM along with an instance of Eclipse containing the toolbox plug-ins. Nested KVM virtualization was used to enable the VMIC to create VMS within the SaaS VM and the nested VMs were backed by a mounted Ceph storage pool accessed via the cephfs Linux kernel module. The Ubuntu 12.04.5 LTS operating system was installed in each VM and ran on the Linux Kernel version 4.5.2. The SaaS VM was allocated 4 CPU cores and 8 Gbyte of memory from a 1U node.

Cloud application & experimental set-up

The chosen application to fulfil the objectives of the experiments is the NewsAsset [38] application that facilitates digital journalism. This is an n-tier application that is composed of a set of VM images as illustrated in Fig. 9. The application has a (fat) client in the front-end, a NewsAsset server implementing the business logic (in the

middle layer) and stores news items data in an Oracle database in the back-end [39].

The load balancer image implemented via HAProxy [40] distributes load between NewsAsset application servers and was installed in a Linux Ubuntu 12.04.5 LTS base image. These application servers running on Windows operating system are comprised of a single binary executable and associated software dependencies. The NewsAsset application stores and retrieves data within a single Oracle database image and single File Server image, both running on Windows. Each VM is allocated 2 CPU cores and 2 Gbytes of memory. Table 1 outlines the software dependencies of each VM image as specified in the OVF passed to the VMIC.

To ascertain the performance of the VMIC when constructing the images for the NewsAsset application four experiments are performed:

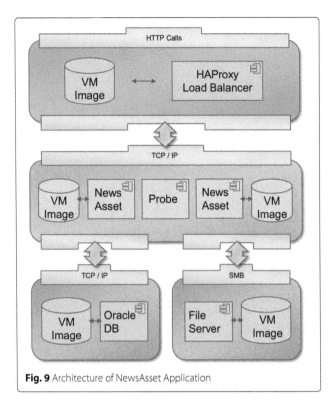

Fig. 9 Architecture of NewsAsset Application

1. The first evaluates the performance of each VMIC phase through the construction of the single image containing the application server component, the independent variable. Dependent variables in this experiment are the fine grained resource utilities of the ASCETiC SaaS VM: CPU utility and network bandwidth.
2. The second evaluates the runtime performance (execution time) of the VMIC. Linux and Windows

components are compared, in addition to the time to generate all News Asset images over 10 consecutive runs.

3. In the third, the runtime performance of the VMIC is evaluated with a range $(1 - 4)$ of concurrently generated HAProxy Linux based images again over 10 consecutive runs.
4. Finally, the fourth demonstrates the VMIC's capabilities to aid in the deployment of NewsAsset energy aware application thanks to monitoring its power consumption.

Results and recommendations

The following section discusses the performance of the VMIC by presenting an analysis of the experimental results and illustrating adequate performance of its tool implementation.

Figure 10 demonstrates the performance characteristics of each VMIC phase. The graphs show the majority of time within the VMIC is spent in three phases. Firstly, the deployment of the cookbooks accounts for nearly 50% of the execution time. Secondly, the copy of the base image accounts for 20% of the execution time and is a factor of the size of the base image. Finally, the bootstrap process that sees the installation of the Chef client accounts for 10% of the runtime and the other phases tally for the remaining 30%. It is worth noting that a very slight delay at the start of the trace before "Copy Image" shows the minimal overhead induced from processing OVF, in the order of 1% of the total runtime.

Reviewing the network bandwidth consumption of the VMIC reveals that the copy of the base image is restricted by the available disk bandwidth over the network (a limitation of the testbed's 1 Gbit network to the Ceph cluster),

Table 1 NewsAsset application software dependencies

| Component | Dependencies | | |
	1	2	3
HAProxy	cpu 0.2.0	build-essential 6.0.0	haproxy 1.6.7
Description	Chef cookbook to manage CPU related actions on linux.	Installs packages required for compiling C software from source.	Installs haproxy and prepares the configuration location.
NewsAsset	chef_handler 1.4.0	windows 1.44.1	newsasset-server
Description	Distribute and enable Chef Exception and Report handlers	Provides a set of useful Windows-specific primitives.	Custom cookbook to install a NewsAsset application server, its .Net dependencies and a monitoring probe
Oracle DB	chef_handler 1.4.0	windows 1.44.1	newsasset-oracle
Description	Distribute and enable Chef Exception and Report handlers	Provides a set of useful Windows-specific primitives.	Custom cookbook to install a Oracle DB server and NewsAsset application server scheme
File Server	newsasset-file		
Description	Custom cookbook to configure CIFS based SMB share		

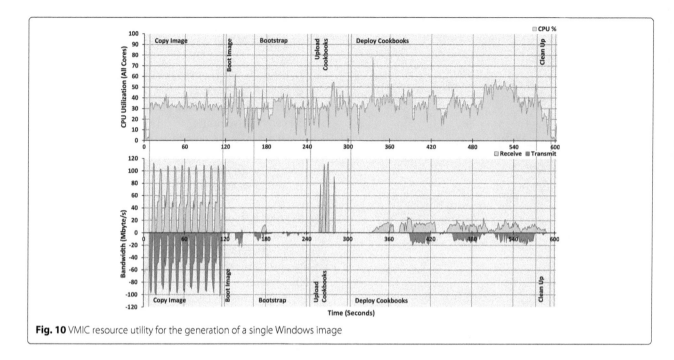

Fig. 10 VMIC resource utility for the generation of a single Windows image

while the deployment of the cookbooks phase is limited by disk I/O. It is recommended that the use of 10 Gbit Ethernet or better and SSD backed storage would dramatically reduce the time to generate images (*recommendation 1*). Furthermore, due to mainly sequential installation processes of the NewsAsset application server, CPU utilization of the VMIC tool is mainly limited to 1 core. Given that the dependency graphs of most software are sequential in nature, we recommend that the VMIC tool be deployed on a machine with the best single thread performance, to reduce runtime further (*recommendation 2*). Finally, the installation of the Chef Client as part of the bootstrapping process could be omitted, if the base images used come with this pre-installed at the expense of additional developer time (*recommendation 3*).

Figure 11 shows the execution time of a range of different NewsAsset components (Windows, Linux, All

Components) generated and includes error bars indicating the standard deviation over 10 consecutive iterations of this experiment. It can be seen that the construction of Windows images takes substantially longer than Linux images. This is due to two factors. Firstly, the Windows base images are twice as larger in size (2.6 GByte Windows vs 1.1 GByte Linux) and take three times longer to boot (45 seconds Windows vs 15 Linux). Given that it is difficult to strip down the Windows Operating System to the levels of a minimal Linux installation, it is recommended that developers limit the use of Windows to legacy applications (*recommendation 4*). Finally, from the error bars it can be seen that the distribution of VMIC invocations is tightly packed suggesting consistent performance.

Figure 12 shows the scalability of a range of concurrent users accessing the VMIC to generating the HAProxy Linux component of the NewsAsset Application. It can

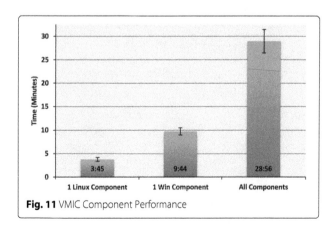

Fig. 11 VMIC Component Performance

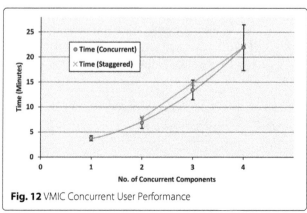

Fig. 12 VMIC Concurrent User Performance

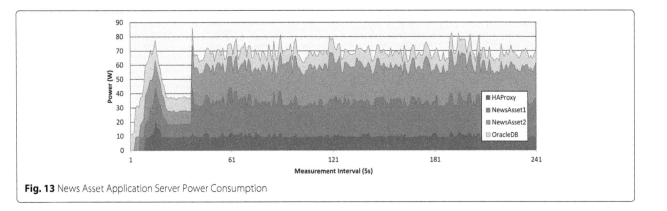

Fig. 13 News Asset Application Server Power Consumption

be seen that as the number of concurrent users increases, the image generation time also increases in a non-linear exponential manner at the same time as variance increases. This is less than ideal if multiple developers wish to share the deployment of a single instance of the VMIC tool. After further investigation of this phenomenon, a second experiment was performed to stagger the arrival rate of concurrent users by 60 seconds. This had the impact of reducing the effect of the Ceph DFS running on 1Gbit connectivity as previously discussed. By spreading its use more evenly, the result of adding 3 minutes of waiting ended in the same runtime for 4 concurrent components generated as without. With this in mind, it is recommended that if the VMIC is to be deployed in a multi-tenant environment, then substantial disk bandwidth and I/O should be available (*recommendation 5*).

In addition to the previous experiments evaluating the performance of the VMIC, Fig. 13 illustrates the benefits of NewsAsset construction with the VMIC and its deployment onto the ASCETiC enabled infrastructure capable of using the embedded monitoring probe. In this experiment the NewsAsset deployment consists of two load balanced application servers driven by a sustained workload. The graph shows the attributed deployment, idle and load power consumption of the NewsAsset VMs during and for a period of a few minutes after deployment. With the VMIC's capabilities to aid in the construction of energy aware cloud applications, the energy efficiency of software can be easily analysed under a variation of loads and deployment configurations (*recommendation 6*).

Conclusion

This paper has highlighted the importance of providing novel methods and tools to support software developers aiming to optimise energy efficiency and minimise the carbon footprint resulting from designing and developing software at the different layers of the cloud stack while maintaining other quality aspects of software to adequate and agreed levels.

We discussed our practical experience during implementation of architectural components relevant to cloud application construction emphasising on automatic image construction, and presented a performance evaluation. The results show that the performance of VM construction is primarily limited by available network and disk I/O. However, for the purpose of a self-adaptive development life-cycle that considers energy awareness the time to generate application components is more than adequate.

Overall, the VMIC is interoperable with cloud providers and technologies that support OVF. It manages software dependency installation and creates cloud provider agnostic VM images in an automated fashion, reducing development effort. Finally, it is shown to be effective through the experimental evaluation of its implementation and is already integrated in a cloud computing toolkit.

Future work on the VMIC will include exploring the integration of third party baseline technologies for the creation of base (master) images such as Vagrant. Integration work will consider the use of containers with the image construction process used in the VMIC such as Docker [41]. We will also consider optimising the energy efficiency of the build process by using DVFS and RAPL policies during the copy-image phase given that it is I/O-bound and can be seen as a possible source of energy saving. This is in addition to research into *intra* and *inter* layer adaptation for the purpose of coordinating the layers of the architecture presented in this paper to further increase cloud application energy efficiency.

Acknowledgments
This work is partly supported by the European Commission under FP7-ICT-2013.1.2 contract 610874 - Adapting Service lifeCycle towards EfficienT Clouds (ASCETiC) project.

Authors' contributions
All authors read and approved the final manuscript.

Competing interests
The authors declare that they have no competing interests.

References

1. Pawlish M, Varde AS, Robila SA (2012) Cloud Computing for Environment-friendly Data Centers. In: Proceedings of the Fourth International Workshop on Cloud Data Management, CloudDB '12. ACM, New York. pp 43–48
2. Mastelic T, Oleksiak A, Claussen H, Brandic I, Pierson J-M, Vasilakos AV (2014) Cloud computing: Survey on energy efficiency. ACM Comput Surv 47(2):33:1–33:36
3. Grech N, Georgiou K, Pallister J, Kerrison S, Morse J, Eder K (2015) Static analysis of energy consumption for llvm ir programs. In: Proceedings of the 18th International Workshop on Software and Compilers for Embedded Systems. SCOPES '15. ACM, USA. pp 12–21
4. (2016) Packer - Identical Machine Images for Multiple Platforms. https://www.packer.io/
5. (2016) Vagrant - Development Environments Made Easy. https://www.vagrantup.com/
6. Götz S, Wilke C, Cech S, Aßmann U (2011) Runtime variability management for energy-efficient software by contract negotiation. In: Proceedings of the 6th International Workshop on Models@run.time, New Zealand
7. Hilty L, Lohmann W (2011) The Five Most Neglected Issues in "Green IT". CEPIS UPGRADE 12(4):11–15
8. te Brinke S, Malakuti S, Bockisch C, Bergmans L, Aksit M (2013) A design method for modular energy-aware software. In: Shin SY, Maldonado JC (eds). Proceedings of the 28th Annual ACM Symposium on Applied Computing (SAC'2013). ACM, New York. pp 1180–1182
9. Grosskop K, Visser J (2013) Identification of Application-level Energy Optimizations. In: Hilty LM (ed). Proceedings of the First International Conference on Information and Communication Technologies for Sustainability (ICT4S'2013), Switzerland
10. Nowak A, Leymann F (2013) Green Business Process Patterns - Part II (Short Paper). In: 6th IEEE International Conference on Service-Oriented Computing and Applications. IEEE, Hawaii. pp 168–173
11. Hönig T, Eibel C, Preikschat WS, Cassens B, Kapitza R (2013) Proactive energy-aware system software design with seep. In: Proceedings of the 2nd Workshop on Energy Aware Software-Engineering and Development. GI Softwaretechnik-Trends. pp 1–2
12. Klingert S, Berl A, Beck M, Serban R, Girolamo M, Giuliani G, Meer H, Salden A (2012) Sustainable Energy Management in Data Centers through Collaboration. In: Energy Efficient Data Centers. volume 7396 of Lecture Notes in Computer Science, Springer Berlin Heidelberg. pp 13–24
13. Mammela O, Majanen M, Basmadjian R, Meer H, Giesler A, Homberg W (2012) Energy-aware job scheduler for high-performance computing. Comput Sci Res Dev 27(4):265–275
14. Armstrong D, Espling D, Tordsson J, Djemame K, Elmroth E (2015) Contextualization: dynamic configuration of virtual machines. J Cloud Comput 4(1):1–15. doi:10.1186/s13677-015-0042-8, http://dx.doi.org/10.1186/s13677-015-0042-8
15. Beloglazov A, Abawajy J, Buyya R (2012) Energy-aware resource allocation heuristics for efficient management of data centers for Cloud computing. Futur Gener Comput Syst 28(5):755–768
16. (2016) CFEngine 3 - Configuration Management Software for Agile System Administrators. http://cfengine.com/
17. Burgess M (2004) Configurable immunity for evolving human computer systems. Sci Comput Program 51(3):197–213
18. (2016) Puppet - IT Automation for System Administrators. http://puppetlabs.com/
19. (2016) Chef - A Systems Integration Framework. http://wiki.opscode.com/display/chef/Home
20. (2015) Open Virtualization Format (OVF) - A standard from the Distributed Management Task Force. http://www.dmtf.org/standards/ovf
21. (2015) OPTIMIS Toolkit. http://optimistoolkit.com
22. Armstrong D, Espling D, Tordsson J, Djemame K, Elmroth E (2013) Runtime Virtual Machine Recontextualization for Clouds. In: Euro-Par 2012: Parallel Processing Workshops. Springer Berlin Heidelberg, Rhodes Islands. pp 567–576
23. Srikantaiah S, Kansal A, Zhao F (2008) Energy aware consolidation for cloud computing. In: Proceedings of the 2008 Conference on Power Aware Computing and Systems, HotPower'08. USENIX Association, Berkeley. pp 10–10
24. Choi K, Soma R, Pedram M (2004) Fine-grained dynamic voltage and frequency scaling for precise energy and performance trade-off based on the ratio of off-chip access to on-chip computation times. In: Proceedings Design, Automation and Test in Europe Conference and Exhibition. IEEE Computer Society, Washington Vol. 1. pp 4–9. doi:10.1109/DATE.2004.1268819
25. Rotem E, Naveh A, Ananthakrishnan A, Weissmann E, Rajwan D (2012) Power-Management Architecture of the Intel Microarchitecture Code-Named Sandy Bridge. IEEE Micro 32(2):20–27
26. Djemame K, Armstrong D, Kavanagh RE, Ferrer AJ, Perez DG, Antona DR, Deprez J-C, Ponsard C, Ortiz D, Macías M, Guitart J, Lordan F, Ejarque J, Sirvent R, Badia RM, Kammer M, Kao O, Agiatzidou E, Dimakis A, Courcoubetis C, Blasi L (2014) Energy Efficiency Embedded Service Lifecycle: Towards an Energy Efficient Cloud Computing Architecture. In: Proceedings of the Energy Efficient Systems (EES'2014) Workshop. CEUR Workshop Proceedings, Stockholm Vol. 1203. pp 1–6. http://ceur-ws.org/Vol-1203/EES-paper1.pdf
27. Badia RM, Conejero J, Diaz C, Ejarque J, Lezzi D, Lordan F, Ramon-Cortes C, Sirvent R (2015) Comp superscalar, an interoperable programming framework. SoftwareX 3:32–36
28. Lordan F, Ejarque J, Sirvent R, Badia RM (2016) Energy-aware programming model for distributed infrastructures. In: Proceedings of the 24th Euromicro International Conference on Parallel, Distributed, and Network-Based Processing (PDP 2016). IEEE, Greece
29. Farokhi S, Jamshidi P, Brandic I, Elmroth E (2015) Self-adaptation challenges for cloud-based applications: a control theoretic perspective. In: Proceedings of the 10th International Workshop on Feedback Computing. ACM, USA
30. Djemame K, Kavanagh R, Armstrong D, Lordan F, Ejarque J, Macias M, Sirvent R, Guitart J, Badia RM (2016) Energy efficiency support through intra-layer cloud stack adaptation. In: Proceedings of the 13th International Conference on Economics of Grids, Clouds, Systems and Services (GECON'2016). Springer, Greece
31. (2016) QEMU - Open Source Machine Emulation and Virtualizer. http://www.qemu.org
32. Bolte M, Sievers M, Birkenheuer G, Niehorster O, Brinkmann A (2010) Non-intrusive Virtualization Management using libvirt. In: 2010 Design, Automation & Test in Europe Conference & Exhibition. Piscataway, USA. pp 574–579
33. Kivity A, Kamay Y, Laor D, Lublin U, Liguori A (2007) KVM: The Linux Virtual Machine Monitor. In: Proceedings of the Linux Symposium, Canada Vol. 1. pp 225–230
34. (2015) OpenStack: Open source software for building private and public clouds. http://www.openstack.org/
35. (2015) Zabbix - An Enterprise-class Monitoring Solution. http://www.zabbix.com/
36. (2013) GEMBIRD Deutschland GmbH. EGM-PWM-LAN data sheet. http://gmb.nl/Repository/6736/EGM-PWM-LAN_manual---7f3db9f9-65f1-4508-a986-90915709e544.pdf
37. (2016) ASCETiC. Adapting Service lifeCycle towards EfficienT Clouds. http://www.ascetic.eu/
38. (2016) Newsasset Agency. http://www.newsasset.com/
39. (2016) Oracle Database. https://www.oracle.com/database/index.html
40. (2015) HAProxy - A Reliable, High Performance TCP/HTTP Load Balancer. http://www.haproxy.org/
41. Docker Inc (2017) Docker - Homepage. https://www.docker.com/

6

VM consolidation approach based on heuristics, fuzzy logic, and migration control

Mohammad Alaul Haque Monil[1] and Rashedur M. Rahman[2*]

Abstract

To meet the increasing demand of computational power, at present IT service providers' should choose cloud based services for its flexibility, reliability and scalability. More and more datacenters are being built to cater customers' need. However, the datacenters consume large amounts of energy, and this draws negative attention. To address those issues, researchers propose energy efficient algorithms that can minimize energy consumption while keeping the quality of service (QoS) at a satisfactory level. Virtual Machine consolidation is one such technique to ensure energy-QoS balance. In this research, we explore fuzzy logic and heuristic based virtual machine consolidation approach to achieve energy-QoS balance. A Fuzzy VM selection method is proposed in this research. It selects VM from an overloaded host. Additionally, we incorporate migration control in Fuzzy VM selection method that will enhance the performance of the selection strategy. A new overload detection algorithm has also been proposed based on mean, median and standard deviation of utilization of VMs. We have used CloudSim toolkit to simulate our experiment and evaluate the performance of the proposed algorithm on real-world work load traces of Planet lab VMs. Simulation results demonstrate that the proposed method is most energy efficient compared to others.

Keywords: Cloud, Datacenter, Dynamic virtual machine consolidation, CloudSim toolkit, Planetlab VM data, Fuzzy logic

Introduction

Cloud computing can be classified as a new era of computing which has revolutionized the IT industry with its pay-as-you-go services. Its dynamic provisioning of computing services by using Virtual Machine (VM) technologies provides opportunity for consolidation and environment isolation. Having the viable business prospect, all the tech-giants have already started providing cloud services. IT companies are now moving from traditional CAPEX model (buy the dedicated hardware and depreciate it over a period of time) to the OPEX model (use a shared cloud infrastructure and pay as one uses it). To enable and ensure the global growth of computing need, cloud service providing companies are now using warehouse sized datacenters to meet user demand which incurs considerable amount of energy. At the beginning of the cloud computing era, cloud service providers focused mainly on catering the computing demand that lead to expansion of cloud infrastructures; hence energy consumption. Therefore, energy consumption by data centers worldwide was risen by 56 % from 2005 to 2010 [4]. In 2010 it was accounted to be between 1.1 and 1.5 % of the total electricity use and carbon dioxide emissions of the ICT industry were estimated to be 2 % of the global emissions which was equivalent to the emissions of the aviation industry [4]. Additionally, an average size data center consumes as much energy as 25,000 households [1]. American Society of Heating, Refrigerating and Air-Conditioning Engineers (ASHRAE) estimated that infrastructure and energy costs contributed about 75 %, whereas IT contributed just 25 %

* Correspondence: rashedur.rahman@northsouth.edu
[2]Department of Electrical and Computer Engineering, North South University, Dhaka, Bangladesh
Full list of author information is available at the end of the article

to the overall cost of operating a data center [2] in 2014. So, to cater the increasing need of computing, energy aware technique should be applied in cloud computing infrastructure otherwise the energy need will be huge and will be threatening to the environment [20]. To handle this problem, datacenter resource needs to be utilized in an efficient manner. An efficient approach will not only reduce the energy consumption but also keep the performance up to the mark. Both in hardware and software there are several techniques being used for energy consumption of a cloud system. In hardware level, Dynamic Component Deactivation (DCD) and Dynamic Performance Scaling (DPS) are two such techniques, while in virtualization level, several techniques have been proposed e.g., the Energy Management for Hypervisor-based VMs and Kernel-based Virtual Machine (KVM) [28].

VM Consolidation is one of the techniques which draw researchers' attention and is an active field of research in recent time. As we know that inactive host or host in sleep mode causes minimal energy; therefore, energy consumption can be reduced considerably. By adopting VM consolidation, more energy could be conserved by shutting down under-utilized datacenters. However, to achieve this outcome, we need to consolidate different VMs in one server and migrate VMs from one host to the other which may lead to SLA (Service Level Agreement) violation. So, algorithms must be designed in such a way that not only reduces power consumption but also serves desired QoS (such as SLA). In a VM consolidation method, selecting the VM to migrate is a challenging job and researchers came up with different solutions. In real world the computation need is very dynamic; therefore, decision is dependent on several criteria. In our research we have applied fuzzy logic. When the overload will be detected, our proposed fuzzy logic and heuristic based algorithm will decide the VM to migrate from the source datacenter to achieve minimum energy consumption by keeping the SLA violation at minimal level.

The remainder of this paper is organized as follows. In section Motivation, motivation has been clarified. In section Proposed method, our proposed methods and algorithms are given. In section Experimental setup, experimental setup is given and in section Experimental result, experimental result and comparisons have been presented. In section Related works, related works are discussed Finally, in section Conclusion, we have discussed about future work and concluded our paper.

Motivation

VM consolidation algorithm needs to be designed in such a way that there will be minimum energy

consumption, minimum violation of SLA, efficient VM migration and minimum number of active hosts in a given time. VM migration causes SLA violation because when a VM is migrated from one host to other it has to transfer its primary memory to the destination host and in the transfer process the requested CPU could not be delivered as the VM will be in a transition state. For this reason, along with power consumption, we need to make sure that the number of VM migration is minimal which will in fact reduce the SLA violation. A desired VM consolidation approach will reduce energy consumption and as well as, it will reduce the negative impact on QoS. To address these issues, VM consolidation has been considered as a bin packing problem in some researches, e.g., [3, 17, 19]. On the other hand, there are researches where VM consolidation has been broken down in separate problems where bin packing solution is considered as one of the sub-problems of VM consolidations, i.e., VM placement [1, 2, 4, 8, 9, 12, 15, 16]. VM consolidation has been broken down in four sub-problems and dealt in researches are the followings:

1. Identify the under loaded datacenter to put them in sleeping mode by migrating all the VMs to other active datacenter (Under load detection).
2. Determine the host that is overloaded. Migrate some VMs from the identified overloaded datacenter to other datacenters while preserving QoS (Overload detection).
3. Decide the VM(s) that should be migrated (VM selection).
4. Place the selected VMs on other active or reactivated hosts\ (VM placement).

Breaking down into sub-problems has two key advantages. (1) Problems get simplified if it is divided into sub-problems and provides the opportunity to break the VM consolidation problem to four problems and devise separate algorithms. By doing that, performance of each algorithm can be measured and analyzed to investigate for identifying the better approach. As in this research we will mostly focus two sub-problems problems, one is host overload detection and another is VM selection. (2) It enables the option of distributed execution of the algorithms by executing the underload/overload detection and VM selection algorithms. Distributed VM consolidation makes the scaling easier. When a new node is added it automatically gets included in the algorithm which is essential for large-scale Cloud providers. These approaches are designed in CloudSim (an open source

Cloud Simulation designed by CLOUDS lab of University of Melbourne [5]). Researchers have developed their algorithms in CloudSim [1, 2, 4] which can be accessed and used for further research. However, there are places where the improvements could be done to yield better results by saving more power yet delivering the expected QoS. The driving factors which motivate to conduct this research are the following:

- For VM selection, there are several VM selection approaches are proposed in research [1, 2, 4], namely Maximum Correlation (MC), Minimum Migration Time (MMT), and Random Selection (RS). The maximum correlation (MC) approach selects the VM to migrate which has the highest correlation value among all the VMs of a host. The minimum migration time approach (MMT) selects the VM to migrate which has the least memory as it will be migrated faster. And the random selection approach (RS) selects the VM randomly from a host. The approaches offer different results. One method (MC) provides more power savings but lacks in QoS. Another method (MMT) provides better performance KPI, i.e., QoS incurring more power [4]. As the situation is uncertain and in real world the computation need is very dynamic, fuzzy logic can be applied with different inputs to achieve the tradeoff between energy consumption and QoS.
- Migration control can be applied to select the VM to migrate. Refraining from steady resource consuming VM migration can lead to better performance in dynamic VM consolidation [3]. But constantly high resource consuming VM should not be migrated as they consume large number of resources. So, migration control can be applied on two types of VMs; steady resource consuming VM and high resources consuming VMs. These phenomena can be taken into account while designing a VM selection method.
- To decide whether a host is overloaded or not, there are several algorithms proposed [1, 2, 4] (e.g., Inter Quartile Range (IQR): which decides the threshold of a host to be marked as overloaded using interquartile range, Median Absolute Deviation (MAD) uses median absolute deviation and THR provides threshold for a host to be marked as overloaded. Local Regression (LR) and Local Robust Regression (LRR) provide prediction of host utilization,). These statistical measures provide a threshold (IQR, MAD and THR) and prediction (LR and LRR) for a host to be identified as overloaded. In parallel, these algorithms rely on mean and standard deviation of resource utilization that gives an indication of future load of a VM which also can be an approach independently for overload detection [15]. However, mean and standard deviation is very much influenced by terminal values. Terminal values indicate the outlier values or the values that are too large or too small and do not represent the normal values. As VM's resource utilization can be very dynamic in real world, instead of mean we can use median and we can modify the formula for standard deviation using median instead of mean. An overload detection algorithm can be designed from this.
- When VM needs to be migrated to another datacenter in VM placement phase or underload detection phase, the destination host needs to be judged whether it will be overloaded in future by using overload detection method.

Proposed method

In this work we have designed Fuzzy VM Selection with migration control algorithm and Mean, Median & standard deviation based over load detection algorithm. However, before going in detail, overview of VM consolidation is presented. The algorithm below portrays the basic VM consolidation approach designed in CloudSim.

Algorithm 1 provides a basic flow of VM consolidation. At first the hosts are created. Then the VM data is taken as input. Based on the real life data of VM and cloudlets are created. Then VMs are assigned to host and cloudlet is assigned to VM. Based on dynamic consolidation technique, status is checked for every scheduled interval. For every scheduled interval, underload detection algorithm is executed and less utilized hosts are put into sleeping mode by transferring all VM to other active VM. Then overload detection is executed, and overloaded hosts are identified. At later steps, VM is selected from the overloaded hosts to migrate. Then those VMs are placed into available hosts or if needed a host is switched on from sleeping mode. After each iteration (the iteration time can be varied in CloudSim, most of the research have used 5 min as iteration interval [1, 2, 4]) a log is created to calculate energy consumption and QoS. At the end of the simulation, Energy consumption and QoS is shown. In next sections our proposed algorithms are discussed. More details of the iteration is discussed in section Experimental setup.

Algorithm 1. Basic VM consolidation

1. Input number of hosts;
2. Interface with real cloud data;
3. VM is created and assigned to hosts;
4. Cloudlet is created and assigned to VMs;
5. for every specified time interval
6.   Execute underload detection;
7.   Identify overloaded host through overload detection.
8.   VM is selected for migration from overloaded host.
9.   VM is placed in available datacenters.
10.   Preserve history and calculate QoS
11. end
12. Simulation ends and provides Energy consumption and other QoS value

A. Fuzzy VM selection with migration control

Fuzzy technique is an attractive approach to handle uncertain, imprecise, or un-modeled data in solving control and intelligent decision-making problems. Different VM selection methods offer different advantages. It will be worthy if we could generate a method which will have the benefits of all of them by combining them together. Fuzzy logic can be an ideal tool for this. It will consider all the options and depending on those options a fuzzy value will be generated based on the predetermined rule of inferences. To develop the fuzzy VM selection method we have selected three distinguished inputs and each of them offers some advantages over others and different researches have already proven them. Minimum migration time and Maximum Correlation can be found at [2, 4] and the idea steady resource consuming VM is adopted from [3]. The following subsections will be focusing on the variables we will be using as input to our fuzzy systems, member ship function generated, inference rules and algorithms for computation.

1) Minimum migration Time

Minimum Migration Time (MMT) policy selects the VM which can be migrated within minimum time limit [2, 4]. The migration time is limited by the memory the VM is using and the spare bandwidth. At any moment t, The MMT with Migration Control policy finds VM x that will be selected for migration by the formula (1). $RAM(x)$ is the Radom Access Memory (RAM) utilization of VM x and $RAM(y)$ is the RAM utilization of VM y. NET_h means the available bandwidth for migration

and V_h is the set of VMs of host h. So the this method comapares the migration time and selects the VM x with minimum migration time among all VMs reside in host h.

$$x \in V_h \mid \forall y \in V_h, \ \frac{RAM(x)}{NET_h} \leq \frac{RAM(y)}{NET_h} \qquad (1)$$

This policy gives us the lowest SLA among all VM selection models. Migration time will be considered as one input of our fuzzy system.

2) Correlation

This method works based on the idea that the higher the correlation between the resource usages by applications running on an oversubscribed server, the higher the probability of server being overloaded [14]. It means that if the correlation of the CPU utilization of VMs of a particular host is high then the probability of this host being overloaded is also high [4, 14]. Based on this research outcome, correlation is considered as a metric as it will provide the information about the VM(s) that is going to cause the host to be overloaded. It is a predictive measure and consequently it will safer if such a VM could be migrated to other host where it will not have higher correlation with other VMs. In the subsequent portion, it is described how the correlations of VMs are calculated. An augmented matrix is created for all VMs of host using last n cycles' CPU utilization and correlation value is calculated. The highest the correlation value of VM, the higher the probability of that VM makes the host to be overloaded.

As described in [4], let there are n number of VMs. Let Y be one out of those n VMs for which we want to determine the maximum correlation with other $n-1$ VMs. Here our objective is to evaluate the correlation of Y with the rest of VMs. The $(n-1)*n$ augmented matrix is denoted by X. Each value in the matrix X represents the observed values of $(n-1)$ VMs and y vector represents $(n-1)$ observations of VM Y.

$$X = \begin{bmatrix} 1 & x_{1,1} & .. & x_{1,n-1} \\ . & . & & \\ . & . & & \\ . & . & & \\ 1 & x_{n-1,1} & . & x_{n-1,n-1} \end{bmatrix} \quad y = \begin{bmatrix} y_1 \\ . \\ . \\ . \\ y_n \end{bmatrix}$$

(2)

A vector of predicted value of VM y is denoted by $\hat{y}$ and expressed in Eq. 3.

$$\hat{y} = Xb, \quad where \ b = \left(X^T X\right)^{-1} X^T y \quad (3)$$

As we can find the predicted vector $\hat{y}$ of Y, the multiple correlation coefficient $(R_{Y, \ 1......N-1})^2$ also can be determined as this is equal to the squared correlation coefficient of the observed values y and predicted values of $\hat{y}$ of VM Y. So the correlation coefficient can be defined by Eq. 4. Here m_y and $m_{\hat{y}}$ are the sample mean of the values of y and $\hat{y}$.

$$R^2_{Y, \ X_1,...X_{n-1}} = \frac{\sum_{i=1}^{n} (y_i - m_y)^2 (\hat{y}_i - m\hat{y})^2}{\sum_{i=1}^{n} (y_i - m_y)^2 \sum_{i=1}^{n} (\hat{y}_i - m\hat{y})^2}$$

(4)

Now the multiple correlation coefficient can be easily found for any VM Xi by $R^2_{X_i, \ X_1,......X_{n-i}, \ X_{n+i} ....X_n}$. According to this method the VM that has the highest correlation with other VMs' CPU utilization will be migrated. More details of this method could be found in [1, 14].

3) Migration control metric for steady resource consuming VM

It has been proven that migration control provides better result in energy aware

VM consolidation and this approach also saves the unwanted traffic load [3]. Migration control can be done in various ways. We can stop migrating the high CPU using VMs or we can restrict steady resourse consuming VM from migration. In this work we will take steady resource consumption as a non-migration factor. If a VM's requirement highly fluctuates over time, then it can cause the host to be overloaded. In dynamic VM consolidation approach, VMs are resized in each iteration according to their need. So when a VM requests CPU which is abruptly high then host may not have such CPU available at that time and SLA violation will occur. As VM migration is triggered from an overloaded host we do not want to to migrate such VM from the overloaded host whose demands of CPU is not changed suddenly. In other words, if a VM is steady resource consuming over some iteration it means that it will be the least possible VM to make this host overloaded and we can expect the same behavior in the next iteration. We have used standard deviation for calculation of steady state resource consumption. If the standard deviation is high it means that the CPU request changes abruptly and we can call VMs with low standard deviation as steady resource consuming VMs. Let us consider a host h and V_h be the set of VMs in host h. $CPU_u(x_t)$ is the CPU utilization of VM X at time t. $CPU_u(x_{t-1})$, $CPU_u(x_{t-2}) ..... CPU_u(x_{t-n})$ are the CPU utilizations of previous n time frames of VM X. Migration control parameter can be given by Eq. 5. Here $CPU_{average}$ means average CPU utilization in last n time frames. The standard deviation of CPU usage of VM X can be determined by this equation. This parameter will surely indicate the fluctuation of CPU usage of the particular VM X.

$$stdev = \sqrt{\frac{1}{n} \sum_{i=1}^{n} \left(CPU_i - CPU_{average}\right)^2} \quad (5)$$

4) Fuzzy Membership function

A FIS (Fuzzy Inference System) is developed to provide fuzzy VM selection decision using three metrics as input. Member ship function needs to be defined to develop the FIS. We are using 4 linguistic variables including VMselection as output. Range of these membership function is chosen from the real cloud simulation data of PlanetLab. In order to do the so, we have run the simulation and collected data of all these variables and proportioned to decide the range. As the ranges have been collected from real world data by doing statistical proportion operation (e.g. top 30 % values are high) for deciding different level (i.e. high, medium and low), using trapezoidal membership function is logical as it deals with ranges with flat region better. As the range of values should be counted as medium or low or high, not a peak value, triangular function is being not used and sigmoid function is not used as it does not define the flat region like trapezoidal function does. Membership function of the linguistic variables are given below:

- RAM: $T(RAM) = \{Low, Medium, High\}$
  - Correlation: $T(Correlation) = \{Low, Medium, High\}$
  - Standard Deviation: $T(Stdev) = \{Low, Medium, High\}$
  - VM selection: $T(Vmselection) = \{Low, Medium, High, Very High\}$

Equation for the Trapezoid membership function [27] can be expressed as Eq. 6.

$$\mu(z) = \begin{cases} 0 & , & z \leq a \\ \left(\dfrac{z-a}{b-a}\right) & , & a \leq z \leq b \\ 1 & , & b \leq z \leq c \\ \left(\dfrac{d-z}{d-c}\right) & , & c \leq z \leq d \\ 0 & , & d \leq z \end{cases}$$

(6)

All the membership function graphs (Figs. 1, 2, 3 and 4) of the linguistic variables are given below and Table 1 shows the type of the membership function, the equation and the parameters.

As mentioned earlier, values and ranges of these membership functions are generated by heuristic approach. The source is 1-day (among 10 days) data of thousands of VM data of PlanetLab cloud network [25] (more discussed in section

Experimental setup). For example, to deduce the standard deviation membership function, we have generated standard deviation value utilization of each of the thousand VMs. As these trace contains 288 (every 5 min from 1 day) data per VM, total sample size is about 288,000 (288 trace data*1000 VMs). Using a

window size of 10, standard deviation is calculated for the total data and by doing ration the high, medium and low ranges are selected. The minimum migration time and correlation is also done in same way.

5) Fuzzy Inference Rule

Fuzzy inference rules are generated from the given linguistic variables. We have given equal weight on the variables to influence the VM selection value. If RAM is low it gets high priority as it makes the migration faster. If correlation is high then it gets high priority in migration as the higher the correlation is, the higher the probability of overloading the host. Finally, if the standard deviation is high then it will get high priority in migration compared to

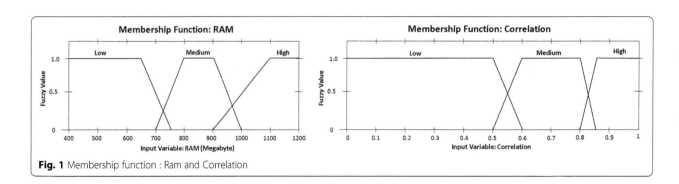

Fig. 1 Membership function : Ram and Correlation

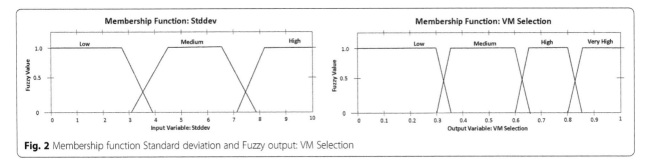

Fig. 2 Membership function Standard deviation and Fuzzy output: VM Selection

its steady state counterparts. The following Table 2 depicts the inference rules.

B. Fuzzy VM selection with migration control Algorithm Combination of Fuzzy VM selection method and migration control is given in Eq. 7 and Eq. 8. These equations indicate that a VM will be nominated for migration if it produces lower CPU usage than the migration control threshold and possesses highest fuzzy output value. If all VMs of an overloaded host produce more CPU usage than the migration control threshold, then the VM that produces highest fuzzy output value will be migrated. It is described in detail below.

Here the VM x is selected for migration if the fuzzy output value of VM x is greater than all other VMs. However, there is a condition that is as follows. If the current time is t and in last n cycles CPU utilization of VM x is $CPU_u(x_t)$, $CPU_u(x_{t-1})$, $CPU_u(x_{t-2})$ ... $CPU_u(x_{t-n})$, then

the average CPU utilization must be less than CPUthreshold to satisfy migration control, i.e., not to migrate the highly utilized VMs. The Eq. 8 means if the average CPU utilization is above threshold for all the VMs then the VM x with maximum fuzzy output value will be selected for migration.

$$x \in V_h \mid \forall y \in V_h, \quad Fuzzy\ Output(x) \geq Fuzzy\ Output(y)$$

Only if;

$$\frac{[CPU_u(x_t) + CPU_u(x_{t-1}) + CPU_u(x_{t-2}) + ...CPU_u(x_{t-n})]}{(n+1)}$$
$$< CPU_{thresold} \tag{7}$$

However, if every VM vm satisfies the following condition that means average utilization is more than the threshold,

---

Algorithm 2. Fuzzy VM selection Algorithm (FS)

Input: *overloaded host h, window size n*
Output: *Virtual Machine to be migrated, VM_m*

1. *Input Overloaded host h ;*
2. *VM_h = GetMigratableVm(h);*
3. *VM_{hex} = ExcludeVmInMigration (VM_h);*
4. *Utilm (VM_{hex})=UtilizationMatrix(VM_{hex});*
5. *Metric(n) =CorrelationCoefficient(UtilM (VM_{hex}));*
6. *for each VM V_i of VM_{hex}*
7.   *CPU_{hist}=GetMcParamFromCpuHistory(V_i);*
8.   *CPU_{mc}=GetMigrationControl(CPU_{hist});*
9.   *$STDEV(V_i)$=StandardDeviation(CPU_{hist});*
10.   *RAM (V_i)=GetRam(V_i);*
11.   *MC (V_i)= Metric(V_i);*
12.   *$Output_{fuzzy}$= EvaluateFuzzy(STDEV(V_i), RAM (V_i), MC (V_i))*
13.   *If $Output_{fuzzy}$ is highest till now*
14.   *$VM_{highest}$ = V_i ;*
15.   *if $CPU_{mc} < CPU_{threshold}$ then $VM_m = V_i$;*
16.   *End;*
17. *End;*
18. *If VM_m is null: VM_m= $VM_{highest}$;*
19. *Return VM_m ;*

Table 1 Memberhip functions

Variables	Parameter		
	Level	Function Type	Parameter
RAM	Low	Trapezoidal	a = 0 b = 0 c = 650 d = 750
	Medium	Trapezoidal	a = 700 b = 800 c = 900 d = 1000
	High	Trapezoidal	a = 900 b = 1100 c = 1800 d = 1800
Correlation	Low	Trapezoidal	a = 0 b = 0 c = .5 d = .6
	Medium	Trapezoidal	a = .5 b = .6 c = .8 d = .85
	High	Trapezoidal	a = .8 b = .85 c = 1 d = 1
Stdev	Low	Trapezoidal	a = 0 b = 0 c = 3 d = .3.75
	Medium	Trapezoidal	a = 3.25 b = 4 c = 6.75 d = 7.5
	High	Trapezoidal	a = 7.5 b = 8.5 c = 100 d = 100
VM Selection	Low	Trapezoidal	a = 0 b = 0 c = .3 d = .35
	Medium	Trapezoidal	a = 0.3 b = 0.35 c = .6 d = .65
	High	Trapezoidal	a = .6 b = .65 c = .8 d = .85
	Very High	Trapezoidal	a = .8 b = .85 c = 1 d = 1

Table 2 Fuzzy inference rule

Input			Output
RAM	Correlation	Stddev	VM Selection
Low	High	High	Very_High
Low	High	Medium	Very_High
Low	High	Low	High
Low	Medium	High	Very_High
Low	Medium	Medium	High
Low	Medium	Low	Medium
Low	Low	High	High
Low	Low	Medium	Medium
Low	Low	Low	Low
Medium	High	High	Very_High
Medium	High	Medium	High
Medium	High	Low	Medium
Medium	Medium	High	High
Medium	Medium	Medium	Medium
Medium	Medium	Low	Low
Medium	Low	High	Medium
Medium	Low	Medium	Low
Medium	Low	Low	Low
High	High	High	High
High	High	Medium	Medium
High	High	Low	Low
High	Medium	High	Medium
High	Medium	Medium	Low
High	Medium	Low	Low
High	Low	High	Low
High	Low	Medium	Low
High	Low	Low	Low

$$\frac{[CPU_u\ (vm_t) + CPU_u\ (vmx_{t-1}) + ... +\ CPU_u\ (vm_{t-n})]}{(n+1)}$$

$$\geq CPU_{thresold}$$

then this technique will select the VM that produces the highest fuzzy output value;

$$x \in V_h \mid \forall y \in V_h, \quad Fuzzy\ Output(x) \geq Fuzzy\ Output(y) \tag{8}$$

The *Algorithm 2* depicts how Fuzzy VM Selection algorithm (FSMC) works. There are two inputs of the algorithm: the host h and window size n (CloudSim Default window size has been used). The overloaded host is detected by previous phase: Overload detection. After having the host h at step-1, at step-2, *GetMigratableVm(h)* function pulls all the VM which are currently placed on that host h. At step-3, *ExcludeVmInMigration* function excludes all the VM which are already in migration for that host and assigned to VM_{hex} . At step-4, the function *UtilizationMatrix* calculates utilization matrix and stores at *UtilM (VM_{hex})*. At step-5, function *CorrelationCoefficient* calculates correlation coefficient based on *UtilM (VM_{hex})* and stores at *Metric(n)*. At step-7, for each VM V_i, CPU usage history of V_i is fetched using the function *GetMcParamFromCpuHistory (V_i)* for last n iteration as per CloudSim settings. At Step-8, Migration control parameter is calculated. To determine the steadiness of a VM's CPU usage,

at Step-9, *STDEV(V_i)*, Standard deviation is calculated using *StandardDeviation* function *from* CPU_{hist}. At Step-10, current usage of RAM will be fetched for V_i and will check for if the one is the lowest up to now. At Step-11, Correlation for this VM will fetched. At Step-12, fuzzy output *Output$_{fuzzy}$* is determined using *EvaluateFuzzy* function where inputs of this function are *STDEV(V_i)*, *RAM (V_i)* and *MC (V_i)*. At step-13, If this one is the highest till now, at step-14, $VM_{highest}$ will be updated. At step-15, VM VM_m will be updated if CPU_{mc} is smaller than $CPU_{threshold}$. If all VM is greater than the threshold and the highest fuzzy output VM is selected for migration at step-18 and finally step-19 returns the VM to be migrated.

C. Mean, Median and Standard deviation based Overload Detection(MMSD)

Algorithm 3. MMSD based overload detection (MMSD)

Input: *host h*
Output: *True or False indicating overloaded or not*
1. *Input Overloaded host h ;*
2. *VM_h = GetVm(h);*
3. *for each VM V_i of VM_h*
4. *TotalRequestedMIPS+=GetCurrentMIPS(V_i);*
5. *Stddev=GetStddevOfUtilization(V_i);*
6. *Mean= GetMeanOfUtilization(V_i);*
7. *Median= GetMedianOfUtilization(V_i);*
8. *$Stddev_{median}$= GetStddevUsingMedian(V_i);*
9. *If Stddev < StdDevThreshold*
10. *TotalPredictedMIPS+= Mean + Stddev;*
11. *Else TotalPredictedMIPS+= Median + $Stddev_{median}$;*
12. *End;*
13. *Utilization= TotalRequestedMIPS /totalMIPSofHost;*
14. *Prediction= TotalPredictedMIPS/ totalMIPSofHost;*
15. *If Utilization>1 or Prediction>1*
16. *Return True;*
17. *Else Return False*

Overload detection algorithm ensures that when a host is overloaded, then the algorithm will find it. Moreover, it will provide intelligent measure so that the datacenter does not get overloaded. There are several overload detection algorithms proposed in [1, 2, 4], 1) A Static CPU Utilization Threshold (THR): where overload decision is based on a static threshold; 2) Adaptive Median Absolute Deviation (MAD): the overload threshold is calculated dynamically using median absolute deviation; 3) Adaptive Interquartile Range (IQR): overload threshold is calculated dynamically using interquartile range method; 4) Local Regression(LR); and 5) Robust local Regression(LRR). LR and LRR are predication methods which will predict whether the host is going to be overloaded or not.

In this work, a new overload detection algorithm has been devised. When overloaded, a host incurs SLA violation. To be precise, a host incurs SLA violation when the required CPU utilization is greater than the actual utilization capacity. To avoid SLA violation, we have to design an overload detection mechanism which will predict this scenario. Host utilization is calculated from the VM utilization. If the summation of mean (μ) and standard deviation (δ) of last n iteration is greater than the maximum capacity of the VM then it can be inferred that this VM will request more utilization than allocated in future [15]. We apply that idea in our research.

$$\mu + \delta > 1 \qquad (9)$$

Equation 9 means that if the summation of mean utilization of a VM for last n cycles and standard deviation of utilization of that VM for last n cycles is higher than the allocated CPU, then in next iteration this VM can go beyond the maximum capacity of that VM. As our objective is to keep SLA violation at the lowest level, we can calculate predicted utilization of all VM of a corresponding host using Eq. (9) and check whether the total predicted utilization of a host is greater than the capacity or not. If the predicted value is greater, then the host is at risk of being overloaded and SLA violation. This technique we are going to apply in our overload detection algorithms. However, mean and standard deviation is very much influenced by terminal values that refer the outlier values or values that are too large or too small. So, when the standard deviation is high (i.e. the value falls in the high range of standard deviation membership function of fuzzy VM selection method) meaning that there is a possibility of high values present in the last n cycles. From the fuzzy membership variable *Stddev*, high range is considered. To avoid terminal values, when standard deviation is high, we replace mean with median and standard deviation formula is changed by replacing mean with median by Eq. (10). Hence, the prediction formula can be represented by Eq. (11). So it ensures, if in last n cycles any sudden fluctuation, i.e., very low or very high CPU utilization is found, this will not impact on the overall decision. δ_{Median} is the standard deviation calculated from median instead of mean. Like Eq. 9, Eq. 11 provides the prediction of a host. If the summation of Median and δ_{Median} is greater than 1 i.e. more than the total CPU then the host is considered to be overloaded.

$$\delta_{Median} = \sqrt{\frac{1}{n}\sum_{i=1}^{n}(CPU_i - CPU_{Median})^2} \qquad (10)$$

$$Median + \delta_{Median} > 1 \qquad (11)$$

Algorithm 3 describes how MMSD works. The input of the algorithm is the host of interest and the output of the algorithm is to determine whether the host is overloaded or not. At second step the VMs are identified which are currently active on the host. For every VM a loop is started at step 3. Total requested MIPS (Million Instructions Per Second) is accumulated to get the total requested MIPS of the host. Then Mean, Standard deviation, Median and Standard deviation from median are calculated. Now the predicted MIPS is calculated by the standard deviation value. If the standard deviation is greater than the threshold (this threshold is taken from the fuzzy member ship variable Stddev's High value which starts from 8.5) then Eq. (11) is followed else Eq. (9) is followed. Then utilization of the host and predicted utilization of the host is calculated. If any of these are beyond 1(meaning 100%) then the host is marked as overloaded by returning true otherwise returning false.

D. Underload detection and handling

There is an underload detection and handling algorithm in CloudSim. The algorithm is simple; it sorts the hosts according to their utilization and starts with the lowest utilized host. If all VMs of a particular low utilized host can be placed to any/ some of active hosts using VM placement method then the host is put to sleep mode by migrating all VMs to other hosts. VM placement will be discussed later section. It is worthwhile to mention that before migrating VM to other active hosts, the destination host is checked whether it will be overloaded by the new assignment with our newly designed overload detection algorithm.

E. VM placement Algorithm

In CloudSim toolkit power aware BFD (Best Fit Decreasing) algorithm is used for VM placement. When overload detection or underload detection finds VMs to migrate, VM placement algorithm assigns the VM in such way that power consumption

is increased minimally [4]. VM is placed in the host with decreasing utilization order. In this work it has been ensured that if a new VM placement is considered, then our newly overload detection algorithm certifies that the destination host will not be overloaded in next iteration.

Experimental setup

In this experiment, we have implemented our algorithms in CloudSim 3.0.3 and analyze the performance of our proposed method. We have considered 800 heterogeneous physical nodes, half of which are HP ProLiant G4 and the rest are HP ProLiant G5 servers. Energy consumption is calculated based on HP ProLiant G4 and HP ProLiant G5 CPU usage and power consumption that is represented in Table 3 [4]. These servers are assigned with 1860MIPS (Million instruction per second) and 2660 MIPS for each core of G4 and G5 servers respectively. Network bandwidth is considered as 1GB/s. The VMs which were created were single core. VM were of 4 types, for example, High-CPU Medium Instance (2500 MIPS, 0.85 GB); Extra Large Instance (2000 MIPS, 3.75 GB); Small Instance (1000 MIPS, 1.7 GB); and Micro Instance (500 MIPS, 613 MB). Fuzzy rules are defined and integrated to Cloud-Sim using JFuzzyLogic Tool [13].

In this work we have used real world work load data that is provided from CoMon project, a monitoring infrastructure for PlanetLab [25]. This data is collected from more than thousand VMs of different servers that are located in 500 different locations. The workload is representative of an IaaS cloud environment such as Amazon EC2, where VMs are created and managed by several independent users. Table 4 presents the day wise VM number for this data. These real world traces contain VM utilization records in every 5-min interval. Ten days' data of year 2011 have been used in this experiment. Each VM contains 288 (=24*(5/60)) data of CPU utilization. The simulation checks CPU data every 5 min interval and those trace data is plugged into dynamic VM consolidation.

The main target of VM consolidation is to reduce energy consumption and at the same time the QoS should be at an acceptable level. The energy consumption metric is discussed below and for QoS parameter, several metrics are stated which are used in several researches [2, 4]. The main QoS is SLA violation. In VM consolidation SLA violation occurs due to host overload and VM

Table 3 Power consumption for diferent level of utilization

Machine type	Power consumption based on CPU utilization					
	0 %	20 %	40 %	60 %	80 %	100 %
HP G4 (Watt)	86	92.6	99	106	112	117
HP G5 (Watt)	93.7	101	110	121	129	135

Table 4 Day wise planet lab data

Date	Number of VMs
3 March	1052
6 March	898
9 March	1061
22 March	1516
25 March	1078
3 April	1463
9 April	1358
11 April	1233
12 April	1054
20 April	1033

migration. To quantify SLA violation for overloaded host, the metric Overload time fraction (OTF) is used and on the other hand to quantify the SLA violation due to VM migration, the PDM (performance degradation due to migration) is defined. SLAV (SLA violation) is the product of OTF and PDM. Moreover, the number of VM migration indicates the efficiency of the consolidation method which is also described as a metric. But the main objective of our research is to obtain Energy-QoS trade off and that is defined by the metric ESV which is the product of energy consumption and SLA violation (SLAV). So the method providing the lowest ESV and at the same, the lowest energy consumption and the lowest SLA violation, is undoubtedly the best method. Based on these six metrics proposed method will be verified and they are described in more detail and mathematically below.

1) Energy Consumption(kWh)

This is the main metric as the target of VM consolidation is to reduce energy consumption. Energy consumption is computed by taking into account all hosts throughout the simulation by mapping of CPU and energy consumption from Table 3. At each iterations the CPU utilization is measured and power consumption is calculated from Table 3 and at the end of the simulation energy consumption is measured by accumulating all hosts' energy consumption.

2) Number of VM migration

This metric counts the number of VMs migrated during the siumaltion. VM migration is an important factor because unnecessary migration causes SLA violation and network traffic.

3) OTF

Overload time fraction [4], OTF is a measure of SLA violatoin. it provides a measure of the fraction of time a host experienced 100 % CPU utilization leading to SLA violation. In Eq. (12), if

N is the number of hosts, T_{si} is the total time when host i experienced 100 % utilizaiton leading SLA Violation, T_{ai} is the total active time of host i, then OTF is defined by:

$$OTF = \frac{1}{N}\sum_{i=1}^{N}\frac{T_{si}}{T_{ai}} \qquad PDM = \frac{1}{M}\sum_{j=1}^{M}\frac{C_{dj}}{C_{rj}}$$

$$(12)$$

4) PDM

Performance degradation due to migration(PDM) [4] is a measure of SLA violation. It measures the total SLA violation due to VM migration. When a host is overloaded, VMs are migrated from that host to non-overloaded host. At the time of migration, that VM is not capable of serving user needs, hence, it causes SLA violation. This metric calculates the SLA violation caused by migration. From Eq. (12), if M is the number of total VMs, C_{dj} stands for the CPU request at the time of migration of VM j and C_{rj} stands for total CPU requested by VM j, then PDM is defined by the Eq. (12).

5) SLAV

Service level agreement violation, SLAV, is combined impact of OTF and PDM. It provides a SLA violation measure for the simmulation which is a product of OTF and PDM i. e., SLAV = OTF*PDM.

6) ESV

Energy consumption and SLA is already defined. It is perceivable that if we try to reduce too much energy consumption the SLA violation will be increased, because consolidating many VMs in a host increase the probability of overload. So it is desirable to obtain a method which will consume less power and still incur less SLA violation. To measure this, ESV is introduced. It is the combination of Energy consumption and SLA violation, i.e., ESV = Energy*SLAV. So this can be treated as one metric to make an overall measurement. If the product of energy consumption and SLA violation is lower, it means that the approach reduces energy consumption and making less SLA violation.

Experimental result

In our experiment, using CloudSim, we have experimented with five Overload detection algorithms (IQR, LR, LRR, MAD and THR) and three VM selection (MC, MMT, RS) methods. So in combination there are 15 methods (IQR_MC, IQR_MMT, IQR_RS, LR_MC, LR_MMT, LR_RS, LRR_MC, LRR_MMT, LRR_RS, MAD_MC, MAD_MMT, MAD_RS, THR_MC, THR_MMT, THR_RS) which will be compared against our proposed MMSD_FS method based on aforementioned performance metrics. Based on the result for 10 days Box grpahs have been prepared to compare the results. It is represented in Figs. 3, 4, 5, 6, 7 and 8. We discuss the performance with respect to each metric are given below.

A. Energy Consumption

Main objective of this research is to design a VM consolidation algorithm so that the energy consumption is reduced. By comparing the proposed and existing methods in the Fig. 3, it is found that energy consumption is significantly reduced in proposed (MMSD_FS) method. Minimum energy consumption by the proposed method is 102 Kwh where the minimum of all other methods is 112 Kwh, therefore we got 8.5 % reduction. If we consider average value, MMSD_FS consumed 136.5 Kwh and all other methods consumed 169 Kwh on average resulting 19 % energy saving. Therefore, we can infer that the basic objective of this research is achieved by saving energy consumption.

B. SLA Violation

SLA violation is one of the key indicators of QoS. SLA Violation is calculated by keeping two scenarios into consideration, i) if any VM got overloaded, and ii) The SLA violation incurred while migration. A method having low SLA violation ensures the desired QoS. From Fig. 4, SLA violation is decreased significantly which is clearly visible. Minimum SLAV by proposed method is 0.0004 % whereas the minimum of all other method is 0.00279 %, resulting 84 % reduction. If we consider average value, MMSD_FS incurred 0.0005 % SLAV and all other methods incurred 0.00617 % on average,

resulting 91 % reduction in SLA violation. This is main achievement of this research. It means that the overload detection method we have used, predicted the overloaded host efficiently and as an outcome, SLA violation was dropped significantly. If host overload is predicted successfully then there will be less number of migration which will reduce SLA violation as well.

C. ESV

As energy consumption has been successfully reduced by the proposed method, now energy-QoS trade off needs to be checked. ESV is the metric which is a product of Energy consumption and SLA violation; hence, provides a tradeoff picture of the proposed method with other existing methods. From previous two sub-sections, we have observed that both energy and SLA violation reduced, so it is inevitable that ESV will also be reduced significantly. From the Fig. 5, ESV is found to be reduced significantly which is clearly visible. If ESV reduces it means that this approach saves energy and at the same time SLA violation is controlled. As ESV is reduced significantly, it means that Energy and SLA trade-off has been achieved. Minimum ESV by proposed method is 0.04 whereas the minimum all other method is 0.49, resulting 91 % reduction. If we consider average value, MMSD_FS incurred 0.07 ESV and all other method incurred 1.09 on average, resulting 93 % reduction in ESV.

D. Number of VM migration

Less number of VM migrations means efficient consolidation, less traffic in cloud network and less SLA violation for VM migration. Reduction in Number of VM migration is also clearly visible

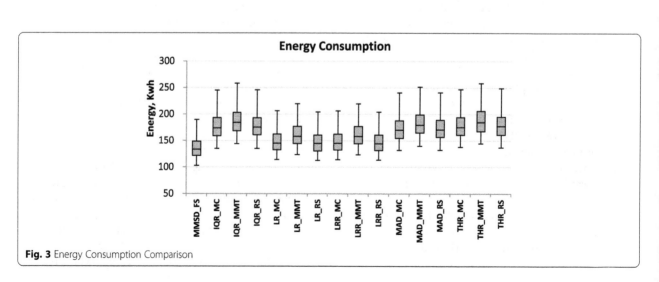

Fig. 3 Energy Consumption Comparison

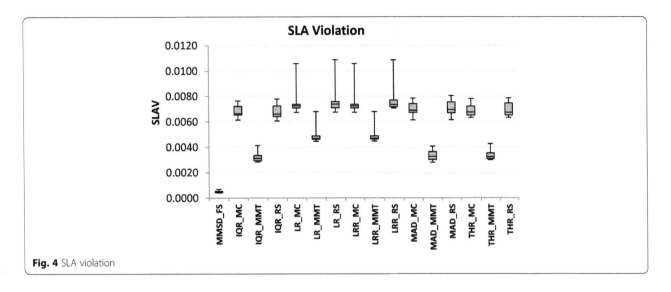

Fig. 4 SLA violation

from Fig. 6. To quantify, minimum number of VM migration caused by MMSD_FS is 5185 whereas the minimum all other method is 16,317, resulting 68 % reduction. If we consider average value, MMSD_FS incurred 7943 migrations on an average and average of all other methods is 24,929, resulting 68 % reduction in migration. From this percentage it is evident that the proposed method provides most optimum VM consolidation compared to the existing VM consolidation approaches.

E. OTF and PDM

From Fig. 7 to Fig. 8, it can be inferred that OTF and PDM is significantly reduced. The proposed method reduced both SLA violation due to overload and SLA violation due to VM migration. Minimum OTF is reduced up to 60 % by the proposed method and Minimum PDM is reduced up to 64 %. On an average OTF is decreased by

67 % and PDM is decreased by 74 % compared to the existing methods.

Finally, we have performed a statistical test namely two-tailed students' t-test on the performance of the proposed method MMSD_FS and IQR_MMT method (the best method in CloudSim as per the ESV, Fig. 4). Our null hypothesis is: "There is no significant difference in the performance between two techniques". Table 5 reports p-values for six performance metrics between MMSD_FS and IQR_MMT generated from 10 days' experimental data. If the p-value is greater than 0.05, then we must accept the null hypothesis, otherwise we must reject the null hypothesis. From Table 5 we find that the p-value is significantly smaller than 0.05 for every performance metric. Therefore, we must reject the null hypothesis and we could conclude that there is significantly difference in performance found.

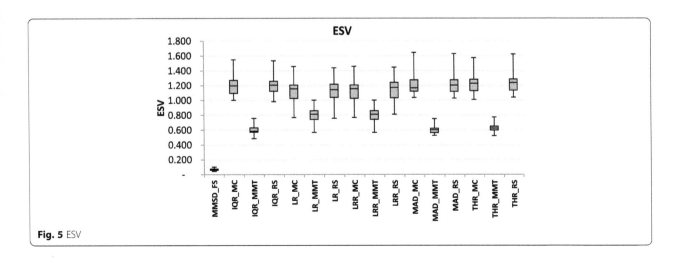

Fig. 5 ESV

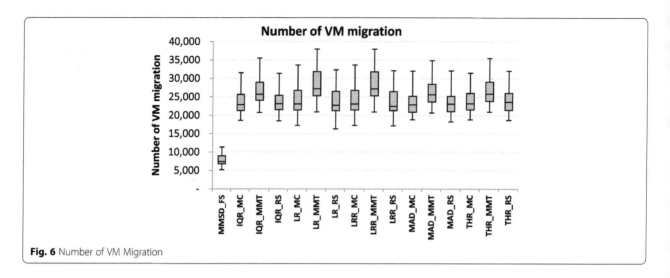

Fig. 6 Number of VM Migration

From all the performance metrics it can be inferred that the proposed method outperforms all other methods.

F. A Deep dive

From the above result analysis, we have found that the proposed method improved significantly. Most of the improvement came from the SLA violation part. This phenomenon indicates that the proposed method identifies the host overload efficiently. To visualize the performance in easier way we have generated two heat maps of MMSD_FS method and another is IQR_MMT method which are given in Fig. 9 and Fig. 10 respectively.

For this experiment, we have used 50 hosts and 50 VMs and random load. In the heat map, if a host is in sleeping mode i.e., 0 % utilization then it is marked by blue color and red color for high utilization. In the X-axis the time is portrayed. As iteration duration is 5 min, so there are total

288(starting from 0 to 8600 s) iterations as the simulation is done for 1-day data. Y-axis represents 50 hosts. From Fig. 9, it is visible that hosts are experiencing ON-OFF frequently and the map seems scattered and the total number of overload occurs 685 times. So this method will invoke VM migration at least 685 times. On the other hand, Fig. 10 shows the heat map for MMSD_FS where we can observe less fluctuation (ON-OFF) of the host. It is easily perceivable that the host is put to sleeping mode and stays in sleeping mode for long. Total number of overload incident is 92, which indicates the efficiency of the algorithm. The main reason behind the performance of MMSD_FS is the prediction done by this algorithm helped to reduce the number overloaded hosts.

Related works

Considerable number of researches has been conducted for VM consolidation using various methods based on

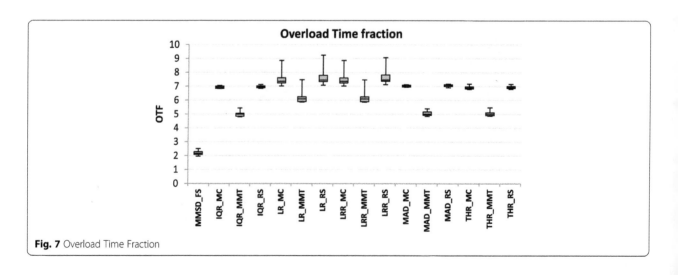

Fig. 7 Overload Time Fraction

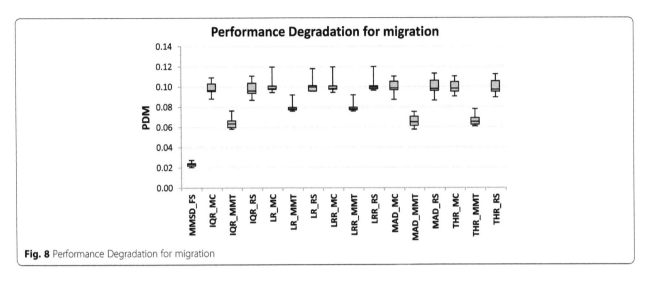

Fig. 8 Performance Degradation for migration

heuristics. In this research, we have worked on two problems, 1) VM selection method, and 2) Overload detection method. Here, we will discuss about various VM selection methods. For Overload detection methods, there are two types of algorithms, a) Threshold based methods, and b) Prediction based method. In threshold based method, researchers apply different statistical or heuristic methods to calculate threshold for a host to be identified as overloaded. On the other hand, there are some predictive methods where researchers use approaches/techniques to predict the future load of a host.

In [1, 2, 4] Beloglazov et al. proposed heuristic based approach to deduce thresholds through different statistical measures. VM Consolidation problem is divided into sub-problems and algorithms for each sub-problem had been designed. Heuristic based algorithms are designed for each sub problems and designed in such a way that they act, adapt and keep their threshold changing based on different scenario in different time so that they can still provide the functionality and consolidation decision in the changed environment. This adaption process allows the system to be dynamic. They designed threshold based (e.g. IQR) and prediction based (e.g. LR) host overload detection mechanisms. We have shown in result section, our proposed algorithms outperformed

Table 5 P-values for performance metrics

Metric	P-value
Energy Consumption	0.004
ESV	2E–09
Number of Migration	1.4E–08
SLAV	6.78E–12
OTF	5.38E–19
PDM	1.44E–12

the algorithms proposed in literature. References [5, 6] describe CloudSim which provides various functionalities of a cloud environment and facilitates in cloud simulation. Reference [1, 2, 4] have also used CloudSim for simulation. The main components of CloudSim are datacenter, Virtual Machine (VM) and cloudlet. Cloudlet can be data from real cloud. The simulator creates datacenter, Virtual Machine and cloudlet based on the defined parameters. When the simulation starts, Virtual Machines are placed in the datacenter for processing. Sub-problems (i–iv) are already developed in CloudSim. To extend it further, one needs to create new class and develop new methods to test it. The VM selection methods and Overload detection methods are compared in this research and the proposed algorithm performs better in all metrics defined in CloudSim. In the previous section we have compared our proposed algorithm with both thresholds based (MAD, IQR and THR) and prediction based approaches (LR and LRR). We have discussed several approaches which are proposed in the literature.

Farahnakian et al. [9] used ant colony system to deduce a near-optimal VM placement solution based on the specified objective function. In [3] VM consolidation with migration control is introduced. Here VMs with steady usage are not migrated and not steady VMs are migrated to ensure better performance. The migrations are triggered and done by heuristic approaches. But this research has not been used the other sub problem rather focused on only the VM placement problem. We have considered all the sub-problems together.

Farahnakian et al. [18] proposed a Reinforcement Learning-based Dynamic Consolidation method (RL-DC) to minimize the number of active host considering the resource requirement. The RL-DC utilizes an agent to learn the optimal policy. The agent uses the past knowledge to take intelligent decision whether to keep

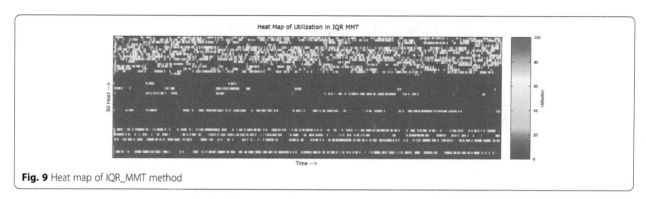

Fig. 9 Heat map of IQR_MMT method

the host in active or sleep mode and improves itself as the workload changes. It also dynamically adapts changes. In [12] linear regression has been used to predict CPU utilization by the same author. These researches are developed in CloudSim and follow the distributed architecture. From result and comparison, it is evident that our proposed algorithm performs better in regression based host overload detection method.

Cao et al. [15] proposed a redesigned energy-aware heuristic framework for VM consolidation to achieve a better energy-performance tradeoff. They designed a Service Level Agreement (SLA) violation decision algorithm which is used to decide whether a host is overloaded with SLA violation or not. SLA violation is determined if the allocated CPU of a particular VM is less than the requested CPU of that VM. In other words, if a host is not capable of assigning CPU resource to all the VMs as per demand, then the SLA violation occurs. There is another type of SLA violation which is SLA violation due to migration. If a particular VM is in migration, at the time of migration, the VM is not capable of serving users need hence it is counted as SLA violation. This research is based on CloudSim and algorithms are developed in CloudSim and they have used mean and standard deviation as the prediction method, whereas in our research we used median and standard deviation derived from median. In the result section we depicted that how our method outperformed. Duy et al. [21] proposed a neural network predictor in a Green scheduling algorithm to predict future resource requirements based on

historical data. Based on the prediction, decision is taken to keep unused servers in sleep mode and keep the high utilized servers in active mode. There are also similar works that can be found in [22, 23]. These works provide a host utilization prediction and one sub problem is discussed which is overload detection. Srikantaiah et al. [24] have studied the interrelationships between energy consumption, resource utilization, and performance of consolidated workloads. The study shows the energy performance trade-off for consolidation. That research did not use all the sub problems of VM consolidation, rather considered the whole problem as a single one.

Mastroianni et al. [19] presented ecoCloud, a self-organizing and adaptive approach for the consolidation of VMs on CPU and RAM. Assignment and migration decisions are driven by probabilistic processes and based on local information. Focusing on the VM placement problem, they experimented in real datacenter. However, all the sub-problems are not addressed. Madani et al. [17] focused on an architecture configuration to manage virtual machines in a data center to optimize the consumption of energy and meet SLA by grafting a tracing component of multiple consolidation plans which ensure minimum number of servers is switched on. In this research, the problem is seen as scheduling problem and sub problems are not discussed.

Sheng at al. [11] designed a method based on Bayes model to predict the mean load over a long-term time interval. Prevost et al. [10] introduced a framework

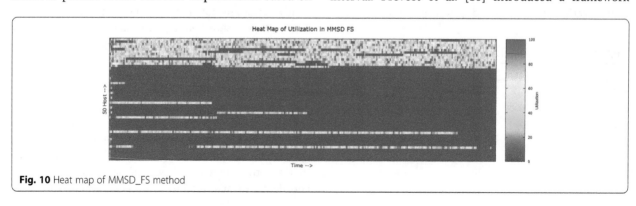

Fig. 10 Heat map of MMSD_FS method

by combining load demand prediction and stochastic state transition models. They used neural network and autoregressive linear prediction algorithms to forecast loads in cloud data center applications. These works used statistical and neural network to predict the host utilization and only focused on overload detection of a host.

In [7] and [8] we worked with basic VM selection algorithm and introduced migration control in the built in CloudSim VM selection methods. In [26] a preliminary study was carried out using fuzzy logic in VM selection. As the initial findings are encouraging, in this research we incorporate all our previous methodologies, e.g., migration control and fuzzy logic together and study the performance on VM selection. Besides, we have introduced a new overload detection algorithm based on mean, median and standard deviation of utilization of VMs. In this research, we study the performance of our proposed VM selection algorithm coupled with the newly designed overload detection algorithm. A comparative study has been also reported to present the performance against previous VM selection algorithms found in CloudSim.

Conclusion

In this research we have devised algorithm for fuzzy VM selection method and introduced migration control in the selection method. Fuzzy VM selection methods take intelligent decision to select a VM to be migrated from one host to the other. Then we designed mean, median and standard deviation based overload detection algorithm. After simulation and making comparison against existing methods, it has been found that the proposed method outperformed other previous methods in both perspectives, i.e., more energy saving and less SLA violation. Therefore, it can be inferred that the objective, energy-SLA tradeoff has been achieved in this work in an efficient manner. As a future work we have plan to improve the default VM placement and underload detection algorithm built in CloudSim to achieve more energy saving and less SLA violation.

Acknowledgement
There is no acknowledgement from authors' side.

Authors' contribution
Monil carried out the survey of literature, the study of energy efficient VM selection algorithms, identified the research problem, proposed the VM selection algorithm and modified the existing overload detection algorithm. Monil carried out the experiments in simulation environment and drafted the manuscript. Rahman discussed and advised to add explanations for few sections. Rahman also provided careful review of the article and helped Monil in answering reviewers' comments. All authors read and approved the final manuscript.

Authors' information
The current research initiative was taken when Mohammad Alaul Haque Monil was doing his Master's program in North South University, Dhaka, Bangladesh. In 2014, he was awarded the M.Sc degree in Computer Science and Engineering from North South University. Currently Monil is a Ph.D. student of University Oregon, Eugene, Oregon, USA. His current research focus is on parallel and distributed computing. Recently he worked on VM placement method for Virtual Machine consolidation. He is also working on applying parallel computing techniques to solve shortest path algorithm in parallel and distributed environment. He received his B.Sc degree on the same major from Khulna University of Engineering and Technology, Bangladesh in 2006. Monil also worked in Grameenphone Bangladesh, a business unit of Telenor for 9 years in different roles including managerial position.
Rashedur M. Rahman is working as an associate professor in Computer and Electrical Engineering department in North South University, Dhaka, Bangladesh. He received his Ph.D. in Computer Science from University of Calgary, Canada and Master's degree from University of Manitoba, Canada in 2007 and 2003 respectively. He has authored more than 100 peer reviewed journals and conference proceedings in the area of parallel, distributed, cloud computing, knowledge and data engineering. He is serving in editorial board of a number of journals. He serves as a program committee member of a number of international conferences organized by IEEE, ACM. His current research interest is in data mining particularly on financial, medical and educational data, VM consolidation in cloud, data replication on grid, computational finance, and image processing.

Competing interests
The authors declare that they have no competing interests.

Author details
[1]Department of Computer and Information Science, University of Oregon, Eugene, OR, USA. [2]Department of Electrical and Computer Engineering, North South University, Dhaka, Bangladesh.

References
1. Beloglazov A, Abawajy J, Buyya R (2011) Energy-aware resource allocation heuristics for efficient management of data centers for cloud computing. Futur Gener Comput Syst (FGCS) 28(5):755–768
2. Beloglazov A, Buyya R (2012) Optimal online deterministic algorithms and adaptive heuristics for energy and performance efficient dynamic consolidation of virtual machines in cloud data centers. Concurrency and Computation: Practice and Experience (CCPE) 24(13):1397–1420
3. Ferreto TC, Netto MAS, Calheiros RN, De Rose CAF (2011) Server consolidation with migration control for virtualized data centers". Futur Gener Comput Syst 27(8):1027–1034
4. Beloglazov A, (2013) PhD Thesis: "Energy-Efficient Management of Virtual Machines in Data Centers for Cloud Computing". Link: http://beloglazov.info/thesis.pdf. Accessed 04 Jul 2016
5. Calheiros RN, Ranjan R, Beloglazov A, Rose CAFD, Buyya R (2011) CloudSim: a toolkit for modeling and simulation of cloud computing environments and evaluation of resource provisioning algorithms. Software: Practice and Experience 41(1):23–50
6. CloudSim link: http://www.cloudbus.org/cloudsim/. Accessed 04 July 2016
7. Monil MAH, Qasim R, Rahman RM (2014) Incorporating migration control in VM selection strategies to enhance performance". Int J Web Appl (IJWA) 6(4):135–151
8. Monil MAH, Qasim R, Rahman RM (2014) "Energy-aware VM consolidation approach using combination of heuristics and migration control", 9th IEEE International Conference on Digital Information Management, pp. 74–79.
9. Farahnakian F, Ashraf A, Liljeberg P, Pahikkala T, Plosila J, Porres I, Tenhunen H "Energy-Aware Dynamic VM Consolidation in Cloud Data Centers Using Ant Colony System" 2014 IEEE 7th International Conference on Cloud Computing (CLOUD), pp. 104–111
10. Prevost J, Nagothu K, Kelley B, Jamshidi M (2011) "Prediction of cloud data center networks loads using stochastic and neural models," in Proc. IEEE System of Systems Engineering (SoSE) Conf., pp. 276–281, 27–30
11. Di S, Kondo D, Cirne W (2012) "Host load prediction in a Google compute cloud with a Bayesian model", in Proc. Of the International Conference for High Performance Computing, Networking, Storage and Analysis (SC), Salt Lake City, UT, Nov. 10–16

12. Farahnakian F, Liljeberg P, Plosila J (2013) "LiRCUP: Linear regression based CPU usage prediction algorithm for live migration of virtual machines in data centers," 2013 39th EUROMICRO Conference on Software Engineering and Advanced Applications (SEAA), pp. 357–364.

13. Cingolani P, Alcala-Fdez J (2012) "jFuzzyLogic: A robust and flexible Fuzzy-Logic inference system language implementation", Proc. Intâl Conf. Fuzzy Systems, pp. 1–8

14. Verma A, Dasgupta G, Nayak TK, De P, Kothari R (2009) "Server workload analysis for power minimization using consolidation," in Proceedings of the 2009 USENIX Annual Technical Conference, pp. 28–28.

15. Cao Z, Dong S (2013) "Energy-Aware framework for virtual vachine vonsolidation in vloud vomputing" High Performance Computing and Communications & 2013 IEEE International Conference on Embedded and Ubiquitous Computing (HPCC_EUC), 2013 IEEE 10th International Conference, pp. pp. 1890–1895

16. Akula GS, Potluri A (2014) "Heuristics for migration with consolidation of ensembles of Virtual Machines" Sixth International Conference on Communication Systems and Networks Communication Systems and Networks (COMSNETS), pp. 1–4

17. Madani N, Lebbat A, Tallal S, Medromi H (2013) "New cloud consolidation architecture for electrical energy consumption management", IEEE Africon 2013 Conference, pp. 1–3.

18. Farahnakian F, Liljeberg P, Plosila J (2014) "Energy-efficient virtual machines consolidation in cloud data centers using reinforcement learning", 22nd Euromicro International Conference on Parallel, Distributed and Network-based Processing (PDP), pp. 500–507

19. Mastroianni C, Meo M, Papuzzo G (2013) "Probabilistic Consolidation of Virtual Machines in Self-Organizing Cloud Data Centers", IEEE Transaction of Cloud Computing, vol.1, pp. 215–228.

20. Barroso LA, Holzle U (2007) The case for energy-proportional computing. Computer 40(12):33–37

21. Duy TVT, Sato Y, Inoguchi Y (2010) "Performance evaluation of a green scheduling algorithm for energy savings in cloud computing", 2010 IEEE international symposium on parallel & distributed processing. Workshops and Phd Forum (IPDPSW), Atlanta, pp. 1–8

22. Feller E, Rilling L, Morin C (2011) "Energy-aware ant colony based workload placement in clouds", Proceedings of the 2011 IEEE/ACM 12th International Conference on Grid Computing, pp. 26–33.

23. Mills K, Filliben J, Dabrowski C (2011) "Comparing VM-placement algorithms for on-demand clouds, IEEE Third International Conference on Cloud Computing Technology and Science (CloudCom), Athens, 2011, pp. 91–98.

24. Srikantaiah S, Kansal A, Zhao F (2008) Energy aware consolidation for cloud computing, Proceedings of the 2008 conference on Power aware computing and systems, pp. 10–10.

25. Park KS, Pai VS (2006) CoMon: a mostly-scalable monitoring system for planet- Lab. ACM SIGOPS Operating Syst Rev 40(1):65–74

26. Monil MAH, Rahman RM (2015) "Fuzzy Logic Based Energy Aware VM Consolidation", 8th International Conference on Internet and Distributed Computing Systems (IDCS 2015), Windsor, U.K., September 2–4, pp. 223–227

27. Fuzzy Trapezoidal membership function. Link: http://www.mathworks.com/help/fuzzy/trapmf.html?requestedDomain=www.mathworks.com. Accessed 04 Jul 2016

28. Beloglazov A, Buyya R, Lee YC, Zomaya A (2011) "A taxonomy and survey of energy-efficient data centers and Cloud computing systems," Advances in Computers, M. Zelkowitz (ed.), vol. 82, Elsevier, pp. 47–111

7

A novel hybrid of Shortest job first and round Robin with dynamic variable quantum time task scheduling technique

Samir Elmougy[1], Shahenda Sarhan[1*] and Manar Joundy[1,2]

Abstract

Cloud computing is a ubiquitous network access model to a shared pool of configurable computing resources where available resources must be checked and scheduled using an efficient task scheduler to be assigned to clients. Most of the existing task schedulers, did not achieve the required standards and requirements as some of them only concentrated on waiting time or response time reduction or even both neglecting the starved processes at all. In this paper, we propose a novel hybrid task scheduling algorithm named (SRDQ) combining Shortest-Job-First (SJF) and Round Robin (RR) schedulers considering a dynamic variable task quantum. The proposed algorithms mainly relies on two basic keys the first having a dynamic task quantum to balance waiting time between short and long tasks while the second involves splitting the ready queue into two sub-queues, Q1 for the short tasks and the other for the long ones.

Assigning tasks to resources from Q_1 or Q_2 are done mutually two tasks from Q_1 and one task from Q_2. For evaluation purpose, three different datasets were utilized during the algorithm simulation conducted using CloudSim environment toolkit 3.0.3 against three different scheduling algorithms SJF, RR and Time Slice Priority Based RR (TSPBRR) Experimentations results and tests indicated the superiority of the proposed algorithm over the state of art in reducing waiting time, response time and partially the starvation of long tasks.

Keywords: Task scheduling, Shortest job first, Round Robin, Dynamic quantum, Starvation

Introduction

The appearance of cloud computing systems represent a revolution in modern information technology (IT) that needs to have an efficient and powerful architecture to be applied in different systems that require complex computing and big-scale. Cloud is a platform that can support elastic applications in order to manage limited virtual machines and computing servers to application services at a given instance of time. The cloud is a suitable environment of multi-tenant computing which allows the users to share resources. In cloud, available resources must be checked and scheduled using an efficient task scheduler to be assigned to clients based on their requests [1–3].

Having an efficient task scheduler became an urgent need with the rapid growth of modern computer systems aiming to reach and achieve the optimal performance. Task scheduling algorithms are responsible for mapping jobs submitted to cloud environment onto available resources in such a way that the total response time and latency are minimized and the throughput and utilization of resources are maximized [3, 4]. Conventional task scheduling algorithms as Shortest-Job-First (SJF) [5], Round Robin (RR) [6], and First-Come-First-Serve (FCFS) [7], Multilevel queue scheduling (MQ) [8], Max-Min [9] and Min-Min [10] had achieved breathtaking results over years in different computer systems types but always suffer from big dilemmas as higher waiting time in RR and FCFS and starvation in SJF and Max-Min.

Starvation problem is one of the major challenges that face task scheduling in cloud where, a task may wait for one or more of its requested resources for a very long time. Starvation is frequently brought on by lapses in a

* Correspondence: shahenda_sarhan@yahoo.com

[1]Department of Computer Science, Faculty of Computers and Information, Mansoura University, Mansoura 35516, Egypt

Full list of author information is available at the end of the article

scheduling calculation, by resource spills, and can be deliberately created by means of a refusal of-administration
assault. For example, if an ineffectively planned multi-
tasking framework dependably switches between the initial two tasks while a third never gets the chance to run,
then the third task is starving [11]. Many hybrids were
introduced to solve the starvation problem as FCFS&RR
and SRTF&RR [12] (note that RR is always a common
denominator in these hybrids) but, no one till now
solves or nearly approach to solve it. A hybrid of SJF and
RR is one of the most used and powerful hybrids for
solving starvation where we can benefit from SJF performance in reducing the turnaround time and from RR
in reducing task waiting time. But the task quantum
value was always the obstacle in having the optimum hybrid. Different researches were proceeded to find the
best methodology to calculate the task quantum value as
having small quantum leads to reducing throughput and
increasing response time while having long quantum
caused a high increase in turnaround time.

From this point and confessing the importance of starvation problem in task scheduling, we introduce in this
paper a novel hybrid scheduling technique of SJF and
RR with Dynamic Quantum, we called SRDQ applied
through having two Queues to schedule processes for
execution. The proposed algorithm is designed to be a
unit based algorithm based on effectively queuing data
structure and optimizing the execution time as possible.
In this proposed technique, a time quantum value is
statically and dynamically determined towards detecting
the impact of quantum dynamicity over starvation and
response time reduction which will be described in details in Section 3.3.

The remainder of this paper is organized as 5 main
sections where, in Section 2, the concepts of task scheduling and some related work are presented. In Section
3.3, the proposed technique is presented enhanced with
examples. While, the simulations settings are analyzed in
Section 4. Section 5 comprises the discussion and results
and finally, our main conclusions and future work are
discussed in Section 6.

Related work

Task scheduling algorithms vary in their technique in
scheduling tasks among cloud nodes statically, dynamically, in batches or even online, eventually they are all trying to achieve the optimal distribution of tasks overs
cloud nodes. Through this section different task scheduling algorithms applied in cloud environment with suitable verification and different aims will be presented and
discussed in details. As Fang et al., in [13] introduced a
two levels task scheduling mechanism based on load balancing in cloud computing. Through the first level a task
description of each virtual machine (VM) is created

including network resources, storage resources and
other resources based on the needs of the tasks created
by the user applications. In the second level scheduler
assigns the adequate resources to each VM considering
its load to achieve load balancing among VMs. According to the authors, this task scheduling mechanism can
not only meet user's requirements, but also get high resource utilization, which was proved by simulation results in the CloudSim toolkit, although this model did
not consider the network bandwidth usability and its impact on VMs load.

In [14] Lin et al., proposed a Dynamic Round-Robin
(DRR) algorithm for energy-aware virtual machine
scheduling and consolidation during which VMs are
moved from the retired physical machine to other physical machines in duty . According to the authors, the
proposed algorithm was compared to GREEDY,
ROUNDROBIN and POWERSAVE schedulers showing
superiority in reducing the amount of consumed power
although it did not consider the load and resources of
the destination physical machines to which the VMs will
be migrated to. Also did not mention any thing about
the rules to consider when the physical machine should
retire and forced its VMs to migrate.

A year after, Ghanbari et al., in [15] introduced a
scheduling algorithm based on job priority named
(PJSC) where each job is assigned resources based on its
priority, in other words higher priority jobs gain access
to resources first. Simulation results as clarified by the
authors indicated that PJSC has reasonable complexity
but sufferer from increasing makespan. In addition to
that PJSC may cause Job starvation as the jobs with less
priority may never gain access to the resources they
need.

In [16] Maguluri et al., considered a stochastic model
for load balancing and scheduling in cloud computing
clusters. Their primary contribution was the development of frame-based non-preemptive VM configuration
policies. These policies can achieve a nearly optimal
throughput through selecting sufficiently long frame durations. Simulations indicate that long frame durations
are not only good from a throughput perspective but
also seem to provide good delay performance but also
may cause starvation.

Gulati et al., in [17] studied the effect of enhancing the
performance of Round Robin with a dynamic approach
through varying the vital parameters of host bandwidth,
cloudlet long length, VM image size and VM bandwidth.
Experimental results indicated that Load had been optimized through setting dynamic round robin by propor-
tionately varying all the previous parameters.

Agha and Jassbi in [18] proposed a RR based technique to obtain quantum time in each cycle of RR using
arithmetic-harmonic mean (HARM), which is calculated

by dividing the number of observations by the reciprocal of each number in series. According to the proposed technique if the burst time of a process is smaller than the previous one, HARM should be utilized for calculating quantum otherwise the arithmetic mean is utilized. The simulation results indicated that in some cases the proposed algorithm can provide better scheduling criteria and improve the average Turnaround Time (TT) and Average Waiting Time (AWT). These results according to the authors may indicate enhancement in RR performance but still missing the consideration of the arrival time of each process to verify the values of TT and AWT besides a real time implementation.

Tsai et al., in [19] introduced an optimization technique named Improved Differential Evolution Algorithm (IDEA) trying to optimize the scheduling of series of subtasks on multiple resources based on cost and time models on cloud computing environment. The proposed technique makes benefit of the Differential Evolution Algorithm (DEA) abilities in global exploration of macro-space and using fewer control parameters and Taguchi method systematic reasoning abilities in exploiting the better individuals on micro-space to be potential offspring. Experimental results were conducted using five-task five-resource and the ten-task ten-resource problems indicating the effectiveness of the IDEA in optimizing task scheduling and resource allocation while considering cost compared to the original DEA, NSGA-II, SPEA2 and IBEA.

Ergu et al., in [20] introduced a model for task-oriented resource allocation where, tasks are pairwise compared based on network bandwidth, complete time, task costs, and reliability of task. Resources are allocated to tasks based on task weight calculated using analysis hierarchy process. Furthermore, an induced bias matrix is used to identify the inconsistent elements and improve the consistency ratio when conflicting weights in various tasks are assigned. According to the authors testing was proceeded using two theoretical and not real time evaluation examples which indicated that the proposed model still needs more testing.

Karthick et al., in [21] introduced a scheduling technique that dynamically schedule jobs through depicting the concept of clustering jobs based on burst time in order to reduce starvation. Compared to other traditional techniques as FCFS and SJF, the proposed technique effectively utilizes the unused free space in an economic way although it hadn't considered consumed energy and the increasing number of submitted jobs.

In [22], Lakra and Yadav, introduced a multi-objective task scheduling algorithm for mapping tasks to VMs via non-dominated sorting after quantifying the Quality of Service values of tasks and VMs. The proposed algorithm mainly considered improving the throughput of the datacenter and reducing the cost without violating the Service Level Agreement (SLA) for an application in cloud SaaS environment. The experiments results indicated an accepted performance of the proposed algorithm although it did not consider many of the Quality of Service factors including awareness of VMS energy.

While Dash et al., in [23] presented a dynamic quantum scheduling algorithm based on RR, named Dynamic Average Burst Round Robin (DABRR). The proposed algorithm was tested and compared to traditional RR, Dynamic Quantum with Re-adjusted Round Robin (DQRRR), Improved Round Robin with Varying time Quantum (IRRVQ), Self Adjustment Round Robin (SARR), and Modified Round Robin (MRR) indicating the superiority of the DABRA. However the authors did not clarify DABRA's response to new arrival processes also sorting processes in an ascending order based on their burst time may cause starvation to processes with long burst time.

Tunc et al., in [24] presented a new metric called Value of Service mainly consider completed tasks within deadline through balancing its value of completing within deadline with energy consumption. They defined the proposed metric as the sum of the values for all tasks that are executed during a given period of time including task arrival time. Each resource was assigned to a task based on the number of the homogeneous cores and amount of memory. The experiments were conducted using IBM blade server using Keyboard-Video-Mouse (KVM), indicating an improvement in performance enhanced by a noticeable reduction in energy consumption only in case of completing tasks within deadline. The authors did not really clarify how their model reacts to the increasing number of tasks especially with the same arrival time.

In the same year Abdul Razaque et al., in [25] introduced a nonlinear programming divisible task scheduling algorithm, allocating the workflow of tasks to VMs based on the availability of network bandwidth. The problem here with this algorithm, it only considered a single criteria of a network for allocating tasks to VMs while neglecting the VMs energy consumption that may cause these machines to retire forcing tasks to terminate.

Recently bio-inspired algorithms as Ant Colony Optimization (ACO), Cuckoo Search (CS), genetic algorithm (GA), Particle Swarm Optimization (PSO) and Bees Life Algorithm (BLA) etc.. have played major role in scheduling tasks over cloud nodes as Mizan et al., in [26] developed a modified job scheduling algorithm based on BLA and greedy algorithm for minimizing make span in hybrid cloud. Based on the authors claim experiments were conducted indicating that the proposed algorithm has outperformed both greedy algorithm and firefly algorithm in make span reduction.

Table 1 Submitted tasks burst and arrival

Task	Burst time	Arrival time
T1	12	0
T2	8	0
T3	23	1
T4	10	2
T5	30	3
T6	15	4

T2	T4	T1	T6	T3	T5

Split based on median $q\tilde{} = 13.5$

T2	T4	T1		T6	T3	T5

In [27] Ge and Wei utilized genetic algorithm (GA) as an optimization technique utilized by the master node to schedule the waiting tasks to computing nodes. Before the scheduling procedure takes place all tasks in the job queue have to be evaluated first. Based on the authors the simulation results indicated reduction in make span and better balanced load across all cloud nodes for the GA over FIFO.

Raju et al., in [28] presented a hybrid algorithm combining the advantages of Ant Colony Optimization (ACO) and Cuckoo Search (CS) in order to reduce make span, based on Job execution within specified time interval. The experimental results clarified that the proposed algorithm achieved better results in terms of makspan reduction over the original ant colony optimization algorithm but not over other related algorithms as RR.

Ramezani et al., in [29] developed Multi-Objective Jswarm (MO-Jswarm) scheduling algorithm to determine the optimal task distribution over the virtual machines (VMs) attempting to balance between different conflicting objectives including task execution time, task

transferring time, and task execution cost. According to the authors the proposed algorithm had the ability to enhance the QOS and to provide a balanced trade-off between the conflicted objectives.

Many other studies have investigated utilizing bio-inspired algorithms in task scheduling over cloud as in [30–40] but most of these studies have suffered from the intricacy and high time and space complexity.

Most of the previous studies concentrated on enhancing one or two of the Qos Standards either by minimizing or maximizing them although in cloud environment, it is highly recommended to consider various criteria as execution time, cost, bandwidth and energy consumption. Other studies even claimed to reach optimality in performance as in [41] and [42], while others have investigated task scheduling from load balancing prospective as in [43–47] concentrating on balancing workload with consumed energy. The experimentations results of all of these studies claimed that they had improved waiting, turnaround time or even throughput but none of them give a real solution to starvation or even approached to

Table 2 Task quantum calculations in first round

T	$B_{ij} = B_{i(j-1)} - q_{i(j-1)}$	$\dfrac{(B_{ij} + q_{i(j-1)})^2}{Q_1, \alpha = 1}$	$\dfrac{(B_{ij} - q_{i(j-1)})^2}{Q_2, \alpha = 0}$	$q_{ij} = q\tilde{} + \dfrac{q\tilde{}}{(B_{ij} + (-1)^{1-\alpha} \cdot q_{i(j-1)})^2}$
T2	8-0= 8	$(8+0)^2$= 64	--------	q_{21} = 13.71
T4	10-0= 10	$(10+0)^2$= 100	--------	q_{41} =13.63
T6	15-0= 15	--------	$(15-0)^2$= 225	q_{61} =13.56
T1	12-0= 12	$(12+0)^2$= 144	--------	q_{11} =13.59
T3	23-0= 23	--------	$(23-0)^2$= 529	q_{31} =13.52
T5	30-0= 30	--------	$(30-0)^2$= 900	q_{51} =13.51
	$\sum B_{i1} = 98$			$\sum q_{i1} = 81.52$

T2	T4	T6	T1	T3	T5

0   8   18   31.56   43.56   57.08   70.59

Gant chart based on table (2)

Table 3 Task quantum calculations in the second round

T	$B_{ij} = B_{i(j-1)} - q_{i(j-1)}$	$(B_{ij} + q_{i(j-1)})^2$ $Q1, \propto = 1$	$(B_{ij} - q_{i(j-1)})^2$ $Q2, \propto = 0$	$q_{ij} = q^{\sim} + \dfrac{q^{\sim}}{(B_{ij} + (-1)^{1-\propto} \cdot q_{i(j-1)})^2}$
T2	--------	--------	--------	--------
T4	--------	--------	--------	--------
T6	15-13.56=1.44	--------	$(1.44-13.56)^2$=146.8	q_{62} =9.79
T1	--------	--------	--------	--------
T3	23-13.52= 9.48	--------	$(9.48-13.52)^2$= 16.32	q_{32} =10.32
T5	30-13.51= 16.49	--------	$(16.49-13.51)^2$= 8.88	q_{52} =10.82
	$\sum B_{i2}$ =27.41	--------		$\sum q_{i2}$=30.93

T6	T3	T5

70.59   80.38   90.7   101.52

Gant chart based on Table 3

solve it. As the starvation problem is considered one of the major scheduling dilemmas, so in this paper we tried to overcome or partially overcome the starvation problem of long tasks though proposing a hybrid scheduling algorithm based on two tradition scheduling algorithms SJF and RR. These two algorithms were intentionally picked to make benefit of SJF fast secluding while solving its starvation problem using RR enhanced with dynamic quantum. Through the proposed algorithm the ready queue is split into two sub-queues Q_1 and Q_2 one for short tasks while the other is for long tasks, which will be discussed in details in next section.

SJF and RR with dynamic quantum hybrid algorithm (SRDQ)

As mentioned before, we are trying in this work to overcome the starvation problem by proposing a new hybrid scheduling technique based on SJF and RR scheduling techniques named SRDQ. SRDQ avoids the disadvantages of both of SJF and RR so that the evaluation of the performance metrics increases rather than decreases the probability of starvation occurrence as far as possible. In the RR stage of SRDQ, the time slice works on avoiding the traditional cons that lead to high waiting times and rare deadlines met. RR time slice or quantum setting is a very challenging process, as if the quantum is too short, too many context switches will lower the CPU efficiency while setting the quantum too long may cause poor response time and approximates First-Come-First-Serve (FCFS) algorithm. So in this paper, the researchers concentrated on calculating the optimal quantum interval at each round of RR algorithm while splitting the tasks ready queue into two sub-queues Q_1 for short tasks and Q_2 for long tasks using the median as the threshold of the tasks length in other words the tasks longer than the median to be inserted in Q_2 while the shorter ones to

Table 4 Task quantum calculations in the third round

T	$B_{ij} = B_{i(j-1)} - q_{i(j-1)}$	$(B_{ij} + q_{i(j-1)})^2$ $Q_1, \propto = 1$	$(B_{ij} - q_{i(j-1)})^2$ $Q_2, \propto = 0$	$q_{ij} = q^{\sim} + \dfrac{q^{\sim}}{(B_{ij} + (-1)^{1-\propto} \cdot q_{i(j-1)})^2}$
T2	--------	--------	--------	--------
T4	--------	--------	--------	--------
T6	--------	--------	--------	--------
T1	--------	--------	--------	--------
T3	--------	--------	--------	--------
T5	16.49-9.73= 6.76	--------	$(6.76-9.76)^2$= 9	9.41
	$\sum B_{ij}$ =6.76	--------		$\sum q_{ij}$=9.41

T5

101.52   108.28

Gant chart based on Table 4

Table 5 The response, waiting and turnaround times of the SRSQ compared to SJF and RR

T	Response time			Waiting time			Turnaround time		
	SRDQ	SJF	RR	SRDQ	SJF	RR	SRDQ	SJF	RR
T1	31.56	18	0	31.56	18	48	43.56	30	60
T2	0	0	5	0	0	30	8	8	38
T3	43.56	45	10	67.7	44	65	90.7	67	88
T4	8	8	15	8	6	38	18	16	48
T5	57.8	68	20	78.28	65	68	108.28	95	98
T6	18	30	25	65.30	26	60	80	41	75
Average time	26.486	28.166	12.5	41.806	26.5	51.5	58.09	42.83	67.833

be inserted in Q_1. Tasks will be executed mutually, two short tasks from Q_1 and one long task from Q_2 will be executed which will lead to reducing long tasks waiting time without the disruption of the SJF in preferring short tasks. SRDQ is designed to be a unit based algorithm based on queuing data structure effectively and optimizing the execution time as possible. SRDQ involves 6 main steps as following:

1. Arrange all submitted tasks, T_i, $i = 1, 2,...$, number of submitted tasks, according to their burst time.
2. Compute the median, $\tilde{q}$, of the burst times of all tasks.
3. If a burst time of a task T, $B(T)$, is less than or equal to the median, insert T into a Q_1 otherwise insert T into Q_2.

Table 6 CloudSim simulation parameters

Number of cloud hosts	1
Number of cloud users	1
Million Instructions Per Second (MIPS)	1000
Number of CPUs per Host	10
Host memory (MB)	2048
Host storage	1,000,000
Host Bandwidth	10,000
Number of CPUs per VM	1,2,3
Virtual Machine Size (MB)	10,000
Virtual Machine Memory (MB)	512
Virtual Machine Bandwidth	1000
System architecture	"x86"
Operating system	"Windows 7"
time zone this resource located	10.0
the cost of using processing	3.0
the cost of using memory	0.05
the cost of using storage	0.001
the cost of using bandwidth	0.0

4. The quantum (q_{ij}) is calculated based on the current executed task source queue (whether it is from Q_1 or Q_2), and the round to be executed in, as following:

$$q_{ij} = \tilde{q} + \frac{\tilde{q}}{\left(B_{ij} + (-1)^{1-\alpha} \cdot q_{i(j-1)}\right)^2} \quad (1)$$

where q_{ij} is the quantum at iteration j, i:1, 2, ..., n and, B_{ij} is burst time of task i at iteration j, $q_{i(j-1)}$, and α is a binary selector $\alpha = \{0,1\}$. In the first round, j = 1, $q_{i(j-1)}$ is set to zero as there is no previous rounds. On the other hand, based on the source queue, α will be set to either zero or one as in:

a. If the resource is taken from Q_1, α will be set to one and thus Eq. (1) will be modified as follows:

$$q_{ij} = \tilde{q} + \frac{\tilde{q}}{\left(B_{ij} + q_{i(j-1)}\right)^2} \quad (2)$$

b. If the resource is taken from Q_2, α will be set to zero and thus Eq. (1) will be modified as follows:

$$q_{ij} = \tilde{q} + \frac{\tilde{q}}{\left(B_{ij} - q_{i(j-1)}\right)^2} \quad (3)$$

5. The first two tasks of Q_1 are assigned to the resources followed by the first task of Q_2.
6. Step 4 is continuously repeated till the Q_1 and Q_2 are empty.
7. In case of the of a new task arrival or a task is finished $\tilde{q}$ will be updated dynamically as following:

Table 7 Data sets

Task	Dataset1		Dataset2		Dataset3	
	Burst Time	Arrival Time	Burst Time	Arrival Time	Burst Time	Arrival Time
T1	49	0	251	0	33	0
T2	98	1	177	1	201	1
T3	143	2	152	2	98	2
T4	187	3	299	3	116	3
T5	244	4	47	4	11	4
T6	252	4	84	5	100	5
T7	199	4	244	3	33	6
T8	67	5	124	3	78	7
T9	83	3	55	4	18	4
T10	75	6	180	6	64	8

a. In case of a new task arrival, it will be inserted in Q_1 or Q_2 based on its burst time and $\tilde{q}$. In this case, $\tilde{q}$ will be updated as follow:

$$\tilde{q} = \tilde{q} + \frac{\tilde{q}}{B_{new}} \qquad (4)$$

Where B_{new} is the new task burst time.

b. In case of a task is finished, $\tilde{q}$ will be updated as:

$$\tilde{q} = \tilde{q} - \frac{\tilde{q}}{B_{terminated}} \qquad (5)$$

Where $B_{terminated}$ is the finished task burst time.

For more explanation, the following illustrative example discusses the case of executing 6 tasks using SRDQ (Table 1).

Round (1) (Table 2)
$\tilde{q}$ = 13.5

Round (2)
T2, T4 and T1 are all finished in the first round so $\tilde{q}$ will be updated as following:

$$\tilde{q} = \tilde{q} - \frac{\tilde{q}}{B_{terminated}}$$

- After finishing T2, $B_{terminated}$ = 8, $\tilde{q}$ = 13.5 −(13.5/ 8) = 11.81
- After finishing T4, $B_{terminated}$ = 10, $\tilde{q}$ = 11.81 −(11.81/10) = 10.62

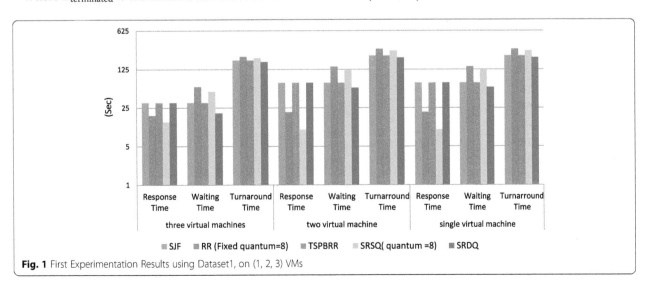

Fig. 1 First Experimentation Results using Dataset1, on (1, 2, 3) VMs

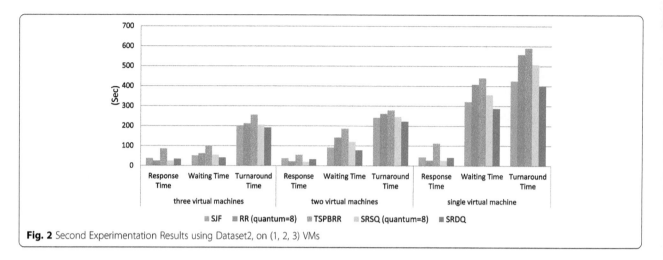

Fig. 2 Second Experimentation Results using Dataset2, on (1, 2, 3) VMs

– After finishing T1, $B_{terminated}$ = 12, $q^\sim$ = 10.62
–(10.62/12) = 9.73

As three tasks finished in the same round, $q^\sim$ will be updated three times and we obtain $q^\sim$ = 9.73 in round 2 (Table 3).

Round (3)

T6 and T3 are finished in the second round so $q^\sim$ will be updated as following:

$$q^\sim = q^\sim - \frac{q^\sim}{B_{terminated}}$$

– After finishing T6, $B_{terminated}$ = 15, $q^\sim$ = 9.73 –(9.73/15) = 9.08
– After finishing T3, $B_{terminated}$ = 23, $q^\sim$ = 9.08 –(9.08/23) = 8.47

Thus $q^\sim$ = 8.47 in this round (Table 4).

Table 5 demonstrates the response, waiting and turnaround times of the SRSQ compared to SJF and RR. We can detect that SRDQ achieved less response time compared to SJF but with higher turnaround and waiting time. Although, RR had really achieved good response time but with comparable waiting time to SRDQ. We can finally say that SRDQ is the balancing point between SJF and RR, in which we tried to overcome or at least reduce RR and SJF problems especially the starvation dilemma.

Simulation settings
Simulation environment

The proposed hybrid algorithm was implemented and tested in the CloudSim environment toolkit 3.0.3 which provides a generalized and extensible simulation framework that enables modeling, simulation, and experimentation of emerging Cloud computing infrastructures and application services, allowing its users to focus on specific system design issues that they want to investigate, without getting

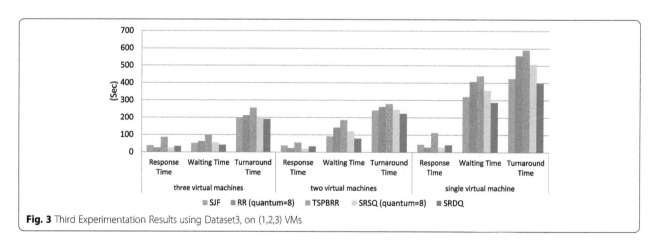

Fig. 3 Third Experimentation Results using Dataset3, on (1,2,3) VMs

Table 8 Cloudlet specification

Cloudlet ID	VM ID	Arrival	Brust time
0	0	0	12
5	0	8	13
2	0	5	44
7	0	11	92
4	0	8	101
8	0	13	144
3	0	7	157
9	0	15	158
6	0	19	179
1	0	5	210

concerned about the low level details related to Cloud-based infrastructures and services [4, 48]. The simulation settings and parameters employed in the CloudSim experiments are summarized in Table 6.

Performance metrics

The following metrics were considered through the evaluation process [49]:

- *Waiting Time:* Average time a process spends in the run queue.
- Response Time: Average time elapsed from when a process is submitted until useful output is obtained.
- Turnaround Time: Average time elapsed from when a process is submitted to when it has completed.

Experimental results & discussion

For evaluation purposes, three different datasets were utilized through testing the proposed algorithm against three different scheduling algorithms: traditional SJF, traditional RR and Time Slice Priority Based RR (TSPBRR) [50]. It was tested in two cases

the first SRSQ with static task quantum through each iteration, while changing from one iteration to the next and the second SRSQ with dynamic quantum through the same iteration and from one iteration to the next. The algorithms performances were evaluated based on turnaround time, waiting time and response time. Each dataset consists of randomly generated and dynamically shuffled ten tasks denoted as T_1, $T_2,......T_{10}$ and each task is characterized by its arrival time and burst time, as shown in Table 7.

To evaluate SRDQ a simulated Cloud computing environment consists of a single data center, a broker and a user, constructed by cloud-based interface provided by CloudSim, series of experiments are performed. The allocation of VMs (Virtual Machine) to hosts utilizes the default FCFS algorithm, while for allocating the cloudlets (tasks) to the virtual machines space-shared policy is used so that the tasks are executed sequentially in each VM. By using this policy each task unit had its own dedicated core therefore number of incoming tasks or queue size did not affect execution time of individual task units as the proposed algorithm is a non-primitive technique.

In CloudSim environment, evaluation experiments were performed in three cases using one VM, two VMs and three VMs. While the assumptions behind the proposed algorithm involve:

- All cloudlets which have to be processed are available,
- At runtime no more cloudlets are added,
- The environment is also static i.e. no more resources are added at runtime.

Finally the inner code of CloudSim was modified to test our proposed algorithm and also to compare it to the traditional RR and SJF. Then our own classes for the scheduling algorithm were defined to extend the basic

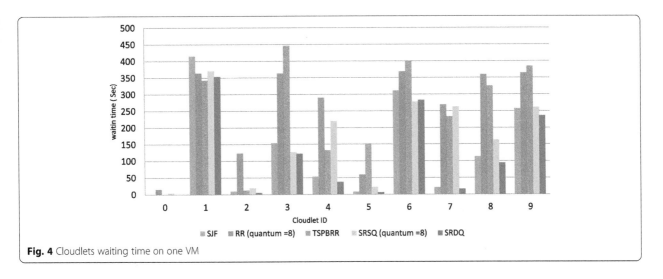

Fig. 4 Cloudlets waiting time on one VM

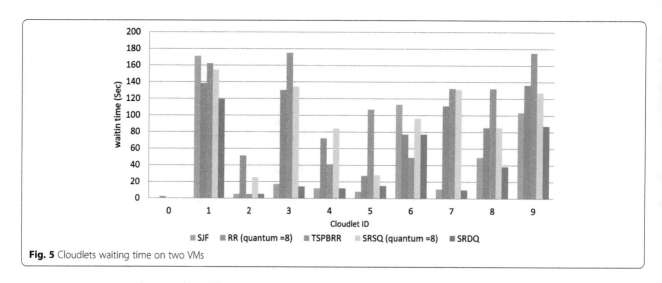

Fig. 5 Cloudlets waiting time on two VMs

CloudSim classes. The same datasets were used in three different cases one VM, Two VMs and three VMs. Each dataset was used in each case as shown in the next figures.

Figure 1 clarifies the experimentation results of the implemented algorithms using dataset1 on one, two and three VMs. It is noticed that SRSQ and RR have the least response time in all phases but suffer from the highest turnaround and waiting time. While SRDQ has the least waiting and turnaround time which is also nearly comparable to the SJF.

From Fig. 2, we can also notice that RR and SRSQ really achieved good comparable response time but still suffer from higher waiting and turnaround time, while TSPBRR suffered from elevated values compared to SJF and SRDQ. Finally the SRDQ is again the winner that achieved the least waiting and turnaround time.

Finally in the third and final experiments using dataset3 as shown in Fig. 3, we can notice that with

the increasing number of VMs, SRDQ performance became better and exceeded the rest in all evaluation metrics, while TSPBRR performance was degrading.

A final test was done through the CloudSim environment using a randomized dataset of 10 cloudlets (tasks) with random arrival and long burst time generated by the environment given in Table 8 to detect the impact of the proposed algorithm on reducing the starvation problem.

It is noticed that the cloudlets (1, 6, 9, 3, and 8) burst time is long which means that theses cloudlets will suffer from starvation if the SJF scheduler was applied and also will suffer if the RR quantum was small. In the proposed algorithms with its two versions, we tried to balance between reducing cloudlets waiting time and increasing quantum value also tried to achieve fairness in selecting cloudlets for execution through having two short cloudlets from Q_1 and one long cloudlet from Q_2.

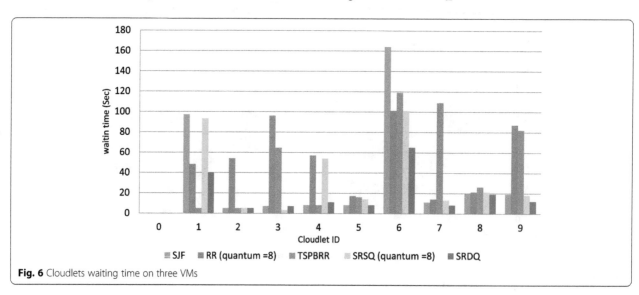

Fig. 6 Cloudlets waiting time on three VMs

Figures 4, 5 and 6 clarifies the waiting time of each cloudlets applied on a 1, 2 and 3 VMs, from which we can see that the proposed algorithm with its two versions had achieved much better reduction in cloudlets waiting time especially cloudlets with long burst time. We can also notice that SRDQ performance exceeds SRSQ or at least comparable to it. SJF achieved the worst waiting time especially with cloudlets with long burst time while TSPBRR achieved better waiting time in most cases that its traditional version.

Reducing the waiting time indicates that the average time a cloudlet spends in the run queue is reduced which leads to reducing cloudlet starvation. SRDQ achieved this waiting time reduction and thus starvation through having the two sub-queues Q1 and Q2 where Q1 for nearly short tasks and Q2 for the rest depending on the tasks median. Many tests and trials have been done by the researchers to find the best methodology for selecting tasks from Q1 and Q2 to be assigned to resources and finally found that as clarified in the algorithm that having two tasks from Q1 and one task from Q2 really have a good impact on reducing task starvation.

From the simulations results, it is obvious that SRSQ and SRDQ had achieved a good performance compared to the traditional RR and SJF and also to TSPBRR in response, turnaround and waiting time. It is also obvious that SRDQ had superiority on SRSQ in reducing waiting and turnaround times while SRSQ exceeds in reducing response time. We can assure that the proposed algorithm in its both versions (SRSQ and SRDQ) had achieved a good reduction in the waiting time of each task and also the overall waiting average, from which we can say that it leads to reducing task starvation which is one of our first priorities.

But one last issue, the experiments results had shown that dynamicity in task quantum had a good impact on reducing task waiting time and turnaround time, while the dynamicity in each task quantum from round to round had a good impact on reducing response time so we can see that SRSQ had exceeds SRDQ in response as it only depends on having a static quantum for all tasks that did not change from round to round. SRDQ works as the balancing point with, waiting, turnaround and starvation reduction especially in tasks with long burst times and with a comparable performance in response to SJF, RR and TSPBRR. From all of the above, we can surely conclude that having the optimum task quantum value is nearly impossible.

Conclusions

Achieving optimality in scheduling tasks over computing nodes in cloud computing is the aim of all researchers interested in both scheduling and cloud. Balancing between throughput, waiting time and response time may provide a way to approach scheduling optimality but on another level it may causes long tasks starvation. Most of the previous studies have concentrated only on one side either starvation or throughput but not both so in this study we have tried to develop a hybrid algorithm based on SJF and dynamic quantum RR, while concentrating on splitting the ready queue into to sub-queues Q1 for short tasks and Q2 long tasks.

Three different datasets were utilized for evaluation conducted using CloudSim environment 3.0.3 in two different versions SJF&RR with Dynamic Quantum (SRDQ) and SJF&RR with Static Quantum (SRSQ) with 1,2 and 3 virtual machines. Experimentations results indicated that the proposed algorithm has outperformed the state of art in minimizing turnaround and waiting times with comparable response time in addition to partially reducing long tasks starvation.

In the future the researchers intend to proceed their experiments in finding a better task quantum calculation methodology that balance between the static and dynamic quantum values to achieved better reduction in waiting and thus reducing task starvation.

Authors' contributions
SS carried out the literature review. SE developed the mathematical models. SS and MJ jointly conducted the simulations and drafted the manuscript. SE provided useful remarks and critically reviewed the manuscript. All authors read and approved the final manuscript.

Competing interests
The authors declare that they have no competing interests.

Author details
[1]Department of Computer Science, Faculty of Computers and Information, Mansoura University, Mansoura 35516, Egypt. [2]University of Al-Qadisiyah, Al-Qadisiyah, Iraq.

References
1. Lu CW, Hsieh CM, Chang CH, Yang CT (2013, July) An improvement to data Service in Cloud Computing with Content Sensitive Transaction Analysis and Adaptation, Computer Software and applications Conference workshops (COMPSACW), 2013 IEEE 37th annual, vol 463-468
2. Azeez A, Perera S, Gamage D, Linton R, Siriwardana P, Leelaratne D, Fremantle P (2010, July) Multi-tenant SOA middleware for cloud computing, Cloud computing (cloud), 2010, IEEE 3rd International Conference on, pp 458–465
3. Demchenko Y, de Laat C (2011, March) Defining generic architecture for cloud infrastructure as a Service model, The International symposium on grids and clouds and the open grid forum Academia Sinica, pp 2–10
4. Calheiros RN, Ranjan R, Beloglazov A, De Rose CA, Buyya R (2011) CloudSim: a toolkit for modeling and simulation of cloud computing environments and evaluation of resource provisioning algorithms. Software: Practice and Experience 41(1):23–50
5. Ganapathi A, Chen Y, Fox A, Katz R, Patterson D (2010, March) Statistics-driven workload modeling for the cloud, Data Engineering workshops (ICDEW), 2010 IEEE 26th International Conference on, pp 87–92
6. Garg SK, Buyya R (2011, December) Networkcloudsim: Modelling parallel applications in cloud simulations, Utility and cloud computing (UCC), 2011 fourth IEEE International Conference on, pp 105–113

7. Buyya R, Ranjan R, Calheiros RN (2009, June) Modeling and simulation of scalable cloud computing environments and the Cloudsim toolkit: challenges and opportunities, High Performance Computing & Simulation, 2009. HPCS'09. International Conference on, pp 1–11

8. Das AK, Adhikary T, Razzaque MA, Hong CS (2013, January) An intelligent approach for virtual machine and QoS provisioning in cloud computing, Information Networking (ICOIN), 2013 International Conference on, pp 462–467

9. Bhoi U, Ramanuj PN (2013) Enhanced max-min task scheduling algorithm in cloud computing. International Journal of Application or Innovation in Engineering and Management (IJAIEM) 2(4):259–264

10. Wang SC, Yan KQ, Liao WP, Wang SS (2010) Towards a load balancing in a three-level cloud computing network, Computer Science and information technology (ICCSIT), 2010 3rd IEEE International Conference on, 1, pp 108–113

11. Venters W, Whitley EA (2012) A critical review of cloud computing: researching desires and realities. J Inf Technol 27(3):179–197

12. Santra S, Dey H, Majumdar S, Jha GS (2014, July) New simulation toolkit for comparison of scheduling algorithm on cloud computing, Control, instrumentation, communication and computational technologies (ICCICCT), 2014 International Conference on, pp 466–469

13. Fang Y, Wang F, Ge J (2010) A task scheduling algorithm based on load balancing in cloud computing. Web information systems and Mining. Springer, Berlin Heidelberg, pp 271–277

14. Lin CC, Liu P, Wu JJ (2011, July) Energy-aware virtual machine dynamic provision and scheduling for cloud computing, CLOUD computing (CLOUD), 2011 IEEE International Conference on, pp 736–737

15. Ghanbari S, Othman M (2012) A priority based job scheduling algorithm in cloud computing. Procedia Engineering 50:778–785

16. Maguluri ST, Srikant R, Ying L (2012) Stochastic models of load balancing and scheduling in cloud computing clusters, INFOCOM, 2012 Proceedings IEEE, pp 702–710

17. Gulati A, Chopra RK (2013) Dynamic round Robin for load balancing in a cloud computing. IJCSMC 2(6):274–278

18. Agha AEA, Jassbi SJ (2013) A new method to improve round Robin scheduling algorithm with quantum time based on harmonic-arithmetic mean (HARM). International Journal of Information Technology and Computer Science 5(7):56–62

19. Tsai JT, Fang JC, Chou JH (2013) Optimized task scheduling and resource allocation on cloud computing environment using improved Differential Evolution algorithm. Comput Oper Res 40(12):3045–3055

20. Ergu D, Kou G, Peng Y, Shi Y, Shi Y (2013) The analytic hierarchy process: task scheduling and resource allocation cloud computing environment. J Supercomput 64(3):835–848

21. Karthick AV, Ramaraj E, Subramanian RG (2014, February) An efficient multi queue job scheduling for cloud computing, Computing and communication technologies (WCCCT), 2014 world congress on, pp 164–166

22. Lakra AV, Yadav DK (2015) Multi-objective tasks scheduling algorithm for cloud computing throughput optimization. Procedia Computer Science 48:107–113

23. Dash AR, Samantra SK (2016) An optimized round Robin CPU scheduling algorithm with dynamic time quantum. International Journal of Computer Science, Engineering and Information Technology (IJCSEIT) 5(1):7–26. doi:10.5121/ijcseit.2015.5102

24. Tunc C, Kumbhare N, Akoglu A, Hariri S, Machovec D, Siegel HJ (2016, December) Value of Service based task scheduling for cloud computing systems, Cloud and autonomic computing (ICCAC), 2016 International Conference on, pp 1–11. doi:10.1109/ICCAC.2016.22

25. Razaque A, Vennapusa NR, Soni N, Janapati GS (2016, April) Task scheduling in cloud computing, Long Island systems, applications and technology Conference (LISAT), 2016 IEEE, pp 1–5. doi:10.1109/LISAT.2016.7494149

26. Mizan, T., Al Masud, S. M. R., & Latip, R. (2012). Modified bees life algorithm for job scheduling in hybrid cloud.

27. Ge Y, Wei G (2010) GA-based task scheduler for the cloud computing systems. In Web Information Systems and Mining (WISM), 2010 International Conference on, Vol. 2. IEEE, Sanya, China, p. 181–186

28. Raju R, Babukarthik RG, Dhavachelvan P (2013) Hybrid ant Colony optimization and cuckoo search algorithm for job scheduling, Advances in computing and information technology. Springer, Berlin Heidelberg, pp 491–501

29. Ramezani F, Lu J, Hussain F (2013, December) Task scheduling optimization in cloud computing applying multi-objective particle swarm optimization, International Conference on Service-oriented computing. Berlin, Springer Berlin Heidelberg, pp 237–251

30. Gan GN, Huang TL, Gao S (2010). Genetic simulated annealing algorithm for task scheduling based on cloud computing environment. In Intelligent Computing and Integrated Systems (ICISS), 2010 International Conference on (pp. 60-63). IEEE, Guilin

31. Wang L, Siegel HJ, Roychowdhury VP, Maciejewski AA (1997) Task matching and scheduling in heterogeneous computing environments using a genetic-algorithm-based approach. Journal of parallel and distributed computing 47(1):8–22

32. Zhao C, Zhang S, Liu Q, Xie J, Hu J (2009) Independent tasks scheduling based on genetic algorithm in cloud computing. In Wireless Communications, Networking and Mobile Computing, 2009. WiCom'09. 5th International Conference on. IEEE, Beijing, p. 1–4

33. Gu J, Hu J, Zhao T, Sun G (2012) A new resource scheduling strategy based on genetic algorithm in cloud computing environment. Journal of Computers 7(1):42–52

34. Mocanu EM, Florea M, Andreica MI, Ţăpuş N (2012) Cloud computing—task scheduling based on genetic algorithms. In Systems Conference (SysCon), 2012 IEEE International. IEEE, Vancouver, p. 1–6

35. Kaur S, Verma A (2012) An efficient approach to genetic algorithm for task scheduling in cloud computing environment. International Journal of Information Technology and Computer Science (IJITCS) 4(10):74

36. Jang SH, Kim TY, Kim JK, Lee JS (2012) The study of genetic algorithm-based task scheduling for cloud computing. International Journal of Control and Automation 5(4):157–162

37. Kruekaew B, Kimpan W (2014) Virtual machine scheduling management on cloud computing using artificial bee colony, Proceedings of the International MultiConference of engineers and computer scientists, vol 1, pp 12–14

38. Bilgaiyan S, Sagnika S, Das M (2014) An analysis of task scheduling in cloud computing using evolutionary and swarm-based algorithms. Int J Comput Appl 89(2):11–18

39. Navimipour NJ, Milani FS (2015) Task scheduling in the cloud computing based on the cuckoo search algorithm. International Journal of Modeling and Optimization 5(1):44

40. Verma, A., & Kaushal, S. (2014) Bi-criteria priority based particle swarm optimization workflow scheduling algorithm for cloud. In Engineering and Computational Sciences (RAECS), 2014 Recent Advances in. IEEE, p. 1–6

41. Alla HB, Alla SB, Ezzati A, Mouhsen A (2017) A novel architecture with dynamic queues based on fuzzy logic and particle swarm optimization algorithm for task scheduling in cloud computing, Advances in Ubiquitous Networking 2, 397, 205–217. Springer, Singapore

42. Sebastio S, Gnecco G, Bemporad A (2017) Optimal distributed task scheduling in volunteer clouds. Comput Oper Res 81:231–246

43. Maharana D, Sahoo B, Sethi S (2017) Energy-efficient real-time tasks scheduling in cloud data centers. International Journal of Science Engineering and Advance Technology, IJSEAT 4(12):768–773

44. Liu Y, Xu X, Zhang L, Wang L, Zhong RY (2017) Workload-based multi-task scheduling in Cloud Manufacturing. Robot Comput Integr Manuf 45:3–20

45. Sofia AS, Kumar PG (2017) Energy efficient task scheduling to implement green cloud. Asian Journal of Research in Social Sciences and Humanities 7(2):443–458

46. Li, K. (2017). Scheduling parallel tasks with energy and time constraints on multiple Manycore processors In A cloud computing environment. Future generation computer systems, http://dx.doi.org/10.1016/j.future.2017.01.010.

47. Rimal BP, Maier M (2017) Workflow scheduling in multi-tenant cloud computing environments. IEEE Transactions on Parallel and Distributed Systems 28(1):290–304. doi:10.1109/TPDS.2016.2556668

48. http://www.cloudbus.org/cloudsim/ [Accessed at : 25/4/2015]

49. http://www.read.seas.harvard.edu/~kohler/class/05s-osp/notes/notes5.html. Accessed 25 Apr 2015

50. Mohapatra S, Mohanty S, Rekha KS (2013) Analysis of different variants in round Robin algorithms for load balancing in cloud computing. Int J Comput Appl 69(22):17–21. doi:10.5120/12103-8221

8

Migration of a SCADA system to IaaS clouds

Philip Church[1,3]* [iD], Harald Mueller[2], Caspar Ryan[1], Spyridon V. Gogouvitis[2], Andrzej Goscinski[1,3] and Zahir Tari[1]

Abstract

SCADA systems allow users to monitor and/or control physical devices, processes, and events remotely and in real-time. As these systems are critical to industrial processes, they are often run on highly reliable and dedicated hardware. Moving these SCADA systems to an Infrastructure as a Service (IaaS) cloud allows for: cheaper deployments, system redundancy support, and increased uptime. The goal of this work was to present the results of our experimental study of moving/migrating a selected SCADA system to a cloud environment and present major lessons learned. To this end, EclipseSCADA was deployed to the NeCTAR research cloud using the "lift and shift" approach. Performance metrics of a unique nature and large scale of experimentation were collected from the deployed EclipseSCADA system under different loads to examine the effects cloud resources and public networks have on SCADA behavior.

Keyword: SCADA, IaaS cloud, Migration, Case study

Introduction

Supervisory Control and Data Acquisition (SCADA) systems are instrumental to a wide range of mission-critical industrial systems, from infrastructure installations like gas pipelines or water control facilities to industrial plants. SCADA systems allow a user to monitor (using sensors) and control (using actuators) an industrial system remotely. As these systems are critical to industrial processes, they are often run on highly reliable and dedicated hardware [1]. This is in contrast to the current trend and state of computing, which is moving from running applications on internally hosted servers to flexible, cheaper, nternal or external cloud systems.

For users, the main benefit of moving applications such as SCADA to the cloud lies in the potential cost savings and reduced setup time. Cloud resources are purchased and accessed on-demand, at a total cost of ownership cheaper than buying and operating hardware; furthermore, as there is no need to install and/or maintain hardware and manage software, the need for technical staff is reduced. For industry, running SCADA on the cloud can lead to new business models, instead of a traditional one-off hardware cost and software licensing fee. Cloud-based

SCADA solutions can provide users with flexible fees based on the amount of computing resources, technical support, and software they use.

One way to provide a cloud-based SCADA system would be the cloud native approach, which means to develop it from scratch, ideally using an appropriate architectural design to make use of cloud inherent features. Another option is to take an existing SCADA implementation and migrate it to a cloud environment. Often this latter approach is an initial step towards the cloud, given that solid and well proven implementations are available.

When moving an open-source SCADA system to cloud infrastructure, there is a need to ensure that the real-time monitoring and control demands of the industrial system can be achieved. Based on a comparison of commercial and open-source SCADA features, EclipseSCADA[1] was selected as an example of a representative SCADA system. Using the "lift and shift" method, EclipseSCADA was migrated to the IaaS cloud, and performance metrics of a unique nature and large scale of experimentation collected. Based on the collected metrics, we provide a number of recommendations, which can benefit users planning to move SCADA systems to cloud infrastructure.

Through the carried out work, the following contributions have been made:

* Correspondence: philip.church@rmit.edu.au
[1]School of Computer Science and Information Technology, GPO, RMIT University, Box 2476, Melbourne, Australia
[3]School of Information Technology, Deakin University, Geelong, Australia
Full list of author information is available at the end of the article

- The presentation of a general migration process and performance metrics of a unique nature and large scale of experimentation collected, which can be applied to move SCADA systems to cloud resources.
- A detailed performance study of EclipseSCADA was carried out to identify how a SCADA system behaves when running across multiple regions of a cloud.
- The presentation of a series of lessons, which can be used to select SCADA parts that should be migrated and location of their deployment, their relationship, influence on execution performance, and even improve the performance of SCADA systems running on the cloud.

The rest of the paper is as follows: Section 3 introduces "generalized" SCADA architecture. Section 3 presents related work in running and migrating SCADA system on the cloud. Section 4 compares open-source SCADA systems with common commercial SCADA products in order to find a representative SCADA system to be migrated. Section 5 shows a case study – it describes the process used to develop and deploy the selected SCADA system (EclipseSCADA) to IaaS cloud resources (NeCTAR [2]). To identify problems regarding the real-time monitoring and control mechanism of SCADA systems when running on the cloud, an analysis of the ported EclipseSCADA system was carried out in Section 6. This section also contains an analysis of collected performance results and migrating lessons. Section 7 concludes the paper.

"Generalized" SCADA architecture

SCADA describes applications, which aim to control and monitor remote equipment via a communication channel [3]. There have been a number of attempts to form a generalized SCADA framework and architecture. Boye [4] defines a simple SCADA architecture that consists of sensors, switches and/or actuators (field devices), connected and read by a device server (see Fig. 1). Data is transferred across a network to a control server, which

handles events (informing a user if sensor data exceeds set boundaries). A user of a SCADA system accesses data via the master server using a workstation.

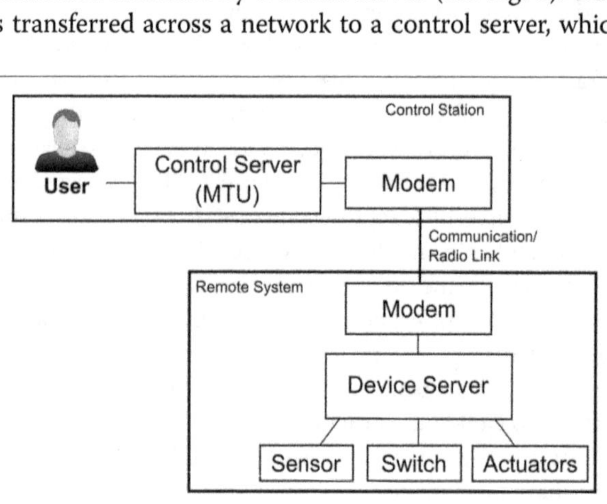

In contrast, IEEE [5] defines an in-depth standard describing the components that make up a SCADA framework. According to the IEEE standard, the system is divided into a remote site and master station (see Fig. 2). The remote site consists of field devices connected to a device server. Communication between the field device and device server makes use of a SCADA communication standard (used by the driver). Collected information is stored in a real-time and historical database on the master station. Communication between components of the master station uses an internal communication protocol. The Master Terminal Unit (MTU) contains a number of tools that interact with the data stored in the databases including:

- An event handler, which reacts to changes to the real time database;
- A device manager, which can modify the behaviour of field devices;
- An alarm manager, which allows users to setup monitoring rules and notify a user if rules have been broken;
- An archiver, which provides analytics of stored data; and
- A GUI or Human Machine Interface, which provides the user with a graphical representation of the remote site.

Every SCADA system uses a large number of field devices. A field device understands and collects data from sensors, switches and actuators. For this reason, field devices make use of a compute device called a Programmable Logic Controller (PLC), or Remote Terminal Unit (RTU) (see Fig. 3). Users can access the PLC or RTU through a network interface or a Human Machine Interface (HMI), allowing for configuration and access to connected sensors, switches or actuators. An inbuilt computer runs code which converts signals from connected sensors, switches or actuators to digital data, or vice versa. The code that runs on field devices falls under two categories: monitoring loops for sensors that may incorporate sampling/averaging, and state diagrams that control the state of output devices such as switches/actuators. Often this code has real time requirements, as it directly monitors and controls the connected field devices.

Field devices are designed to be reliable, often incorporating backup power and redundancy in the form of backup I/O cards. If a device is connected to an I/O card that fails, the device automatically gets connected to the redundant I/O. In the absence of this feature, if an input card fails, signals would be lost until the card is replaced.

Fig. 1 Simple SCADA System

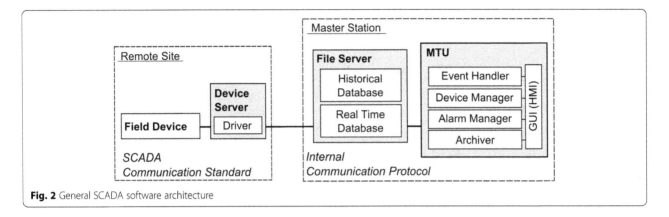

Fig. 2 General SCADA software architecture

Through the use of SCADA and Field Devices, it becomes possible to monitor and control large scale systems (such as gas pipelines, which cover very large distances) cheaply and efficiently.

To transfer data between a field device and SCADA system, communication protocols are used. Protocols are either Polling or Event Driven (see Fig. 4). Polling protocols transfer data on a timed loop, where the time between each transfer is called the polling interval. Event driven protocols transfer data on sensor change. Commonly used polling protocols include Modbus [6] and Profibus [7]. Commonly used event driven protocols include S7 [8] and iec104 [9].

Related work

There are a number of papers, which discuss how to build cloud-based SCADA architectures. They focus on implementing a solution from the ground up, as opposed to utilizing pre-existing SCADA solutions.

- Liu, et al. presents a generalized overview of clouds and SCADA and proposes the possibility of running SCADA in the cloud [10].
- Gligor and Turc recommend exposing each SCADA component as a service and deploying them through

a Local Directory Service (LDS) [11]. The LDS stores a description of available SCADA resources, access methods, and description. The use of a broker allows some components can be replaced by cloud services; for example the database service can utilize Data Center as a Service (DaaS). This approach is very flexible; allowing users to extending the SCADA system by adding new functionalities to existing services or defines new ones in accordance with needs and formulated requirements.

Based on these concepts, a web-based SCADA system is implemented on Rackspace cloud resources. Data was transferred using a simple protocol, consisting of a few numerical and process monitoring variables. Data transfer rates were measured from a local database to a cloud database, results measured were between 125 to 156 ms.

- Goose et al. present a secure SCADA cloud framework called SKYDA [12]. This SCADA system is designed to take advantage of the scalability and reliability offered by a cloud-based infrastructure. This paper focuses on providing a high level understanding of SCADA replication using clouds, moving all SCADA components (except the field devices) as a single service. Field devices are connected to the cloud

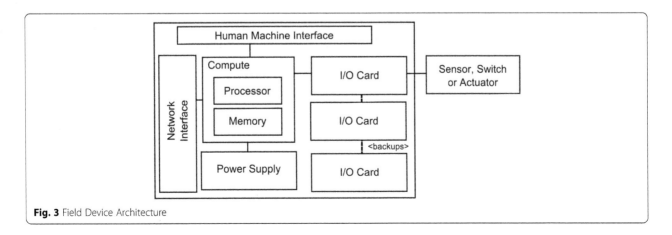

Fig. 3 Field Device Architecture

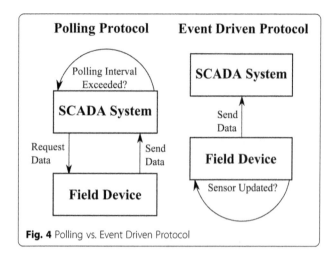

Fig. 4 Polling vs. Event Driven Protocol

based SCADA system directly or (for legacy devices) via a proxy. The framework utilizes multiple cloud providers, running multiple copies of the SCADA Master application in multiple clouds to provide fault tolerance.

There also are solutions provided by commercial cloud-based SCADA providers; the two major commercial solutions are Ignition and XiO's Cloud SCADA.

- Ignition SCADA is a SCADA solution that has been built from the ground up using Java to take advantage of cloud features [13]. Ignition interfaces with most Programmable Logic Controllers (PLC), allowing users to take advantage of existing sensors/actuators. Ignition users do not maintain hardware themselves; instead they access systems remotely via web interfaces. Users are charged based on the number of servers used instead of via software licensing fees. Ignition allows users to customize their architecture by choosing to deploy components individually.
- XiO Cloud SCADA [14] consists of two components, a local (customizable) hardware module called a Soft-I/O, which contains the sensors and actuators, and the cloud component, the SCADA application which runs on secure commercial servers. Users subscribe to a Cloud Service, for a monthly fee, giving them access to the SCADA system through web and mobile apps. Users can customize the priorities of their XiO SCADA system, for example to priorities energy efficiency.

In general, there is a trend to develop SCADA systems specifically for cloud infrastructure. The fact that existing SCADA solutions have not been used alludes to potential issues with migrating SCADA solutions. However, it is not clear if issues are performance or deployment related. The solution presented by Gligor and Turc addresses performance through the use of a simple data transfer protocol,

while the local directory service addresses deployment issues. The SKYDA cloud framework only addresses deployment issues through the use of automated replication.

Common open-source SCADA solutions include EPICS, TANGO, EclipseSCADA and IndigoSCADA. EPICS (Experimental Physics and Industry Control System) [15] is a SCADA system designed to operate devices such as particle accelerators, large experiments, and major telescopes. TANGO [16] is an object orientated distributed control system supported by a consortium of European Synchrotrons in Germany, Spain, Italy, Poland, and France. EclipseSCADA [17] is a key eclipse foundation project used commercially, the details of which have not been made public. IndigoSCADA [18] is a light weight SCADA system for Linux and Windows. While some of these solutions have been run on cloud infrastructure, no major performance study has been carried out on how these solutions behave. This paper focuses on the process of migrating and understanding, based on the nature and scale of experimentation undertaken, the feasibility and outcomes of migrating existing open SCADA solutions to run on cloud infrastructure.

Open-source SCADA selection

It was the goal to ensure that the results of this migration study would be able to be applied to a wide range of open and commercial systems. Therefore there was a need to select an open-source SCADA package which would: provide similar architecture and features to commercial packages, have manageable code with minimal coupling between components, and be widely adopted and supported.

Most commercial solutions focus on detailing features of their product rather than the system architecture, which is making comparisons difficult. One commercial SCADA package which provides a detailed description of the system architecture and provided features is WinCC. As WinCC has an open architecture [19], it has been selected as the focus of architecture and feature comparison. By choosing an open-source SCADA solution with similar features and structure to WinCC, we make the claim that our outcomes are applicable to commercial SCADA systems.

SCADA architecture and feature comparison

The WinCC open architecture [20] is a theoretical model that consists of a number of software components called managers. There are three key managers that make up the core WinCC functionality: event, device, and database managers. Similar features are provided by the open-source SCADA solutions presented in section 3.

- Event managers handle notifications and alarms. The EPICS solution provides alarm handling through an application, which notifies the user when information is stored in a distributed database. Users of TANGO build event notification through access to databases. EclipseSCADA and IndigoSCADA perform checks on data stored in the real-time database.

- The Device manager handles connection of field devices and incorporates drivers. Similar functions are provided by all open-source SCADA solutions; each solution provides a system node which listens to connected devices via drivers.
- Database managers handle both historical and real-time data using relational databases. This approach is most similar to IndigoSCADA, which also uses relational database storage for both historical and real-time data. EclipseSCADA, EPICS, and TANGO store historical data in a relational database, but real-time data is stored in memory in the form of blocks.

Device support is another key feature, which can be compared (see Table 1). WinCC supports drivers in four categories: Open Platform Communications (OPC), Field bus, telecontrol systems, and TCP/IP drivers. Most open-source solutions provide similar support for field devices; EPIC, TANGO and EclipseSCADA support all but telecontrol systems. IndigoSCADA provides support for all but field bus devices.

SCADA code manageability comparison

Related work (see section 3) alludes to the need to modify a SCADA system to take advantage of cloud. For this reason a study of code manageability was carried out. Manageability of code can be based on static code metrics measuring coupling (see Table 2). Solutions with fewer modules and fewer links between modules will be easier to analyze and port. CppDepend [21] and Eclipse Metrics [22] were used to identify the number of modules, links, and shared functions.

Of the studied solutions, results show that EPICS is the most complex, having on average 2.2 links per module. TANGO and EclipseSCADA have around 1 link per module; however, EclipseSCADA is more manageable, consisting of fewer modules. IndigoSCADA is the simplest solution having on average 0.7 links per module.

Measuring the variance of shared functions can also give an indication of code manageability. Solutions, in which code is weakly coupled across many modules, can

be difficult to partition, while modules with few tightly coupled links are easier to partition. EPICS and EclipseSCADA are loosely coupled solutions with few strong links. EPICS having more modules and links, has code-reuse spread across more modules. TANGO and IndigoSCADA have modules, which are highly coupled, only a few modules which reuse code.

The last aspect of manageability is the type of SCADA package; TANGO and EclipseSCADA are toolkits and require development be carried out before migration. EPICS and IndigoSCADA are out-of-the-box systems and do not require further development, reducing the time needed to carry out migration.

SCADA adoption comparison

SCADA adoption and support differs depending on the solution.

- TANGO is supported by a consortium of European Synchrotrons in Germany, Spain, Italy, Poland, and France. Key projects that utilized TANGO include: the C3 Prototype of the European Mars Analog Station, the diagnostics of the Laser Mégajoule and the laser facility CILEX-APOLLON. TANGO has a large community of users, contributing a large number of device drivers, at time of writing over 558 different devices are supported, including sensors, motors, vacuums and lasers (beam lines).
- EPICS is a collaborative project between Argonne and Los Alamos national labs. As of 2015, EPICS is deployed in over one hundred research lab across the globe; key research institutes using EPICS include Fermilab, Australian Synchrotron, and the Lawrence Berkeley National Labs. Commercial companies also provide services for EPICS, in the form of consulting, by providing device drivers for their hardware or by selling instruments with an embedded IOC.
- EclipseSCADA is part of the Eclipse IoT Industry Working Group initiative. EclipseSCADA has been deployed in a number of productive installations around the world. Commercial support is available through a company called IBS SYSTEMS, which uses the EclipseSCADA toolkit to build SCADA solutions targeted to users' industrial requirements.

Table 1 Comparison of supported SCADA drivers

Drivers	WinCC	EPICS	TANGO	EclipseSCADA	IndigoSCADA
OPC	Yes	Yes	Yes	Yes	Yes
Field Bus	Yes	S7, Profibus	S7, Profibus	S7	No
Telecontrol	Yes	No	No	No	DNP3, iec104, iec61850
TCP/IP	Yes	Modbus, Ethernet	Modbus	Modbus	Modbus, RFC1006

Table 2 Manageability of open-source SCADA solutions

SCADA Solutions	# Modules	Avg. # of Links	Variance of Shared Functions	SCADA System Type
EPICS	9	2.2	134	Out-of-the-box
TANGO	9	1.1	5598	Toolkit
EclipseSCADA	6	1	113	Toolkit
IndigoSCADA	9	0.7	7163	Out-of-the-box

- IndigoSCADA is supported by a company called Enscada, little is known about deployment of this SCADA system in research and/or commercial environments.

Conclusion

A summary of open-source SCADA packages in terms of their features, manageability and adoption/support is as follows (see Table 3):

- Similarity of WinCC has been measured based on features and driver support. Of the selected SCADA systems, both IndigoSCADA and EclipseSCADA share features in terms of event, device and storage managers, while TANGO and EPICS implement event handling and data storage differently than WinCC. Driver support across all open-source solutions is similar, supporting 3 out of 4 categories. As a toolkit with features similar to WinCC, EclipseSCADA would allow for a SCADA configuration similar to WinCC to be developed.
- Manageability is measured in terms of coupling and required development. IndigoSCADA, TANGO and EclipseSCADA had significantly less coupling then EPICS. Out of the solutions with low coupling, only Indigo is an out-of-the-box solution which does not require further development. Out of the toolkits, EclipseSCADA has fewer modules compared to TANGO and is therefore more manageable.
- EPICS and TANGO are widely used in research areas, and have a large support base. EclipseSCADA is not as well-known as EPICS and TANGO, but used commercially, and has links to the eclipse foundation, which are points in its favor. IndigoSCADA has limited adoption in research or industry, and is ranked last.

Based on these criteria, the open source EclipseSCADA was chosen. As a toolkit, EclipseSCADA is flexible enough to build a SCADA solution that is similar to WinCC. The low coupling score suggests a modular solution, which could be modified to suit cloud infrastructure.

Migration of EclipseSCADA

The open source EclipseSCADA toolkit was chosen as a representative SCADA system. Using EclipseSCADA, a SCADA system was developed, which consisted of a remote sever, a master server, and a file server. Using the "lift and shift" method, EclipseSCADA was ported to the NeCTAR research cloud.

EclipseSCADA solution development

Development of a SCADA solution using the EclipseSCADA toolkit is carried out using the EclipseIDE. Through the toolkit, users are provided with a configuration template that they can use to define the structure of the SCADA system, by creating and configuring servers and devices (see Fig. 5).

The configuration template defines two type of servers, external or system nodes: the remote server is where real time storage of data is performed, and the system node is where device drivers are run. Users modify these templates by specifying the running IP address of each server. Users can link any number of devices to a system node. Device templates are available for a number of communication protocols, which can be modified by specifying port numbers and data types, and communication period.

When compiled, the SCADA system defined by the user takes the form of OSGi services [23], which are bundled Java code that can be installed, started, stopped, and updated through a simple API. A separate service is built for each IP address defined by the user, and is designed to be deployed on the specified machine. Users

Table 3 Examination of open-source SCADA solutions

SCADA Solutions	Criteria					
	Similarity to WinCC		Manageability			Widely Used
	Features	Driver Support	Coupling	Toolkit		
EPICS	Through Extensions	3/4 categories	Low	No		Yes
TANGO	Through Extensions	3/4 categories	High	Yes		Yes
EclipseSCADA	Through Customization	3/4 categories	Low	Yes		Yes
IndigoSCADA	Yes	3/4 categories	High	No		No

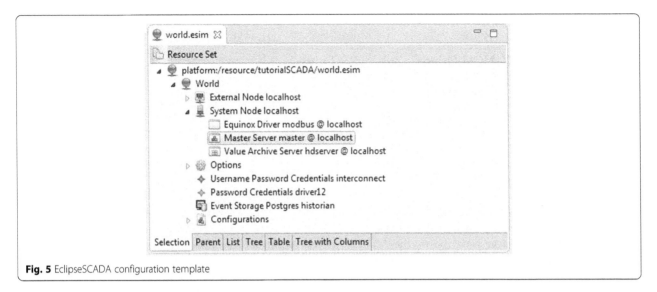

Fig. 5 EclipseSCADA configuration template

can access these compiled OSGi services through a GUI, which implements Human Machine Interface (HMI) features. This GUI can link to system node and file server, giving end-users access to real time and historical data, alarm and event handling.

Using the EclipseSCADA toolkit, the core components shown in Fig. 6 were developed. The core components consist of a remote server, a master server, and file server.

- The remote server provides real-time collection of sensor, switch, and actuator information. Data is stored in memory (data blocks) and converted to the EclipseSCADA internal protocol, Next Generation Protocol (NGP [24]).
- The master server provides event and alarm handling for NGP formatted data.
- The file server provides data archival. A relational database service is used to store and manage data.

Migration methodology

When migrating EclipseSCADA to the cloud, three different deployment paths can be considered: re-hosting, re-factoring, and revising [25]. The quickest and simplest approach is achieved by simply re-hosting an application in the cloud ("lift & shift" method). Re-hosting is the process of installing an existing application in a cloud environment and mainly relying on Infrastructure as a Service (IaaS) offerings. This can be the first step in a gradual approach, enabling to perform initial analysis and to improve the application during multiple iterations.

To better benefit from the characteristics of cloud computing, e.g., making an application scalable or more reliable, re-engineering might be necessary. This can be a simple refactoring, i.e. a modification of one or a few features. An example is adding monitoring capabilities, which enable elastic behavior such as adding new resources when the application is heavily used or releasing resources when they are not needed. It might also require revising an application, i.e. making major modifications at its core; examples would be using a Platform as a Service (PaaS) database offering or changing an application into a multi-tenancy SaaS offering. To fully benefit from the cloud, it might also be necessary to rebuild an application and integrate, for example automation for scaling in and out. Driven by the increasing number of SaaS offerings, an option might be to replace an existing application with a cloud-based SaaS solution [26].

We used a combination of re-hosting and performance testing to deploy EclipseSCADA to the NeCTAR research cloud [2] (running OpenStack [27]). The steps used to carry out "lift and shift" are as follows:

1. Create and upload an Ubuntu VM image to the NeCTAR cloud.
2. Deploy the Ubuntu VM and carry out installation of EclipseSCADA.
   a. Install the EclipseSCADA dependencies (Java, Eclipse, etc.).
   b. Copy each EclipseSCADA component into the VM.
   c. Configure EclipseSCADA links by specifying the location of each sensor/switch and SCADA component.
3. Start each EclipseSCADA component.

Following these instructions each EclipseSCADA component (field device, remote server, master server, and file server) was deployed to the NeCTAR cloud as a standalone virtual machine.

Sensor and actuator simulation

EclipseSCADA was configured to use simulated Modbus/TCP devices. Modbus is one of the most commonly

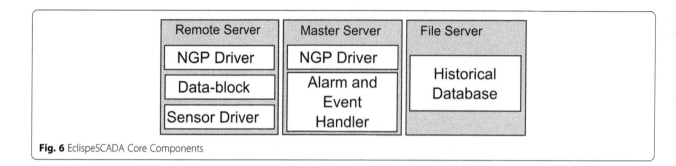

Fig. 6 EclispeSCADA Core Components

used polling protocols, with numerous simulators and libraries. While the original version of the Modbus protocol is designed for use over serial ports, the Modbus/TCP variant enables communication using the Internet Protocol Suite.

A Modbus device consists of registers that are used to hold data. Request messages are sent from the SCADA system to a Modbus device to carry out operations on registers. The Modbus device also sends response messages back to the SCADA system. A message consists of a number of fields;

- Transaction Identifier - Incrementing ID for synchronization of messages.
- Protocol Identifier - Set to 0, reserved for future extensions.
- Length Field - Remaining bytes in message.
- Unit Identifier - The register ID to carry out the operation.
- Function Code - The function to be carried out (read, write, etc.).
- Data Bytes - Data for response or commands (data which was read or to be written).

The operation of the Modbus/TCP Protocol and five sensors is illustrated in Fig. 7. The EclipseSCADA system requests data by sending a message to the connected field device. The field device retrieves the requested sensor data and sends sensor data back to the EclipseSCADA system. Sensors are polled sequentially until data from each connected sensor is retrieved by the SCADA system.

When measuring the time taken to transfer Modbus data, there are two terms that must be defined: Round Trip Time (RTT) and the Polling Interval. Round Trip Time (RTT) is the time between sending a request until receiving the respective response with the sensor data. The Polling Interval is the time between sending requests to the same sensor. The Polling Interval is configured by the user and is often implemented in the form of a timer.

Analysis of EclipseSCADA metrics

To study the real-time monitoring and control mechanism of SCADA systems when running on the cloud, an analysis of the migrated EclipseSCADA system was carried out. Metrics were collected which focus on understanding the influence of the size of a monitored environment and EclipseSCADA specific delays, the influence of the location

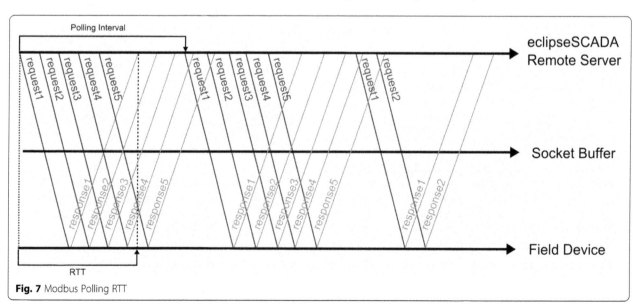

Fig. 7 Modbus Polling RTT

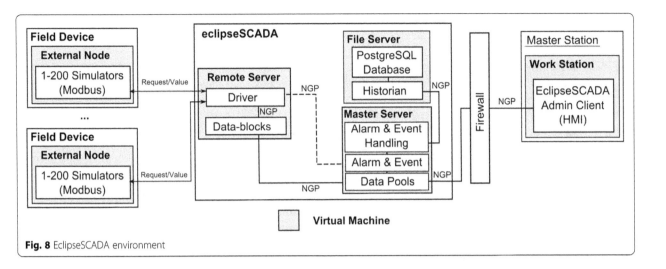

Fig. 8 EclipseSCADA environment

of EclipseSCADA components on EclipseSCADA performance, and the relationship between processing time and communication time.

Cloud and SCADA environment setup

Each EclipseSCADA component was deployed on an individual virtual machine hosted on the NeCTAR research cloud [2], which runs OpenStack (Kilo Release), configured with Neutron with Linux bridge networking. Each virtual machine (m1.medium) had 2 virtual CPUs, 8GB RAM and 60GB secondary disk. Each virtual CPU consisting of a single core running at 2.6 GHz clock speed.

Performance metrics were collected while EclipseSCADA was placed under different sensor loads (200, 400, 600 and 800). Modbus/TCP simulators were deployed on each field device to represent sensors. As each field device could only contain 200 simulated sensors (due to implementation restrictions of the used Modbus simulator), additional field devices (running on separate virtual machines) were added to the EclipseSCADA system for the 400, 600 and 800 sensor load experiments (see Fig. 8).

The EclipseSCADA system was deployed across Melbourne and Tasmania cloud regions, where simulated field devices were deployed in Tasmania, and SCADA components were deployed in Melbourne. There was an estimated distance of 429 km between these two sites. Table 4 shows the speed of the internal and external network, where the internal Melbourne network is over twice as fast as the public (Melbourne to Tasmania) network.

The study of the influence of the size of a monitored environment

In order to understand the influence the size of a monitored environment has on the performance of EclipseS-CADA, the Modbus/TCP Round Trip Time (RTT) was measured using Wireshark [28] (see Table 5). As mentioned above, simulated field devices were deployed in Tasmania, while SCADA components were deployed in Melbourne.

The numbers of simulators were varied between 1 and 800, with a polling rate of 1 millisecond. Typically SCADA systems are setup with a slower polling interval of seconds, but with thousands of sensors. A polling rate of 1 millisecond was deliberately chosen to put more load on the system, in order to adjust for the number of sensors.

Results showed that the RTT changes depending on the number of simulated sensors attached to the eclipseS-CADA system. In a rather small SCADA system consisting of a single simulator sensor, the time taken to transfer a single Modbus/TCP sensor of data is on average 11 milliseconds, where 4 milliseconds are spent sending a request and 7 milliseconds are spent sending sensor data. As the size of a monitored environment increases, i.e., more simulator sensors are added to the SCADA system, the average time to retrieve a single point of sensor data increases.

In conclusion, the majority of the RTT time is spent retrieving data from the simulator. In order to understand the cause of this behavior, experiments were

Table 4 Comparison of network speed (TCP)

Location	Download (Gbits/sec)	Upload (Gbits/sec)
Internal Melbourne Network	3.77	3.30
Melbourne to Tasmania	1.52	1.07

Table 5 Average Time to Transfer Modbus Data (ms)

# Simulated Sensors	Request	Response	Total RTT
1	4	7	11
200	4	3630	3634
400	4	5996	6000
600	4	9034	9038
800	4	13,961	13,965

carried out to investigate how the network and SCADA components interact.

The study of the influence of component location

In order to understand how the distribution of SCADA components affects network communication, "field devices" and "remote server" components were deployed across the Melbourne and Tasmania cloud regions. Modbus/ TCP Round Trip Time (RTT) was measured: between Melbourne and Tasmania (Remote Region), within the Melbourne region (Single Region), and on a single machine (Single Machine) (see Fig. 9).

Results indicate that changing how EclipseSCADA is deployed geographically has minimal overall effect on Modbus/TCP data transfer. The single machine setup eliminates the network completely, resulting in an average RTT reduction of ~0.5 seconds (when compared with the remote region setup). Likewise, EclipseSCADA running in a single region performs only slightly better with an average RTT reduction of ~0.3 seconds.

In conclusion, network transfer and delays are responsible for a small percentage of the total Modbus/TCP RTT. To further reduce RTT, it is necessary to reduce the number of sensors managed by a single remote server, or use a more efficient communication protocol. By using event-driven protocols, it is possible to remove the need for request messages.

Processing time vs. communication

Results presented in Fig. 9, show that eliminating the network (single machine) has a minimal effect on Modbus/TCP RTT. From this, it is possible to conclude that most of the observed delay when requesting data (see Table 5) is due to processing rather than network delays. Furthermore, as the time to retrieve sensor data increases with the number of monitored sensors, it is

likely that the delay is due to the implementation of the Modbus/TCP protocol sending all requests before receiving sensor data.

In conclusion, network communication can be neglected in comparison to the time spent processing. Results show that the migrated SCADA system spent more time generating and sending polling requests than storing data. For this reason, Modbus/TCP requests and responses should be managed by an event queue or on separate threads.

Distinctive features of experimentation

Sections 6.1–6.4 show a unique nature and large scale of experimentation. First, the experiments were carried out using two production clouds, the NeCTAR research clouds; each ran OpenStack. Second, the experiments were carried out across Melbourne and Tasmania cloud regions; the distance between them, 429 km, is impressive in terms of industry, business, and research applications. Third, the speed of the internal and external network, where the internal Melbourne network is over twice as fast as the public (Melbourne to Tasmania) network; such a difference creates some buffering problems. Fourth, since we wanted to carry out experiments in boundary computation and communication conditions, with a huge number of devices, it was necessary to use simulated field devices. That allowed us to run experiments with load of up to 800 sensors deployed in Tasmania (SCADA components were deployed in Melbourne). Fifth, the numbers of simulated devices were varied between 1 and 800, with a polling rate of 1 millisecond. Typically, SCADA systems are setup with a slower polling interval of seconds. A polling rate of 1 millisecond was deliberately chosen to put more load on the system. Sixth, all experiments were carried out during normal exploitation of clouds and connected them public networks; that formed normal business/industry conditions.

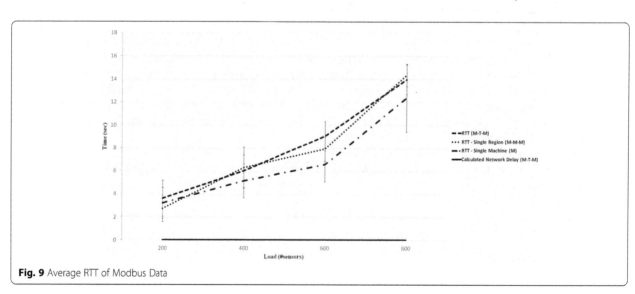

Fig. 9 Average RTT of Modbus Data

Recommendations

Based on these observations, we make the following recommendations when moving and configuring SCADA to make use of cloud resources:

- Use event-driven protocols (where a sensor informs the SCADA system on change) – Polling in general is not efficient; to retrieve a sensor value, a request message and response message must be sent; additionally as a timer is used there is a tendency for a polling based system to flood a network with repetitive sensor data. Event-driven protocols reduce the amount of data sent across a network.
- If a legacy SCADA system is used it needs to be ensured that processing of the messages does not incur excessive delays. Our results, for example, indicate that for larger system loads, network communication can be neglected in comparison to the time spent processing and storing data. When using device protocols that are built for serial devices (like Modbus), it is sometimes a design limitation of the device or protocol, that there cannot be requests in parallel. For the other cases, proper techniques, such as use of an event queue or multi-threading, need to be employed to minimize processing delays.
- When the above cannot be influenced and polling protocols with serial processing need to be used (like Modbus TCP in certain configurations), field devices should be spread across many remote servers – The amount of sensors per remote server depends on the processing and transfer time required by the SCADA system. This also means that the remote server should be able to scale horizontally. It can also be concluded that the network transmission time influences the performance, and that protocol conversion - at least for polling protocols - should be done close to the field devices.

Conclusion and future work

Monitoring and control of industrial complexes is of critical importance. Each individual complex is in the majority of cases distributed, e.g., a gas pipeline, industrial plant. Therefore, there is a need for a system that can provide services in real time and is distributed. SCADA systems are instrumental to a wide range of mission-critical industrial systems. These systems allow a user to monitor (using sensors) and control (using actuators) an industrial system remotely.

Currently, SCADA systems run on highly reliable and dedicated hardware. This is in contrast to the current state of computing, which is moving from running applications on internally hosted servers to flexible, cheaper, internal or external cloud systems. The problem is to identify factors that affect performance of cloud-based SCADA systems.

Experiments were carried out to examine the effects cloud resources and public networks have on SCADA systems. Using the "lift and shift" approach, EclipseSCADA was deployed to the NeCTAR research cloud in multiple locations. Performance metrics were collected from the deployed EclipseSCADA system under different loads.

When moving a SCADA system to cloud infrastructure, there is a need to ensure that the real-time monitoring and control demands of the industrial system can be achieved. By carrying out analysis of the EclipseSCADA system we made a series of recommendations that should be taken into consideration when migrating SCADA systems to the cloud. In general, latencies introduced by running SCADA system components in the cloud are not a limiting factor, given that response time requirements are usually in the order of several hundred milliseconds to seconds. While scalable compute power in a cloud-based system tempts to centralizing functionalities, this may lead to problems in given system designs. We have specifically discovered limitations with polling protocols processed in a serialized way. We propose in particular the adoption of event-driven communication protocols to reduce network transfer, doing protocol conversion close to the field devices, and replication of remote servers, to ensure polling intervals are met.

Adaption of event-driven protocols for cloud based SCADA systems would require the use of smart sensors that would be able to respond to requests made by the cloud. The complexity of these field devices means that simulators are not readily available. Polling protocols are based on timers transfer the same amount of data every polling interval. When working with event driven simulators, the amount of data being transferred would change depending on the registered events (which is depended on the size of the system and application). For this reason experiments with event driven protocols must include the simulation of realistic datasets, and ideally under different applications and scenarios. Future work would extend the experimental methodology to event driven protocols, which would require the collection of datasets from large scale SCADA installations and the development of simulators which would playback these datasets.

Endnote

[1]As of the 19th of November 2015, EclipseSCADA has been renamed to Eclipse NeoSCADA (https://www.eclipse.org/eclipsescada/news/2015/11/19/a_new_name__eclipse_neoscada.html).

Acknowledgments

The work presented in this paper was funded by Siemens AG, Corporate Technology, Munich.

A NeCTAR research grant, provided access to the IaaS cloud resources necessary to deploy EclipseSCADA in the cloud.

The authors are also grateful for the support of Deakin University, for providing a working environment, and wish to express their gratitude to the anonymous reviewers and Editor in Chief for their constructive comments.

Authors' contributions

PC carried out the experimental work and wrote the manuscript. AG, CR, ZR participated in study design and coordination, as well as the validation of experimental results. HM and SVG contributed to the selection of the open source SCADA system. All authors have read and approved the final manuscript.

Competing interests

The authors declare that they have no competing interests.

Author details

[1]School of Computer Science and Information Technology, GPO, RMIT University, Box 2476, Melbourne, Australia. [2]Corporate Technology, CT RDA ITP, Siemens AG, Otto-Hahn-Ring 6, 81739 Munich, Germany. [3]School of Information Technology, Deakin University, Geelong, Australia.

References

1.   A. Alharthi, Z. Tari, A. Goscinski, and I. Khalil, "PPFSCADA - Privacy Preserving Framework for SCADA Data Publishing," *Int. Journal on Future Generation Computer Systems (FGCS)*, 2014.
2.   J. Kirby. (2012). *NeCTAR - Australian Research Cloud*. Available: http://www.nectar.org.au/. Accessed 6 June 2017.
3.   Ken Barnes BJ, Nickelson R (2004) Review Of Supervisory Control And Data Acquisition (SCADA) Systems. Idaho National Engineering and Environmental Laboratory, Idaho Falls, Idaho
4.   Stuart A, Boye E (2010) SCADA: supervisory control and data acquisition, Research Triangle Park. International Society of Automation, NC
5.   IEEE Power Engineering Society, "IEEE Standard for SCADA and Automation Systems," 2008.
6.   Modicon, "Modicon Modbus Protocol Reference Guide," ed, 1996, p. 121.
7.   Real Time Automation. (2016, 21/4). *PROFIBUS Protocol Overview - Real Time Automation*. Available: http://www.rtaautomation.com/technologies/profibus/. Accessed 6 June 2017.
8.   Siemens. (2016, 21/4). *Siemens communications overview*. Available: http://snap7.sourceforge.net/siemens_comm.html. Accessed 6 June 2017.
9.   IPCOMM GmbH. (2016, 21/4). *IEC 60870–5-104*. Available: http://www.ipcomm.de/protocol/IEC104/en/sheet.html. Accessed 6 June 2017.
10. Liu M, Guo C, Yuan M (2014) The Framework of SCADA System Based on Cloud Computing. In: Leung V, Chen M. (eds) Cloud Computing. CloudComp 2013. Lecture Notes of the Institute for Computer Sciences, Social Informatics and Telecommunications Engineering, vol 133. Springer, Cham
11. Gligor A, Turc T (2012) Development of a Service Oriented SCADA System. *Procedia Economics and Finance* 3:256–261
12. S. Goose, J. Kirsch, and D. Wei, "SKYDA: cloud-based, secure SCADA-as-a-service," *International Transactions on Electrical Energy Systems*, pp. n/a-n/a, 2014.
13. Inductive Automation. (2014). *Ignition by Inductive Automation*. Available: https://www.inductiveautomation.com/scada-software/. Accessed 6 June 2017.
14. XiO. (2015). *XiO Cloud SCADA® Control System*. Available: http://www.xioio.com/wp/. Accessed 6 June 2017.
15. A. Johnson. (2014). *EPICS - Experimental Physics and Industrial Control System*. Available: http://www.aps.anl.gov/epics/index.php. Accessed 6 June 2017.
16. TANGO Consortium, "The TANGO Controls website," 2014.
17. IBH Systems GmbH. (2014). *openSCADA | We are the good guys*. Available: http://openscada.org. Accessed 6 June 2017.
18. apaatsf. (2015). *IndigoSCADA*. Available: http://sourceforge.net/projects/indigoscada/?source=navbar. Accessed 6 June 2017.
19. Siemens. (2014). *SCADA System SIMATIC WinCC*. Available: http://w3.siemens.com/mcms/human-machine-interface/en/visualization-software/scada/pages/default.aspx. Accessed 6 June 2017.
20. ETM professional control GmbH (2015) SIMATIC WinCC Open Architecture [Brochure]. Austria, 2015, p 8
21. CoderGears. (2015). *CppDepend: : C/C++ Static Analysis and Code Quality tool*. Available: http://www.cppdepend.com/. Accessed 6 June 2017.
22. sauerf. (2015). *Eclipse Metrics plugin*. Available: http://metrics.sourceforge.net/. Accessed 6 June 2017.
23. OSGi™ Alliance. (2015). *The OSGi Architecture*. Available: https://www.osgi.org/developer/architecture/. Accessed 6 June 2017.
24. J. Reimann. (2013, 22 Jan). *openSCADA Protocol Description*. Available: http://download.openscada.org/documentation/l/1.2.0/html/protocol/. Accessed 6 June 2017.
25. Gartner. (2011). *Gartner Identifies Five Ways to Migrate Applications to the Cloud*. Available: http://www.gartner.com/newsroom/id/1684114. Accessed 6 June 2017.
26. Philip Church, Harald Mueller, Caspar Ryan, Spyridon V. Gogouvitis, Andrzej Goscinski, Houssam Haitof, et al., (2017) "SCADA systems in the Cloud," in Handbook of Big Data Technologies, ed: A.Y. Zomaya and S. Sakr, Springer, Cham, pp. 691–718
27. OpenStack Project. (2012). *OpenStack - Open source software for building private and public clouds*. Available: http://www.openstack.org/. Accessed 6 June 2017.
28. Wireshark Foundation. (2015). *Wireshark - Go Deep*. Available: https://www.wireshark.org/

9

Multi-objective dynamic management of virtual machines in cloud environments

Mahdi Mollamotalebi* (iD) and Shahnaz Hajireza

Abstract

The management strategy of a data center needs access to sufficient resources in order to handle different requests of applications, while minimizing the consumed energy. With regard to high and varying resource demands, Virtual Machines (VM) management necessitates dynamic strategies. Dynamic management of VMs includes VM placement and VM migration. The management approach presented in this paper aimed to reduce the energy consumption and the violation of service level agreements (SLA) simultaneously in data centers. The simulation results indicate that proposed approach improved the VM management 40% compared to the previous single-goal approaches based on the energy consumption and SLA violation rates.

Keywords: Cloud computing, Dynamic management, Energy consumption, SLA violation, Virtual machine placement

Introduction

Nowadays, computing tends to handle large-scale data centers and provides the resources for client applications as pay-per-use. The data center managers attempt to reduce the consumed energy while providing the required resources to user applications.

The resource allocation can be handled statically by assigning the peak number of required resources to the application. However, such allocation may lead to over-provisioning [1], which results in wasting of data centers' resources. Virtualization technology enables a physical machine to host multiple virtual machines. Each virtual machine can handle different client applications. Even if the peak amount of demanded resources is allocated to the application, still some resources of physical machine may be underutilized. Resource utilization can be improved by allocating only necessary resources to handle the typical demands. However, this may result in resource access competition between VMs in high demand conditions.

The applications with high and variable requirements necessitate frequent changes in their VMs [2] and dynamic management. By such manner of management, a running VM is migrated to another physical host (live migration). In a typical VM management solution, there are following operations as coordinated: (1) VM Placement (Allocation): the placement of a VM to a host machine in response to a VM creation request; (2) VM Relocation: the migration of VMs from a host when their overall resource requirements exceed the available resources of host; and (3) VM Consolidation: the migration of VMs from an under-utilized host so that the machine powers off in order to reduce the costs.

This paper focuses on two important issues in dynamic management of virtual machines: SLA violations reduction, and energy consumption reduction. These issues are often in contrast because reducing the energy consumption is usually reached through in-use (powered on) host reduction. But this leads potentially to more SLA violations. This is because that lower energy consumption can be achieved by placing as many VMs as possible on each host. However, sudden increasing of workload on a host may result lack of resources and subsequently SLA violations. Conversely, reducing the SLA violations typically necessitates VMs to be spread across more number of hosts, often each having a significant amount of unused resources. This manner potentially leads to more energy consumption. Designing a management strategy able to achieve both of the above

* Correspondence: mmahdi2@live.utm.my
Department of Computer, Buinzahra Branch, Islamic Azad University, Buinzahra, Iran

goals is difficult, as getting better performance considering one of the goals typically leads to degradation of performance towards the other goal. The management approaches often focus on a single goal, or prioritize the goals as a primary goal and some secondary goals [1, 3, 4, 5].

This paper proposes two single-goal approaches, Energy-Reduction to reduce the energy consumption and SLAV-Reduction to reduce the SLA violation rates. It then presents a double-goal approach, ESDR, achieving the above two goals simultaneously. The remainder of this paper is organized as follows: Related work section reviews the related work of VM Placement, VM Relocation, and VM Consolidation. The details of proposed approaches are described in The proposed management approaches section. Implementation and evaluation section presents and discusses the simulation results of the proposed approaches, and Conclusion and future work section concludes the paper.

Related work

The efficient allocation of VM to host machines while ensuring sufficient access to computing resources for applications (a requirement of quality of service), has been the subject of much attention in recent years. The reviewed approaches in literature are categorized as *static* and *dynamic* allocation. In static allocation, VMs' service requests are issued as fixed, or they are variable but a one-time mapping of some VMs into empty hosts is performed.

Cardosa et al. [6] developed a VM placement algorithm that leveraged the CPU allocation features min, max, and shares which are presented in modern hypervisors. The algorithm aimed to make balance between VMs' performance and overall energy consumption. Four techniques were provided for VM placement exploiting the inherent features of virtualization technology (Max, Min, and Share). Setting a min metric for a VM ensures that it receives at least the specified minimum amount of resources when it powered on. Also, setting a max metric for low-priority applications ensures no overflowed resource usage and keeping the resources available for high-priority applications. The metric Share enables distributing the resources between contending VMs. Lack of continuous optimization of data center during the live migration of virtual machines can be mentioned as the weakness of this algorithm.

Speitkamp and Bichler [7] proposed a static server consolidation approach that analyses the data mathematically to characterize variations of real-world workload traces. Linear programming was used for optimal mapping of VMs and host machines; however, the approach was not easily adaptable to changes of data centers' workloads.

Stillwell et al. [8] worked on mapping a set of static workloads into hosts to optimize the VMs' resource allocation in terms of fairness. They analyzed different algorithms, and indicated that a vector (or multi-dimensional) bin packing algorithm [9, 10, 11] is able to reach almost optimal result for the problem.

Bobroff et al. [1] presented the First Fit Decreasing heuristic algorithm that periodically re-calculates mapping of VMs to a set of empty hosts, based on forecasts of VMs' demands. The aim was to keep average number of active hosts as minimum while having probabilistic SLA guaranty for VMs. But the relationship between several resources such as CPU and I/O are not considered in the algorithm. It acts as static while considering variable demands to re-calculate VMs mapping periodically.

Khanna et al. [3] showed that the number of servers can be reduced in VM relocation using virtualization technology. VMs and hosts can be selected for migration by developing a mathematical optimization model. They presented a heuristic method that sorts the VMs as ascending on CPU and memory utilization to minimize the migration costs. Then hosts list is sorted as ascending on remaining capacity (i.e. available resources) to maximize resource utilization. After that, the least loaded VMs (in terms of CPU and memory usage) are migrated to the highest loaded hosts. The First Fit heuristic is used as selection algorithm with the primary goal of energy consumption reduction. The authors considered neither additional sorting strategies, nor the impact of their heuristic on the number of migrations issued.

Verma et al. [5] relied on a First Fit Decreasing heuristic that to place VMs in the most power efficient servers. The main goal was reducing the migration costs and energy consumption in data centers while meeting the QoS requirements; despite no reduction in SLA violations. The presented system is able to work in a heterogeneous environment that supports virtualization, and VMs are allocated to a physical machine in terms of consumed energy.

Wood et al. [7] presented a management system named *Sandpiper* using the First Fit Decreasing heuristic [12, 13, 14]. The hosts are sorted in an increasing order based on resource utilization, the workload is balanced among the hosts, and SLA violations are reduced subsequently. Also, monitoring and detection of hotspot servers are performed automatically.

Moreover, a new mapping to physical and virtual resources is applied and essential migration in virtualized data centers is set up.

Gmach et al. [15] developed a fuzzy logic based controller as part of their proposed management system. The controller does not distribute migrations when a host became stressed or underutilized. The appropriate host for migration is the least loaded one with enough resources to fit the VM. However, VM selection for migration is not clearly explained.

Keller et al. [16] studied variants of the First Fit heuristic to address the VM relocation problem. They showed that the order of VMs/hosts migration affects the performance metrics of data centers, such as energy consumption and SLA violations.

Beloglazov and Buyya [17] proposed Best Fit Decreasing heuristic algorithm to deal with both stressed and underutilized hosts. In the case of stressed hosts, the algorithm selects VMs with the least memory allocation to migrate, and selects as much VMs as needed in order to reduce hosts' CPU utilization to a specified value. When hosts are underutilized, all hosts' VMs are selected for migration. The selection of target host is based on a Best Fit Decreasing heuristic. The migrating VMs are sorted as descending on CPU utilization. They are then placed on the appropriate host having minimum energy consumptions.

In [18], Foster et al. attempt to switch between two single goal (minimizing SLA violations or energy consumption) strategies dynamically. They aimed to get better adaption of changing data center conditions. They proposed three strategies to handle dynamic switching between different strategies; however their situation identification process to handle the replacements is time consuming.

Zhen Xiao et al. [19] presented a system that uses virtualization technology to allocate datacenter resources dynamically based on application demands. The system is adapted to green computing by optimizing the number of servers in use. They introduced *skewness* as a metric to measure unevenness for multi-dimensional resource utilization of a server. By minimizing the skewness, different types of workloads are combined. Also, overall utilization of server resources is improved. In overall, the system is able to prevent overloads effectively while saving the energy.

Ferdaus et al. [20] addressed the resource and energy related issues in datacenters by tackling through datacenter level resource management. They focused on high resource wastage and energy consumption. To this aim, they proposed a method using the Ant Colony Optimization (ACO) metaheuristic and a vector algebra-based multi-dimensional resource utilization model. Optimizing network resource utilization is handled by an online network-aware VM cluster placement strategy to localize data traffic among VMs communication. By this manner, traffic load in data center interconnects and subsequently communication overhead in upper layer network switches are reduced.

With regard to the above review of literature, allocation of VMs to physical machines while keeping the access to computing resources as efficient is handled by many of recent researches. The provided allocation approaches are categorized as *static* and *dynamic*. Most of the algorithms aimed to make balance between VMs' performance and overall energy consumption. They try to allocate the minimum amount of resources to low-priority applications and keep the resources available for high-priority ones. With regard to the dynamic nature of cloud environments, some approaches recalculate mapping of VMs to a set of empty hosts periodically based on VMs' demand forecasts. Such approaches are able to minimize the number of active hosts while keeping SLA for VMs in a reasonable level. Choosing VMs and hosts for migration can be performed by a mathematical optimization model. Also, heuristic methods are used to sort VMs based on CPU/memory utilization in order to minimize the migrations and reduce the consumed energy.

The dynamic behavior of cloud environment necessitates having a dynamic and adapted strategy to switch between SLA violation and energy consumption dynamically in VM migrations. Most of the existing algorithms have focused on one aspect of efficiency. This paper provides three dynamic approaches (first one to reduce the energy consumption, the second one to reduce SLA violations, and third one to handle both of energy and SLA violations simultaneously) to manage the virtual machines in data centers. With regard to changes of data center's state, the provided double-goal approach switches between different policies at run-time if it is necessary. SLA violation and power efficiency are measured in order to decide for activate the appropriate approach.

The proposed management approaches

With regard to the dynamic nature of virtualized data centers, designing a management system with different goals is a challenging task. In this section, three dynamic approaches are proposed to manage the virtual machines in data centers. In the following, first the terms and metrics of management approaches are introduced. Then, two single-goal approaches (one to reduce the energy consumption, and another to reduce SLA violations) are proposed. After that, a double-goal approach is proposed achieving the above two goals simultaneously.

i) The status *SLA violation* occurs when resources required by a VM are not available. This status subsequently leads to performance degradation. It is typically defined by the percentage of a VM's required CPU time which is not available currently. ii) The *overall utilization* of a data center is the percentage of CPU capacity that is currently in use by data center. Iii) A limited capacity of CPU's processing capabilities is specified as *CPU_Shares*. In our work, the CPU_Shares assigned to each core, is related to its frequency. For example, the CPU_Shares for a 1GHZ CPU is assigned to 1000. iv) For a host h, the *power efficiency*, per_h, refers to in-use processing per consumed energy, and it is measured by CPU-shares-per-watt (CPU/W). The power efficiency of a single host is calculated by Eq. 1:

$$per_h = \frac{\Phi_h}{\Psi_h} \qquad (1)$$

Where Φ_h is the number of CPU_Shares currently is in-use across all cores in the host, and Ψ_h refers to current power consumption of the host in watts. Moreover, an active host consumes a significant amount of power even if it has little or no CPU load (i.e., very low power efficiency). Equation 2 calculates the power efficiency for the entire data center, per_{dc}:

$$per_{dc} = \frac{\Sigma_{h \in hosts}\Phi_h}{\Sigma_{h \in hosts}\Psi_h} \qquad (2)$$

Such that *hosts* indicates a collection of all hosts in data center. v) *Maximum Power Efficiency* represents the best amount of power efficiency a host can achieve. It is calculated as power efficiency of the host at maximum CPU utilization. vi) *HostUtilization* refers to the average amount of CPU utilization for all hosts in the state "On". The higher value of host utilization leads to more efficient usage of resources and energy consumption reduction.

This paper supposes that each time a management operation takes place, hosts are classified to three different power states: *power on, power suspended, and power off*. The powered on hosts are further classified to *stressed, partially-utilized, under-utilized,* and *empty* based on their CPU utilization. The state of hosts may be changed according to workload changes of hosted VMs, or migrations performed by management operations. To do this, two threshold values are used as $stress_{cpu}$ and min_{cpu}. The classification is carried out based on average CPU utilization of hosts. Hosts with average CPU utilization ranged in ($stress_{cpu}$, 1], (min_{cpu}, $stress_{cpu}$], and

[0, min_{cpu}) are supposed as stressed, partially-utilized, and under-utilized hosts respectively. Moreover, hosts with no assigned VMs are empty ones; hosts in suspended or power off state are also included in this category.

Energy-reduction and SLAV-reduction approaches

Energy-Reduction and SLAV-Reduction are two single-goal candidates. In the next subsections, the process of VM Placement, VM Relocation and VM Consolidation policies that form the above approaches are explained. The placement management operation runs each time a new VM creation request is received, and selects a host in which to instantiate the VM. Algorithm 1 shows the process of virtual machine placement policy for the proposed Energy-Reduction approach.

Algorithm 1 VM Placement process for Energy-Reduction approach

Data: H,VM

1: $H^!, H^+, H^-, H^\phi \leftarrow classify(H)$
2: $targets \leftarrow combine(sort(H^+), sort(H^-), sort(H^\phi))$
3: **for** $h_t \in targets$ **do**
4:     **if** has_capacity(h_t, VM) **then**
5:         place (VM, h_t)
6:         break
7: **end**

The VM Placement policy for Energy-Reduction approach (see Algorithm 1), first classifies *hosts* in appropriate categories (line 1) as stressed ($H^!$), partially-utilized (H^+), under-utilized (H^-) or empty (H^ϕ). Each host category is then sorted (lines 2). H^+, and H^- are sorted as descending on maximum power efficiency and CPU utilization respectively. The category H^ϕ is also sorted as descending on maximum power efficiency and power state respectively. Such sorting ensures focus of placement on power efficiency. Then a list of *targets* hosts is prepared by concatenating *(sort (H^+), sort (H^-), sort (H^ϕ))*. Finally, following a First Fit approach, the policy assigns VM to the first host in *targets* with enough capacity (lines 3-6). The method *has_capacity (h_t, VM)* checks the ability of host to meet resource requirements indicated in the VM creation request (line 4) without becoming stressed.

The VM Placement policy for SLAV-Reduction approach differs from the Energy-Reduction policy in the way that H^+ and H^- are sorted. H^+ and H^- are sorted as ascending and descending respectively on CPU utilization and then maximum power efficiency. Such sorting causes the placement to be focused on distributing the load across the hosts, and leaving spare resources to handle spikes in resource demand over other considerations.

The VM relocation operation runs frequently over short intervals of time in order to detect stress situations as soon as possible. For both approaches, the interval is set to 10 min. The VM relocation determines which hosts are prone to be in a stress situation. Then it removes such hosts by migrating one VM from a stressed host into a non-stressed one. Algorithm 2 shows the process of virtual machine relocation policy for the proposed approach Energy-Reduction.

Algorithm 2 VM Relocation process for Energy-Reduction approach

Data: H

1: $H^{!}, H^{+}, H^{-}, H^{\phi} \leftarrow classify(H)$

2: $sources \leftarrow sort(H^{!})$

3: $targets \leftarrow combine(sort(H^{+}), sort(H^{-}), sort(H^{\phi}))$

4: **for** $h \in sources$ **do**

5:     $success \leftarrow FALSE$

6:     VM-$candidates \leftarrow sort(Vm_h)$

7:     $i = 1$

8:     **for** $v_i \in VM$-$candidates$ **do**

9:         **for** $h_t \in targets$ **do**

10:             **if** $has\_capacity(h_t, VM)$ **then**

11:                 $migrate(h, v_i, h_t)$

12:                 $i = i+1$

13:                 $success \leftarrow TRUE$

14:                 break

15:         **if** $success$ **then break**

16: end

As shown in Algorithm 2, the VM Relocation policy for Energy-Reduction approach first classifies *hosts* to appropriate categories (line 1) performing a *stress check* on all hosts. A host is stressed if its CPU utilization has remained above the $stress_{cpu}$ threshold throughout the last CPU load monitoring window. The hosts are categorized as stressed ($H^{!}$), partially-utilized (H^{+}), under-utilized (H^{-}), or empty (H^{ϕ}). Then each host category is sorted (line 3). $H^{!}$ is sorted as descending on CPU utilization, H^{+} and H^{-} are sorted as descending on maximum power efficiency and CPU utilization respectively. H^{ϕ} is sorted as descending on maximum power efficiency and power state respectively. After that, a list of *targets* hosts is formed by concatenating *(sort (H^{+}), sort (H^{-}), sort (H^{ϕ}))*. Following the First Fit heuristic, one VM is chosen from each host h in *sources* and a corresponding *host* in *targets* to which one to migrate VM (lines 4-13). For each host h in *sources* (which is stressed), VMs with less CPU load are filtered. The remaining VMs then are sorted as

ascending on CPU load (line 6). After that, all VMs are sorted as descending on CPU load, and finally the migration process is launched (line 10).

VM Relocation policy for SLAV-Reduction approach differs from Energy-Reduction in the way of sorting $H^{!}$ and H^{-} ($H^{!}$ is sorted as ascending on CPU utilization and maximum Energy-Reduction efficiency respectively. H^{+} is sorted as descending on CPU utilization and maximum power efficiency respectively). In addition, SLAV-Reduction policy performs a different stress check such that a host is considered as stressed if its last two monitored CPU load values are more than $stress_{cpu}$ threshold, or its average CPU utilization throughout the last CPU load monitoring window exceeds $stress_{cpu}$.

The purpose of VM consolidation policy is to control the load that VM Placement and VM Relocation have distributed across the data center. This is performed by migrating VMs from under-utilized hosts (through suspending or powering them off) to partially-utilized ones. This management operation runs less frequently than VM Relocation. The interval is set to 1 and 4 h for Energy-Reduction and SLAV-Reduction strategies respectively. Algorithm 3 shows the steps of virtual machine consolidation process for the proposed approach Energy-Reduction.

Algorithm 3 VM Consolidation process for Energy-Reduction approach

Data: H

1: $H^{!}, H^{+}, H^{-}, H^{\phi} \leftarrow classify(H)$

2: $:sources \leftarrow sort(H^{-})$

3: $targets \leftarrow combine(sort(H^{+}), sort(H^{-}))$

4: $usedTargets \leftarrow \emptyset$

5: $usedSources \leftarrow \emptyset$

6: **for** $h \in sources$ **do**

7: **if** $h \in usedTargets$ **then** continue

8: **for** $v \in VM_h$ **do**

9:     **for** $h_t \in targets$ **do**

10:         **if** $hasCapacity(h_t, v)$ **&** $\wedge h_t \neq h$ **&** $\wedge h_t \notin usedSources$ **then**

11:             $usedTargets \leftarrow usedTargets \cup h_t$

12:             $usedSources \leftarrow usedSources \cup h$

13:             $migrate(h, v, h_t)$

14:             breake

15: **end**

As shown in Algorithm 3, the VM consolidation policy for Energy-Reduction approach first classifies *hosts* (line 1) as stressed ($H^{!}$), partially-utilized (H^{+}), underutilized (H^{-}), and power off (H^{ϕ}). Host machines in Power-off state are grouped as Empty. The policy then sorts H^{+} and H^{-} as descending on power efficiency and CPU utilization respectively, and

Table 1 The characteristics of used workload patterns

The workload pattern	Description	Monitoring time period (sec)	Measurement time period (sec)
ClarkNet	Based on the Log file prepared from the access to ClarkNet during two weeks	1,209,400	100
EPA	The file prepared from web Log based on EPA during one day	86,200	100
SDSC	The file prepared from Log center of Santiago supercomputers during one day	86,200	100
Google cluster data	Tracking 7 h the workload of Google cluster with different jobs	22,200	300

creates new lists. Then it forms a list of *targets* hosts by concatenating *sort (H⁺)*, *sort (H⁻)* (line 3). Afterwards, H^- is sorted again this time as ascending on power efficiency and CPU utilization respectively. Using a First Fit heuristic, the policy attempts to release all hosts *h* in *sources* by migration of their VMs to *hosts* in *targets* (lines 6-14). For each host *h* in *sources*, the policy sorts its VMs as descending on overall resource capacity (memory, number of CPU cores, and core capacity) and CPU load respectively. It is necessary to avoid using a host both as source and target for migrations.

The VM Consolidation policy for SLAV-Reduction approach differs from Energy-Reduction in the way that H^+ and H^- are sorted such that first, H^+ is sorted as ascending on CPU utilization and maximum power efficiency respectively. Also, H^- is sorted as descending on CPU utilization and maximum power efficiency respectively. Then, H^- is sorted as ascending on CPU utilization to form the source host machines.

The approaches use different values for $stress_{cpu}$ threshold: Energy-Reduction uses 95% and SLAV-Reduction uses 85%. The lower threshold for the SLAV-Reduction approach allows additional resources to be available for workload variations. Both strategies use the min_{cpu} threshold of 60%. Selected

values for the above thresholds have been obtained experimentally and based on the average CPU utilization of host machines. The characteristics of workload patterns are shown in Table 1.

Energy-reduction and SLAV-reduction dynamic run-time replacement (ESDR)

ESDR attempts to meet two objectives simultaneously. With regard to changes of data center's state, ESDR switches between different policies at run-time if it is necessary. It checks data center metrics monitored during different executions in order to determine if current in-use approach (*ActiveApproach*) needs changes. It uses SLA violation and power efficiency ratio metrics to evaluate whether the active approach should be switched. The power efficiency ratio is calculated as the ratio of optimal power efficiency to current power efficiency [21]. The switching approach is triggered when the metric's value related to the goal of the active approach (i.e. sla^v for the SLA violation, *per* for the Power efficiency ratio) is less than the threshold value (sla^v_{normal} or per_{normal}), while the metric related to inactive approach exceeds the threshold value. Algorithm 4 shows the steps used to change active approach in ESDR.

Algorithm 4 Conditions to change the active approach in ESDR

Data: ActiveApproach, per, sla^v

1: *if* $per < per_{normal}$ & $sla^v < sla^v_{normal}$ *then* state ← *Energy*
2: *if* $sla^v >= sla^v_{normal}$ *then*   state ← *SLAV*
3: *if ActiveApproach == Energy_Approach & state == SLAV then*
4:        *Using SLAV_Approach*
5: *else if ActiveApproach == SLAV_Approach & state == Energy then*
6:        *Using Energy_Approach*
7: *end*

The switching used in ESDR allows the data center to respond to a situation in which performance in one metric has deteriorated. Table 2 shows the default value of ESDR's parameters.

As shown in Table 2, choosing the best running interval as well threshold values (sla^v_{normal} |per_{normal}) is performed based on the results of Energy-Reduction and SLAV-Reduction experiments. The default values are

Table 2 Default values of ESDR's parameters

Parameter	Normal Value	Description	Calculation method
per_{normal}	71.817	Normal value for power efficiency threshold	The average value of energy efficiency in both Energy-Reduction and SLAV-Reduction approaches
sla^v_{normal}	1.644	Normal value for SLA violations threshold	The average value of SLA violation in both Energy-Reduction and SLAV-Reduction approaches
Interval Running Approach	1 h	Time interval for running ESDR approach	—

Table 3 The features of hosts used in data centers

Hosts	Number of CPUs	Number of cores	Min CPU share	Max CPU share	Power consumption at 100% efficiency	Maximum power efficiency	Memory capacity
Large	2	4	2500	20,000	W233	85.84	GB16
Small	2	2	3000	12,000	W258	46.51	GB8

obtained after 12 iterations of Energy-Reduction and SLAV-Reduction process with 5 randomly generated workload patterns. The average of 30% least values of consumed energy and SLA violations are considered as the default values.

Implementation and evaluation

In order to evaluate the performance of proposed algorithms, they are implemented in DCSim [22] simulation environment which is found as a common and efficient simulation tool in the literature. Two metrics, power efficiency (*per*) and SLA violation (sla^v), are considered to evaluate the performance. Making decision only based on the above metrics is difficult because if one approach performs well with respect to SLA violations at the expense of high power (and vice versa), it is hardly possible to conclude about the preferable approach [18, 23]. The decision depends on relative changes in each area as well as the importance assigned to each metric by data center operators according to their business objectives, and costs of energy and SLA violations.

To measure the performance of proposed double-goal approach, an experiment is planned such that the Energy-Reduction and SLAV-Reduction approaches are used as benchmarks. SLAV-Reduction approach provides the bounds for the best SLA violation ($sla^v_{best} = sla^v_{SLAV\text{-}Reduction}$) and the worst power efficiency ($per_{worst} = per_{SLAV\text{-}Reduction}$). The Energy-Reduction approach provides the bounds for worst SLA violation ($sla^v_{worst} = sla^v_{Energy\text{-}Reduction}$) and best power efficiency ($per_{best} = per_{Energy\text{-}Reduction}$). The values for selected approach i (Energy-Reduction, SLAV-Reduction or ESDR), are then used to create the normalized vector v_i, represented as [per_{norm}, sla_{norm}]. The values of sla^v_{norm} and per_{norm} are calculated through the following equations [18]:

$$sla^v_{norm} = \frac{sla^v_i - sla^v_{best}}{sla^v_{worst} - sla^v_{best}} \quad (3)$$

$$per_{norm} = \frac{per_{best} - per_i}{per_{best} - per_{worst}} \quad (4)$$

$$v_i = (per_{norm}, sla^v_{norm}) \quad (5)$$

per_{norm} and sla^v_{norm} indicate normalized power efficiency and normalized SLA violation respectively. It is noteworthy that $per_{best} > per_{worst}$, but $sla^v_{best} < sla^v_{worst}$. By having the normalized vector v_i, it is possible to calculate L^2-*norm* and use it as an overall score ($Score_i$).

$$Score_i = |vi| = \sqrt{sla^v_{norm}{}^2 = + per_{norm}{}^2} \quad (6)$$

Equation 6 calculates the score of selected approach i. Lower value for the score is considered as the better one, as it is construed as a smaller distance to the *best* bounds of each metric (defined by sla^v_{best} and per_{best}). The Energy-Reduction and SLAV-Reduction approaches always achieve the score 1, as each one achieves the *best* score for one metric and the *worst* score for the other one. Scores less than 1 indicate that overall performance of the candidate approach has improved relative to the baseline approaches. Different workload patterns of data center are considered, and the average amount of all tests' score is calculated to be used in comparisons.

Experimental setup for evaluation

In order to evaluate the proposed approaches, they are simulated along with similar latest ones using DCSim [22] that is an extensible simulator able to model the multi-tenant virtualized data centers efficiently. Also, DCSim includes virtualization features such as CPU scheduling used in modern Hypervisors, resource allocation and virtual machine migrations. Moreover, it is able to model a continuous and interactive workload that is necessary in experiments.

The simulated data center consists of 200 host machines of two types (*small* and *large*). The *small* hosts are considered as HPProLiant DL380G5, with 2 dual-core 3 GHz CPUs and 8 GB of memory. The *large* hosts are considered as HP ProLiantDL160G5, with 2 quad-core 2.5 GHz CPUs and 16 GB of

Table 4 Properties of virtual machines in the data center

Type of VMs	Number of virtual cores	Min CPUShare	Memory capacity
Small	1	1500	512 MB
Medium	1	2500	512 MB
Large	2	2500	1 GB

Table 5 The best values of ESDR parameters

Parameter	Value	Description
per_{normal}	71.817	Normal value of power efficiency threshold
sla_{normal}^v	1.644	Normal value of SLA Violation threshold

memory. Table 3 shows detailed features of the above mentioned hosts used in performed experiments.

The power consumption of both hosts is calculated by SPECPower benchmark [24] and results indicate that maximum power efficiency of *large* hosts (85.84 CPU/W) doubles the *small* host ones' (46.51 CPU/W). Three different sizes are considered for virtual machines in simulated data center as shown in Table 4.

The hosts are able to use a work-conserving CPU scheduler which is available in virtualization technology. This means that each shared CPU that is not used by a VM can be used by other ones. For CPU contention, the shares are assigned to VMs as round-robin until all the shares be allocated. The metrics used by management policies (e.g. host CPU utilization and SLA violation) are measured every 2 min from each host, and evaluated by the policy over a sliding window of 5 measurements.

Workload pattern

Data centers experience a highly dynamic workload, driven by frequent VMs' arrivals/departures, as well as resource requirements of VMs. In this paper, to evaluate the proposed approach, random workload patterns are generated each one having a set of VMs. The VMs are assigned a specific start/stop time and a dynamic trace-driven resource requirement. Each VM is driven by one of the individual traces (*ClarkNet*, *EPA*, and *SDSC* [25]), and two different job types from the *Google Cluster Data* trace [26]. For each workload pattern, incing requests are calculated with 100 s interval. The requests rate is used to define current workload of each VM. The CPU requirement of each VM is calculated through a linear function of current input rate. Each VM starts its trace with a random selected offset time.

The number of VMs in data centers varies during simulation process frequently to form dynamicity of the environment. Within first 40 h of activity, 600 VMs are

created and remain as running throughout simulation period in order to keep at least a low level of loads existing. After 2 days of simulation, the rate of new arrival VMs begins to change, and it stops changing after about 1 day. The arrivals are generated as one per day. The total number of VMs in data center is set by a random generated number with normal distribution between the values of 600 and 1600. The reason to choose value 1600 for maximum number of VMs is that beyond this value, the SLAV-Reduction denies admission of some incoming VMs due to insufficient available resources. The simulation continues for 10 days and then the experiment finishes.

Evaluation of per_{normal} and sla_{normal}^v in ESDR

Switching between two approaches Energy-Reduction and SLAV-Reduction in ESDR occurs when the metrics related to the goal of active approach (sla^v for SLA violations or per for power efficiency) is within the normal/acceptable range considering the threshold values (sla_{normal}^v or per_{normal}). But the metrics of non-active approach exceeds its normal/acceptable threshold value. ESDR uses $\{sla_{normal}^v | per_{normal}\}$ threshold values. These values are derived from the experiments performed on different workload patterns for Energy-Reduction and SLAV-Reduction approaches. Table 5 shows the best values of above mentioned parameters.

Discussion and evaluation of the experimental results

The experiments with the same workload patterns are repeated five times for each proposed approach and the average values of results are obtained. Table 6 shows the results of five different workload patterns for each approach.

The columns of Tables 6 are evaluation metrics introduced in Section III-I. The results show measured values of different metrics as well the reported normal values of Energy-Reduction and SLAV-Reduction.

As shown in Fig. 1, the highest and lowest host utilization values result from Energy-Reduction and SLAV-Reduction approaches respectively.

Given that the Energy-Reduction and SLAV-Reduction approaches use different values for $stress_{cpu}$ threshold (95% in Energy-Reduction approach, and 85% in SLAV-Reduction approach), lower threshold allows SLAV-Reduction approach access to more resources while

Table 6 The results of 5 workload patterns for each approach

Approach	Host Unit	Power (KWH)	PwrEff (CPU/W)	SLA	Migration	sla_{normal}^v	per_{normal}	Score
SLAV-Reduction	83.505	4531.190	68.811	1.403	57,459	0	1	1
Energy-Reduction	84.686	4094.201	74.695	2.087	37,863	1	0	1
ESDR	84.583	4404.442	70.712	1.476	50,417	0.307	0.514	0.599

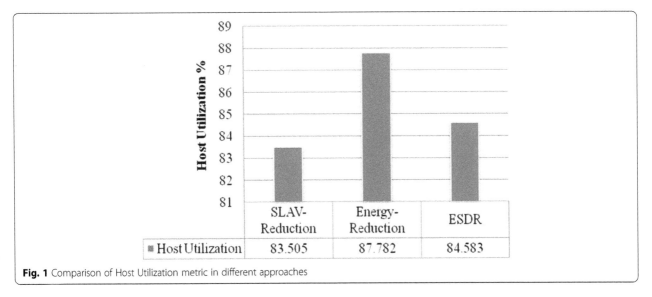

Fig. 1 Comparison of Host Utilization metric in different approaches

workload changes. This subsequently leads to low utilization of the active host. Figure 2 and Fig. 3 compare the metrics power consumption and power efficiency for different approaches.

With regard to primary goal of SLAV-Reduction and Energy-Reduction approaches which are reducing SLA violations and increasing energy efficiency respectively, SLAV-Reduction approach consumes the highest amount of power (its power efficiency is low) and Energy-Reduction approach acts as contrary. Figure 4 compares the SLA violations of three proposed approaches.

Corresponding to power consumption results, Fig. 4 shows that SLAV-Reduction approach has the lowest amount of SLA violations while Energy-Reduction approach suffers from highest amounts of violations. The

number of migrations for different approaches is compared in Fig. 5.

The results indicate that SLAV-Reduction approach caused by the highest number of virtual machine migrations while Energy-Reduction approach gained the least ones. SLAV-Reduction approach attempts to reduce the SLA violations through migration strategies, and thus the resource requests of VMs rarely fail. On the other hand, Energy-Reduction approach avoids migrations as much as possible in order to increase the hosts' utilization.

The migration overhead and its effects on SLA violation and host utilization are also investigated. Switching between Energy-Reduction and SLAV-Reduction approaches with different stress thresholds increases the migrations from ESDR to Energy-

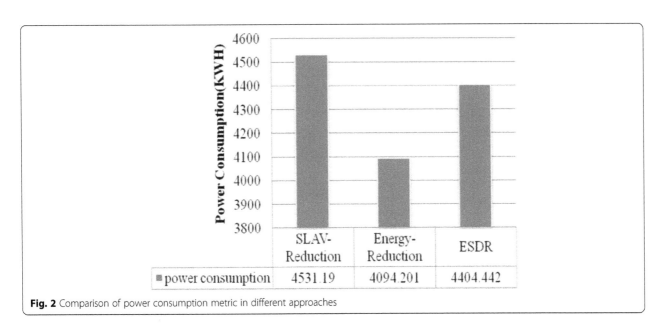

Fig. 2 Comparison of power consumption metric in different approaches

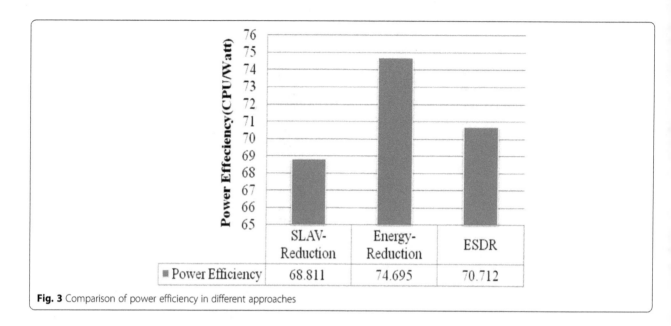

Fig. 3 Comparison of power efficiency in different approaches

Reduction as a side-effect. The value of stressed threshold varies in different approaches. The Energy-Reduction approach uses a large number of hosts efficiently while considering the stress threshold. It switches to SLAV-Reduction approach close the stress threshold, causing a large number of hosts become stressed and migrations increasing.

In order to evaluate the success rate of ESDR approach considering both goals (SLA violation reduction and power efficiency), a new metric is introduced named as score (see Eq. 6). The values obtained for score of different approaches are compared in Fig. 6.

As shown in Fig. 6, double-goal ESDR approach has achieved fewer score compared to single-goal SLAV-Reduction and Energy-Reduction approaches. This means difference reduction for best values of SLA violation and power efficiency. The graphical representation vectors of score can be also useful to show and analyze the results. L2-Norm (Euclidean) vector representation in two-dimensional space is as the unit circle which is shown in Fig. 7.

Both Energy-Reduction and SLAV-Reduction approaches that have been selected as benchmark, gained the score 1. The smaller radius of the circle gets better results because it means that the shorter distance is created for the best values of SLA violation and power efficiency. As shown in Fig. 7, ESDR has gained better score than other single-goal approaches, Energy-Reduction and SLAV-Reduction.

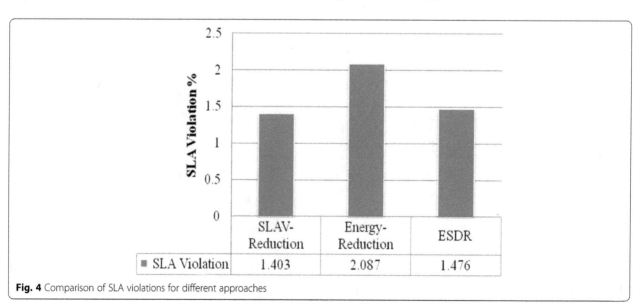

Fig. 4 Comparison of SLA violations for different approaches

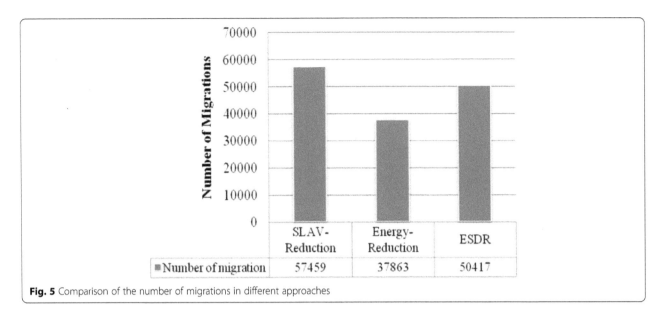

Fig. 5 Comparison of the number of migrations in different approaches

The ESDR improved the score about 40% compared to Energy-Reduction and SLAV-Reduction. This is due to regular calculations of SLA violations and power efficiencies at specified intervals and then, comparing them with per_{normal} and sla^v_{normal} parameters.

Conclusion and future work

This paper aimed to manage virtual machines dynamically which is useful in cloud environment data centers. The provided approaches handle both major goals of dynamic management in data centers, maximizing power efficiency and minimizing SLA violations, considering the inherent trade-off between these goals. It is difficult to manage data centers with conflicting goals simultaneously. It becomes worse by lack of an efficient method to do a straightforward comparison based on various metrics. This paper provided two single-goal approaches Energy-Reduction and SLAV-Reduction, and also ESDR as a double-goal approach. The double-goal approach reduces the consumed energy and SLA violations simultaneously.

All approaches are experimented in the same simulation conditions. The experimental results indicated that ESDR handles the mentioned goals more effectively compared to other approaches. ESDR improved the score about 40% compared to Energy-Reduction and SLAV-Reduction.

Some directions can be chosen as future work. One possible plan is to focus on a management approach able to switch between two single-goal approaches considering entire efficiency of data center and according to its current workload. Moreover, this paper relied only on

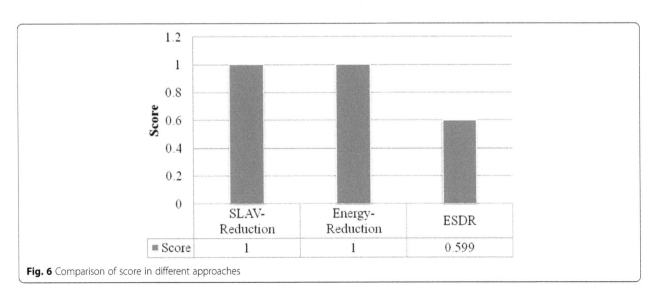

Fig. 6 Comparison of score in different approaches

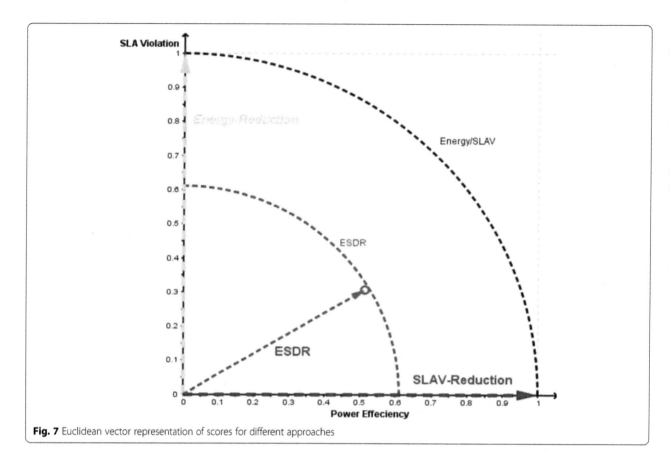

Fig. 7 Euclidean vector representation of scores for different approaches

CPU loads to measure host or VM loads. In future works, the memory and bandwidth loads can be taken into account additionally.

Acknowledgements
We are also thankful to anonymous reviewers for their valuable feedback and comments for improving the quality of the manuscript.

Authors' contributions
This research work is part of SH (second author) dissertation work. The work has been primarily conducted by SH under the supervision of MM (first author). Extensive discussions about the algorithms and techniques presented in this paper were carried between the two authors over the past year. Both authors read and approved the final manuscript.

Authors information
Mahdi Mollamotalebi is an Assistant Professor in the Department of Computer, Buinzahra branch, Islamic Azad University, Buinzahra, Iran. He received his Ph.D. from the University Teknology Malaysia (UTM) in the area of Grid computing resource discovery. He has authored and coauthored several technical refereed and non-refereed papers in various conferences, journal articles, and book chapters in research and pedagogical techniques. His research interests include parallel and distributed system performance, Grid and Cloud computing, and IoT. Dr. Mollamotalebi is a member of IEEE. Shahnaz Hajireza is pursuing towards his M.Sc., Department of Computer, Buinzahra branch, Islamic Azad University, Buinzahra, Iran. Shahnaz's interests are in Cloud computing, Virtualization, and Cloud localization. She has authored and coauthored some technical papers in various conferences, and journal articles.

Competing interests
The authors declare that they have no competing interests.

References
1. Bobroff, N., Kochut, A., & Beaty, K. (2007). Dynamic placement of virtual machines for managing sla violations. In Integrated Network Management, 2007. IM'07. 10th IFIP/IEEE International Symposium on (pp. 119-128). IEEE
2. Kochut, A., & Beaty, K. (2007). On strategies for dynamic resource management in virtualized server environments. In Modeling, Analysis, and Simulation of Computer and Telecommunication Systems, 2007. MASCOTS'07. 15th International Symposium on (pp. 193-200). IEEE
3. Khanna, G., Beaty, K., Kar, G., & Kochut, A. (2006). Application performance management in virtualized server environments. In Network Operations and Management Symposium, 2006. NOMS 2006. 10th IEEE/IFIP (pp. 373-381). IEEE
4. Wood T, Shenoy PJ, Venkataramani A, Yousif MS (2007) Black-box and gray-box strategies for virtual machine migration. In: NSDI Vol. 7, pp 17–17
5. Verma, A., Ahuja, P., & Neogi, A. (2008). pMapper: power and migration cost aware application placement in virtualized systems. In Proceedings of the 9th ACM/IFIP/USENIX International Conference on Middleware (pp. 243-264). Springer-Verlag New York, Inc.
6. Cardosa, M., Korupolu, M. R., & Singh, A. (2009). Shares and utilities based power consolidation in virtualized server environments. In Integrated Network Management, 2009. IM'09. IFIP/IEEE International Symposium on (pp. 327-334). IEEE
7. Speitkamp B, Bichler M (2010) A mathematical programming approach for server consolidation problems in virtualized data centers. IEEE Trans Serv Comput 3(4):266–278
8. Stillwell M, Schanzenbach D, Vivien F, Casanova H (2010) Resource allocation algorithms for virtualized service hosting platforms. J Parallel Distributed Comput 70(9):962–974
9. Panigrahy, R., Talwar, K., Uyeda, L., & Wieder, U. (2011). Heuristics for vector bin packing. Research. Microsoft. Com

10. Kou LT, Markowsky G (1977) Multidimensional bin packing algorithms. IBM J Res Dev 21(5):443–448
11. Frenk H, Csirik J, Labbé M, Zhang S (1990) On the multidimensional vector bin packing. University of Szeged. Acta Cybernetica, pp 361–369
12. Yue M (1991) A simple proof of the inequality FFD (L)≤ 11/9 OPT (L)+ 1,∀ L for the FFD bin-packing algorithm. Acta Mathematicae Applicatae Sinica (English Series) 7(4):321–331
13. Dósa G (2007) The tight bound of first fit decreasing bin-packing algorithm is FFD (I)≤ 11/9OPT (I)+ 6/9. In: Combinatorics, algorithms, probabilistic and experimental methodologies. Springer, Berlin Heidelberg, pp 1–11
14. Kao, M. Y. (Ed.). (2008). Encyclopedia of algorithms. Springer Science & Business Media. Springer Berlin Heidelberg. doi:10.1007/978-3-642-27848-8.
15. Gmach, D., Rolia, J., Cherkasova, L., Belrose, G., Turicchi, T., & Kemper, A. (2008). An integrated approach to resource pool management: Policies, efficiency and quality metrics. In Dependable Systems and Networks With FTCS and DCC, 2008. DSN 2008. IEEE International Conference on (pp. 326-335). IEEE
16. Keller, G., Tighe, M., Lutfiyya, H., & Bauer, M. (2012). An analysis of first fit heuristics for the virtual machine relocation problem. In Network and service management (cnsm), 2012 8th international conference and 2012 workshop on systems virtualiztion management (svm) (pp. 406-413). IEEE
17. Beloglazov A, Buyya R (2012) Optimal online deterministic algorithms and adaptive heuristics for energy and performance efficient dynamic consolidation of virtual machines in cloud data centers. Concurrency Comput 24(13):1397–1420
18. Foster, G., Keller, G., Tighe, M., Lutfiyya, H., & Bauer, M. (2013). The right tool for the job: Switching data centre management strategies at runtime. In Integrated Network Management (IM 2013), 2013 IFIP/IEEE International Symposium on (pp. 151-159). IEEE
19. Xiao Z, Song W, Chen Q (2013) Dynamic resource allocation using virtual machines for cloud computing environment. IEEE Trans Parallel Distributed Syst 24(6):1107–1117
20. Ferdaus, M. H. (2016). Multi-objective virtual machine Management in Cloud Data Centers (Doctoral dissertation, Monash University)
21. Tighe, M., Keller, G., Shamy, J., Bauer, M., & Lutfiyya, H. (2013). Towards an improved data centre simulation with DCSim. In Network and Service Management (CNSM), 2013 9th International Conference on (pp. 364-372). IEEE
22. Tighe, M., Keller, G., Bauer, M., & Lutfiyya, H. (2012). DCSim: A data centre simulation tool for evaluating dynamic virtualized resource management. In Network and service management (cnsm), 2012 8th international conference and 2012 workshop on systems virtualiztion management (svm) (pp. 385-392). IEEE
23. Foster, G. (2013). UTIL-DSS: utilization-based dynamic strategy switching for improvement in data Centre operation (Doctoral dissertation, The University of Western Ontario)
24. (2014) SPECpower ssj2008. Standard Performance Evaluation Corporation. Available on: https://www.spec.org/power_ssj2008/. Accessed 7 July 2017.
25. (2014) The Internet Traffic Archive. Available on: http://ita.ee.lbl.gov/. Accessed 7 July 2017.
26. (2014) Google Cluster Data. Google Inc. Available on: https://github.com/google/cluster-data. Accessed 7 July 2017.

10

High availability in clouds: systematic review and research challenges

Patricia T. Endo[1,2*], Moisés Rodrigues[2], Glauco E. Gonçalves[2,3], Judith Kelner[2], Djamel H. Sadok[2] and Calin Curescu[4]

Abstract

Cloud Computing has been used by different types of clients because it has many advantages, including the minimization of infrastructure resources costs, and its elasticity property, which allows services to be scaled up or down according to the current demand. From the Cloud provider point-of-view, there are many challenges to be overcome in order to deliver Cloud services that meet all requirements defined in Service Level Agreements (SLAs). High availability has been one of the biggest challenges for providers, and many services can be used to improve the availability of a service, such as checkpointing, load balancing, and redundancy. Beyond services, we can also find infrastructure and middleware solutions. This systematic review has as its main goal to present and discuss high available (HA) solutions for Cloud Computing, and to introduce some research challenges in this area. We hope this work can be used as a starting point to understanding and coping with HA problems in Cloud.

Keywords: Cloud computing, High availability, Systematic review, Research challenges

Introduction

Cloud Computing emerged as a novel technology at the end of the last decade, and it has been a trending topic ever since. The Cloud can be seen as a conceptual layer on the Internet, which makes all available software and hardware resources transparent, rendering them accessible through a well-defined interface. Concepts like on-demand self-service, broad network access, resource pooling [1] and other trademarks of Cloud Computing services are the key components of its current popularity. Cloud Computing attracts users by minimizing infrastructure investments and resource management costs while presenting a flexible and elastic service. Managing such infrastructure remains a great challenge, considering clients' requirements for zero outage [2, 3].

Service downtime not only negatively effects in user experience but directly translates into revenue loss. A report [4] from the International Working Group on Cloud Computing Resiliency (IWGCR)[1] gathers information regarding services downtime and associated revenue losses. It points out that Cloud Foundry[2] downtime results

in \$336,000 less revenue per hour. Paypal, the online payment system, experiences in a revenue loss of \$225,000 per hour. To mitigate the outages, Cloud providers have been focusing on ways to enhance their infrastructure and management strategies to achieve high available (HA) services.

According to [5] availability is calculated as the percentage of time an application and its services are available, given a specific time interval. One achieves high availability (HA) when the service in question is unavailable less than 5.25 minutes per year, meaning at least 99.999 % availability ("five nines"). In [5], authors define that HA systems are fault tolerant systems with no single point of failure; in other words, when a system component fails, it does not necessarily cause the termination of the service provided by that component.

Delivering a higher level of availability has been one of the biggest challenges for Cloud providers. The primary goal of this work is to present a systematic review and discuss the state-of-the-art HA solutions for Cloud Computing. The authors hope that the observation of such solutions could be used as a good starting point to addressing with some of the problems present in the HA Cloud Computing area.

*Correspondence: patricia.endo@upe.br
[1]University of Pernambuco (UPE), BR 104 S/N, Caruaru, Brazil
Full list of author information is available at the end of the article

This work is structured as follows: "Cloud outages" section describes some Cloud outages that occurred in 2014 and 2015, and how administrators overcame these problems; "Systematic review" section presents the methodology used to guide our systematic review; "Overview of high availability in Clouds" section presents an overview regarding HA Cloud solutions; "Results description" section describes works about HA services based on our systematic review result; "Discussions" section discusses some research challenges in this area; and "Final considerations" section delineates final considerations.

Cloud outages

Cloud Computing has become increasingly essential to the live services offered and maintained by many companies. Its infrastructure should attend to unpredictable demand and should always be available (as long as possible) to end-clients. However, assuring high availability has been a major challenge for Cloud providers. To illustrate this issue, we describe four (certainly among many) examples of Cloud services outages that occurred in 2014 and 2015:

Dropbox

Dropbox's Head of Infrastructure, Akhil Gupta, explained that their databases have one master and two replica machines for redundancy, and full and incremental data backups are performed regularly. However, on January 10th, 2014[3], during a planned maintenance scheduled intended to upgrade the Operating System on some machines, a bug in the script caused the command to reinstall a small number of active machines. Unfortunately, some master-replica pairs were impacted which resulted in the service going down.

To restore it, they performed the recovery from backups within three hours, but the large size of some databases delayed the recovery. The lesson learned from this episode was the need to add a layer to perform distributed state verification and speed up data recovery.

Google services

Some Google services, such as Gmail, Google Calendar, Google Docs, and Google+, were unavailable on January 24th, 2014, for about 1 hour. According to Google Engineer, Ben Treynor, "*an internal system that generates configurations - essentially, information that tells other systems how to behave - encountered a software bug and generated an incorrect configuration. The incorrect configuration was sent to live services over the next 15 minutes, caused users' requests for their data to be ignored, and those services, in turn, generated errors*".

Consequently, they decided to add validation checks for configurations, improve detection, and diagnose service failure.

Google Apps

The Google Apps Team schedules maintenance on data center systems regularly and some procedures involve upgrading groups of servers and redirecting the traffic to other available servers. Typically, these maintenance procedures occur in the background with no impact on users. However, due to a miscalculation of memory usage, on March 17th, 2014 the new set of backend servers lacked of sufficient capacity to process the redirected traffic. These backend servers could not process the volume of incoming requests and returned errors for about three hours.

The Google Engineering team said that they will "*continue work in progress to improve the resilience of Hangouts service during high load conditions*".

Verizon Cloud

Verizon Cloud[4] is a Cloud provider that offers backup and synchronization data to its clients. On January 10th, 2015 Verizon provider suffered a long outage of approximately 40 hours over a weekend. The outage occurred due to a system maintenance procedure which, ironically, had been planned to prevent future outages.

So, as we can see, Cloud outages can occur from different causes and can be fixed using different strategies. However, in most cases, in addition to the loss of revenue, such service disruptions pushed Cloud providers to rethink their management strategies and sometimes to re-design their Cloud infrastructure design altogether.

Financial losses due to Cloud outages foment studies about HA solutions, in order to minimize outages for Cloud providers. In the next Section, we describe the systematic review approach that we used to undertake research about HA solutions.

Systematic review

In this work, we adapted the systematic review proposed by [6], in order to find strategies that address HA Clouds. Next, we describe each activity (see Fig. 1) in detail and describe how we address it.

Activity 1: identify the need for the review

As stated previously, high availability in Clouds remains a big challenge for providers since Cloud infrastructure systems are very complex and must address different services with different requirements. In order to reach a certain level of high availability, a Cloud provider should monitor its resources and deployed services continuously.

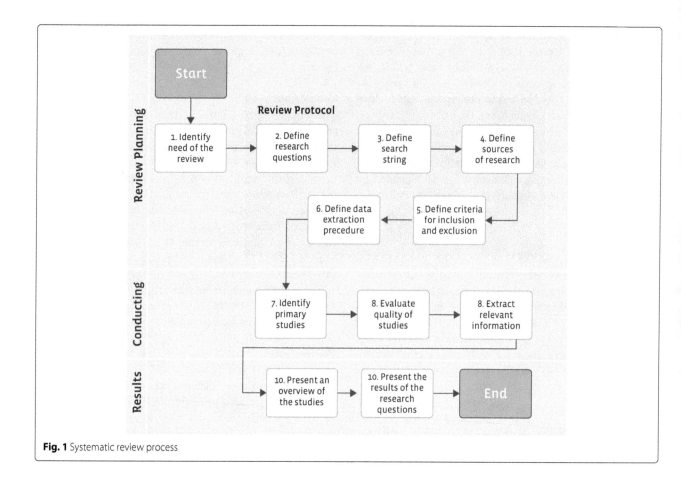

Fig. 1 Systematic review process

With information about resources and service behaviors available, a Cloud provider could make good management decisions in order to avoid outages or failures.

Activity 2: define research questions

In this activity, we need to define which questions we want to answer. The main goal of this work is to answer the following research questions (RQ):

- RQ.1: What is the current state-of-the-art in HA Clouds?
- RQ.2: What is the most common definition of HA?
- RQ.3: What are the HA services implemented by HA Cloud solutions?
- RQ.4: What are the most common approaches used to evaluate HA Cloud solutions?
- RQ.5: What are the research challenges in HA Clouds?

Activity 3: define search string

In this activity, we need to define which keywords we will use in selected search tools. For this work, we used the following expressions: "cloud computing" AND "high availability" AND "middleware".

Activity 4: define sources of research

For this work, we chose the following databases: IEEE Xplore[5], Science Direct[6], and ACM Digital Library[7].

Activity 5: define criteria for inclusion and exclusion

In order to limit the scope of this analysis, we considered only journals and conferences articles published between 2010 and 2015. The keywords "cloud computing" and "middleware" or "framework" were required to be in the article.

Activity 6: define data extraction procedure

Data extraction is based on a set of items to be filled for each article: keywords, proposal, and future works.

Activity 7: identify primary studies

The search returned 9, 63, and 145 articles in IEEE Xplore, Science Direct, and ACM Digital Library, respectively, totaling 217 works.

By reading all abstracts and using the criteria for inclusion or exclusion, we selected 19 papers for data extraction and quality evaluation. This number is justified because the keyword "high availability" is very common in Cloud Computing, especially in its own definition, and so most of articles had this keyword in them. However, in most cases high availability was not their research focus.

Activity 8: evaluate quality of studies
The quality evaluation was based on checking if the paper is related to some HA Cloud proposal for middleware or framework.

Activity 9: extract relevant information
This activity involves applying the data extraction procedure defined in Activity 6 to the primary studies selected in Activity 7.

Activity 10: present an overview of the studies
In this activity, we present an overview of all articles we selected in Activity 8, in order to classify and clarify them according to the research questions presented in Activity 2. The result of this activity is presented in "Overview of high availability in Clouds" section.

Activity 11: present the results of the research questions
After an overview about studies in HA Clouds, we had a discussion in order to answer the research questions stated in Activity 2. The results of this activity are presented in "Overview of high availability in Clouds" section.

Overview of high availability in Clouds
In this Section, we present an overview about Activity 10, presenting some characteristics of the selected articles in HA Cloud. Figure 2 shows the number of articles published per year from 2010 to 2015.

Concerning research source (Fig. 3), we can see that ACM has more articles published in HA Cloud area.

Some articles define the term "high availability". For instance, authors in [7] say "the services provided by the

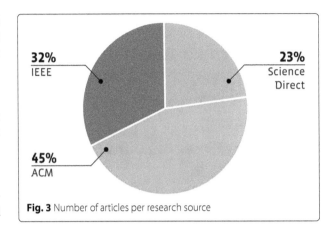

Fig. 3 Number of articles per research source

applications are considered highly available if they are accessible 99.999 % of the time (also known as five 9's)". The Table 1 outlines the various definitions of "high availability" we identified through our research, as well as the source of each definition.

We also observed that many services are implemented in conjunction in order to offer a HA Cloud. Figure 4 shows monitoring, replication, and failure detection are the most implemented services, identified in 50 % of studies in the research. Please, note that there are more services than published works because it is common to implement more than one service in a proposal.

Figure 5 shows how solutions were evaluated in the studies we analyzed. We can see experimentation is the most popular technique used. These results indicate that research about this topic is working to derive proposals with fast application to the cloud computing industry.

Table 1 High availability definitions

Reference	Definition
Achieving High Availability at the Application Level in the Cloud [7]	The services provided by the applications are considered highly available if they are accessible 99.999 % of the time (also known as five 9's)
Managing Application Level Elasticity and Availability [25]	High availability is achieved when the outage is less than 5.25 minutes per year
Scheduling highly available applications on cloud environments [35]	High availability systems are characterized by fewer failures and faster repair times
Are clouds ready for large distributed applications? [36]	High availability is defined in terms of downtime that is the total number of minutes the site is unavailable for events lasting longer than 5 minutes over a 1-year period
Software aging in the eucalyptus cloud computing infrastructure: Characterization and rejuvenation [37]	Availability is defined as the ability of a system to perform its slated function at a specic instant of time.

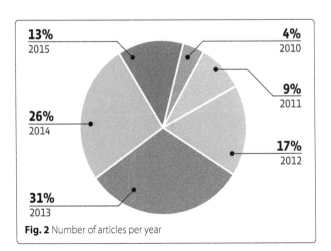

Fig. 2 Number of articles per year

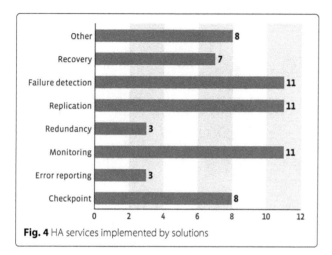

Fig. 4 HA services implemented by solutions

Our classification is a simplified view of the framework proposed by Service Availability Forum (SAForum) (Fig. 7). SAForum is focused on producing open specifications to address the requirements of availability, reliability and dependability for a broad range of applications (not only Clouds).

There are three types of services in its Application Interface Specification (AIS): Management Services, Platform Services, and Utility Services. According to [10], Management Services provide the basic standard management interfaces that should be used for the implementation of all services and applications. Platform Services provide a higher-level abstraction of the hardware platform and operating systems to the other services and applications. Utility Services provide some of the common interfaces required in highly available distributed systems, such as checkpoint and message.

SAF also proposes two frameworks: Software Management Framework (SMF), which is used for managing middleware and application software during upgrades while taking service availability into account; and Availability Management Framework (AMF), which provides functions (e.g. a set of APIs) for availability management of applications and middleware [10], such as component registration and life cycle management, error reporting and health monitoring.

We understand our 3-layer classification covers the SAF framework, because SAF specifications can be allocated between our layers. The next sub-sections will present solutions found in our systematic review focusing on services layer.

The analysis should be performed based on comparison metrics. Work presented in [8] defines some metrics used to evaluate HA solutions, as shown in Table 2.

Results description

As we found in this systematic review, Cloud providers can make use of several technologies and mechanisms to offer HA services. Authors in [9] classify HA solutions into two categories: middleware approaches and virtualization-based approaches. They propose a framework to evaluate VM availability against three types of failures: a) application failure, b) VM failure, and c) host failure. Authors use OpenStack, Pacemaker, OpenSAF, and VMware to apply their framework, which considers stateful and stateless-HA applications.

However, in our research, we organize solutions into three layers (underlying technologies, services, and middlewares), and keep in mind that layers can be composed of (one or many) solutions from bottom layers to perform their goals (Fig. 6).

Underlying technologies

The bottom layer is a set of underlying technologies that enable a Cloud provider offering a plethora of possibilities to provide high availability using commodity systems.

Virtualization is not a new concept but Cloud providers use it as key technology for enabling infrastructure

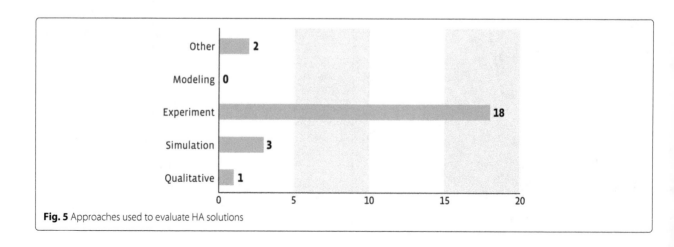

Fig. 5 Approaches used to evaluate HA solutions

Table 2 Metrics for HA evaluation from [8]

Metric	Definition
Reaction time	Delay between the occurrence of the failure and the first reaction of the availability management solution.
Repair time	Duration from the first reaction until the faulty entity is repaired.
Recovery time	Duration from the first reaction until the service is provided again
Outage time	Time between the failure happening and the service recovery. In other words, outage time is the amount of time the service is not provided and it is the sum of the reaction and recovery times.

operation and easy management. According to [11], the main factor that increased the adoption of server virtualization within Cloud Computing is the flexibility regarding reallocation of workloads across the physical resources offered by virtualization. Such flexibility allows, for instance, for Cloud providers to execute maintenance without stopping developers' applications (that are running on VMs) and to implement strategies for better resource usage through the migration of VMs. Also, server virtualization is adapted for the fast provisioning of new VMs through the use of templates, which enables providers to offer elasticity services for application developers [12].

Virtualization can also be used to implement HA mechanisms at the VM level, such as failure and attack isolation, checkpoint and rollback as recovery mechanisms. Beyond that, virtualization can also be used at the network level with the same objectives by virtualizing network functions (see about Network Function Virtualization (NFV) in [13]).

There are several hypervisor options, such as from the open-source community, Xen[8] and Kernel-based Virtual Machine (KVM)[9]. As well, there are those from proprietary solutions, including VMWare[10] and Microsoft's HyperV[11].

Services
The second layer is composed of many services that can be implemented and configured according to Cloud provider requirements or management decisions. For instance, if a provider has a checkpoint mechanism implemented in its infrastructure, it should configure the checkpoint service, which could mean setting it as an active or a passive checkpoint, and configuring the update frequency, for instance. The next subsections describe the main services and report how related studies used them.

Redundancy
The redundancy service can offer different levels of availability depending on the redundancy model, the redundancy strategy, and the redundancy scope (Fig. 8).

The redundancy model refers to the many different ways HA systems can combine active and standby replicas of hosted applications. AMF describes four models: 2N, N+M, Nway, and Nway active [14]. The 2N ensures one standby replica for each active application.

The N+M model is an extension of the 2N model and ensures that more than two system units (meaning a virtual machine, for instance) can handle taking active or standby assignments from an application. N represents the number of units able to handle active assignments and M represents those with standby assignments. It is important to notice that, considering the N+M model, a unit that handles active assignments will never handle standby assignments.

Furthermore, the N-way is similar to the N+M model with the difference that it allows in the N-way model

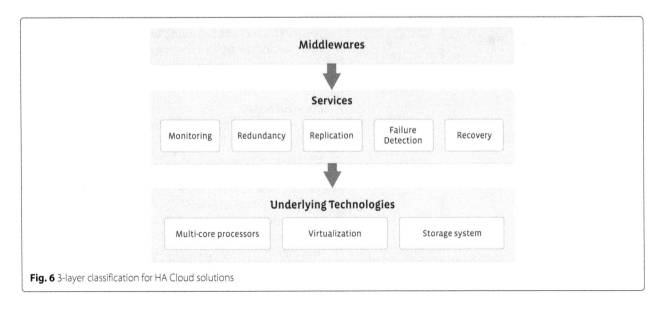

Fig. 6 3-layer classification for HA Cloud solutions

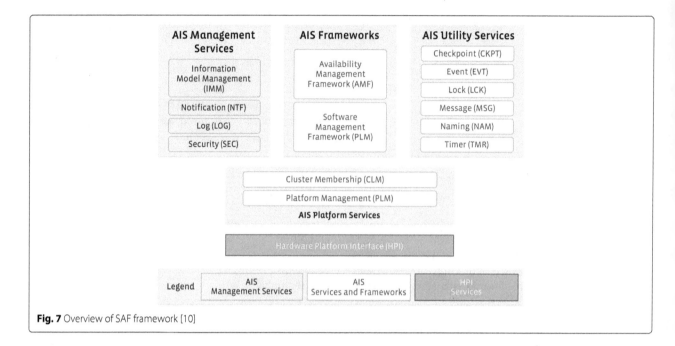

Fig. 7 Overview of SAF framework [10]

unit to handle both active and standby assignments from diverse applications instances.

Lastly, the N-way Active redundancy model comprehends only active assignments from unit applications; it does not allow standby assignments, but permits an application instance to be allocated as active into various units. Due to its simplicity, the 2N model is preferred in terms of implementation [15, 16].

The redundancy strategy is divided in two classes: active and passive redundancy [17]. In active strategy, there are no standby replicas and all application replicas work in parallel. When one node fails, tasks executing at the failed node can be resumed in any remaining node. In passive redundancy, there is one working replica whereas remaining replicas are standby. When the main node fails, any standby replica can resume failed node tasks. Please note that this active strategy helps to provide load balancing to applications. However, maintaining consistency in the passive model is simpler, and so this strategy is used in different proposals [15].

In respect to scope, one can replicate the application itself, the VM that hosts the application, or the complete physical server hosting the application. Authors in [15] propose to use all these approaches in a model-based framework to select and configure High Availability mechanisms for a cloud application. The framework constructs a model of the running system and selects the proper HA services according to the benefits and costs of each service, as well as the required availability level. In contrast, the proposal described in [16] focuses on the VM scope only.

Data replication

Data replication is used to maintain state consistency between replicas. The main problem associated with this service is the question of how to govern the trade-off between consistency and resource usage [18]. In Clouds, the replication may be achieved either by copying the state of a system (checkpoint) or by replaying input to all replicas (lock-step based) [16] (see Fig. 9).

The lock-step strategy is also called "State Machine Replication" and its main goal is to send the same operations to be executed by all replicas of an application in a coordinated way, thus guaranteeing message order and

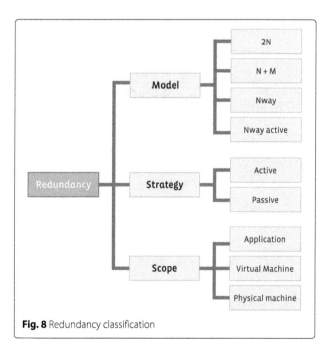

Fig. 8 Redundancy classification

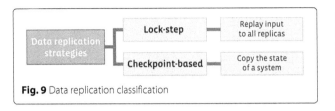

Fig. 9 Data replication classification

state. This strategy can be found in the TClouds plataform [19], which is applied to the state maintenance of application replicas and is also applied to maintain the consistency of objects stored in a set of cloud storage services. The same strategy is applied in the Cloud-Niagara middleware [20] in order to offer a monitoring service to check resource usage and send failure notifications with minimal delay. Following this same strategy, Perez-Sorrosal et al. [21] propose a multi-version database cache framework to support elastic replication of multi-tier stateless and statefull applications. In this framework, application and database tiers are installed at each replica and a multicast protocol maintains data consistency between replicas. The main focus of this proposal is elasticity, but the solution can also cope with failures since the replication protocol uses virtual synchrony to guarantee the reliable execution of the replicas.

Checkpoint-based replication involves propagating frequent updates of an active application to its standby replicas. It is desirable that an application have some checkpoint replicas distributed over different entities to increase reliability, guarding it against failures [10]. Checkpoint service can be implemented in a centralized fashion, when all checkpoint replicas are allocated to the same entity, and in a distributed one, where replicas are located in different entities of a cluster.

Remus is a production level solution implemented at Xen to offer High Availability following this strategy [22]. Authors of that solution point out that lock-step replication results in an unacceptable resource usage overhead because communication between applications must be accurately tracked and propagated to all replicas. In contrast, checkpoints between active and standby replicas occurs periodically, in intervals of milliseconds, providing better tradeoff between resource usage overhead and updates. Taking a similar approach, Chan and Chieu [23] introduce a cost effective solution which utilizes VM snapshots coupled with a smart, on-demand snapshot collection mechanism to provide an HA in the virtualization environment. The main idea behind this proposal is to extend the snapshot service (a common service offered by virtualized infrastructures) to include checkpoint data of a VM.

While Remus and similar approaches fit well to IaaS Clouds because they provide an application-agnostic VM-based checkpoint, Kanso and Lemieux [7] argue that

in a PaaS Cloud the checkpoint service must be performed at the application level in order to cope with internal application failures that may remain unnoticed in a VM-based HA system. Therefore, the authors propose that each application send its current state to the HA system through a well-defined checkpoint interface.

In [24], authors propose BlobCR, a checkpoint framework for High Performance Computing (HPC) applications on IaaS. Their approach is directed at both application and process checkpoint levels through a distributed checkpoint repository.

In [16] authors present a solution focusing on HA for real-time applications. The middleware proposed is derived from others technologies, such as Remus, Xen and OpenNebula. For instance, continuous-checkpoint, in which asynchronous checkpoints are made in a security VM to provide HA in case of failures, was inherited from Remus.

Monitoring

Monitoring is a crucial service in an HA Cloud. Through this service, applications' health is continuously observed to support others services. The primary goal of this service is to detect when a replica is down, but robust implementations can also follow the health indicators of an application (CPU and memory utilization, disk, and network I/O, time to respond requests) which will help to detect when a replica is malfunctioning [17]. It can also be done at virtual and physical machine level (Fig. 10).

Papers surveyed showed there are two basic types of monitoring: push-based monitoring and polling-based monitoring. The latter is the most common type of monitoring and involves a set of measuring controllers periodically sending an echo-signal to the hosted applications. This check can be sent to the operating system that hosts the application (through standard network protocols like ICMP or SNMP) or directly to the application through a communication protocol, e.g., HTTP in the case of web applications [17].

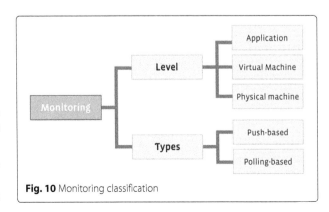

Fig. 10 Monitoring classification

Polling-based monitoring can also be sent from a backup replica to an active replica in order to check its status and to automatically convert it from backup to active when necessary [15] and [20]. This type of monitoring can be made by a monitoring agent that is external to the application or an agent can be implemented directly in the application by a standardized API that handles messages sent by the Cloud. Through this intrusive approach the internal state of the applications can be monitored, enabling the earlier detection of adverse conditions and making it possible to offer services such as checkpointing [7].

Push-based monitoring consists of the application (or a cloud monitoring agent deployed with the application) being the one responsible for sending messages to the measuring controller, when necessary. In this case, the controller is informed when a meaningful change occurs in the monitored application [25]. Push-based monitoring can also be implemented following a publish/subscribe communication model. This type of monitoring is employed by Behl et al. [26] to provide fault-tolerance to web service workflows. The fault monitoring is implemented through ZooKeeper's Watches, which are registered to check if a Zookeper's ephemeral node (an application in this case) is active. In the case of failure, the monitoring controller is notified about the crash. An et al. [16] point out that the highly dynamic environment of cloud computing requires timely decisions that can be achieved by publish/subscribe monitoring. In this case, the monitoring controllers are subscribers and the monitoring agents are publishers.

One important aspect to observe is that both approaches (push and poll) can be implemented in a Cloud environment. The high availability platform proposed by Chan and Chieu [23] uses polling to check periodically for host failures, and monitoring agents running in the hosts push notifications to the monitoring controller. An et al. [16] propose a hierarchical monitoring strategy combining the publish/subscribe communication model for global-level monitoring with polling at the local level.

Failure detection

Failure detection is an important service contained in most HA solutions, which aims to identify systems' faults (application, virtual or physical machine level) and provide needed information for services capable of treating problems to maintain service continuity (Fig. 11).

In [17] the authors list some mechanisms used to detect faults like ping, heartbeat and exceptions. From this perspective, failure detection can be classified in two categories according to detection mechanisms: reactive [23, 26]) and proactive [20]. The first approach waits for

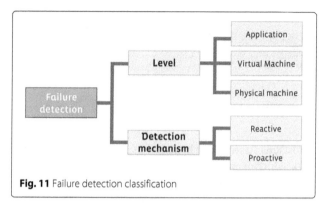

Fig. 11 Failure detection classification

KEEP ALIVE messages, but it identifies a failure after a period of time waiting without any KEEP ALIVE message. The second approach is more robust and is capable of identifying abnormal behaviors in the environment, checking the monitoring service and interpreting collected data to verify whether there are failures or not.

For simplicity, the reactive type is implemented more often. The work presented in [26] proposes a fault-tolerant service through replication processes with BPEL implementation, which means that Zookeeper is responsible for detecting crashed replicas using a callback mechanism called watches. As well [23], authors treat failure detection through heartbeats hosted in each node, and so the absence of heartbeats after a period of time has passed indicates a failure and hence the recovery process begins.

Authors in [20] propose an intelligent system that depends on a proactive mechanism of monitoring and notification, as well as a mathematical model which is responsible for identifying the system faults.

Others studies lack many details about the failure detection process. For instance, in [27], failure detection is implemented together with failure mitigation (recovery) in a process called Fault Injection. This process aims to evaluate the framework capacity to handle failover possibilities. Also, in [7], authors proposed a HA middleware inside VMs for monitoring and restarting in case of failures.

In [16], authors proposed an architecture with an entity called LFM (Local Fault Manager), located in all physical host. It is responsible for collecting resource information such as memory, processes, etc. and transferring it to the next layer, which is responsible for decision making, similar to a monitoring service. Moreover, LFM also runs HAS (High-Availability Service) that keeps synchronization between primary and backup VMs, and is responsible for making backup VM active when a failure is detected in the primary VM.

Recovery

The recovery service is responsible for ensuring fault-tolerant performance through some services like redundancy [17], which means preserving HA even during crashes at application, virtual or physical machine level. It can be classified into smart [15, 16, 20] and simple [23, 28] (Fig. 12). The smart recovery uses other services and mechanisms (such as monitoring and checkpoint) to provide an efficient restoration with minimum losses for the application. Meanwhile, considering simple recovery, the broken application is just rebooted in a healthy node, so that the service continues to be provided, but all state data are lost.

The smart recovery proposed in [15] is guaranteed through a fault tolerant mechanism that keeps an application backup synchronized with active applications but deployed in a different VM. Authors in [16] work in a similar way, starting with the Remus project as base and applying a technique for VM failover using two VMs (primary and backup) that periodically synchronize states and are able to change from primary VM to backup, when needed. In [20], recovery is reached using an active replication technique, where a controller manages a priority list through Backup-ID from resources. Therefore, after a failure, broadcast communication is made and other nodes at the top of the list must assume the execution.

Furthermore, authors in [23] decided to use the simple recovery after a failure by using merged snapshots, in which faulty agent requires the manager any of snapshot available. In addition, work in [28] also uses simple recovery, in which the VMS are monitored by a VM wrapper that identifies unavailability and makes reboots.

Middleware

At the upper layer, we have middleware that uses services to provide HA to applications. The main goal is to manage how these services will operate, configure them, and take decisions according to information acquired.

OpenSAF [10] is an open source project that offers some services that implement the SAForum Application Interface Specification (AIS). For instance, OpenSAF implements the Availability Management Framework (AMF), which is the middleware responsible for maintaining service availability. Is also implements the checkpoint service (CPSv) that provides a means for processes to store checkpoint data incrementally, which can be used to protect applications against failures. For a detailed description of all SAF services implemented by OpenSAF, please see [10].

Since OpenSAF is used for general purpose, some studies use it to implement their Cloud solutions. For instance, authors in [7] propose an HA middleware for achieving HA at application level by using an SAF redundancy strategy. The middleware is responsible for monitoring physical and virtual resources, and repairing them or restarting VMs in case of failure. They also propose an HA integration. Basically, there is an integration-agent, which a Cloud user interacts with in order to provide information about its application and its availability requirements (such as number of replicas and redundancy model); and there is an HA-agent, which is responsible for managing the state of state-aware applications, and abstracting the complexity of APIs needed to execute the checkpoint service.

OpenStack[12] is an open source platform for public and private Clouds used to control large pools of computation, storage and networking resources. OpenStack has several components, and each component is responsible for a specific aspect of the Cloud environment. For instance, the component named Nova is responsible for handling VMs, and providing different flavors and images that describe details about the CPU, memory and storage of a VM. Another component is Neutron, which responsible for network management functions, such as the creation of networks, ports, routers and VMs connections. Considering the HA scope, we highlight the component called Heat that is OpenStack's orchestration tool. Using Heat, one can deploy multiple composite Cloud applications into OpenStack's infrastructure, using both the AWS CloudFormation template and the Heat Orchestration Template

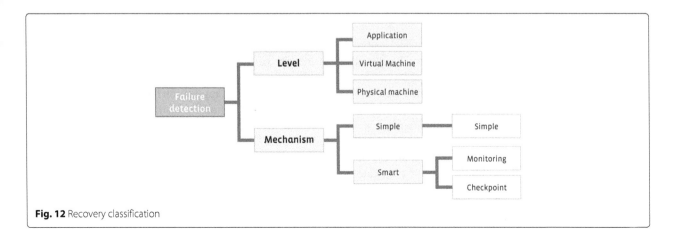

Fig. 12 Recovery classification

(HOT). In terms of HA, with Heat it is possible to monitor resources and applications from three basic levels[13]: 1) application level; 2) instance level; and 3) stack level (group of VMs). In case of failure, Heat tries to solve the problem in the current level. If the problem persists, it will try to solve it in a higher level. However, restarting resources can take up to a minute. Heat can also automatically increase or decrease the number of VMs, in conjunction with Celiometer (which is another OpenStack service) [25].

The paper [28] presents an OS-like virtualization cloud platform. They offers a dual stack API in the shell. One is called "Kumoi" and is used to manipulate data centers directly, while the other is called "Kali" and is used to build up the stack of cloud computing. With this cloud platform authors provide several HA services, such as checkpoint, monitoring, failure detection, recovery and elasticity. One should notice that services are provided at the VM level. They also present a qualitative evaluation between their tool and several others, such as Openstack, Nimbus, and OpenNebula.

The proposed solution in [20] is a high availability and fault tolerance middleware through the checkpoint, watchdog and log services for applications in a cloud environment. The authors claim that two issues are responsible for reaching middleware objectives: notifications without delay and monitoring of resources, which is achieved through an analytic model that identifies the fault nature. The Cloud-Niagara algorithm is shown and performs adjustments at nodes through resources calculation. The mean time to recover of the proposed solution is compared to other systems and evaluated on OpenStack, where Cloud-Niagara operates, by executing processes from real applications (PostgreSQL Database (DB), File Transfer Protocol (FTP), etc). This evaluation shows the CPU usage variation through different loads from the execution of applications processes execution, presenting the importance of monitoring the effective replica instantiation.

Discussions

In the previous sections, we presented a 3-layer classification for HA Cloud solutions that use many techniques to apply HA requirements at the infrastructure level. Since these technologies are key-enablers for Cloud operation and management, it is crucial that we go beyond the advantages to understand their specific challenges.

Regarding the underlying technologies, despite the fact that we presented virtualization as a good alternative for providing HA, some authors do not completely agree that this technology is a good solution for this purpose. In [7], the authors state that virtualization can hide some failures at the software level and that failures

at the operating system level can affect both active and standby VMs if running in a lock-step way. Beyond that, virtualization introduces additional software layers imposing additional delays to network datagrams [29]. Consequently, performance measurements can also be affected by virtualization; authors in [29] show that clock-related measurements are affected by CPU load in the host as well as in the network load.

Regarding the offered services - the main focus of this work -, we can find several proposals in the literature for improving them, such as ([5, 30, 31]). Here, we highlight the issues surrounding automatic configuration and test of these services. As it was observed in "Cloud outages" section , Cloud outages can occur due to the misconfiguration of management services. Commonly, enterprises add validation checks for automatic configurations and improve mechanisms for detection and recovery of service failures.

Another important aspect is the feasibility of the service implementation. For instance, authors in [7] implemented their proposal; their algorithms run in polynomial time and the middleware consumes approximately 15MB of RAM and a moderated amount of CPU. On the other hand, Always On solution [32] proposes an HA architecture but does not provides insights on the feasibility of its implementation, nor does it treats how to deploy it. Beyond that, in this solution, applications need to implement their own HA mechanisms because they do not use a modular approach.

In terms of the middleware layer, its main shortcomings are its lack of compatibility to a standard specification and its dependency on a specific technology platform. These characteristics make these solutions inflexible, since once an application is developed to comply with such a middleware, the application cannot be migrated to other alternative solutions without major modifications. In this way, these solutions do not represent the desired interoperability (portability) requirement. The middleware presented in [7] overcomes this problem by offering HA at the application level by using an open-source and standardized implementation, named OpenSAF, which is a flexible and platform-independent solution.

Security is also an essential aspect for HA Clouds; however, none of the presented solutions deals with security mechanisms, such as those protecting against malicious attacks at the VM or application level. This occurs because detection and treatment of security breaches depends on different mechanisms. Even when an attack leads to a failure condition, dealing with this issue can propagate the consequences of the attack to the standby units. For example, in the case of a Denial-of-Service (DoS) attack, the middleware can proactively detect the active unit is out of service, failover to the standby unit, and transfer all requests to the standby unit. This strategy would propagate the denial of service to the standby unit. Therefore, the integration of HA and security services is an essential requirement when implementing a cloud middleware.

The advancement of standardization and improvement of HA strategies in a cloud computing system leads to the concept of HA-on-demand. Authors in [7] discuss this idea. They point out that not all applications need HA requirements during all the time. Thus, users can request HA services for their applications according to their current real needs. An online store can, for example, program different HA levels according to the chronogram of an announced promotion (e.g. Black Friday), changing the robustness of the system in respect to its calendar, clients demand, and allocated budget. In this way, authors state that it is feasible to have HA-as-a-service per applications in the Cloud.

NoPaas: proposal of a high available cloud for PaaS provisioning

Considering all of this related work, we have defined a set of requirements for implementing a high available framework to provide PaaS, which we named NoPaaS (Novel PaaS).

We grouped these requirements into two categories: a) application requirements, and b) framework requirements. **Application requirements** represent mandatory characteristics that all applications require in order to work properly within the NoPaaS framework (Table 3). In turn, **framework requirements** are a set of services and characteristics that the NoPaaS framework itself must provide for applications and/or developers (Table 4).

The application requirements are necessary to provide a unique interface to developers. In this way, the proposal provides strategies to allow developers to handle some HA resources provided by the NoPaaS. At the same time, applications need to be adapted in order to comply with all these requirements, as stated in REQ A.1, in which developers should use NoPaaS API to implement their applications. Despite application requirements making application development a little bit hard, this is a very common requirement in PaaS environments, such as Google App Engine[14]. Those PaaS cloud environments provide user APIs for building scalable web applications and mobile backends. Furthermore, REQ A.2 was defined in order to guarantee the multi-tier and stateful applications handling by the NoPaaS, and REQ A.3 was stated

Table 3 Application requirements

REQ A.1	Must implement the API as described by the framework
REQ A.2	Must always include the session ID in messages exchanged between tiers of the application
REQ A.3	RESTful communications between tiers

Table 4 Framework requirements

REQ F.1	Must define the API for north bound communication with applications
REQ F.2	Must support different profile configurations
REQ F.3	Must plan resource allocation based on different profile configurations
REQ F.4	Must support multi-tier applications
REQ F.5	Must support stateful applications
REQ F.6	Must deal with sticky sessions
REQ F.7	Must assure HA
REQ F.8	Must provide scaling
REQ F.9	Must provide resource management
REQ F.10	Must rely on Cloud infrastructure compatible with current standards

to facilitate and standardize the communication between application' tiers.

The framework requirements were defined in order to achieve high availability focused on provisioning multi-tier stateful applications. REQ F.1 allows an unique form of communication with different types of applications, making this process simple for the developer. REQ F.2 and F.3 are related to profile configurations (economy, business, and custom) in order to incoporate different available budgets and requirements into response time and availability levels. These requirements facilitate the resource management from the PaaS provider perspective. From REQ F.4 to F.6, we have determined that the framework must deal with a specific type of application: multi-tier and stateful. It is our big distinction, since we did not find other studies considering such an application type. From REQ F.7 to F.9, we state the main services in order to ensure high availability. These are the big challenges for us, since we are considering multi-tier and stateful applications. The REQ F.10 guarantees compatibility with existing Cloud IaaS providers.

Considering all of these requirements, we propose our NoPaaS framework for high available clouds, shown in Fig. 13. The NoPaaS was designed to support the deployment of multi-tier and stateful applications deployment, providing services that include checkpoint, session migration, and failure recovery.

App deployment module

The App Deployment module is responsible for the interface between the application developer and our NoPaaS framework. NoPaaS proposes a set of modules, in which each module must act as a gateway between the PaaS service and NoPaaS internal services. Applications which will be deployed within NoPaaS must accomplish REQs A.1, A.2, and A.3 regarding the application requirements, and REQ F.1 regarding the framework requirements.

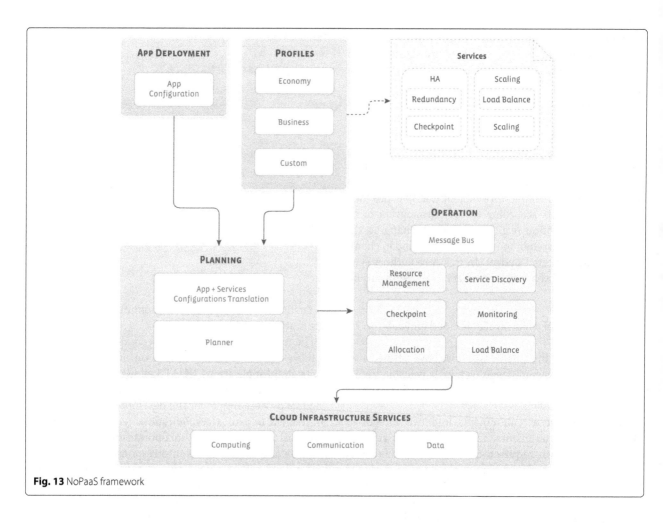

Fig. 13 NoPaaS framework

For the developers, it is mandatory to provide a configuration file specifying all information needed to deploy their applications in NoPaaS. Such a configuration file is very similar to what is usually provided to traditional PaaS in order to deploy a new application (e.g., git repository address and multi-tier architecture).

Profiles module

NoPaas makes use of profiles to represent and map the available budget provided by the developer and application requirements into response time and availability levels. The NoPaaS defines and provides, but it is not limited to, three different profiles: a) economy; b) business; and c) custom. For each profile, there is a specific configuration of load balance, scaling, checkpoint mechanism, and redundancy model based on the Service Availability Forum (SAForum or just SAF) model. REQs F.2 and F.3 are obeyed by this module.

NoPaaS uses the SAF reference because it produces open specifications to address the requirements of availability, reliability and dependability for a broad range of applications. In the SAF specification, there are five redundancy models: no redundancy, 2N, N+M, Nway, and

Nway active. These redundancy models differ from each other in the number of active and standby assignments each service has [33], and consequently in terms of the availability level that each model is able to reach.

Planning module

The set of information provided by the developers regarding their applications' configurations and profiles is sent to the App + Services Configurations Translation in the Planning module, which is responsible for translating this information so it can be used by the Planner. The Planner analyses all requirements and available resources on the Cloud infrastructure and plans the resource allocation, choosing the SAF redundancy model in order to satisfy **REQs F.4, F.5, and F.6**. The Planner also communicates with the Resource Management (in the Operation module) in order to ensure information about resource availability is always updated.

The Planner is responsible for executing two main activities: calculating the availability estimation based on SAF redundancy models, and defining the application allocation by trying to minimize the total cost while reaching a minimum availability level defined by the developer.

Each tier of an application is named as Service Instance (SI), and each SI is assigned into a Service Unit (SU). We modeled the solution for mapping SI into SU as an integer program and solved it using algorithms to find the best SAF model (with minimum cost). The Planner uses an analytic worst-case models to estimate the availability of each SAF redundancy model. For a detailed explanation about the analytic models and some simulation results and analysis, please see [34].

Operation module

The Operation module provides many services to deal with the Cloud infrastructure. Resource Management is responsible for supervising the infrastructure, reporting on application failures and generating scaling in/out triggers. The Checkpoint stores backups of deployed applications, recovering their states in case of failure, and also deals with session migrations. The Allocation enforces the reservation of resources designed by the Planner. The Monitoring keeps track of applications and physical resources, maintaining a map of resource usage. The Load Balance is used to distribute the load among multiple tiers of an application, dealing with session stickiness, server failure, and session migration. We define the Message Bus entity for communication purposes, and it is responsible for receiving and delivering messages for all entities. **REQs F.7, F.8, and F.9** should be attended by services of this module.

For instance, we have the **resource management** that handles application failures and is also responsible for issuing alerts regarding scaling needs. **Monitoring** is a basic service responsible for monitoring all applications and (virtual and/or physical) resources. Data generated by the monitor entity is stored and used a posteriori to measure which resources are available and to calculate the ideal configuration needed to deploy a new application (or if scaling is needed).

Cloud infrastructure module

The Cloud Infrastructure services comprise the IaaS services that NoPaaS uses to allocate the developers' applications. The main idea is to use Cloud facilities in order to avoid unnecessary work. For that, NoPaaS needs to contract some IaaS provider or configure our own private IaaS. With this, we comply with **REQ F.10**.

Final considerations

Cloud outages, no matter how long, are responsible for large financial losses. Cloud providers look for solutions that provide high availability even in failure cases. In this paper, we proposed a classification for HA Cloud solutions based on 3 layers. We also described and discussed some existing commercial and non-commercial solutions focused on middlewares.

High availability is a great challenge for Cloud providers due to its complexity (from the infrastructure to the application level). There are many issues to study in order to minimize Clouds outages, such as portability, feasibility, and security. A next step could be the implementation of HA-as-a-service, highlighting even more the importance of this research area for Cloud providers.

Endnotes

[1] http://iwgcr.org/

[2] https://www.cloudfoundry.org

[3] https://blogs.dropbox.com/tech/2014/01/outage-post-mortem/

[4] http://www.verizonwireless.com/solutions-and-services/verizon-cloud/

[5] http://ieeexplore.ieee.org/Xplore/home.jsp

[6] http://www.sciencedirect.com/

[7] http://dl.acm.org/

[8] https://www.xenproject.org/

[9] http://www.linux-kvm.org/page/Main_Page

[10] http://www.vmware.com/

[11] https://www.microsoft.com/en-us/cloud-platform/virtualization

[12] http://docs.openstack.org/developer/heat/

[13] https://wiki.openstack.org/wiki/Heat/HA

[14] https://cloud.google.com/appengine/

Acknowledgements

This work was supported by the RLAM Innovation Center, Ericsson Telecomunicaçõs S.A., Brazil.

Authors' contributions

Our contribution is a systematic review regarding existing high availability solutions for Cloud Computing. We considered studies done from 2010 to 2016; and we provided an overview and description about them based on 3-layer classification. Furthermore, we proposed a framework for providing high availability services, and also presented requirements to deal with multi-tier and stateful applications. All authors read and approved the final manuscript.

Competing interests

Cloud computing, high availability, resource management.

Author details

[1] University of Pernambuco (UPE), BR 104 S/N, Caruaru, Brazil. [2] Federal University of Pernambuco, GPRT, Recife, Brazil. [3] Rural Federal University of Pernambuco, Recife, Brazil. [4] Ericsson Research, Kista, Sweden.

References

1. Dillon T, Wu C, Chang E (2010) Cloud computing: issues and challenges. In: Advanced Information Networking and Applications (AINA), 2010 24th IEEE International Conference On. IEEE. pp 27–33. http://ieeexplore.ieee.org/document/5474674/?arnumber=5474674&tag=1

2. Puthal D, Sahoo B, Mishra S, Swain S (2015) Cloud computing features, issues, and challenges: a big picture. In: Computational Intelligence and Networks (CINE), 2015 International Conference On. IEEE. pp 116–123. http://ieeexplore.ieee.org/document/7053814/?arnumber=7053814
3. da Fonseca NL, Boutaba R (2015) Cloud Architectures, Networks, Services, and Management. In: Cloud Services, Networking, and Management. Wiley-IEEE Press. http://ieeexplore.ieee.org/xpl/articleDetails.jsp?arnumber=7090261
4. Cérin C, Coti C, Delort P, Diaz F, Gagnaire M, Gaumer Q, Guillaume N, Lous J, Lubiarz S, Raffaelli J, et al. (2013) Downtime statistics of current cloud solutions. International Working Group on Cloud Computing Resiliency, Tech. Rep. http://iwgcr.org/wp-content/uploads/2013/06/IWGCR-Paris.Ranking-003.2-en.pdf. Accessed Oct 2016
5. Toeroe M, Tam F (2012) Service Availability: Principles and Practice. John Wiley & Sons. http://www.wiley.com/WileyCDA/WileyTitle/productCd-1119954088.html
6. Coutinho EF, de Carvalho Sousa FR, Rego PAL, Gomes DG, de Souza JN (2015) Elasticity in cloud computing: a survey. Ann. Telecommunications-annales des télécommunications 70(7–8):289–309
7. Kanso A, Lemieux Y (2013) Achieving high availability at the application level in the cloud. In: Cloud Computing (CLOUD), 2013 IEEE Sixth International Conference On. IEEE. pp 778–785. http://ieeexplore.ieee.org/document/6740222/?arnumber=6740222
8. Heidari P, Hormati M, Toeroe M, Al Ahmad Y, Khendek F (2015) Integrating open saf high availability solution with open stack. In: Services (SERVICES), 2015 IEEE World Congress On. IEEE. pp 229–236. http://ieeexplore.ieee.org/document/7196529/?arnumber=7196529
9. Hormati M, Khendek F, Toeroe M (2014) Towards an evaluation framework for availability solutions in the cloud. In: Software Reliability Engineering Workshops (ISSREW), 2014 IEEE International Symposium On. IEEE. pp 43–46. http://ieeexplore.ieee.org/document/6983798/?arnumber=6983798
10. OpenSAF Overview Release 4.4 Programmer's Reference. http://sourceforge.net/projects/opensaf/files/docs/opensaf-documentation-4.4.1.tar.gz/download. Accessed Oct 2016
11. Gonçalves GE, Endo PT, Cordeiro T, Palhares A, Sadok D, Kelner J, Melander B, Mangs J (2011) Resource allocation in clouds: concepts, tools and research challenges. XXIX SBRC-Gramado-RS. http://sbrc2011.facom.ufms.br/files/anais/shortcourses-12.html. http://sbrc2011.facom.ufms.br/files/anais/files/mc/mc5.pdf
12. Marshall P, Keahey K, Freeman T (2010) Elastic site: Using clouds to elastically extend site resources. In: Proceedings of the 2010 10th IEEE/ACM International Conference on Cluster, Cloud and Grid Computing. IEEE Computer Society. pp 43–52. http://dl.acm.org/citation.cfm?id=1845214
13. Cui C, Xie Y, Gao G, Telekom D, Martiny K, Carapinha J, Telecom S, Lee D, Argela TT, Ergen M Network functions virtualisation (nfv). White paper, available at: https://portal.etsi.org/Portals/0/TBpages/NFV/Docs/NFV_White_Paper3.pdf. Accessed Oct 2016
14. Availability Management Framework. http://devel.opensaf.org/SAI-AIS-AMF-B.04.01.AL.pdf. Accessed Oct 2016
15. Wu Y, Huang G (2013) Model-based high availability configuration framework for cloud. In: Proceedings of the 2013 Middleware Doctoral Symposium. ACM. p 6. http://dl.acm.org/citation.cfm?id=2541595
16. An K, Shekhar S, Caglar F, Gokhale A, Sastry S (2014) A cloud middleware for assuring performance and high availability of soft real-time applications. J Syst Arch 60(9):757–769
17. Alexandrov T, Dimov A (2013) Software availability in the cloud. In: Proceedings of the 14th International Conference on Computer Systems and Technologies. ACM. pp 193–200. http://dl.acm.org/citation.cfm?id=2516814
18. Chen T, Bahsoon R, Tawil A-RH (2014) Scalable service-oriented replication with flexible consistency guarantee in the cloud. Inform Sci 264:349–370
19. Bessani A, Cutillo LA, Ramunno G, Schirmer N, Smiraglia P (2013) The tclouds platform: concept, architecture and instantiations. In: Proceedings of the 2nd International Workshop on Dependability Issues in Cloud Computing. ACM. p 1. http://dl.acm.org/citation.cfm?id=2506156
20. Imran A, Ul Gias A, Rahman R, Seal A, Rahman T, Ishraque F, Sakib K (2014) Cloud-niagara: A high availability and low overhead fault tolerance middleware for the cloud. In: Computer and Information Technology (ICCIT), 2013 16th International Conference On. IEEE. pp 271–276. http://ieeexplore.ieee.org/document/6997344/?arnumber=6997344

21. Perez-Sorrosal F, Patiño-Martinez M, Jimenez-Peris R, Kemme B (2011) Elastic si-cache: consistent and scalable caching in multi-tier architectures. VLDB J Int J Very Large Data Bases 20(6):841–865
22. Cully B, Lefebvre G, Meyer D, Feeley M, Hutchinson N, Warfield A (2008) Remus: High availability via asynchronous virtual machine replication. In: Proceedings of the 5th USENIX Symposium on Networked Systems Design and Implementation, San Francisco. pp 161–174
23. Chan H, Chieu T (2012) An approach to high availability for cloud servers with snapshot mechanism. In: Proceedings of the Industrial Track of the 13th ACM/IFIP/USENIX International Middleware Conference. ACM. p 6. http://dl.acm.org/citation.cfm?id=2405152
24. Nicolae B, Cappello F (2013) Blobcr: Virtual disk based checkpoint-restart for hpc applications on iaas clouds. J Parallel Distrib Comput 73(5):698–711
25. Toeroe M, Pawar N, Khendek F (2014) Managing application level elasticity and availability. In: Network and Service Management (CNSM), 2014 10th International Conference On. IEEE. pp 348–351. http://ieeexplore.ieee.org/document/7014191/?arnumber=7014191
26. Behl J, Distler T, Heisig F, Kapitza R, Schunter M (2012) Providing fault-tolerant execution of web-service-based workflows within clouds. In: Proceedings of the 2nd International Workshop on Cloud Computing Platforms. ACM. p 7. http://dl.acm.org/citation.cfm?id=2168704
27. Ooi BY, Chan HY, Cheah YN (2012) Dynamic service placement and replication framework to enhance service availability using team formation algorithm. J Syst Softw 85(9):2048–2062
28. Sugiki A, Kato K (2011) An extensible cloud platform inspired by operating systems. In: Utility and Cloud Computing (UCC), 2011 Fourth IEEE International Conference On. IEEE. pp 306–311. http://ieeexplore.ieee.org/document/6123513/?arnumber=6123513
29. Dantas R, Sadok D, Flinta C, Johnsson A (2015) Kvm virtualization impact on active round-trip time measurements. In: Integrated Network Management (IM), 2015 IFIP/IEEE International Symposium On. IEEE. pp 810–813. http://ieeexplore.ieee.org/document/7140382/?arnumber=7140382
30. Patel P, Bansal D, Yuan L, Murthy A, Greenberg A, Maltz DA, Kern R, Kumar H, Zikos M, Wu H, et al. (2013) Ananta: cloud scale load balancing. ACM SIGCOMM Comput Commun Rev 43(4):207–218
31. Singh D, Singh J, Chhabra A (2012) High availability of clouds: Failover strategies for cloud computing using integrated checkpointing algorithms. In: Communication Systems and Network Technologies (CSNT), 2012 International Conference On. IEEE. pp 698–703. http://ieeexplore.ieee.org/document/6200714/?arnumber=6200714
32. Anand M (2012) Always on: Architecture for high availability cloud applications. In: Cloud Computing in Emerging Markets (CCEM), 2012 IEEE International Conference On. IEEE. pp 1–5. http://ieeexplore.ieee.org/document/6354593/?arnumber=6354593
33. Availability Management Framework - Application Interface Specification SAI-AIS-AMF-B.04.01. Available at: http://devel.opensaf.org/SAI-AIS-AMF-B.04.01.AL.pdf. Accessed Oct 2016
34. Gonçalves G, Endo P, Rodrigues M, Sadok D, Curesco C Risk-based model for availability estimation of saf redundancy models. http://ieeexplore.ieee.org/stamp/stamp.jsp?tp=&arnumber=7543848
35. Frîncu ME (2014) Scheduling highly available applications on cloud environments. Future Generation Comput Syst 32:138–153
36. Sripanidkulchai K, Sahu S, Ruan Y, Shaikh A, Dorai C (2010) Are clouds ready for large distributed applications? ACM SIGOPS Oper Syst Rev 44(2):18–23
37. Araujo J, Matos R, Alves V, Maciel P, Souza F, Trivedi KS, et al. (2014) Software aging in the eucalyptus cloud computing infrastructure: characterization and rejuvenation. ACM J Emerg Technol Comput Syst (JETC) 10(1):11

11

Green spine switch management for datacenter networks

Xiaolin Li, Chung-Horng Lung* and Shikharesh Majumdar

Abstract

Energy consumption for datacenter has grown significantly and the trend is still growing due to the increasing popularity of cloud computing. Datacenter networks (DCNs), however, are starting to consume a greater portion of overall energy in comparison to servers used in datacenters due to advanced virtualization techniques. On the other hand, devices in a DCN often remain under-utilized. There are various DCN architectures. This paper proposes an approach called Green Spine Switch Management System (GSSMS) for Spine-Leaf topology based DCNs. The objective of the approach is to reduce energy consumption used by the network for a Spine-Leaf topology-based datacenter. The primary idea of GSSMS is to monitor the dynamic workload and only keep Spine switches that are necessary for handling the current network traffic. We have developed an adaptive management system to control the number of Spine switches in a Spine-Leaf DCN for efficient energy consumption. Further, we have performed extensive simulation using CloudSim for a number of scenarios. The simulation results demonstrate that our proposed GSSMS can effectively save energy by as much as 63 % of the energy consumed by a datacenter comprising a fixed static set of Spine switches.

Keywords: Datacenters, Datacenter Networks, Spine-Leaf Topology, Resource Management, Energy Efficiency

Introduction

The usage of third party datacenters for provisioning of services is becoming more widespread. More and more small and medium scale enterprises (SMEs) choose to host their services on datacenters managed by datacenter providing companies because of the convenience and decrease in cost in comparison to acquiring and maintaining their own equipment. The service providers endeavor to support reliable, secure, scalable and multi-tenant services with massive datacenters. To serve more and more tenants, the size of a datacenter has to increase. While the size of such a datacenter increases continually, the power consumed by datacenter also increases dramatically. According to [1], from 2000 to 2005, electricity consumed by world datacenters has doubled, and from 2005 to 2010, there is a 56 % increment in power consumption for datacenters across the world, and 36 % for the US datacenters. The report also indicates that, in 2010, electricity used by datacenters is about 1.3 % of the total world electricity usage, and for

US, it is about 2 % of the total US electricity usage. The energy consumed by datacenters still remains substantial and it is important for datacenter service providers to minimize electricity usage for protecting the environment as well as for reducing operational cost.

As mentioned in [1], the deceleration of the growth in electricity usage from 2005 is caused by the increased deployment of virtualization in datacenters and the industry's efforts to improve efficiency of datacenter facilities. The sources of the inefficiencies in datacenters include energy non-proportional servers and over-provisioned servers as well as the power infrastructure. The energy non-proportional servers [3] cannot control their energy consumption in accordance with the workload. In other words, servers always consume an almost fixed amount of energy irrespective of whether the workload is low or high. With over-provisioned servers and the supporting power infrastructure, e.g., cooling systems, that are used for handling (the temporary) peak workloads, datacenter devices typically remain under-utilized for most of the time. Researchers have performed a great deal of research on reducing energy consumed by servers and their cooling systems. On the

* Correspondence: chlung@sce.carleton.ca
Department of Systems and Computer Engineering, Carleton University, Ottawa, Canada

other hand, the energy consumed by datacenter *networks* (DCNs) has not received adequate attention although it is 10–20 % of datacenter's total power [2].

Previous studies show that as servers are becoming more energy-proportional, DCNs will consume a greater proportion of the overall power. Although a DCN with a fat tree topology consumes only 12 % of overall power when the datacenter is at its full utilization, with fully energy-proportional servers the the network will consume nearly 50 % of overall power when datacenter is 15 % utilized [3]. Devices in a DCN are typically under-utilized. The utilization of Edge links, aggregation links and core links, remains below 10 % during 95 % of the time, and does not exceed 30 % for more than 99 % of the time [4]. Hence, an effective management of network devices can save energy, and the most efficient way of saving energy consumed by networks is minimizing the number of active network devices [2].

To minimize the number of active switches, a DCN topology must support the ability to shift the traffic on one switch to any other switch on the same layer. Access switches can never achieve this requirement because they are connected to different servers, and their state (on or off) depends on whether or not all the servers they are connected to are inactive. Therefore, this research focuses on aggregation switches in a DCN with a topology called Spine-Leaf (as shown in Fig. 1). A detailed discussion of the Spine-Leaf topology is presented in the next section.

A preliminary report described the basic idea of a novel Green Spine Switch Management System (GSSMS) [20] for Spine-Leaf topology [5, 6] based DCNs. The aim of GSSMS is saving energy by dynamically controlling the number of active Spine switches and maintaining only a minimal set of active Spine switches that is necessary to handle the current workload. This paper extends the experiments and thoroughly investigates the effect of various system parameters.

The main contributions of this paper are summarized:

○ A new technique for energy aware Spine switch management is introduced. The technique comprises algorithms to control the number of active Spine switches according to current network traffic.
○ A simulation-based performance analysis of the technique for three different traffic patterns is presented.
○ Insights into the relationship between various system as well as workload parameters and performance are described.
○ A simulation-based analysis of the impact of the various parameters controlling the behavior of the algorithms on performance is presented.
○ A set of guidelines for choosing the various parameters controlling the behavior of the algorithms
is discussed.

The rest of the paper is organized as follows. The next section presents the description of the Spine-Leaf topology and some approaches for saving energy in

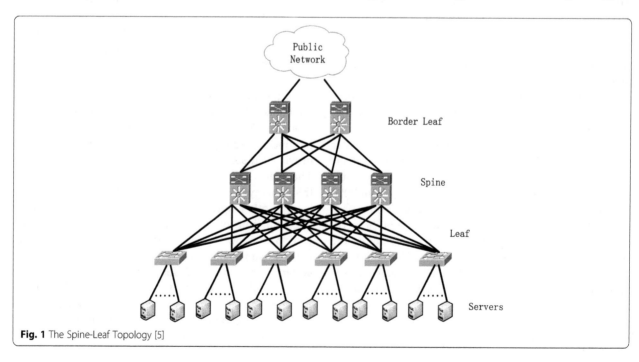

Fig. 1 The Spine-Leaf Topology [5]

datacenters. In Section III the algorithm of GSSMS is introduced. Section IV discusses the simulation methodology and results. The conclusions and future works are presented in Section V.

Related works
Spine-leaf topology
The Spine-Leaf topology, proposed by Cisco [5, 7], is used in massively scalable data centers. As shown in Fig. 1, the Spine-Leaf topology has two types of switches: Spine switch and Leaf switch. Spine switches work as aggregation switches in the traditional 3-tier network architecture. They only connect with Leaf switches and do not connect directly with servers. Every Spine switch connects with all Leaf switches. Leaf switches are access switches. They connect with Spine switches and a number of servers. As shown in Fig. 1, there are also some Leaf switches called Border Leaf switches which are responsible for connecting to public networks.

The Spine-Leaf topology has many advantages that include the following:

O Overcoming oversubscription: In the traditional 3-tier datacenter network, one access switch only connects to one core switch; therefore, the traffic capacity between servers under different access switches depends on the link capacity between the access layer and the core layer. Sometimes the available bandwidth between the access layer and the core layer is not enough to handle traffic spikes, which may lead to unexpected oversubscription. One way to mitigate the oversubscription problem is to use higher link capacity between the access layer and the core layer than that between servers and the access layer. However, oversubscription using the tree-based topology can still exist and result in the blocking server-to-server connectivity problem which can have severe performance impact on data centers due to increasing east-west traffic.
In contrast, in the Spine-Leaf topology, one Leaf switch connects to multiple Spine switches; therefore, the traffic capacity is not limited by the link capacity of a single link between the Leaf layer and the Spine layer. When one Spine switch alone is unable to handle the traffic spikes, there are other Spine switches available to share the traffic load. With high-performance switches incorporating high link capacity, a Spine switch can connect to hundreds of Leaf switches (e.g., 384 or 768) and a Leaf can connect to 32 Spine switches, which give rise to an oversubscription ratio of up to 1:1 (i.e., no oversubscription) [7, 21]. The Spine-Leaf topology represents a reasonable balance among various design considerations, including development cost, east-west vs. north-south traffic, complexity and the number of cables needed [21].

O Providing a predicable amount of delay: The topology only consists of two layers, the Spine layer and the Leaf layer. Further, a Leaf switch is connected to each and every Spine switch. As a result, the delay or latency for traffic inside the data center, i.e., east-west traffic, is predicable and a non-blocking server-to-server connectivity can be realized [7].

O Improving robustness for the network: Because every Spine switch connects with all Leaf switches, the Spine-Leaf topology can reduce failures for the network. If one Spine switch fails, the traffic routed through the failed Spine switch can be distributed to other Spine switches [5].

O Making scaling out easy on datacenters: If the datacenter providers need additional servers in the datacenter, 100 servers or lower for example, they can simply add one or two new Leaf Switches and new servers without making any change to existing Spine switches or servers in the network. If more than 100 servers need to be added or when oversubscription occurs, an additional Spine switch may be added and connected to every Leaf switch. Alternatively, multiple Spine switches may be added at the same time, if needed. The process can be repeated until the either port capacity of a Spine switch gets exhausted or oversubscription becomes an issue. If the ports for Spine switches are exhausted, then as suggested in [7], an additional super Spine switch connecting Spine switches may be considered.

To the best of our knowledge, there is no research reported in the literature addressing the energy reduction for Spine-Leaf topology. However, the Spine-Leaf topology has many advantages, such as simplifying VM placement, reducing network failures and making datacenters easy to scale out [5].

Some protocols used in the traditional 3-tier DCN, such as Spanning Tree Protocol (STP), are not suitable for the Spine-Leaf topology. Instead, for the Spine-Leaf topology, datacenter providers can use multipath to scale bandwidth [5]. FabricPath is a multipath protocol used in the Spine-Leaf topology. It basically is multipath Ethernet. It can work on NX-OS (a datacenter operating system proposed by Cisco). FabricPath combines a number of layer 3 features with current layer 2 attributes to enhance efficiency. In other words, FabricPath makes some capabilities in layer 3 routing available in the traditional layer 2 switching.

Energy saving approaches in datacenters

Researchers have proposed some algorithms for saving energy in DCNs. These algorithms save energy by minimizing the number of network devices, managing port rate or using traffic engineering schemes.

In [2], the authors proposed Elastic Tree which is a system for minimizing the DCN power consumption by shutting down unneeded switches and links. Elastic Tree chooses a subset of network devices that must be active to achieve the required performance and fault tolerance objectives based on the traffic matrix, DCN topology and the power model for each switch. Kakadia et al. [8] proposed a SDN based method for the fat tree topology to incrementally calculate the network devices required to support the current load. Preter et al. [9] presented a spanning tree based algorithm in the SDN paradigm to reduce the network electric energy consumption. Both the fat tree topology and the spanning tree based approaches suffer from the blocking of a server-to-server communications problem at high traffic, rendering the system inefficient for handling the increasing level of east-west network traffic inside of a data center. As stated in Section I, the blocking problem can be mitigated or avoided using the Spine-Leaf topology.

Both [3] and [10] proposed to save energy by managing the port rate. Abts et al. [3] proposed a topology called Flattened Butterfly (FBFLY) and exploited managing the port rate with FBFLY to save energy consumed by the DCN. The authors combined load prediction with link's dynamic traffic range to ensure that each link has the appropriate link speed to satisfy the traffic load. The approach presented in [10] focused on saving energy by traffic merging with FBFLY. The authors presented the design of a hardware called traffic merge network, which merges traffic from multiple links prior to feeding the merged traffic to the switch. The merged traffic enters the switch through several ports which are assigned maximum port rate, and other ports are assigned lower port rate.

Traffic engineering methods have been used in [11] and [12] to save energy. Vasic et al. [11] proposed a system which pre-computes energy-critical paths off-line for the network, and then uses online traffic engineering to deactivate and activate network elements on demand. In [12], the authors used a traffic off-balancing algorithm which behaves oppositely to the load-balancing algorithm to minimize the number of active network devices. Shi et al. [13–15] have proposed approaches managing resource in wireless network.

In this paper, we propose an algorithm that minimizes the number of active Spine switches to dynamically manage the number of Spine switches needed according to the traffic load in datacenters. Based on an investigation on energy consumption, a high end switch can save tremendous energy (e.g., 84 %) when it is in the Hibernation mode [19]. The main difference between our algorithm and aforementioned approaches is that our algorithm uses the Spine-Leaf topology. Our current focus is not specifically for SDN. But the concept can be integrated with SDN, as our approach also makes use of a controller to Spine switches, as shown in Section III.

Green spine switch management system

The basic concepts underlying GSSMS are summarized. When the network traffic increases and the active Spine switches do not have enough available bandwidth for the traffic, GSSMS activates an additional Spine switch that is available; when the network traffic drops and one or more active Spine switches are idle, GSSMS deactivates those Spine switches for energy saving.

GSSMS comprises of four main modules: Routing, Spine Switch Controller, Network Monitor and Power

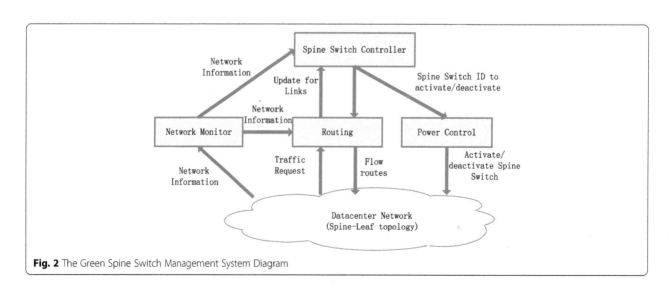

Fig. 2 The Green Spine Switch Management System Diagram

Control, as shown in Fig. 2. The Routing module is responsible for choosing one Spine switch from the available active Spine switches to forward traffic that comes from Leaf switches. The Spine Switch Controller module is used to monitor the utilizations of all links and all Spine switches, and make the decision of activating or deactivating a Spine switch and the decision of which Spine switch should be activated or deactivated as well. The Network Monitor module is responsible for collecting network information. The Power Control module is in charge of toggling the power states (active or sleep) of Spine switches.

Routing module

The Routing Module selects the active Spine switch with the highest link utilization (the link connecting the Spine and the Leaf switches) that has enough available bandwidth to handle the new flow. The algorithm is shown in Algorithm 1.

The Routing Module's inputs are the requests coming from the DCN. The requests are of two types: (i) New Flow Request – the source Leaf switch asks for bandwidth reservation for a new flow and (ii) End Flow Request – the source Leaf switch asks to release the bandwidth reservation for the finished flow.

As shown in Algorithm 1, for both types of requests, the Routing Module determines whether the flow's destination is outside or inside the datacenter. Requests will be treated in different ways based on their destination. A flow with a destination outside the datacenter only needs bandwidth reservation on one link between a Spine switch and a Leaf switch. A flow with a destination inside the datacenter needs bandwidth reservation on two links between a Spine switch and two Leaf switches.

Algorithm 1: Routing

Input : Requests from the datacenter network

Output: flow routes and link utilization update

```
1.   receive a request
2.   switch(request)
3.     case New Flow:
4.       if (request.dest is outside datacenter)
5.         find the proper Spine switch
6.         make the bandwidth reservation on the link
7.       else find the proper Spine switch
8.         make bandwidth reservations on two links
9.         send the flow route & link utilization increase update
10.    case End Flow:
11.      if (request.dest is outside datacenter)
12.        delete the reservation on one link
13.      else delete the reservations on two links
14.        send the link utilization decrease update
```

For a New Flow request, the Routing Module finds the proper Spine switch to transmit the new flow. Inside the Routing Module, for each Leaf switch, all

utilizations of links are sorted in non-increasing order in a queue. If the new flow goes outside of the datacenter, the Routing Module just needs to select the first Spine switch that has enough available bandwidth in the link utilization queue. Otherwise the Routing Module needs to choose the first Spine switch that has enough available bandwidth for two links; one is the link between the source Leaf switch and the Spine switch, and the other one is the link between the Spine switch and the destination Leaf switch. Then the Routing Module makes the bandwidth reservations on both the links. Finally, the Routing Module sends the flow route with the Spine switch ID back to the source Leaf switch, and sends a message to update the Spine Switch Controller with the increased utilization of the link between source Leaf switch and the chosen Spine switch.

For an End Flow request, besides the destination of the flow, the Routing Module can also acquire information about the Spine switch which transmits the flow. If the flow's destination is out of the datacenter, the Routing Module only needs to remove the bandwidth reservation on the link between the source Leaf switch and the Spine switch. Otherwise, the Routing Module needs to release the bandwidth reservation on two links – one is between the source Leaf switch and the Spine switch and the other one is between the Spine switch and the destination Leaf switch. Finally, the Routing Module sends a link utilization update to the Spine Switch Controller.

Spine switch controller

The Spine Switch Controller module which is the key component of GSSMS uses eight parameters:

1. The high First Utilization Threshold (FUT-H)
2. The low First Utilization Threshold (FUT-L)
3. The high Control Threshold (CT-H)
4. The low Control Threshold (CT-L)
5. The high Second Utilization Threshold (SUT-H)
6. The low Second Utilization Threshold (SUT-L)
7. The Time Duration for Activating (Tda)
8. The Time Duration for Deactivating (Tdd)

FUT-H and FUT-L are used for starting the timer for activating or deactivating decision making, respectively. SUT-H and SUT-L are used to decide if the respective timer for activating and deactivating Spine switches should stop. CT-H and CT-L are ratios of the number of links between a Leaf switch and Spine switches that cross those aforementioned thresholds. Tda is the time duration used for activating a Spine switch, while Tdd is the time duration used for deactivating one or more Spine switches. Tda and Tdd are used to avoid frequent changes in the number of Spine switches due to temporary spikes in traffic.

Algorithms for activating/deactivating spine switches

The algorithm for activating a Spine switch is presented in Algorithm 2. For each Leaf switch, when the link utilizations of a given number (Na) of links connected with the given Leaf switch exceed FUT-H, and remain higher than SUT-H for the given time duration Tda, a Spine switch is activated.

Algorithm 2: Increasing the number of active Spine switches

---

1. Na = round-up (number of active Spine switches × CT-H)
2. **foreach** Leaf switch
3.   **if** the link utilization of Na links connected with the given Leaf switch ≥ FUT-H
4.   start timer T
5.   **if** T ≥ Tda
6.   Activate a Spine switch

Algorithm 3: Decreasing the number of active Spine switches

---

1. Nd = round-up (number of active Spine switches × CT-L)
2. **foreach** Leaf switch
3.   **if** the link utilization of Nd links connected with the given Leaf switch ≤ FUT-L
4.   add the Leaf switch into *timingmap*
5.   **if** *timingmap.size()* == number of Leaf switches
6.   start timer T
7.   **foreach** Leaf switch
8.   **if** the link utilization of Nd links connected with the given Leaf switch ≥ SUT-L and T ≤ Tdd
9.   remove the Leaf switch from timingmap and stop timer T
10. **if** *timingmap.size()* == number of Leaf switches for T ≥ Tdd
11.   deactivate at least Nd Spine switches

The algorithm for deactivating Spine switches is presented in Algorithm 3. For each Leaf switch, when the link utilizations of a given number (Nd) of links connected with the given Leaf switch fall below FUT-L, the Leaf switch is put into a list *timingmap*. If all Leaf switches are in *timingmap* for the given time duration Tdd, a number of Spine switches are deactivated.

Operations of the spine switch controller

The main operation performed by the Spine Switch Controller comprises two steps: (i) making decision of starting the timer for activating/deactivating a Spine switch and (ii) checking the time duration.

Algorithm 4 presents the steps for making the decision for starting the timer used in Algorithm 2 and 3. The input of the Spine Switch Controller is the link utilization update, including link utilization increase update and link utilization decrease update.

Algorithm 4: Making decision of starting the timer

Input   : link utilization updates

---

1. **switch**(*update*)
2.   **case** increase update:
3.   **if** the utilization of the updated link ≥ FUT-H and the number of busy links of the Leaf switch ≥ Na
           start the activating timer for the Leaf switch
5.   **else if** the utilization of the updated link ≥ SUT-L and the number of idle links of the Leaf switch < Nd
6.   remove the Leaf switch from *timingmap* and stop the deactivating timer if needed
7.   **case** decrease update:
8.   **if** the utilization of the updated link ≤ FUT-L and the number of idle links of the Leaf switch ≥ Nd
9.   add the Leaf switch into *timingmap*
10.   **if** (*timingmap.size* == number of Leaf switches)
11.   start the deactivating timer
12.   **else if** the utilization of the updated link ≤ SUT-H and the number of busy links of the Leaf switch < Na
13.   stop the activating timer for the Leaf switch
14. Checking the time duration

For a link utilization increase update, the Spine Switch Controller needs to check the number of links with utilization that is equal to or higher than FUT-H for the source Leaf switch to determine if the timer for activating a Spine switch needs to start. If the number of links reaches Na, the timer for activating a Spine switch starts. Because any Leaf switch can trigger the timer for activating, Leaf switches have separate timers. Then the Spine Switch Controller updates the information related to the timer for deactivating Spine switches and switches OFF the timer if the requirement of deactivating is not satisfied any more.

Algorithm 5: Checking the time duration

Output: Spine switches' ID to activate or deactivate

---

1. **foreach** Leaf switch
2.   **if** the activating timer for the Leaf switch is on for Tda
3.   add a Spine switch and send the Spine switch's ID to the Routing Module and the Power Control
4. **if** the deactivating timer is on for Tdd
5.   **foreach** Leaf switch
6.   **if** (*min_num* > *num_of_idle_links*[*leafswitchID*])
7.   *min_num*= *num_of_idle_links*[*leafswitchID*]
8.   choose *min_num* Spine switches with the lowest utilization to deactivate

---

For a link utilization decrease update, the Spine Switch Controller updates the link utilization and checks if the timer for deactivating Spine switches should start. The Spine Switch Controller has one timer for deactivating Spine switches and a timingmap (shown in line 6&9 in Algorithm 4, which is a list of Leaf switch IDs) to record the Leaf switches that satisfy the requirement of deactivating Spine switches. Only when all Leaf switches' IDs are in timingmap, the Spine Switch Controller starts the timer for deactivating Spine switches. Then the Spine Switch Controller updates the information related with the timer for activating a Spine switch and switches OFF the timer if the requirement of activating is not satisfied any more.

After confirming the timer's state, the Spine Switch Controller checks the time duration, as shown in Algorithm 5. Each Leaf switch has a timer for activating a Spine switch. If any one of those timers is on and Tda is exceeded, the Spine Switch Controller makes the decision of adding a new one. The Spine Switch Controller sends the Spine switch's ID to the Power Control to inform it that the Spine switch should be activated, and sends the Spine switch's ID to the Routing Module to tell it that traffic can be distributed on the new active Spine switch.

If the timer for deactivating Spine switches is on and Tdd is exceeded, the Spine Switch Controller calculates the number (*min_num*) of Spine switches that should be deactivated (as shown in lines 5–7 in Algorithm 5) and determines which Spine switches should be deactivated. The Spine Switch Controller sends the Spine switches' ID to the Power Control Module to inform that the Spine switches should be deactivated, and sends the Spine switch's ID to the Routing Module to inform that traffic is not to be distributed on those Spine switches.

Backup spine switch

Because the Spine Switch Controller does not activate a Spine Switch immediately when the traffic load increases, it is possible that during the respective time duration, the traffic load exceeds the capacity of the DCN. In this scenario, there is no active Spine switch to transmit the extra traffic; and the DCN will drop all extra traffic, which is unacceptable. Therefore, GSSMS

chooses one active Spine switch as the backup Spine switch, which is always on. The Backup Spine Switch's responsibility is to transmit traffic when there is no other active Spine switch with enough available bandwidth, as shown in Fig. 3.

After GSSMS decides to activate a Spine switch, there is an expected delay (1–3 min as noted for EnergyWise in [16]) before the Spine switch can accept new flows. During this time duration, GSSMS distributes new flows on the Backup Spine Switch. After the newly activated Spine switch becomes active, GSSMS distributes new flows on the Spine switch. GSSMS never move existing flows from one Spine switch to another.

Simulation setup and results

We use CloudSim [17] for simulation. The traffic model used in this paper is the ON/OFF model. The ON/OFF traffic model is observed in real DCNs [4]. This paper uses the same distribution used in [18] for the durations of ON/OFF period – Pareto distribution. In the simulation, the DCN configuration used is adopted from Cisco's practices [7]. The DCN consists of 16 Leaf switches and 8 Spine switches, and the link capacity is set to10Gbps. One Leaf switch connects to 15 servers. One server has 10 VMs and each VM is a traffic source.

Metrics used in simulation evaluation include: the average number of active Spine switches (ANASS), the percentage of power consumed by GSSMS over the total number of Spine switches (POPC) and the percentage of failures (PF). They are calculated by Eqs. (1), (2) and (3). In Eq. 2, N represents the total number of Spine switches, and we assume that a switch in the Hibernation mode can lead to a significant power saving, e.g., 84 % as reported in [19].

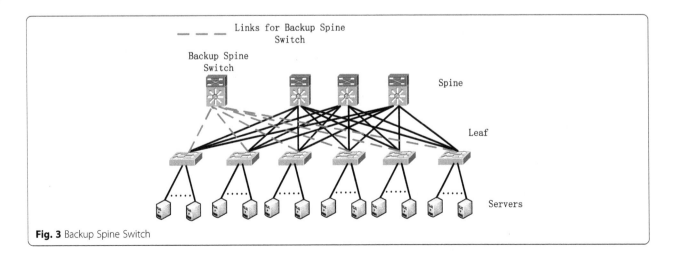

Fig. 3 Backup Spine Switch

$$\text{ANASS} = \frac{\sum \text{number of active Spine switches} \times \text{duration}}{\text{total duration}} \tag{1}$$

$$\text{POPC} = \frac{\text{ANASS} + (\text{N--ANASS}) \times 0.16}{\text{N}} \times 100\% \tag{2}$$

$$\text{PF} = \frac{\text{the number of failed flows}}{\text{the number of all flows}} \tag{3}$$

A failure is said to occur when a VM intends to send data, but there is not enough available bandwidth for the data flow. In GSSMS, the minimum number of active Spine switches is two. One of the two Spine switches is the backup Spine switch.

Input traffic patterns

This paper uses three types of traffic pattern for GSSMS's input. These three types of traffic pattern are: Uniform Traffic, Sine-Wave Traffic and Random Traffic.

Uniform traffic

For the uniform traffic [2], the traffic rate is fixed for each traffic source. Based on the traffic's destination, this paper considers three types of uniform traffic: Near traffic, Far traffic and Half-Far/Half-Near traffic.

Near traffic (Near): For each data flow, the flow's source and destination connect with the same Leaf switch.

Far traffic (Far): For each data flow, the flow's source and destination connect with different Leaf switches.

Half-Far/Half-Near traffic (Half-Half): 50 % of the traffic is Near traffic, and 50 % of the traffic is Far traffic.

These traffic types are adapted from [2]. The simulation results for the Uniform traffic are presented in Fig. 4. In Fig. 4a, for the Near traffic case, ANASS is two all the time, because the traffic is not routed through Spine switches for Near traffic. Thus, ANASS is not affected by the traffic change. For Far traffic, as expected, ANASS increases as the traffic rate for each traffic source increases. The total traffic routing through Spine switches increases while the traffic rate for each traffic source increases. The increase of the total traffic causes the increase of ANASS. For Half-Far/Half-Near traffic, ANASS also increases as the traffic rate for each traffic source increases. The reason is same as the reason provided for Far traffic. Compared with the Far traffic case, for a given traffic rate, the total traffic of the DCN is approximately half of that in the Far traffic scenario. Therefore, ANASS is approximately half of ANASS in the Far traffic scenario. Figure 4a also shows that POPC is determined by the traffic routing through Spine switches. For Near traffic, there is no traffic routing through Spine switches. Therefore, only two Spine switches are active and POPC is 37 % all the time. For Far

traffic, POPC increases while the traffic rate for each traffic source increases. That means that the saved energy decreases as the traffic rate increases. When the traffic rate is 30Mbps, POPC is 37 %, which means GSSMS saves 63 % energy in comparison to a static system. When the traffic rate is 310Mbps, POPC is 100 %, which means GSSMS cannot save energy. For Half-Far/Half-Near traffic, GSSMS can save energy from 42 to 63 %. GSSMS can save more energy for Half-Far/Half-Near traffic at a given traffic rate because Half-Far/Half-Near traffic has lower traffic routing through Spine switches.

In Fig. 4b, failures appear when the traffic rate increases (e.g., traffic rate from 150Mbps to 190Mbps, from 210Mbps to 230Mbps and from 250Mbps to 290Mbps) while ANASS remains the same value. For instance, the four points shown in Fig. 4b: A, B, C and D, but the values of PF are small. Because GSSMS does not activate Spine switches immediately, it is possible that the network does not have enough available bandwidth for the traffic at a given time; hence failures occur on the system. The increase in PF is caused by the increase in the traffic rate. With the same ANASS, the network in the case of a higher traffic rate has less available bandwidth; as a result, more flows cannot receive adequate bandwidth. If the traffic rate keeps increasing, ANASS increases, such as the points E, F, and G shown in Fig. 4b. The increase of ANASS means that the available bandwidth of the network increases. Therefore, the network can handle the traffic without failures most of the time.

Sine-wave traffic

For the Sine-Wave traffic, the traffic rate for each traffic source varies as a sine wave [2].

$$\text{Traffic Rate} = {}^1/_2 \times \text{ max rate } \times (1 + sin(t)) \tag{4}$$

There are three types of Sine-Wave traffic: Near traffic, Far traffic and Half-Far/Half-Near traffic. These three types of Sine-Wave traffic have a similar meaning as their respective Uniform traffic counterparts.

NASS in Fig. 5 represents the number of active Spine switches. Figure 5 shows the simulation results for Far traffic. The number of Spine switches changes as the traffic rate for each traffic source changes. The results show that NASS changes according to the total traffic of the DCN. As the total traffic of the DCN increases, more Spine switches are activated in the DCN. As the total traffic of the datacenter decreases, NASS of the DCN is observed to decrease.

The Half-Far/Half-Near traffic gives rise to a similar results, except that the value of NASS at a given point in time seems to be smaller than that achieved with the Far traffic scenario.

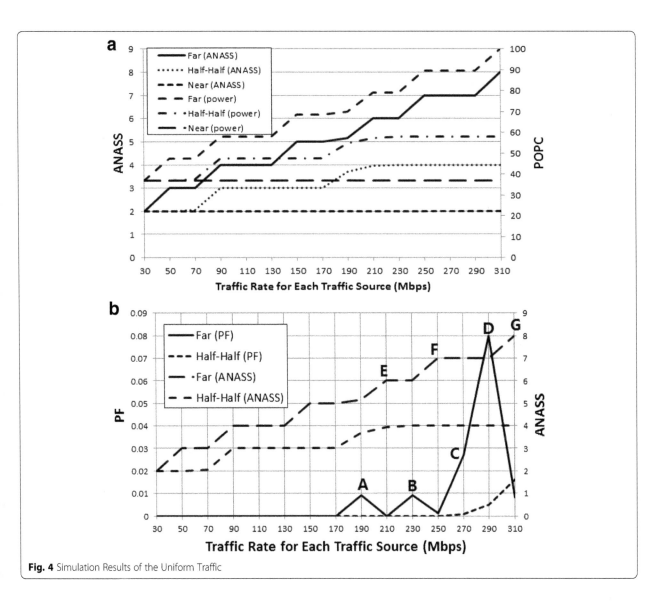

Fig. 4 Simulation Results of the Uniform Traffic

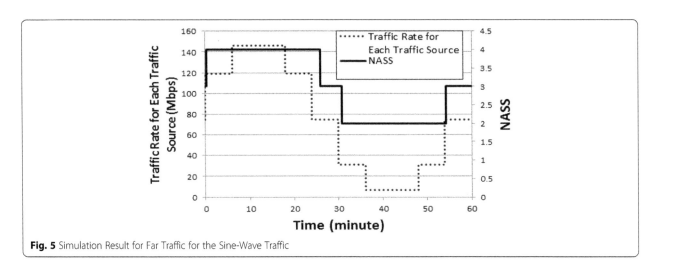

Fig. 5 Simulation Result for Far Traffic for the Sine-Wave Traffic

Random traffic

Random traffic is used to simulate the scenario observed in datacenters where 95 % of the time, the traffic is 10 % of the DCN capacity, and during 5 % of the time, the traffic is higher than 10 % of the DCN capacity [4]. In the simulation setup, each link has a capacity of 10Gbps. Therefore, in the random traffic scenario, the traffic rate for each traffic source is 9Mbps for 95 % of the time, and uniformly varies within the range between 50Mbps and 200Mbps for the rest 5 % of the time.

The results for Random traffic are shown in Fig. 6. The traffic bursts last for approximately 1 min and GSSMS increases the number of active Spine switches for the duration of the traffic bursts and decreases the number of active Spine switches when the traffic bursts finish. Time duration Tda is 5 s and Tdd is 10 s in the simulation. NASS increases approximately 5 s after the traffic rate for each traffic source increases. NASS decreases approximately 10 s after the traffic rate for each traffic source decreases. Because the x-axis values in the graph are in minutes, it is very difficult to visualize these delays clearly in the figure.

For Sine-Wave traffic and Random traffic, we expect that the shapes of ANASS and POPC graphs would be similar to those in Fig. 4a.

Comparison between GSSMS and fixed numbers of spine switches

In this section, the simulation results present the difference between GSSMS and fixed numbers of Spine switches as captured by ANASS and PF for a datacenter. Because for the Near traffic case, the number of Spine switches never changes, the simulation results for Near traffic are not discussed.

Figures 7 and 8 present the simulation results for Uniform-Far and Uniform-Half-Far/Half-Near (Uniform-Half/Half) traffic. NSS in Fig. 7 represents the number of Spine switches used in a datacenter that does not use

GSSMS and deploys a fixed number of Spine switches. In Fig. 7, compared to the datacenter with six Spine switches, GSSMS can save energy when the traffic rate is < 210Mbps. When the traffic rate is higher than 250Mbps, GSSMS leads to an ANASS that is higher than six. Although GSSMS consumes more energy than the datacenter with a fixed set of six Spine switches when the traffic rate is higher than 250Mbps, it has much lower PF than that with six Spine switches. When the traffic rate is 270Mbps, PF of GSSMS is only 0.03 while PF of the datacenter with six Spine switches is more than 0.3. Compared with the datacenter deploying a fixed number of eight Spine switches, GSSMS can save energy when not all the Spine switches are active and has an acceptable PF at the same time. In Fig. 8, compared to the datacenter with a fixed set of four Spine switches, GSSMS produces an ANASS lower than four when the traffic rate is < 210Mbps. When the traffic rate is > 210Mbps, ANASS for GSSMS is four and it produces a PF that is similar to the datacenter using a fixed set of four Spine switches.

The simulations for Sine-Wave-Far (Sine-Far) and Sine-Wave-Half-Far/Half-Near (Sine-Half/Half) traffic produce similar results, except that the value of ANASS and PF at a given traffic rate is smaller than that for the Uniform-Far and Uniform-Half/Half scenarios.

The simulation results reveal that compared with the datacenter with a fixed numbers of Spine switches, GSSMS can save energy consumed by Spine switches with an acceptable increase in PF (<0.09) and reduce PF significantly (100 to 82 %) by having one or more active Spine switches when the PF of GSSMS is compared with the PF of the datacenter with a fixed set of two, four and six Spine switches.

Effect of system parameters

A detailed simulation-based investigation of the impact of various system and workload parameters on performance was performed.

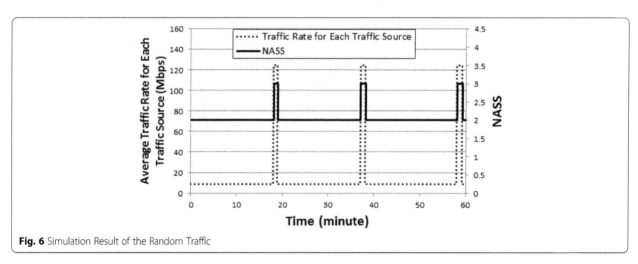

Fig. 6 Simulation Result of the Random Traffic

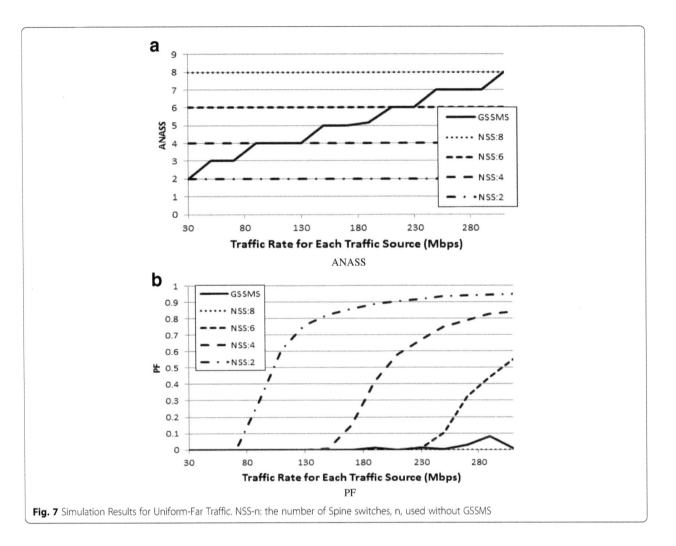

Fig. 7 Simulation Results for Uniform-Far Traffic. NSS-n: the number of Spine switches, n, used without GSSMS

The system parameters are the aforementioned parameters: FUT-H, FUT-L, CT-H, CT-L, SUT-H, SUT-L, Tda and Tdd.

Figure 9 presents the simulation results which demonstrate the impact of FUT-H. Figure 10 shows the impact of FUT-L. FUT-H is used for activating a Spine Switch in response to an increase in traffic. FUT-L is used for deactivating Spine switches in response to a decrease in traffic.

The simulation results shown in Fig. 9a demonstrate that ANASS increases as FUT-H decreases. The reason is that compared with GSSMS with a high FUT-H, GSSMS with a low FUT-H is more likely to activate a Spine switch under the same situation. For instance, consider a situation in which the traffic increases to 96 % of a link capacity and then decreases to 70 % of a link capacity within the time duration Tda. In this scenario, when the traffic increases to 96 % of a link capacity, the traffic can trigger the timer of activating a Spine switch for both GSSMS with FUT-H of 95 % and GSSMS with FUT-H of 80 %. However, when the traffic decreases to 70 % of a link

capacity, the timer of GSSMS with FUT-H of 95 % turns to OFF (SUT-H is 20 lower than FUT-H, and 70 % is lower than SUT-H of 75 %). On the other hand, the timer of GSSMS with FUT-H of 80 % is still ON because 70 % is higher than SUT-H of 60 %. As a result, after the time duration Tda, GSSMS with FUT-H of 80 % activates a Spine switch while GSSMS with FUT-H of 95 % does not.

The simulation results shown in Fig. 9b illustrate that when FUT-H is 100 %, PF of Far traffic increases dramatically. A 100 % FUT-H means that only when the active Spine switches are fully used, GSSMS can trigger the timer for activating a Spine switch. As a result, when the current active Spine switches do not have enough available bandwidth for the traffic, a Spine switch cannot be activated in time, which leads to the occurrence of failures. PF of Half-Far/Half-Near traffic increases slightly because compared with the Far traffic case, the Half-Far/Half-Near traffic case has lower traffic. To summarize, the simulation results demonstrate that high FUT-H leads to a low ANASS and a high PF compared with a low FUT-H.

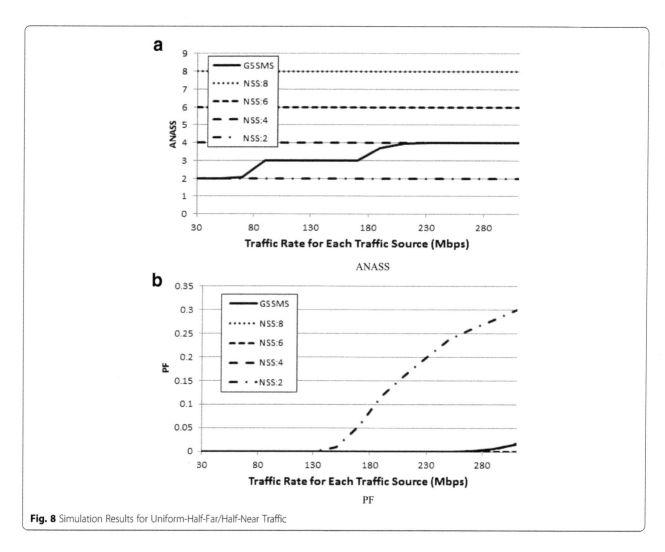

Fig. 8 Simulation Results for Uniform-Half-Far/Half-Near Traffic

In Fig. 9a, ANASS of Uniform-Far traffic for given FUT-H and FUT-L is higher than ANASS of Uniform-Half-Far/Half-Near traffic except for 100 % FUT-H, and ANASS of Sine-Wave-Far traffic is higher than ANASS of Sine-Wave-Half-Far/Half-Near traffic except for 100 % FUT-H. The reason is that compared with Far traffic, Half-Far/Half-Near traffic has less traffic routing through Spine switches. The number of active Spine switches of GSSMS at a given time is determined by the traffic routing through Spine switches. Thus, the number of active Spine switches of GSSMS for Half-Far/Half-Near traffic at a given time is lower than that for Far traffic. For the 100 % FUT-H case, there is no difference in ANASS for the four traffic patterns because 100 % is too high and GSSMS never has a chance to increase the number of active Spine switches during the simulation.

Figure 9a also shows that ANASS of Uniform-Far traffic for given FUT-H and FUT-L is higher than ANASS of Sine-Wave-Far traffic except for 100 % FUT-H, and ANASS of Uniform-Half-Far/Half-Near traffic for given FUT-H and FUT-L is higher than ANASS of Sine-Wave-

Half-Far/Half-Near traffic except for 100 % FUT-H. This is caused by the difference in traffic routing through Spine switches in the Uniform traffic case and the Sine-Wave traffic case. As introduced in Section IV.A, in the Uniform traffic case, the traffic rate for each traffic source is fixed. In the Sine-Wave traffic case, the traffic rate at a given time varies as a sine wave, and the traffic rate assigned as the traffic rate for each traffic source is the maximum traffic rate. The traffic rate at a given time can reach the maximum traffic rate during only one fifth of the simulation time. Therefore, for Uniform traffic and Sine-Wave traffic with the same traffic rate for each traffic source, the traffic routing through Spine switches in the Uniform traffic case is higher than that in the Sine-Wave traffic case.

Figure 10a demonstrates that ANASS decreases as FUT-L increases except for the Uniform-Far traffic case. The reason is that compared with GSSMS using a low FUT-L, a GSSMS using a high FUT-L can deactivate a Spine switch more easily. For instance, consider a situation in which the traffic decreases to 3 % of a link

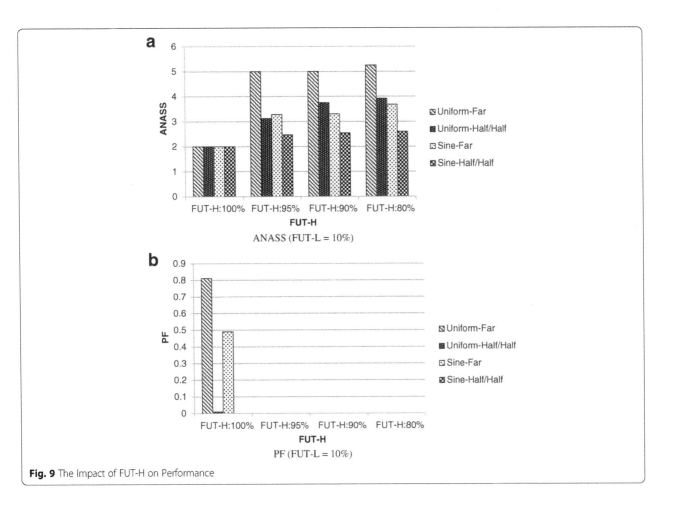

Fig. 9 The Impact of FUT-H on Performance

capacity and then increases to 26 % of a link capacity within the time duration Tdd. In this scenario, when the traffic decreases to 3 % of a link capacity, the traffic can trigger the timer of deactivating a Spine switch for GSSMS with FUT-L of 5 % and GSSMS with FUT-L of 20 %. However, when the traffic increases to 26 % of a link capacity, the timer of GSSMS with FUT-L of 5 % turns to OFF (SUT-L is 10 higher than FUT-L, and 26 % is higher than SUT-L of 15 %). On the other hand, the timer of GSSMS with FUT-L of 20 % is still ON because 26 % is lower than SUT-L of 30 %. Therefore, GSSMS with FUT-L of 20 % has higher probability of deactivating a Spine switch than GSSMS with FUT-L of 10 % under the same situation. For Uniform-Far traffic, the utilizations of all links are much higher than FUT-L. GSSMS does not have a chance to deactivate a Spine switch for the Uniform-Far traffic case. Therefore, the simulation results for Uniform-Far traffic cannot show the impact of FUT-L.

The simulation results shown in Fig. 10b illustrate that when FUT-L is 100 %, PF of Far traffic increases dramatically. A 100 % FUT-L means that GSSMS can start the timer for deactivating Spine switches at any time and can always deactivate Spine switches after the time duration Tdd. As a result, GSSMS deactivates Spine switches even when the Spine switches are needed to handle the traffic. The inappropriate deactivation of Spine switches leads to the occurrence of failures. PF of Half-Far/Half-Near traffic increases slightly for an FUT-L of 100 % because compared with the Far traffic case, the Half-Far/Half-Near traffic case leads to a lower traffic. To summarize, the simulation results demonstrate that high FUT-L leads to a low ANASS and a high PF compared with a low FUT-L.

Figure 10a also shows that ANASS of GSSMS for Uniform-Far traffic for given FUT-H and FUT-L is always higher than that for Uniform-Half-Far/Half-Near traffic, and ANASS of GSSMS for Sine-Wave-Far traffic for given FUT-H and FUT-L is always higher than that for Sine-Wave-Half-Far/Half-Near traffic. ANASS of GSSMS for Uniform-Far traffic for given FUT-H and FUT-L is always higher than that for Sine-Wave-Far traffic and ANASS of GSSMS for Uniform-Half-Far/Half-Near traffic for given FUT-H and FUT-L is always higher than that for Sine-Wave-Half-Far/Half-Near traffic. As discussed before, the difference between ANASSs

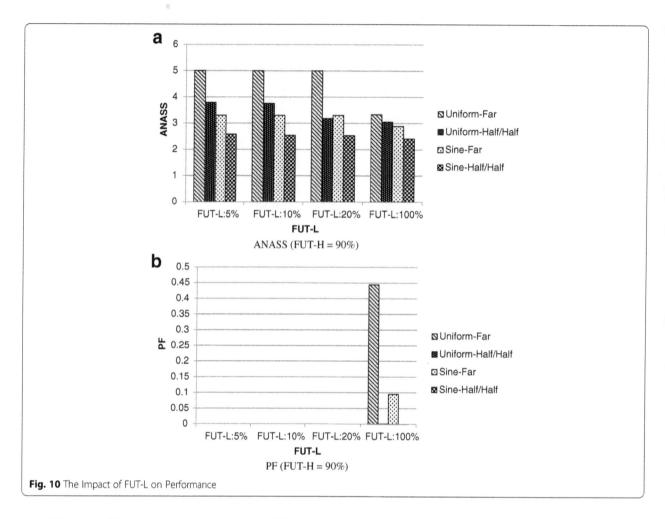

Fig. 10 The Impact of FUT-L on Performance

for different traffic patterns is caused by the difference between the traffic routing through Spine switches in the different traffic pattern cases.

Simulation results show that SUTs have similar impact on performance with FUTs. The difference is that SUTs have less impact on performance than FUTs, especially on PF. In the simulation for SUT-H, the highest PF is 0.005, and the highest PF is 0.0002 in the simulation for SUT-L. The highest PF in the simulation for FUTs are 0.8 and 0.44 respectively.

Figures 11 and 12 present the impact of CT-H and CT-L on performance. Like FUTs, CT-H is used for activating a Spine Switch in response to an increase in

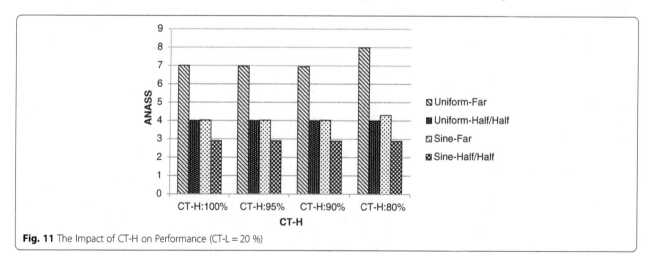

Fig. 11 The Impact of CT-H on Performance (CT-L = 20 %)

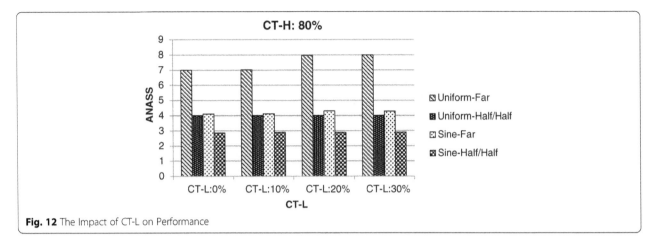

Fig. 12 The Impact of CT-L on Performance

traffic. CT-L is used for deactivating Spine switches when traffic reaches a predetermined low value.

The simulation result for the Far traffic case in Fig. 11 illustrates that ANASS increases while CT-H decreases. The reason is that a lower CT-H value is easier to reach. For example, consider a situation in which there are six active Spine switches in the network and a Leaf switch has five links with utilization higher than FUT-H. In this situation, if CT-H is 90 %, the given number Na is six, and Na is five if CT-H is 80 %. That means that when CT-H is 80 %, GSSMS sets the timer for activating a Spine switch ON; when CT-H is 90 %, the timer for activating a Spine switch is still OFF. Figure 11 shows that the performance for Half-Far/Half-Near traffic is not very sensitive to CT-H. The reason is that the number of active Spine switches is too small which makes Na be the same when CT-H has different values.

Changes in CT-H do not seem to have much impact on PF. The simulation results demonstrate that when CT-H is 100 %, it only has slight impact on the Sine-Wave Far traffic case (PF is 0.0002). The reason for the occurrence of failures is that GSSMS cannot activate a Spine switch in time because of the high CT-H. The reason of no failures in the Uniform Far traffic case is that seven active Spine switches are enough to handle the traffic without failure.

Similar to the previous results, Fig. 11 shows the same difference between Far traffic and Half-Far/Half-Near traffic and the same difference between Uniform traffic and Sine-Wave traffic.

The simulation results in Fig. 12 demonstrate that ANASS increases while CT-L increases. The reason is that a lower CT-L value is easier to reach. For instance, consider a situation in which there are six active Spine switches in the network and all Leaf switches have one link with utilization lower than FUT-L. In this situation, if CT-L is 10 %, the given number Nd is one, and Nd is two if CT-L is 30 %. That means that when CT-L is 10 %, GSSMS sets the timer for deactivating a Spine

switch ON; when CT-L is 30 %, the timer for deactivating a Spine switch is still OFF.

The change of CT-H does not have much impact on PF. The simulation results demonstrate that when CT-L is 0 %, it only has a slight impact on the Sine-Wave Far traffic (PF is 0.0001).

The Time Durations Tda and Tdd are used to filter out the instantaneous traffic. Tdd is held at twice the value of Tda in the simulation. That Tdd is longer than Tda is good for the situation that the traffic increases in a short time after it decreases. The simulation results shown in Fig. 13a illustrate that ANASS decreases as Tda increases for the Uniform traffic. For Uniform traffic, ANASS for the small Tda is higher than that for the large Tda. The reason is that with small Tda, GSSMS activates a Spine switch for the short time traffic increase while GSSMS with large Tda does not activate a Spine switch for such a short time traffic increase. For Sine-Wave traffic, when Tda is smaller than 100 s, ANASS decreases as Tda increases. The reason is same with Uniform traffic. The simulation results shown in Fig. 13b demonstrate that when Tda is 100 s or 20 s, the Far traffic case has failures. The reason is that if Tda is too long, and GSSMS can be too late for activating a Spine switch and some packets may be dropped.

There is another difference between Uniform traffic and Sine-Wave traffic shown in Fig. 13a. As Tda increases, ANASS of GSSMS for Uniform traffic decreases while ANASS of GSSMS for Sine-Wave traffic decreases first and then increase slightly. For Sine-Wave traffic, ANASS increases when Tda is 100 s. For the Sine-Wave traffic, the traffic rate for each traffic source changes with time as a sine wave, and the number of the active Spine switches is the minimum number two for half of the simulation time because of the low traffic rate part (the traffic rate is lower than half of the maximum traffic rate) in Sine-Wave traffic. When Tda is 100 s, the number of active Spine switches decreases to two 200 s after the decrease of the traffic

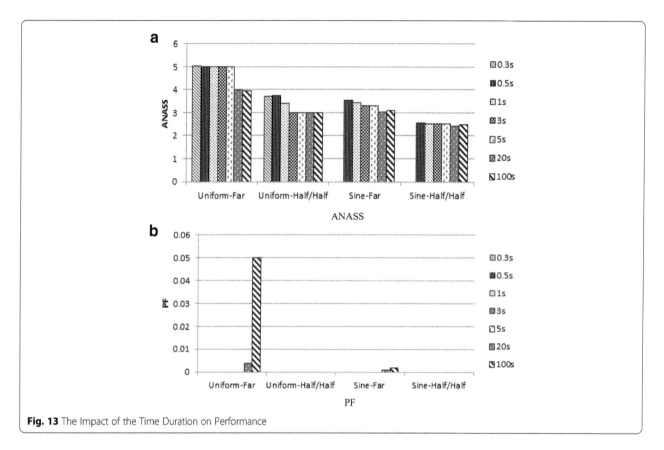

Fig. 13 The Impact of the Time Duration on Performance

rate. The 200 s delay is the reason for the increase of ANASS.

The workload parameters include the number of Leaf Switches, ON/OFF Duration-ON and ON/OFF Duration-OFF.

Figure 14 presents the impact of the number of Leaf switches (NLS). The simulation results illustrate that ANASS decreases as NLS decreases. The reason is that with more Leaf switches, the probability of traffic concentrating on one Leaf switch is higher. For instance,

assuming that the traffic on each Leaf switch is i.i.d and the probability of the traffic on one Leaf switch exceeding the link capacity is p, eight Leaf switches in the network means that the total probability of the traffic on one or more Leaf switches exceeding the link capacity is $8 \times p$. If the network has 24 Leaf switches, the total probability of the traffic exceeding the link capacity is $24 \times p$. GSSMS activates a Spine switch as long as any one Leaf switch satisfies the requirement of activating an additional Spine switch. Therefore, if the total probability of the traffic

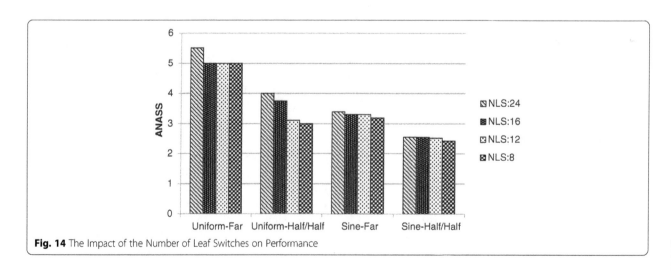

Fig. 14 The Impact of the Number of Leaf Switches on Performance

exceeding the link capacity increases, the probability of GSSMS activating a Spine switch increases.

The simulation results in Fig. 15 demonstrate that, as expected, ANASS decreases while the ON Duration decreases. The reason is that when the ON Duration decreases, the number of the concurrent flows decreases, thus the total traffic in the DCN decreases. ANASS decreases when the total traffic decreases.

The simulation results in Fig. 16 demonstrate that ANASS increases while the OFF Duration decreases. The reason is that when the OFF Duration decreases, the number of the concurrent flows increases, thus the total traffic in the DCN increases. As a result, ANASS increases when the total traffic increases.

Guidelines for choosing the control parameters

A few guidelines for choosing the parameters have been developed and are presented in this section. Only those parameters that have demonstrated an impact on performance during the simulation studies are considered. Although the exact values of these parameters depends on the other system and workload parameters including the pattern of network traffic in the datacenter, a general set of rules that can aid in making such parameter choices is discussed. A simulation-based study can be used to choose appropriate parameter values for a given datacenter.

FUT-H and SUT-H: jointly control the activating of Spine switches on the system. FUT-H is to be chosen to be low enough such that the desired value of PF is achieved. SUT-H can then be chosen such that the lowest possible value of ANASS for the selected FUT-H is achieved.

FUT-L and SUT-L: jointly control the deactivation of the Spine switches on the system. Once again, values of these two parameters need to be chosen in such a way that PF does not exceed the desired value and ANASS is minimized. Note that higher values for both of these parameters are expected to lead to a lower ANASS. However, the system administrator needs to be aware between the potential tradeoff between ANASS and PF while making a choice of these parameters.

Tda and Tdd: smaller values of these parameters tend to increase the sensitivity of GSSMS to change in traffic intensity, but may also lead to frequent changes in the number of Spine switches leading to an increase in system overhead. Values of these parameters that strike an effective compromise between sensitivity and undesirable frequency of changes in the number of Spine switches need to be used.

Conclusions and future directions

This paper proposed GSSMS to save energy consumed by the DCN using the Spine-Leaf topology which has received increasing attention in practice. GSSMS can dynamically manage the number of Spine switches according to the current DCN traffic. The purpose is to save energy consumption without a significant decrease in reliability when the traffic intensity is low. The GSSMS algorithm used six parameters to determine the number of active Spine switches in a DCN. The threshold parameters FUTs and SUTs are used to control the activating and deactivating of Spine switches. The time duration Tda and Tdd are used to avoid frequent changes in the number of active Spine switches. Unlike the traditional DCN, which has a fixed number of switches, GSSMS uses two Spine switches when the network traffic is lower than the capacity of two Spine switches, and activates additional Spine switches when the number of Spine switches is not enough to handle the increased traffic in the DCN.

The simulation results show that GSSMS can work efficiently for different input traffic patterns. In comparison to Far traffic, GSSMS can save more energy for the Half-Far/Half-Near traffic because the Half-Far/Half-Near traffic

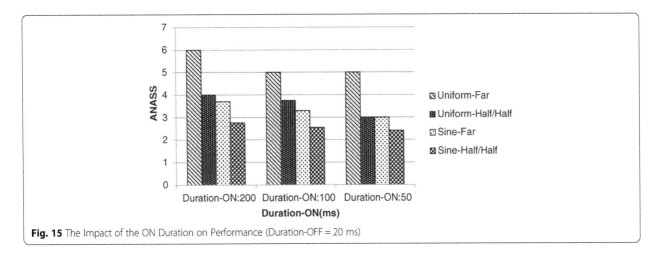

Fig. 15 The Impact of the ON Duration on Performance (Duration-OFF = 20 ms)

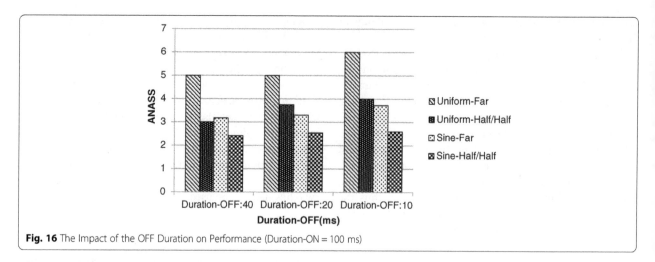

Fig. 16 The Impact of the OFF Duration on Performance (Duration-ON = 100 ms)

results in lower traffic through Spine switches. Compared with Uniform traffic, GSSMS can save more energy for Sine-Wave traffic because the traffic routed through Spine switches with the Sine-Wave traffic is lower than that achieved with the Uniform traffic. Specifically, GSSMS can save energy (up to 63 %) with a slight increase (0.08) in PF (shown in Fig. 4) or reduce PF significantly by dynamically adjusting the number of active Spine switches (see Fig. 7). Similar conclusions are expected when DCNs have different number of Leaf and Spine switches than those used in our simulations.

The simulation results also show the limitations of GSSMS. First, if the traffic burst exceeds the link capacity, activating one Spine switch may not be enough to handle the traffic burst. The current algorithm needs to wait for another monitoring duration to activate an additional Spine switch if the high traffic demand persists. To handle the scenario more effectively, the algorithm can be extended by incorporating another high threshold. Once this high threshold value is exceeded, two or more Spine switches can be activated at the same time. Second, if the traffic is complex (e.g., when the traffic is mixed with slow increase and spikes which can last longer than Tda occasionally), it is challenging to find a Tda that works efficiently for the complex traffic. As shown in simulation, a small Tda works efficiently for large traffic bursts, whereas a large Tda works efficiently for the stable traffic.

Further research is warranted for addressing the issues outlined in the previous paragraph. Directions for future research include the following:

(i). Investigating the effect of activating/deactivating multiple Spine switches at the same time.
(ii). Investigating the use of a variable Tda to improve GSSMS's performance when subjected to other traffic patterns forms an interesting direction for future research.

(iii). Investigating the use of Network Function Virtualization (NFV) for the proposed approach: Although GSSM is not specifically targeted for the SDN or the NFV paradigm, the proposed approach could be seen as one of the network functions for a datacenter network. Hence, it is worthy of further investigation using NFV for GSSM.

Abbreviations
DCN, Datacenter network; FBFLY, Flattened Butterfly; GSSMS, Green Spine Switch Management System; STP, Spanning tree protocol.

Authors' contributions
The work is mostly based on XL's Master's research and thesis, which was co-supervised by CL and SM. All authors contributed to each aspect of the technical areas and the writings. XL designed and implemented the simulation on CloudSim. All authors read and approved the final manuscript.

Competing interests
The authors declare that they have no competing interests.

References
1. Koomey J. Growth in Data center electricity use 2005 to 2010 [Online]. Analytics Press. Available: http://www.analyticspress.com/datacenters.html, [Last Accessed on 19 May 2016]
2. Heller B, Seetharaman S, Mahadevan P (2010) Elastic Tree: Saving Energy in Data Center Network. Proc. of 7th USENIX Conf. on Net. Sys. Design and Imple. (NSDI). San Jose, CA, USA, pp 17-17
3. Abts D, Marty MR, Wells PM, Klausler P, Liu H (2010) Energy Proportional Datacenter Networks. Proc of the 37th Int Symp Comput Architecture. Saint-Malo, France, pp 338–347
4. Benson T, Akella A, Maltz D (2010) Network Traffic Characteristics of Data Centers in the Wild. Proc of 10th ACM SIGCOMM Conf Internet Measurement Melbourne, Australia, pp 267–280
5. Beck P et al (2013) IBM and Cisco: Together for a World Class Data Center. IBM Redbooks. [Online], Available: http://www.redbooks.ibm.com/redbooks/pdfs/sg248105.pdf, [Last Accessed on 4 Jul 2016]
6. Alizadeh M, Edsall T (2013) On the Data Path Performance of Leaf-Spine Datacenter Fabrics. Proc of IEEE 21st Symp High-Performance Interconnects (HOTI), San Jose, CA USA, pp 71–74
7. Cisco. Cisco's Massively Scalable Data Center. [Online], Available: http://www.cisco.com/c/en/us/solutions/enterprise/data-center-designs-data-center-networking/landing_msdc.html, [Last Accessed on 19 May 2016]

8. Kakadia D Varma V (2012) Energy Efficient Data Center Networks – A SDN based Approach. Bangalore, IBM Collaborative Academia Research Exchange (I-CARE) IISC, Report No: IIIT/TR/2012/-1

9. Prete L, Farina F, Campanella M, Biancini A (2012) Energy Efficient Minimum Spanning Tree in OpenFlow Networks. Proc of European Workshop on Software Define Networking, Darmstadt Germany, pp 36-41

10. Carrega A, Singh S, Bruschi R, Bolla R (2012) Traffic Merging for Energy-Efficient Datacenter Networks. Proc of Int Symp on Performance Evaluation of Computer and Telecommunication Systems (SPECTS), Genoa Italy, pp 1–5

11. Vasic N, Bhurat P, Novakovic D, Canini M, Shekhar S, Kostic D (2011) Identifying and Using Energy-Critical Paths. Proc of the 7th Conf on Emerging Networking Experiments and Technologies Article No. 18 Tokyo, Japan

12. Lee C, Rhee JK (2012) Traffic Off-Balancing Algorithm: Toward Energy Proportional Datacenter Network. Proc Opto-Electronics Commun Conf (OECC), Busan, Korea, pp 409–410

13. Shi Z, Beard C, Mitchell K (2013) Analytical Models for Understanding Space, Backoff, and Flow Correlation in CSMA Wireless Networks. Wireless Networks 19(3):393–409

14. Shi Z, Beard C, Mitchell K (2008) Tunable Traffic Control for Multihop CSMA Networks. Proc of the 28th Military Communications Conf (MILCOM), San Diego, CA, 1–7

15. Shi Z, Beard C, Mitchell K (2011) Competition, Cooperation, and Optimization in Multi-Hop CSMA Networks. Proc of the 9th ACM Symposium on Performance Evaluation of Wireless Ad Hoc, Sensor, and Ubiquitous Networks (PE-WASUN) Paphos, Cyprus, pp 117–120

16. Cisco. Configuring EnergyWise. [Online], Available: http://www.cisco.com/c/en/us/td/docs/switches/lan/catalyst2960x/software/15-0_2_EX/energywise/configuration_guide/b_ew_152ex_2960-x_cg/b_ew_152ex_2960-x_cg_chapter_010.pdf, [Last Accessed in on 19 May 2016]

17. The Cloud Computing and Distributed Systems (CLOUDS) Laboratory, University of Melbourne, http://www.cloudbus.org/cloudsim/

18. Calabretta N, Centelles RP, Di Lucente S, Dorren TJS (2013) On the Performance of a Large-Scale Optical Packet Switch Under Realistic Data Center Traffic. Opt Commun Networking 5(6):565–573

19. Miercom Report. Cisco Catalyst 2960-X/2960-XR Switches. Nov. 2013, Available: http://miercom.com/pdf/reports/20131112.pdf, [Last Accessed on 19 May 2016]

20. Li X, Lung C, Majumdar S (2015) Energy Aware Green Spine Switch Management for Spine-Leaf Datacenter Networks. Proc IEEE Int Conf Communications (ICC), London, UK, pp 116–121

21. Cisco. Massively Scalable Data Center (MSDC) Design and Implementation Guide. Oct. 2014, http://www.cisco.com/c/en/us/td/docs/solutions/Enterprise/Data_Center/MSDC/1-0/MSDC_Phase1.pdf, [Last Accessed on 19 May 2016]

12

IO and data management for infrastructure as a service FPGA accelerators

Theepan Moorthy* ⓘ and Sathish Gopalakrishnan

Abstract

We describe the design of a non-operating-system based embedded system to automate the management, reordering, and movement of data produced by FPGA accelerators within data centre environments. In upcoming cloud computing environments, where FPGA acceleration may be leveraged via Infrastructure as a Service (IaaS), end users will no longer have full access to the underlying hardware resources. We envision a partially reconfigurable FPGA region that end-users can access for their custom acceleration needs, and a static "template" region offered by the data centre to manage all Input/Output (IO) data requirements to the FPGA. Thus our low-level software controlled system allows for standard DDR access to off-chip memory, as well as DMA movement of data to and from SATA based SSDs, and access to Ethernet stream links. Two use cases of FPGA accelerators are presented as experimental examples to demonstrate the area and performance costs of integrating our data-management system alongside such accelerators. Comparisons are also made to fully custom data management solutions implemented solely in RTL Verilog to determine the tradeoffs in using our system in regards to development time, area, and performance. We find that for a class of accelerators in which the physical data rate of an IO channel is the limiting bottleneck to accelerator throughput, our solution offers drastically reduced logic development time spent on data management without any associated performance losses in doing so. However, for a class of applications where the IO channel is not the bottle-neck, our solution trades off increased area usage to save on design times and to maintain acceptable system throughput in the face of degraded IO throughput.

Keywords: Infrastructure as a service, FPGA acceleration in data centres, Heterogeneous computing

Introduction

Parallel and heterogeneous computing with the use of discrete device accelerators like GPUs, FPGAs, and even ASICs, are some of the recent system level attempts that have addressed an increasing demand for computational throughput [1, 2]. However, heterogeneous computing is challenging at both the systems level implementation and resource management aspects of deployment. Therefore, data centres are starting to fill a market need for computing horsepower—without end users having to tackle such challenges directly. This sort of market has been termed Infrastructure as a Service (IaaS) within the more general category of cloud computing services.

Within the IaaS domain, there have been recent attempts in literature to facilitate the integration of device accelerators into cloud computing services [3–6]. These works primarily focus on scaling the use of accelerators in IaaS in three different ways; firstly, by treating the accelerator as a virtualized hardware resource, secondly in the case of FPGAs, by making use of their dynamic reconfigurable capabilities directly without virtualization, or thirdly, by offloading greater portions of traditionally host CPU based code onto accelerator based soft or hard processor cores. The work in this article is complementary to these efforts to integrate accelerators into cloud computing services, but we focus on a singular aspect of this broader challenge. We deal with the systems level implementation of integrating accelerators. We draw attention to the fact that present day accelerators may rely on direct access to IO data channels to offer effective acceleration.

High Level Synthesis (HLS) has gained some traction in offering acceptable levels of performance relative to

*Correspondence: tmoorthy@ece.ubc.ca
The Department of Electrical and Computer Engineering, The University of British Columbia, Vancouver, BC, Canada

manual RTL design for FPGA based hardware accelerators. More specifically, HLS is presently capable of transforming task specifications in a high-level programming language (such as C or Java) into near optimal hardware implementations for the compute portions of hardware acceleration [7]. However, successful acceleration of the compute portions alone does not translate into the desired application level acceleration as well. The increases in computational throughput must be supported by a corresponding increase in Input/Output (IO) data throughput to achieve system level acceleration. Unfortunately, HLS at present offers very little support or design abstraction for implementing custom IO data transfers and their corresponding organization in the memory subsystem, leaving system designers to still fall back on manual Register Transfer Level (RTL) design for these tasks. In fact, managing ingress and egress data across multi-level on-chip and off-chip memory hierarchies is an open HLS problem [7].

To mitigate some of these existing limitations of HLS in virtualizing FPGA usage in the cloud, recent work has provided further innovation [8, 9]. Ma et al. in their work [8], have combined existing development on Domain Specific Languages and the use of FPGA overlays to offer a run-time interpreter solution to managing FPGA resources. However, because they have taken an overlay approach, as they have cited, they also must offer standard accelerator *interface* templates for any IO to the FPGA. Such IO interfaces would indeed provide a great amount of flexibility for FPGA accelerator usage, but would suffer on optimality for any specific accelerator's data access pattern. Chen et al. [9] in their related work on FPGA based cloud computing, go further to recognize that there may be miscellaneous peripherals such as Ethernet controllers and various memory controllers required by specific accelerators. As such they make reference to a context controller switch to handle varying IO sources, but do not elaborate on whether any optimization is being made on this IO interface on a per accelerator application case basis.

In IaaS, this issue of customized IO and memory throughput for accelerators is further exacerbated by the fact that an end-user of a cloud computing environment does not have access to modify the bare underlying hardware's IO in any way. This is due to security limitations in the case of FPGAs [3], and in the case of GPUs and ASICs once their IO controller data-paths are designed and deployed they are fixed. Thus even if an end-user is willing to commit the manual RTL development hours required to customize the IO interfaces for their accelerated application, their lack of control and visibility over the underlying physical IO channels would prohibit them from doing so. Moreover, it is sometimes desirable to *virtualize* accelerators and enable time-sharing, and allowing

for significant user customization may not be possible in this scenario.

With such limitations in mind, if IaaS is to be a viable option for those seeking FPGA based acceleration, a flexible method to access IO data channels must be offered by the infrastructure itself. Furthermore, a level of abstraction must also be offered by any such method in order for the underlying infrastructure to be upgraded or changed and not require changes in the end user's applications as a result.

We seek to complement HLS based acceleration by abstracting the design efforts required to integrate IO and memory data channels. We do so by investigating the use of the existing embedded ecosystem on modern FPGAs to handle IO data channels in software. Although this approach may not offer the same performance when compared to automated custom configuration methods [10], and far less effective relative to manual RTL design, it still offers design times that are comparable to an HLS approach. More importantly, it allows for data transfers to be handled in software. Certain classes of FPGA devices today have an embedded ecosystem as hardened components readily available; making use of these embedded resources via software control abstracts away the exact details of the embedded processor and physical IO channels. This gives IaaS providers the freedom to carry out infrastructure upgrades without disrupting their customer workloads. And for the end user customers, this provides the option to harness any future hardware upgrades or changes in underlying IO technology at a software level should they wish to do so.

Towards demonstrating the value of an embedded IO processor in FPGA-based accelerators, we use two case studies to demonstrate the value of IO management in data-intensive applications as well as the possible performance implications of embedded IO processors. *Although we have focused on FPGAs as the substrate for implementing accelerators, we believe that the central idea of utilizing an embedded IO processor will be an attractive approach for other accelerator implementations as well.*

FPGAs as managed hardware in IaaS data centres

Whether FPGAs are integrated into data centres via proposed virtualized methods [3] or by more direct Open-CL based methods [11, 12] the FPGA fabric itself will need to consist of two separate regions. A static region of logic will exist in order for the FPGA to bootstrap itself and configure the minimum communication protocols necessary for it to interact with the host system. The second (dynamic) region will be an area of the fabric that is partially reconfigurable at runtime to allow for custom logic to be placed onto the device. This custom logic will then accelerate a specific compute-intensive task call of the application's algorithm, or run the application as a whole entirely on the FPGA.

The dynamic region of the FPGA will be accessible to the end user to configure via the FPGA vendor's partial reconfiguration tool flow. The static region's base "template", however, will not be accessible to the end user and must be provided for and maintained by the data centre host. The boundary (Fig. 1) between these two static and dynamic regions of the FPGA fabric is what this article concerns itself with.

We refer to the static region as a template above because this region is what defines the structure of external IO data channels that the FPGA end user sees and has access to. The static region accomplishes this by instantiating the necessary DRAM memory controllers, PCI express end-point blocks, and any other specific IO controllers that it wishes to provide. It is worthy to note here that although the FPGA device itself may be physically wired to multiple IO channels on the Printed Circuit Board (PCB) that was manufactured for its data centre usage (Fig. 2), the static region itself does not necessarily need to instantiate a controller for all of the available IO channels. What this allows for is different price points within IaaS for a data centre to rent its FPGA resources at, while keeping their actual physical FPGA infrastructure uniform with a fixed cost. For example, a data centre may have all of its FPGA PCBs designed with four Ethernet ports available, but intentionally restrict an end user from only accessing one or two based on what level of access they have paid for. In Fig. 2 this is illustrated by depicting multiple IO protocols and channels that may be physically wired to FPGA boards, however, the actual IO resources that an end user has access to can easily be limited by a static region bitstream

in the SDAccel flow. The static region bitstream will not have an IO controller for all of the available IO protocols such as Ethernet, SATA, JESD, or SERDES, unless the end-user has subscribed to a design flow that includes these options (at a cost).

Apart from the business side advantages that mandating a static region on the FPGA provides, a static region also allows physical IO channel upgrades in technology while offering minimal disruption to existing applications and customers. Consider that the data centre upgrades the solid state storage devices that its FPGA customers have access to from SATA 2 to SATA 3 SSDs. In this scenario, only the SATA controllers within the static template would need to be redesigned and deployed, while keeping the partially reconfigurable dynamic portion of FPGA logic unaffected. However, this begs the question as to whether this is feasible or even possible in the actual implementation of these static and dynamic regions. Given that there is to be very tightly linked and high throughput communication between these two regions, if a component within the static region changes even slightly will this not necessitate a redesign in the modules of the dynamic region that it interacts with. The answers to these questions rest completely on what the boundary logic between these two regions consists of.

The boundary region at the implementation level merely represents the set of architectural choices that are made to design and determine the type of interfaces that the static and dynamic regions will use to accomplish data transfers between them. This work contributes an embedded method to manage data channels that strays away from what conventional RTL design practices would dictate. We also put forth the novelty of using our embedded

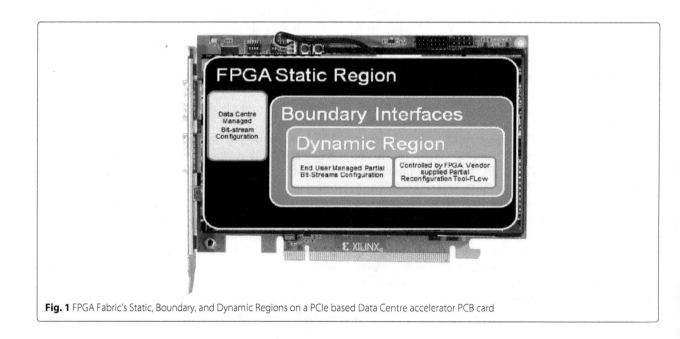

Fig. 1 FPGA Fabric's Static, Boundary, and Dynamic Regions on a PCIe based Data Centre accelerator PCB card

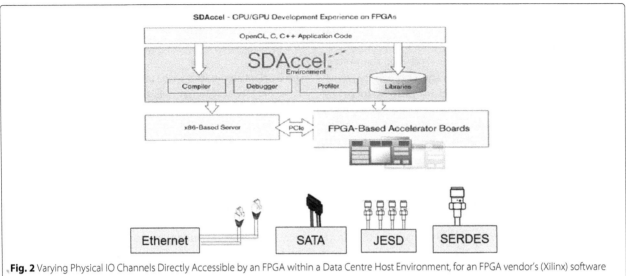

Fig. 2 Varying Physical IO Channels Directly Accessible by an FPGA within a Data Centre Host Environment, for an FPGA vendor's (Xilinx) software development flow

method in data centres where FPGAs may contribute as managed hardware resources within IaaS environments. This domain is an emerging and rapidly evolving field where end users are given increasingly less control over the bare-metal hardware that they seek to use. They must also accept certain levels of abstraction in their usage if they are to reap the economically cheaper rewards of scaling their FPGA acceleration based needs.

We explain our solution to IO data channel management in this environment by way of two use case examples that follow in "Bioinformatics application study" and "Video application study" sections. Towards demonstrating the value of our solution, in the first case we show that there are no performance penalties in adopting IaaS acceleration for the majority of data intensive or IO bound applications. In the second case, where IO performance loss does present itself as a problem, we successfully show that the acceleration itself can be scaled to compensate/offset IO performance loss at the application level if need be.

Bioinformatics application study
Application characteristics
Applications that require access to, or that produce, large volumes of data are presently loosely defined as "Big Data" applications. Big Data type applications, where FPGAs are utilized for acceleration, can be found in various application domains, ranging from Financial Computing, Bioinformatics, and conventional Data Center usages [13–15].

The particular application chosen for the experiments of this section falls under the Bioinformatics domain. However, the IO, memory, and data volume characteristics of this application allow for the results to be prevalent across most FPGA accelerated Big Data applications in

general. Traditional, in house, computing-cluster based infrastructures for such applications may not be economical as their data needs continue to scale, and can be costly to maintain. The take away that we would like to stress in this section is that, in IO constrained cases of these applications, performance does not have to be sacrificed when moving to IaaS.

The underlying common denominator, from a hardware perspective, of such applications, is that they all require the use of a non-volatile storage device to handle the large data sets. The use of non-volatile devices, such as Solid State Drives (SSDs) or other flash memory based hardware, often necessitates a memory hierarchy within the system design process. A typical hierarchy will include off-chip flash memory for large data sets, followed by off-chip DRAM for medium sized data sets, and finally on-chip SRAM.

For the off-chip memory components, the physical IO data channel by which these components are accessed also adds a lot of variation to the system level design. For example, in the Financial Computing domain of applications, large volumes of off-chip data might be streaming in from multiple Ethernet channels, whereas in Data Centers the incoming data might be arriving over PCI-express links connected to SSD storage. This variation in the physical IO channels creates the need for multiple IO controllers that rely on different IO protocols for communication, which in turn results in varying interface requirements for each controller.

The FPGA application accelerators in this class will require the IO controllers to supply a high throughput of data that at least matches the targeted scale of acceleration throughput. This required acceleration throughput can often be much greater than the physical bandwidth of the underlying IO device, the throughput rate of the controller that is accessing the underlying device, or any combination of the two. This dynamic results in the high throughput potential of the accelerator being limited by low IO throughput at the systems level. For the system architects that have the financial resources to do so, overcoming this problem might be a possibility by investing in higher throughput IO channels (i.e. converting from 2nd generation SATA to 3rd generation, or increasing the number of lanes in a PCI-express link). However, cases, where even state of the art physical IO channels cannot match accelerator throughput requirements, are not rare [16].

The use case application chosen for this section demonstrates the operation of two different IO protocols, Ethernet and SATA, and more importantly illustrates the effort that is required to integrate their respective controllers into the FPGA-accelerated data path. In doing so, we find that indeed the limitations in controller throughput do become the bottleneck to system level performance. Within the latter part of this section, we move to demonstrating how such IO bottlenecks in the system can be exploited to create interfaces to these controllers that are software driven and less complex to design.

The DIALIGN algorithm

Bioinformatics algorithms generally lend themselves well to hardware acceleration due to their inherent amount of parallelization. DIALIGN [17] takes an input query sequence against another input reference sequence, and aligns/matches segments of the query sequence to the regions of the reference sequence that offer the highest (optimal) degree of similarity. The output of DIALIGN is a mapping of the query sequence coordinates to various reference sequence coordinates (i.e. regions).

The input data to DIALIGN is a series of 1-byte characters that represent either DNA or protein strands of query and reference sequences for comparison (cross comparisons between DNA strands and protein strands are never made). DNA representation requires only 4 distinct characters thus a 2-bit data representation would suffice, however, protein variations require greater than 16 characters to represent. Thus an 8-bit data representation is favoured to accommodate these two types of input sequences.

Acceleration in hardware is achieved by a systolic array architecture implemented by Boukerche et al. [18]. Their systolic array architecture (Fig. 3) stores each character of the query sequence within each PE, then streams the reference sequence across the chain of PEs to compute a matrix scoring scheme. Ideally, this architecture performs best when all of the characters of the query sequence can entirely fit into the total number of synthesizable PEs. Given that query-sequence sizes of interest today are in the mega characters range, this ideal scenario is not feasible even with relatively large FPGA devices. Thus several passes of the reference-sequence must be made across multiple partitions of the query-sequence.

DIALIGN implemented with fully RTL based IO interfaces

There are two IO channels that the DIALIGN application running on our FPGA platform relies on. The first is the Ethernet channel for external communication, and the second is the SATA channel for internal deep storage access.

Between the two IO channels, the Ethernet channel has the simpler interface to the accelerator. Here we are using the word interface, not in the sense of a standard protocol by which the ports of two or more communicating hardware modules must be connected, but in the more general sense of any necessary changes in frequency, data-width, or timing that must be performed in order to achieve a viable data-path between any two hardware components. The two primary components of interest in this article are the accelerator (or more specifically, the systolic array for this particular application) and an IO controller. The interface is then, the mechanism by which the IO controller transfers data to the native input or output ports of the accelerator. This mechanism, by definition, should at a minimum support two basic features—data width conversions and cross clock domain stability.

Our system was implemented on the Digilent XUP-V5 development board [19], which features a 1-Gbps physical Ethernet line, two SATA header/connectors, and the Xilinx XC5VLX110T Virtex 5 FPGA. Our system consumed 88% of the device logic with the accelerator and the (hardware) IO interfacing resources combined. With the accelerator synthesized to utilize 50 PEs, the system is capable of operation at 67.689 MHz. The SSD connected to our board is the Intel SSD_SA2_MH0_80G_1GN model, with a capacity of 80 GBs. It offers SATA 2 (3 Gbps) line rates, and states 70 and 250 MB/s sequential write and read bandwidths respectively under technical specifications by the manufacturer. A 1-gigabyte-reference and 200-character-query synthetic sequence were generated on the Host side for experimentation (Fig. 4).

The reference sequence is at most 1 byte per character, and at our synthesized accelerator operational speed of 67.689 MHz, this requires only 68 MB/s of Ethernet controller throughput to sustain the accelerator's maximum throughput level. Therefore, this required Ethernet throughput rate of 68 MB/s does not become a bottleneck to the system, and thus the Ethernet interface specifications will not be discussed further.

In comparison to the Ethernet controller the SATA controller, however, does pose significant system bottleneck issues.

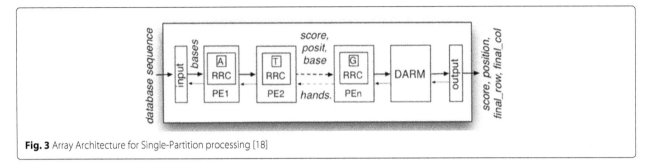

Fig. 3 Array Architecture for Single-Partition processing [18]

Intermediate data storage support between partitions

Given that partition switches across the PEs are necessary to support increasing lengths of query-sequences, the demand that this process places on intermediate storage requirements when gigabyte reference sequences are streamed is now described. Three partition switches across a systolic-array architecture of 50 PEs daisy chained together, effectively creates the logical equivalent of 200 PEs being used in a similar daisy chain fashion [20]. Thus, all of the data being produced by the last (50th PE) at each clock cycle of a single partition's operation must be collected and stored. This stored data will then be looped back and fed as contiguous input to the 1st PE when the next partition is ramped up, thereby creating the required illusion that 200 PEs are actually linked together (Fig. 5).

During the systolic-array based operation of the PEs, there are seven pieces of intermediate data that flow from one pipeline-stage to the next. The abstract Load/Store FIFO Blocks (Fig. 5) are implemented as 7 banks of 32-bit wide FIFOs (Fig. 6), with each bank capturing 1 of the 7 values of output from the terminal-PE. This flow of intermediate data generated by the DIALIGN accelerator is outputted or inputted at a significantly

high throughput rate of 1896 MB/s. There are seven native accelerator ports in each direction that push and receive this intermediate data to and from external storage, with each port being 4-bytes wide. The accelerator operates at 67.689 MHz and at 28 bytes every clock cycle (assuming no stalls by the Ethernet controller) this produces the one-way throughput of 1896 MB/s.

The fourteen accelerator ports mentioned above are what feed the Store FIFO Block and receive data from the Load FIFO Block in Fig. 6. At the very bottom of Fig. 6, data heading downstream is received by the SATA controller ports. The native port-width of our particular SATA controller [21] is 16-bits. The controller clock runs at a frequency of 150 MHz such that its 2-byte input port then offers a bandwidth of 300 MB/s, which is the maximum bandwidth of SATA 2 devices. Observed SATA throughput, however, is a combination of the controller's implementation and the particular drive that it is connected to. With the Intel SSD used in our system, we experimentally observed maximum sequential write and read throughput rates of 66.324 and 272.964 MB/s respectively.

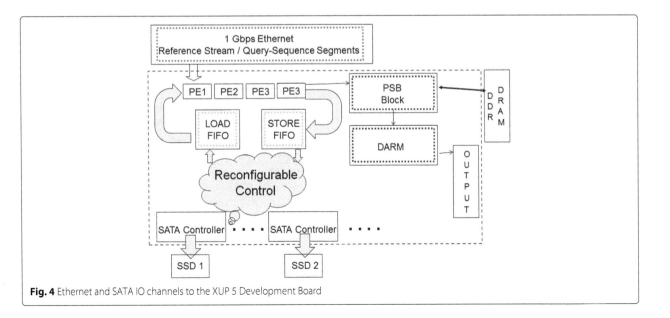

Fig. 4 Ethernet and SATA IO channels to the XUP 5 Development Board

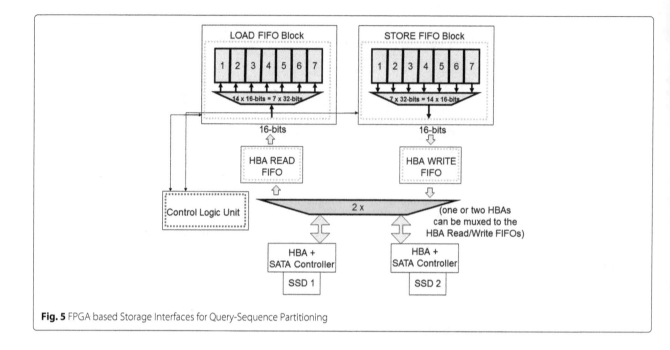

Fig. 5 FPGA based Storage Interfaces for Query-Sequence Partitioning

The accelerator to IO controller interface, for this channel, consists of all the data path and control units depicted in Fig. 6. It serves all three of the functions within our definition of an interface: data-width conversion, clock domain crossing, and flow control. Figure 6 is an intentionally simplified block diagram of this interface that hides the details of implementation. In this section, such details will be elaborated so that they may be fairly compared to alternative software interfaces in future sections.

Within the Store FIFO Block of Fig. 6, below the 7 FIFO segments, a multiplexer is depicted to convert the 224-bit (7x32-bit) data path from the accelerator to only 16-bits. This is an oversimplification, and in reality, a

mux-control-FSM in conjunction with seven other 2-to-1 muxes are used to accomplish this task. The FSM also helps to perform another mandatory task of framing the data for SATA protocol writes. The SATA controller writes to disk in single sector segments of 512-bytes per sector. The 28-bytes of data produced by the accelerator at each cycle cannot be evenly packed into 512-byte frames. Every 18 cycles of accelerator operation, will only produce 504-bytes of data that must be packed into a 512-byte frame. The FSM packages the payload data with 4-bytes of Start of Frame and End of Frame encoding, such that a single frame can be successfully detected, and stripped of its payload data, during the return backward path of data flow.

Stuffing the remaining 8 bytes of a 512-byte sector with the first 8 bytes from another cycle of accelerator operation would create the additional overhead of realigning FIFO-bank lines when the sectors are eventually read back. Moreover, if a FIFO-bank line crosses two sectors, and the controller has not returned the 2nd sector yet, this would cause some individual FIFOs within the bank to become empty while others are not, and thus further exacerbate the synchronization issues that would have to be resolved.

Lastly, the mentioned mux-control-FSM is designed to operate at the faster SATA controller clock frequency of 150 MHz, such that 16-bits of output can be produced at the maximum bandwidth of 300 MB/s. Note that the 224-bits to 16-bits ratio, means that an accelerator running at even 1/14th of the SATA frequency is capable of providing enough data to sustain a throughput of 300 MB/s by this FSM.

Fig. 6 Data flow to and from the Load/Store FIFOs to SSDs (Not all connections to the CLU are depicted)

To briefly recap the primary hardware components that went into this interface, there were two FSMs, one at the front end to perform data-width conversion and data framing, and a back end FSM to issue SATA commands and handle error recovery. Alongside these primary FSMs, non-trivial arrangements of FIFOs and muxes were utilized to assist with data packing and flow control. The most important aspect of these hardware considerations is that all of these components were designed with the architectural requirement of running at the native SATA controller frequency of 150 MHz, such that data bandwidth was never compromised due to interfacing. However, the much slower SATA write throughput limitation imposed by the actual physical SSD negates the over-provisioning of the interface logic. This then allows for other simpler (and slower) IO interfacing options to be considered while still achieving a comparable system level runtime.

The question that we are soon to resolve is that given that the SATA controller's actual end write throughput is much lower than its input-port bandwidth capacity, can we relax the aforementioned frequency requirements of the interface for a simpler architectural solution.

DIALIGN implemented with software IO interfaces

Adapting to software controlled IO interfaces, by definition requires at least one embedded processor to execute the software control. As such, the IO controllers in the system must also support communication over whatever bus standard that is supported by the chosen processor.

The development board that was used in the hardware interface experiments is held as a constant, and used within this section as well. As such, the Xilinx MicroBlaze [22] softcore processor is the embedded processor around which our software solution will be explored. The MicroBlaze ISA supports the following three bus protocols for external communication. They are

a) Local Memory Bus
(LMB, low latency direct access to on-chip memory block-ram modules),
b) Processor Local Bus
(PLB, a shared bus intended for processor peripherals and memory-mapped IO),
c) Xilinx Cache-Link
(XCL, similar to the PLB, however, it supports burst transactions and is exclusive to the processor's instruction and data caches).

The two IO controllers used for the DIALIGN application, with fully RTL interfaces, in "DIALIGN implemented with fully RTL based IO interfaces" section were the SIRC based Ethernet controller [23] and the corresponding Groundhog SATA controller [21]. Because the Ethernet controller makes use of only block-rams at its top level

for data intake and delivery, it can be adapted to connect with the MicroBlaze LMB interface. However, the Groundhog SATA controller, which although allows for a lot of design flexibility to interface directly with its SATA command layer via custom hardware, is not capable of being connected directly to a PLB interface without significant design additions. As such, the SATA2 controller [24], another open source SATA controller that is more amenable to embedded solutions is adopted in this section. Both controllers are comparable in their SATA 4 KiB write tests, with the SATA2 controller performing slightly worse using comparable SSDs. Therefore, the alternative software solution being explored in this section is not unfairly biased in its favour via a better SATA controller.

The SATA2 controller makes available the following two bus protocols for communication with the core—PLB and Native Port Interface (NPI). The PLB has been previously introduced, however, the NPI is another protocol exclusive to Xilinx's DRAM controller that is being introduced here. For embedded systems' use, Xilinx makes available their Multi-Port Memory Controller (MPMC). Furthermore, the MPMC supports various interfaces on its ports, with two of them being PLB and NPI interfaces in this case. An NPI port, as its name implies, is meant to provide the closest matching signals and data-width to that of the physical DRAM being controlled. For example, the off-chip DRAM modules on the XUP5 development board have a 64-bit wide combined data path, and thus the NPI, in this case, would also accommodate a 64-bit port. This is in contrast to the PLB port, which would be set to a 32-bit port as dictated by the MicroBlaze ISA. Therefore, an MPMC instantiated with both PLB and NPI ports allows the MicroBlaze processor access to DRAM, and also allows a Direct Memory Access (DMA) module or peripheral access to native memory widths respectively (Fig. 7).

With the addition of a complementary NPI based DMA, the SATA2 core has direct access to DRAM with little MicroBlaze intervention; thereby not having the throughput to the SSD restricted by PLB limitations as well.

HW/SW partitioned architecture

Given the feasibility of interconnecting the Ethernet and SATA controllers utilized by the DIALIGN algorithm to standard bus protocols, the existing EDA tools offered by FPGA vendors for embedded systems design can be leveraged to manage data flow in software, while allowing for the computationally intensive accelerator portions to remain in hardware.

Newer interfaces such as AXI [25] exist to interconnect the programmable logic data-path to an embedded processor; however, due to the limitations on IP for the Virtex 5 development board, our architecture utilizes Fast Simplex Link (FSL) [26] based communication. Our

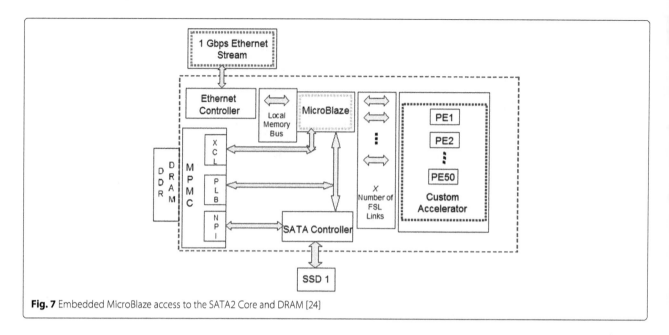

Fig. 7 Embedded MicroBlaze access to the SATA2 Core and DRAM [24]

architecture combines a varying amount of FSL channels, along with the Ethernet and SATA controllers, to form a flexible and easily controllable data-path for hardware acceleration (Fig. 8).

The number of FSL links used to connect the configurable accelerator to the embedded system depends on the needs of the application being accelerated. Each link, as mandated by the FSL interface, has configurable FIFOs built in. Although a minimal dual cycle latency for data is possible via the FSL links, the total bandwidth between the accelerator and the processor will be limited by the lower clock speed of the MicroBlaze processor. Nonetheless, the potential for ease of automated configuration is high due to the fact that the FSL lanes can be scaled according to the number of input and output ports that are required by

the accelerator, and by the fact that the data-width of each port can be set accordingly as well.

The low aggregate bandwidth between the accelerator and the processor that comes with the use of FSL lanes does not introduce a new throughput bottleneck into the system for all applications. If the application already has an IO channel throughput bottleneck that is lower than the FSL channel rate, the ease of automation gained by using the FSL lanes will have no adverse effect on the overall system throughput.

Soft-processor data management

As depicted in Fig. 8 all input to the alignment accelerator is received over the Ethernet channel. During accelerator operation, one DNA character (a single byte) of the

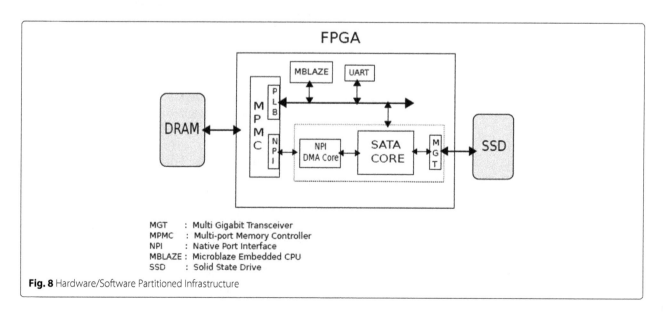

MGT   : Multi Gigabit Transceiver
MPMC   : Multi-port Memory Controller
NPI   : Native Port Interface
MBLAZE : Microblaze Embedded CPU
SSD   : Solid State Drive

Fig. 8 Hardware/Software Partitioned Infrastructure

reference sequence is required per cycle. The accelerator runs at a maximum frequency of 67.689 MHz and thus requires 68 MB/s of input bandwidth to sustain operation at full throughput. Through experimentation, we have verified that the SIRC Ethernet controller can provide a stream bandwidth rate between 58.88 MB/s and 60.35 MB/s. However, this does not cause the SIRC stream to become the bottleneck of the system. The greater bottleneck is discussed below.

The SATA 2 (3 Gbps line rate) protocol allows for a maximum theoretical bandwidth of 300 MB/s. Real SSDs, however, offer much lower rates, especially on write bandwidth. The SSD used in our experiments revealed maximum sequential write rates of 66 MB/s. The DIALIGN accelerator produces seven 32-bit words per cycle of intermediate data at a clock rate of 67.689 MHz, or rather 1895 MB/s of write data.

The design goal of this section is to capture the 1895 MB/s of data produced by the accelerator logic, bring it into the soft-processor based embedded system domain, and feed it to the SSD controller. As long as this process can be successfully implemented without dropping below the physical SSD data write rate of 66 MB/s, the use of an embedded system for data management does not degrade system performance relative to custom RTL based data management. Given that a conventional MicroBlaze softcore processor can be run at a frequency of 125 MHz and that it operates on 32-bit word operands, this provides for an upper bandwidth limit of 500 MB/s to work within. Realistic bus transfer rates along with actual DRAM write/read rates in implementation will be considered to determine the degradation to this 500 MB/s upper limit.

The first stage of data transfer is achieved via seven FSL links that give the MicroBlaze core access to each of the seven accelerator output operands using distinct FSL channel ID numbers in software. The Xilinx FSL link interface includes built in FIFOs on each channel. All seven FIFOs on the links are all set to the same depth. The accelerator concurrently writes to all FIFOs on each clock cycle of its operating frequency, however, the processor will read from the FIFOs in round robin fashion. Accelerator operation can be paused in response to any almost-full control signals from the FSL FIFOs.

The XUP5 development board used in our design uses DDR2 DRAM and is controlled by the Multi-Port Memory Controller (MPMC) IP [27]. Although the PLB [28] interface supports burst-mode data transfers to the MPMC, MicroBlaze does not support burst-transfers over the PLB. As a workaround, a data-cache can be incorporated into the MicroBlaze design, and then the Xilinx Cache Link (XCL) [22] can be utilized for burst-mode data transfers to DRAM. This is the optimization we have employed to achieve native 64-bit wide data writes into DRAM via write bursts issued by the MicroBlaze

data cache. We also ensured that the "Use Cache Links for all Memory Accesses" parameter was set so that data is pushed onto the XCL even if the data-cache was disabled.

Software functions to read/write to the FSL channels are provided within Xilinx's SDK environment and 32-bit words of data can be accessed within single cycle speeds. Thus the processor running at 125 MHz can consume data from the FSL links at a bandwidth of 500 MB/s. From there, the data rate at which the data-cache-bursts write to the MPMC will be the first bandwidth funnel. The upper bound on throughput from the MicroBlaze to the MPMC is affected by several factors. From the source (MicroBlaze) side, data may not always be injected at the upper limit of 500 MB/s due to the fact that some MicroBlaze overhead cycles will be used to gather the data from multiple FSL channels. On the sink (MPMC) side, write throughput will depend on any other concurrent reads or writes occurring to the same physical DRAM (via the SATA controller) and how effectively the arbitration policy of the MPMC is executed. These complexities prohibit derivations of any practical analytical methods to infer reasonable throughput levels between the MicroBlaze and the MPMC.

After the data has been streamed by the MicroBlaze from the FSL channels into DRAM, the SATA2 core can begin to consume it from there. The modified SATA2 core [24] that we employ uses the Native Port Interface (NPI) [27] of the MPMC for its own internal DMA based transfers. The DMA setup and start commands are still issued in software by the MicroBlaze communicating with the core over the PLB. The SATA2 core's internal NPI based DMA engine can obtain data from the MPMC at a throughput of 240 MB/s. This rate has been experimentally verified, and also drops down to no less than 200 MB/s when the MicroBlaze is simultaneously issuing data writes to the MPMC via its XCL port. In this scenario, the MPMC internally performs round-robin arbitration between the XLC writes and the NPI reads. Nonetheless, even a 200 MB/s rate of data delivery to the SATA2 controller far exceeds the 66 MB/s write rate of the actual SSD. Thus these empirical results, which could not have been obtained in a practical analytical manner, establish that the system throughput is not degraded by this software solution.

In creating this embedded system based data-path, all of the custom logic depicted in Fig. 6 for the hardware interface in "DIALIGN implemented with fully RTL based IO interfaces" section is no longer necessary. FIFOs to collect the data from an accelerator at variably wide data-widths (up to sixteen 32-bit wide words) are automatically available within the FSL IP, transfer of that data into DRAM is then controlled in software, and finally the repacking of data words for the appropriate sector write frames into SSDs can also be handled in software.

Furthermore, should the underlying physical SATA-core be changed to support future SATA-3 generation devices or merely wider data-widths of the transceivers used even within SATA-2 devices, these changes can be supported by software. For example, Virtex 5 transceivers (GTP tiles) utilize 16-bit SERDES (Serializer-Deserializer) circuits for their SATA physical-layer links, however, Virtex 6 transceivers (GTX tiles) were upgraded to 32-bit SERDES transceivers. These changes propagate all the way up to the command layer of the SATA HBA controller and require the buffers or FIFOs that supply data to the controller to also be converted to matching 32-bit words. If our data-path was solely an RTL design ("DIALIGN implemented with fully RTL based IO interfaces" section), then the muxes, FIFOs, and more importantly the FSMs would all have to be accordingly modified to pack wider words. In the presently described embedded solution, not only can the 32-bit upgrade be supported entirely in software, but we can also maintain full backward compatibility with any legacy 16-bit SATA controllers, through 32-bit input-word conversions into half-word data writes to DRAM in software.

Resource utilization across interface solutions

In this section, the hardware utilization associated with the solely hardware, and the HW/SW partitioned interface solutions will be compared and discussed.

Table 1 lists the amounts and percentages of resources consumed on the Virtex 5, XUP5 development board [19], for both interface options. It can be observed that there is roughly a 20% overhead increase in LUT and DFF logic that is consumed when moving to a HW/SW partitioned solution. The majority of this extra logic can be attributed to not only the MicroBlaze softcore itself but also to the MPMC, its supporting busses, the FSL channels, and the extra DMA unit within the SATA2 controller itself. As expected for this application, the actual run time performance of the DIALIGN accelerator is equal between the custom HW and HW/SW interfaces, and thus is not reported in the table for comparison.

What is gained by this increase in hardware is the significant reduction in design time and debugging efforts. The custom hardware interfaces are very resource efficient,

however, they can require 6 months of design to architect, implement, and verify. Furthermore, they cannot easily be reused when an IO controller update is required.

Video application study

Motion estimation implemented with fully RTL based IO interfaces

As a motivator for the case study described in this section the reader is urged to consider the system level challenges of a commercial application such as Netflix [29]. Although an application such as Netflix in its infancy may start out with a fully customizable computing cluster environment, as its customer base and data requirements expand, a full warehouse data-centre infrastructure is often inevitable [30]. In this scenario, customized acceleration for the encoding required for all standards of input video sources, and the output video stream resolutions produced, will be challenging. Therefore, cloud-based solutions are often sought to handle the scale and possible automation of the encoding workloads [31]. It is precisely this sort of environment that our solution aims to target. In this environment, the flexibility to scale the accelerators that handle the compute bound portions of the application's code can be leveraged to manage IO constraints *if*, and only if, the IO interface architecture is appropriately designed and matched.

Acceleration of Motion Estimation (ME), for the H.264 video encoding standard [32], on FPGAs uses only a memory controller for off-chip DRAM access as its single channel for IO data. We examine ME in this section because, from an IO perspective, it is fundamentally different from the previously covered DIALIGN application in that neither its physical IO channel device (DDR2 DRAM) nor its IO controller (the Multi-Port-Memory-Controller) are bottlenecks to accelerator performance. Nonetheless, ME is still a relatively IO dependent application. However, what will be demonstrated in this section is that the requirements of this application, and how these requirements are exploited, combine to prevent IO throughput from becoming an issue. We show that this form of application requirement exploitation can be achieved through the careful customization of its interface to the memory controller.

Table 1 DIALIGN alignment accelerator with custom HW interfaces vs. HW/SW IO interfaces

	Area[a]				LUTs %	DFFs %	Accelerator	MicroBlaze
	LUTs		DFFs		Increase	Increase	frequency (MHz)	frequency (MHz)
	#(K)	%	#(K)	%				
HW Interface	51.0	73.8	36.9	53.4			67.7	N/A
HW/SW Interface with Microblaze	64.5	93.3	52.0	75.2	19.5	21.8	67.7	125

[a]Xilinx's Virtex 5 devices use 4 DFFs & 4 6-input LUTs per Slice

External DRAM throughput requirements

A memory hierarchy (Fig. 9) is used to move portions of a large data set stored at the non-volatile level (i.e. a video file), into a medium data set stored in DRAM (video frames), and then finally into small data sets of on-chip buffering (sub-frame blocks) to support acceleration. It will soon be detailed that a throughput of only 620 MB/s from off-chip DRAM to on-chip block rams suffices for this application. Thus even using a modest DDR2 memory controller will not become a bottleneck based on the required 620 MB/s of read throughput (to supply data to the accelerator) and the required 125 MB/s of write throughput (to load video data coming in from the SSD at a speed of at most 60 fps).

A single pixel is often encoded as a single byte. Thus a single 1920 × 1088 High Definition (HD) frame occupies 2.09 MB of memory. Since on-chip FPGA memory is commonly limited to be between 2 to 6 MB, video frames must be encoded in partial segments sequentially. The 1920×1088 frame can be encoded as eight equal segments of 960×272 Sub-Frame (SF) portions at a time. The 960×272 SF allows for a more manageable 261.1 KB of pixels to be encoded within on-chip memory at a time.

The VBMSE algorithm [32, 33] requires the video frame that is to be encoded (the present frame) to be compared to at least four other (reference) frames, before conclusive calculations on its corresponding motion vectors are reached. Therefore in addition to the 1/8th portion of the present frame (PSF), four other such portions of reference frames (RSFs) must be held within on-chip memory as well (Fig. 10), which brings the total memory space thus far to 1.3 MB. Here, we introduce the design concept of double buffering—the first buffer is initially loaded with data to be processed, processing then commences, simultaneously the second buffer is loaded with the next set of sub-frame data, thereby overlapping memory access

latency with processing time. This then brings the total required on-chip memory allocation to 2.6 MB for double buffering, which even modest FPGA devices can support.

FPGA devices with larger amounts of on-chip memory can opt to double buffer larger sub-frame portions, but we wish to note that doing so only reduces the required memory-controller throughput rate. This is due to the fact that for VBSME an increase in data to be processed is not linearly proportional to processing times. Therefore, double-buffering larger sub-frame segments allows for the acceleration to be more compute-bound than IO bound, and thus lowers the required external memory throughput.

The basic building blocks for which motion vectors are produced as outputs in motion estimation are 16×16 blocks of pixels, commonly referred to as a macro-block. Within the 960 × 272 sub-frame portion size that we are using in this work there will be 1020 macro-blocks that need to be encoded. For reasons that will be clarified in the next sections to come, the number of required clock cycles to encode a single macro-block against a single reference frame is 99 cycles, when the accelerator is scaled to its highest level of acceleration. We intentionally use the highest level of scaling here in these calculations to demonstrate the upper bound on the required external memory throughput. Next, recall that VBSME requires the present frame to be compared against four other reference frames when calculating the motion vectors for its macro-blocks. Therefore, the 99 cycles become 396 cycles in total per macro-block. We can now state the entire processing time of a sub-frame portion in cycles to be equal to 403 920 (1020 macro-blocks x 396 cycles per macro-block).

As detailed earlier in this section, the total data required to process a sub-frame against its four reference frames is 1.3 MB (1.3056 MB exactly, Fig. 10). The maximum

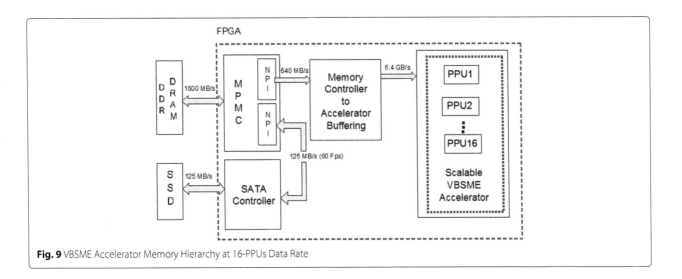

Fig. 9 VBSME Accelerator Memory Hierarchy at 16-PPUs Data Rate

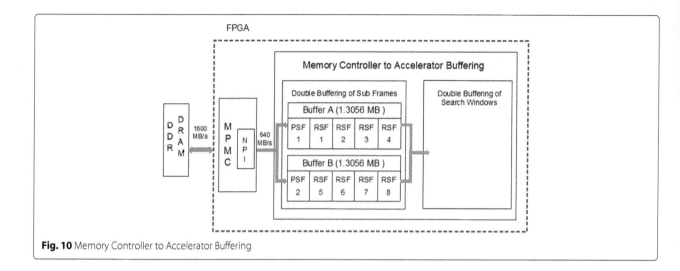

Fig. 10 Memory Controller to Accelerator Buffering

frequency of the implemented VBSME accelerator on our chosen FPGA device is 200 MHz. Thus the final required external memory throughput with the use of double buffering can now be derived as 646.5 MB/s (1.3056 MB / 403 920 cycles * 200 MHz).

VBSME accelerator operation

For the purposes of this article, it suffices to view the VBSME accelerator as a scalable black-box accelerator. The scalability of our black-box accelerator is measured in terms of the number of Pixel Processing Units (PPUs) that it is instantiated (synthesized) with. In our system implementation, the offered set of scaling levels is 1, 2, 4, 8, or 16 PPUs. Looking into this black-box slightly for the purpose of understanding its IO requirements, each PPU can be viewed as a single 16×16 two-dimensional array of Processing Elements (PEs) (Fig. 11). A single PPU requires two separate memory busses, each being 16-bytes wide. The necessity of this dual-bus architecture stems from the need to avoid any pipeline bubbles within

the hardware architecture for VBSME [34]. These dual-buses are each independently connected to two physically separate Memory Partitions A and B that contain two vertically segregated logical partitions of the search-window memory space (Fig. 12).

Although each PPU requires, in total, an input path of 64-bytes across its two buses, fortunately, this relationship is not held when scaling the VBSME architecture to use multiple PPUs in parallel. The relationship between the number of bytes required when scaling upwards to n number of PPUs is $15 + n$ bytes on each bus [35]. Thus an instance of a VBSME accelerator scaled to 16-PPUs would only require 31-bytes on each bus. This derives from the fact that each additional PPU always shares 15-pixels in common with its preceding PPU (Fig. 13).

Search-window buffer scaling

Due to the fact that the input bus-width requirements of the VBSME accelerator vary when it scales, as discussed previously, the search-window buffers must also be scaled

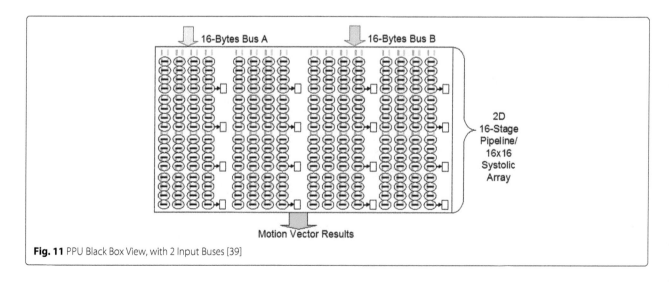

Fig. 11 PPU Black Box View, with 2 Input Buses [39]

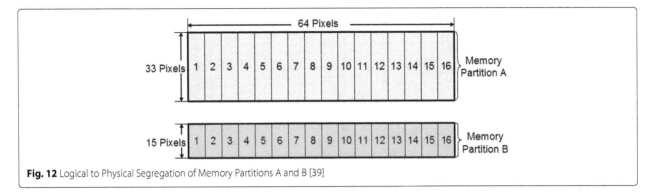

Fig. 12 Logical to Physical Segregation of Memory Partitions A and B [39]

(synthesized) in varying patterns of data organization to accommodate the scaling.

The VBSME accelerator processes a search window by accessing its rows (top to bottom) one cycle at a time. Accesses to the last 15 rows of the search window, coming from Memory Partition B (Fig. 12), are always overlapped with the 33 rows being accessed from Memory Partition A [34]. Thus 33 cycles are all that is required to finish a vertical sweep of the search-window. However, not all of the 64 columns of the pixels within a 64×48 search-window are read per each row access.

The number of columns $(15 + n)$ that are read per row depends on the number of PPUs that the accelerator is scaled to. Once a vertical sweep of these columns is performed, a horizontal shift to the right is performed to start the next vertical sweep. The granularity of this horizontal-shift to the right is exactly equal to the number of PPUs being employed. Therefore, the number of vertical sweeps that are required to sweep a search window of width w, in a top-down left-to-right manner is given by $\lceil (w - (15 + n))/n \rceil$.

Thus in our implementation, the VBSME accelerator when scaled to 16-PPUs will require a total of 3 vertical sweeps to process the search window ($\lceil (64 - (15 + 16))/16 \rceil$). These 3 vertical sweeps of 33 cycles each, result in a total of 99 cycles needed to completely process the search window. As another example, if the VBSME accelerator is scaled down to use only a single PPU the number of required vertical sweeps is 48 ($\lceil (64 - (15 + 1))/1 \rceil$), resulting in a total of 1584 cycles required to complete the search.

Figures 14 and 15 represent the logical columns (Lx_A) of the horizontal shifts that are required when the VBSME accelerator is scaled to 16-PPUs and 8-PPUs respectively. In both cases, the widths of each Lx_A partition is equal to the number of PPUs being used. The number of vertical sweeps, and thus the total processing time, is also labeled in the figures for each case according to the previously explained formula.

In order to support the access of these logical partitions, which are in turn based on the granularity of the PPUs being scaled, different mappings of these logical partitions into a varying number of physical block-ram banks must be implemented. The number of block-ram banks required for this logical to physical translation of search window data is determined by $\lceil (15 + n)/n \rceil$ [35].

The logical to physical implementation of search window buffering for the 16-PPUs and 8-PPUs cases of scaling are represented in Figs. 16 and 17 respectively. As shown in the figures, the required hardware includes both block-rams and multiplexers to implement the required

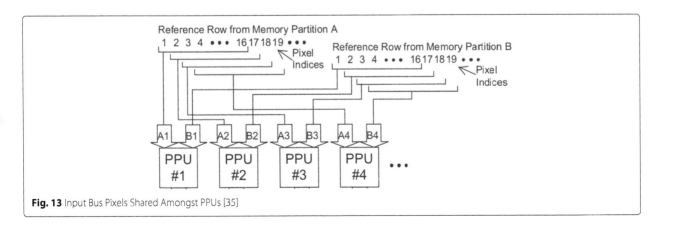

Fig. 13 Input Bus Pixels Shared Amongst PPUs [35]

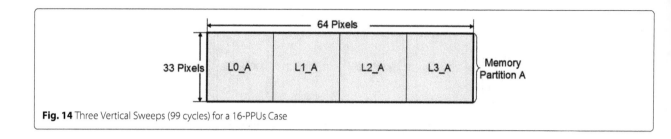

Fig. 14 Three Vertical Sweeps (99 cycles) for a 16-PPUs Case

data path flexibility during the various clock cycles of search window processing. An important component not depicted in the figures is the Control Logic Unit (CLU). These CLUs are implemented as Finite State Machines (FSMs) for each level of accelerator scaling, and perform the duties of generating the appropriate block-ram addresses and mux selection control signals.

A custom RTL implementation consisting of the above-mentioned block-rams, muxes, and FSMs must exist within the "Double Buffering of Search Windows" functional block of Fig. 10, within each of the search windows shown. This requires a significant amount of RTL development and debugging that must be performed for each level of VBSME accelerator scaling that is to be implemented.

In the following section, an embedded soft-core approach to memory organization that will obviate the need to redesign these hardware components for each level of scaling is presented.

Motion Estimation implemented with Software IO interfaces

Before any video compression algorithm can be run it is, of course, necessary for the raw video frames to be available within DRAM. From the details of the previous section, it is clear as to how the FPGA device itself within our proposed embedded system can directly access raw video data from a secondary storage device such as SATA SSDs. Once video data is held within DRAM, the 256 MB or more of DRAM capacity is enough to sustain the buffering of frames in a manner that does not render the SATA-core to DRAM bandwidth to be the bottleneck [35].

To support the VBSME algorithm introduced in "External DRAM throughput requirements" section in

terms of physical design within the embedded system, only two main parameters need to be resolved. The first one being how many FSL channels need to be instantiated per each level of accelerator scaling, and secondly what the data-width of each channel needs to be. If this is done correctly, the manner in which the memory subsystem is implemented will be transparent to the accelerator logic. Apart from answering these two parameter questions, the data pattern by which pixels should be loaded into the FSL FIFOs is another important algorithmic challenge.

The number of FSL channels to be instantiated can be resolved via the following formula for VBSME scaling.

$x = 2 \times \lceil (15 + n)/4 \rceil$

Here x refers to the number of FSL channels that need to be instantiated, and n refers to the number of PPUs that are implemented according to the level of accelerator scaling. $15 + n$, are the number of pixels that need to be forwarded to the accelerator unit respective of its n units of scaling ("Search-window buffer scaling" section). Since each pixel is 8-bits in representation, a single 32-bit FSL channel can forward 4 pixels of information. The multiple of 2 derives from the accelerator requirement of having dual memory partitions ("VBSME accelerator operation" section).

If the number of pixels required per clock cycle by the accelerator (the numerator in the above equation) is exactly divisible by 4, then each FSL channel will be set to the maximum width of 4-bytes (32-bit words). However, if the quotient leaves a remainder when dividing by four then a modulus function can be applied to determine the data width of the last FSL channel. Since the FSL widths are configurable, this customization can be achieved.

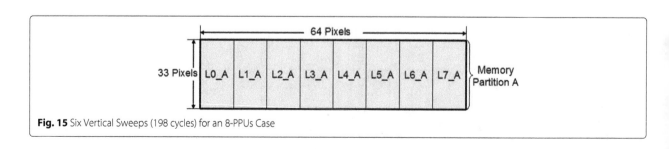

Fig. 15 Six Vertical Sweeps (198 cycles) for an 8-PPUs Case

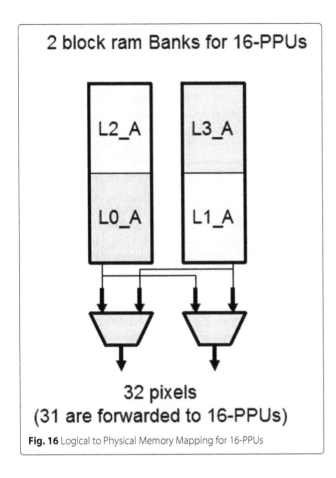

Fig. 16 Logical to Physical Memory Mapping for 16-PPUs

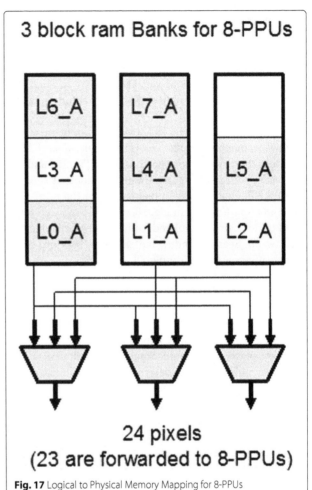

Fig. 17 Logical to Physical Memory Mapping for 8-PPUs

In "Search-window buffer scaling" section block-rams and muxes were introduced as the components that constituted the underlying memory substructure. In this section, we will detail the use of the built in FIFOs in the FSL channels as a transparent substitute for the custom RTL-designed components. In a pure block-rams based buffering system, memory addressing can be used to repetitively access data. However, if the block-rams are instantiated as FIFOs, once a specific memory-data read occurs, it can not be accessed again without it being re-pushed into the FIFO queue again. Thus, although a memory interface based on FIFOs is simpler to integrate and control, the continual loading of data into these FIFOs will follow a more complex pattern. This is the trade-off that is to be made, and this is also where we will leverage the flexibility of soft-core based transfers from DRAM to support the complex patterns of FIFO loading.

Once the number of FSL channels has been set according to the previous formula, columns of pixel data from the search window of interest must be initially transferred into these channels in a left to right manner. After this initial filling of the FIFOs within the FSL channels, the sweeps across the search window by the accelerator ("Search-window buffer scaling" section) are accomplished by horizontal pixel-column shifts in the search

window that equate to the number of PPUs the accelerator is scaled to. In Figs. 14 and 15, this shift-width can be logically viewed as the partition width (e.g. block L0_A, L1_A, etc.). In the case of the accelerator scaled to 16 PPUs their partition widths will be 16-pixels, in the case of 8 PPUs, it will be 8-pixels and so forth.

When using the FSLs for pixel-column shifts, since their channel width is set to the maximum of being 4-pixels wide (to optimize data transfers), shifts that occur in multiples of 4 can be handled by relatively straight forward 32-bit memory word reads from DRAM. Such is the case for the accelerator scaling levels of 16, 8, and 4 PPUS. However, as the accelerator scaling falls to 2-PPUs or even a single PPU, the required FSL granularity of shifting becomes $1/2$ FSL width and $1/4$ FSL width respectively. Since the Microblaze ISA is byte addressable, word accesses from DRAM can be packed/re-ordered such that a finer granularity of shifting pixels is supported. At the micro-architectural level, Microblaze may make use of barrel shifting within its ALU to get the desired byte from a 32-bit data bus read. Therefore the Microblaze core was synthesized with its additional barrel-shift logic parameter enabled.

Four-pixel (32-bit word) reads from memory for a 2-PPUs accelerator are realigned before being pushed into the FSL channel FIFOs at various time steps, such that they hold the appropriately shifted pixel columns within them (Fig. 18).

For simplicity's sake Fig. 18 above shows only the logical to physical mapping of pixel-rows 1 to 33 in a Search Window (i.e. Physical Memory partition A in Figs. 14 and 16), the reader is urged to keep in mind that another separate set of 5 FSL channels are implemented for the pixel-rows 34 to 48 of partition B. In Fig. 18, a single time step refers to 33 cycles being completed, or in other words one vertical sweep (Search-window buffer scaling section) of the Search Window being completed.

Experimental results

Before we present the experimental results of the measured bandwidths in our soft-core controlled system, we would like to address why experiments are necessary in the first place. One could argue that analytical analysis alone could suffice to determine the feasibility of our system, since the bandwidths and operational frequencies of our embedded system components are already published within their respective technical data sheets. This is true in that such an analysis would result in an upper theoretical bound on what level of system performance is possible. However, this estimate is likely to be overly optimistic and may downplay the realistic result of accelerator throughput degradation in actual implementation.

Many of the embedded system components have non-deterministic latencies and throughput. These components included the MPMC (Multi-Port Memory Controller), the PLB and XCL buses to the MPMC, and even the Microblaze processor itself given the varying loads on the buses that it interacts with. All of these factors combine to make the throughput of an embedded system based data transfer mechanism highly variable in nature. This is even more pronounced when the accelerators that draw data from this system belong to varying application domains.

The Virtex 5 device used in the synthesis results for the VBSME accelerator is the XC5VLX330. This chip contains 51 840 Virtex 5 slices (each slice has four 6-input LUTS and FFs). Table 2 above presents the area and performance results of the VBSME accelerator when paired with custom RTL implementations of a memory substructure for each level of scaling; Table 3 then compares the area and performance of the accelerator paired with our soft-processor based system of memory data delivery.

Similar results for the DIALIGN DNA Alignment accelerator were previously listed in Table 1 (the table is reproduced below as Table 4 for reader convenience). Unlike the VBSME application, DIALIGN did not suffer any performance degradation in the adoption of a HW/SW MicroBlaze interface, and thus performance metrics are not listed in the table for comparison. The DIALIGN accelerator was implemented on the 5vlx110tff1136-1 Virtex 5 device, on the XUP 5 development board [19]. As seen in the table, moving to the easier development flow of a HW/SW solution does come at the cost of roughly a 20% increase resource utilization. This device is a relatively smaller chip with 17 280 Virtex 5 slices.

Total development hours for the embedded-system based design of data movement for both of these application accelerators was measured in weeks, and less than a month at a maximum including debug time. In comparison, custom RTL based interface design and memory management for these accelerators was closer to 6 months exclusive of debugging hours. Furthermore, the RTL designs cannot easily be reused when an IO controller update is required.

For the embedded-system the development time is quantifiable under two different steps. The first step, which is the actual configuration of the embedded system can take up to a week or two to design and test, to ensure that the FSLs are connected to the accelerator correctly. The 2nd step is the writing of the embedded software itself, to transfer data from the SSD to the accelerator. This resulted in roughly only 500 to 1000 lines of code, between the two applications, with the debug hours being greater than the code writing hours.

In contrast, the previous work on custom RTL interfaces [35] consisted of five different Verilog modules for

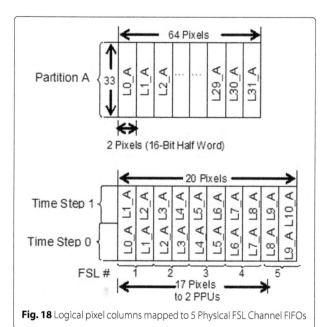

Fig. 18 Logical pixel columns mapped to 5 Physical FSL Channel FIFOs

Table 2 VBSME accelerator area and performance results with a custom RTL-designed memory subsystem

| # of PPUs | Area[a] | | | | Performance | | |
| | LUTs | | DFFs | | Target resolution | Freq | fps |
	#(K)	%	#(K)	%		(MHz)	
1	8.71	4.20	3.42	1.65	640×480 (VGA)	200.6	28
2	18.5	8.92	5.49	2.65	800×608 (SVGA)	199.0	34
4	37.8	18.2	9.64	4.65	1024×768 (XVGA)	198.3	42
8	76.4	36.8	18.0	8.68	1920×1088 (HD Video)	198.3	31
16	154	74.3	34.6	16.7	1920×1088 (HD Video)	198.3	62

[a]Xilinx's Virtex 5 devices use 4 DFFs & 4 6-input LUTs per Slice

each level of memory subsystem scaling. Then, five other top-level Verilog modules were also required to accomplish the correct wiring of the scalable accelerator to the chosen memory subsystem module. Each of the Verilog memory subsystem modules contained sub-components previously described such as block rams, muxes, and the most time consuming of all—an FSM based sub-component acting as the CLU. On average there were close to 600 lines of RTL across the five Verilog memory subsystem files.

For the DIALIGN accelerator use case example, the hardware interface to the SATA controller consisted of eight Verilog modules, each consisting of roughly 500 lines of RTL code. Since these lines of RTL code interact with a physical external device, often simulation alone is not enough to diagnose bugs during the debug process. Thus internal logic analyzers were required to pinpoint issues at run time. This level of hardware debugging requires multiple iterations to complete and suffers from high synthesis and place and route times between iterations. Visibility into simultaneous variables (i.e. registers) is also limited and confined to within usually 1024 clock-cycle sample windows at a time. Thus the verification process quickly becomes on the order of months before the system is functional as intended.

In contrast, the MicroBlaze HW/SW partitioned interface solutions can be implemented and verified within less than a month, inclusive of debugging hours, since

debugging the interfaces in software does not require the FPGA device to be synthesized nor placed and routed for each debug iteration. It is also highly flexible towards future IO controller updates, while also retaining backwards compatibility in software. Above all of these factors that favour an embedded system approach—when custom RTL designed access to bare metal IO controllers in IaaS environments is not permitted at all, an embedded solution may be the only viable option to provide end customers with a flexible method to manage to their IO data.

The Microblaze processor chosen for the experiments was implemented using the minimum-area tool setting in XPS (Xilinx Platform Studio) and was clocked at 125 MHz. It also included barrel-shift logic as the only additional hardware component to its ALU. The VBSME accelerator using its stand-alone custom RTL memory substructure could be clocked at least at 198.3 MHz at 16-PPUs scaling, and at a maximum frequency of 200.6 MHz at the single PPU level of scaling. The required bandwidth to support its native operating frequency is far above what the FSL channels are capable of supporting (up to 500 MB/s). Thus the accelerator was underclocked down to 100 MHz, to run slower than the Microblaze and thus allowing for the Microblaze processor to keep up with data delivery demands. This results in a roughly 50% frame rate drop in performance across all the levels of scaling.

Table 3 VBSME accelerator area and performance results with MicroBlaze (125 MHz) based data delivery

| # of PPUs | Area* | | | | LUTs % Increase | DFFs % Increase | Performance | |
| | LUTs | | DFFs | | | | Freq (MHz) | fps |
	#(K)	%	#(K)	%				
1	22.7	10.9	6.70	9.11	6.70	7.46	100	15
2	32.5	15.7	6.78	10.1	6.78	7.45	100	16
4	51.8	25.0	6.80	12.1	6.80	7.45	100	20
8	90.4	43.6	6.80	16.1	6.80	7.42	100	15
16	168	81.0	6.70	24.2	6.70	7.50	100	30

*Xilinx's Virtex 5 devices use 4 DFFs & 4 6-input LUTs per Slice

Table 4 DIALIGN alignment accelerator with custom HW interfaces vs. HW/SW IO interfaces

	Area[a]				LUTs % Increase	DFFs % Increase	Accelerator frequency (MHz)	MicroBlaze frequency (MHz)
	LUTs		DFFs					
	#(K)	%	#(K)	%				
HW interface	51.0	73.8	36.9	53.4			67.7	N/A
HW/SW interface with Microblaze	64.5	93.3	52.0	75.2	19.5	21.8	67.7	125

[a]Xilinx's Virtex 5 devices use 4 DFFs & 4 6-input LUTs per Slice

Discussion

For the VBSME accelerator system, its custom memory substructure was never the bottleneck of the system. The IO channel that its memory substructure relied on was DDR2 or greater device memory, which always supplied a surplus of memory bandwidth than what was required by the accelerator [35]. Thus, in this case, transitioning to a Microblaze soft-core data delivery method hurt its system performance by 50% or more (i.e. the Microblaze based FSL channels became a new IO bottleneck).

Despite the less than acceptable frame rates (< 26 fps) of Table 3 across all but one level of resolution scaling, an important piece of insight is still gained from the data within Tables 2 and 3 when analyzed together. In Table 2, the RTL designed interface, at the highest 1920×1088 HD target resolution, scaling to 16-PPUs results in a frame rate of 62 fps. The 62 fps rate, for most video applications, is beyond what is necessary (2630 fps). However, the same level of scaling, using a software IO interface in Table 3 still produces a useable frame rate of 30 fps. What this reveals is an important tradeoff—dialing up the computational performance of the accelerator can indeed compensate for limited IO throughput, and compensate well enough to achieve acceptable system performance.

At first, this revelation seems fairly counter-intuitive. One would expect that as the computational power of an accelerator is scaled up, this would then cause existing IO bottlenecks to be exacerbated further, resulting in unacceptable system performance. However, what we see in the frame rates of Table 3 is the opposite. As the accelerator performance is scaled higher from a single PPU up to 16 PPUs the frame rates increase correspondingly as well (except in the 8-PPUs row, which is an outlier in both Tables 2 and 3 that will be explained shortly). The reason for this lies in the architecture of the VBSME accelerator, and how it correlates a doubling in computational performance with only a single byte increase in the required input bandwidth. Based on this, one could reason that at some unknown level of accelerator scaling even a modest amount of IO throughput, such as that offered via a MicroBlaze solution, will produce the required frame rate for the system.

The 8-PPUs row is an outlier with respect to correlating increases in frame rates as the number of PPUs is increased. This is due to the fact that we are not measuring frame rate performance while holding the frame resolution as a constant. In other words the frame rate that we measure is against a targeted resolution per number of PPUs used. When video industry standards moved to 1080 HD video from previous VGA resolutions, the screen aspect ratio was widened. This widening of the frame means there are many more columns of macro-blocks that must be processed during VBSME. Thus the number of computations is significantly higher for HD video. As a result, even though we increase the number of PPUs to 8, the increase in HD resolution workload outweighs the extra PPUs and thus we do not see an increase in frame rate relative to the preceding row. However, when the HD resolution is held constant and the number of PPUs is further increased to 16, we see a significant doubling of the frame rate as expected.

For the DIALIGN DNA alignment accelerator, even with a custom memory/data delivery system, the slow SSD write rates of 66 MB/s were the IO bottleneck. In this case, transitioning to a Microblaze software controlled data infrastructure offered significant advantages in design time, testing, and future flexibility with no performance loss at all. However, the area overhead costs to include the Ethernet and SATA controllers as software driven microprocessor peripherals (versus custom FSM based controller logic) was just under 20% (for the LUTs used).

It should also be noted that the particular Virtex 5 device used did not contain a hardcore processor or memory controller, thus the MicroBlaze softcore and its required IP peripherals needed to consume programmable fabric resources in order to be implemented. This, however, is not the case with all of the modern FPGA devices on the market today. FPGA vendors have adopted the System-on-Chip model, where a hardened processor and memory-controller are well integrated with the programmable logic by default. Furthermore, volume of sales does not necessarily place such devices at higher price points either. In the case of such devices, the programmable logic overhead cost of 20% reported here would not exist, and the reduction in development time and effort could be gained without incurring the increased logic area penalty.

Present advances and shortcomings to hardware IO interfaces

On the path of making FPGA design more amenable to software developers, FPGA vendors have adopted software frameworks such as OpenCL [11, 36] for accelerator development. These frameworks, as a side effect of having raised the abstraction level in the hardware design process, have also made it easier to integrate certain IO devices.

As an example, the Ethernet channel that was used in this article's DIALIGN application was integrated using third party open-source SIRC cores that made the controller and a suitable interface for Ethernet access available. Today, FPGA vendors, such as Xilinx, have made Ethernet controllers directly available via their OpenCL development platforms (Fig. 19).

This step certainly solves the first problem of having at least a controller readily available to access the IO channel. However, the application requirements of how the IO data should be organized and buffered, or when back pressure should be asserted and released still falls into the user design space. These design choices falling into the user design space in itself is not a shortcoming. From an architectural point of view, requirements that will vary per application, should of course fall into that application user's design space. But the fact that no abstractions in software are available to manage the IO data stream within the application accelerator's design space is the real limitation.

The present means to emulate the same level of control that an embedded soft-core or hardened processor

would have over the data within the OpenCL environment is as follows. The user must first create custom data structures such as arrays to contain the incoming IO data. For DIALIGN the query-sequence and reference-sequence Ethernet data would be segregated, for example, into two separate arrays. Then the control sequences by which the data stream is fed to these two arrays would also be written. Since all of this is still performed in software there is no drawback between our proposed solution and this framework as of yet.

After all of the data organization and control has been programmed according to the available OpenCL APIs, the burden will completely fall on the High Level Synthesis (HLS) tool to implement the fine-grained data movement that is desired. And as discussed previously, having HLS efficiently manage data across varying clock-domains and interfaces is still an open-ended problem [7]. Due to this limitation, the fine-grained data pattern that was intended by the accelerator developer may not match what is actually implemented, thereby making throughput and latency worse off compared to manual implementation. This degradation, as shown in this article, may not affect the overall application performance. However, in scenarios where it does, an embedded core solution will offer better IO performance relative to HLS.

Using an embedded IO solution also offers other significant benefits to the FPGA vendor or the data centre that is offering FPGA nodes as Infrastructure as a Service (IaaS). The integration of future IO controllers yet to be released (such as SATA controllers), will not require their own individual FIFO and Bridge IP logic for integration to the accelerator design. Furthermore, these IO resources can be virtualized over multiple users' accelerators without comprising on security by allowing each user to access the IO controller directly.

The same arguments that we have made so far towards IO controllers also applies to the device DRAM memory controller as well. And in the context of device DRAM being shared by multiple accelerator users, the case for security over the bare metal controller is even stronger.

One of the more recent interfaces to FPGA vendor provided memory controllers is the AXI Stream interface [25]. This type of interface, allows custom accelerators and OpenCL based accelerators alike access to DRAM memory via accompanying AXI interconnect infrastructure (Fig. 20).

However, as can be seen in the architecture of Fig. 20, there is no inherent support for memory data buffering organization beyond relying on HLS or custom RTL development. As this article has shown, this organization and control of DRAM data onto on-chip buffers can significantly affect the application level performance.

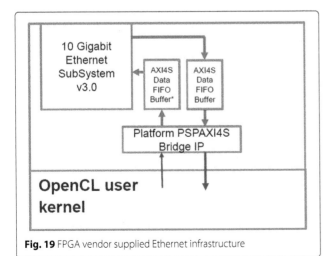

Fig. 19 FPGA vendor supplied Ethernet infrastructure

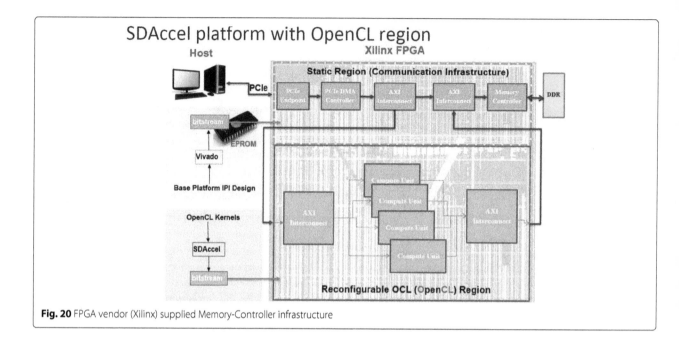

Fig. 20 FPGA vendor (Xilinx) supplied Memory-Controller infrastructure

Conclusion

This article has highlighted the need for standardized mechanisms to handle IO and data transfers to FPGA accelerators within data centers that offer their Infrastructure as a Service. This need arises from the fact that the end-user of such environments will never have full access to the underlying FPGA hardware. Thus data transfer methods that can be controlled in software while still offering performance levels equal to that of custom RTL interfaces are necessary.

To this end corporations such as Amazon (F1 Instances [37]) and Microsoft (Azure [38]) at present, for no extra cost, already offer FPGA "shells" as wrappers that developers can call to gain IO functionality on their cloud based FPGA instances. This shell is similar in concept to the static-region "template" described within this work. It is similar in that it too eases the pain of handling IO on FPGAs to the end-customer by providing pre-implemented IO controllers to standard interfaces such as PCIe, DDR memory, or even Ethernet in the case of Microsoft's Azure. However, this is where the similarity ends. What is proposed in this article goes another step beyond the abstraction of providing the IO controllers, we have presented a method by which the incoming data from the IO controllers can be effectively tailored to the performance needs of a particular accelerated algorithm. In contrast, Amazon and Microsoft defer the end-customer to the use of the FPGA vendor's HLS tool to handle the data after it crosses the IO controller boundary. And if HLS fails to provide optimal data partitioning and management of IO at the on-die buffering level for a unique application's data path, then the end-user is left to implement their own custom solution in RTL; if they have the skills and development time to do so.

We on the other hand have demonstrated an embedded system solution for data transfer, and more importantly, have shown that for a class of applications that have physical IO devices as their system level bottleneck, the system level performance is not degraded. For other classes of applications that have no such IO bottlenecks to begin with, our embedded solution does degrade system performance, however, we have also shown that in such cases scaling the acceleration is enough to counterbalance the IO performance loss caused by our solution.

Within this work, we have also compared the development time effort, performance, and area tradeoffs between the custom RTL design methodology used when end-users have full access to their FPGAs, and our embedded solution to be offered by data centres when such levels of access can not be granted to the end-users. Through our comparisons of experimental results, we make an argument in favour of the embedded-system approach. That conclusion was derived based not only on the ease of automation available within the current embedded-system EDA space of FPGA vendors but by the experimentally verified validity in aggregate performance and throughput of the accelerators not being compromised. The total effect on power consumption through the use of our embedded system approach to data transfers is predicted to be higher; however, it was beyond the scope of this paper to perform any detailed power analysis, and that remains to be completed as a future work in progress.

Authors' contributions

TM performed all of the RTL and embedded systems design that were necessary to conduct the experiments discussed in this article. SG conceived of the study to contrast embedded systems based IO control with purely RTL based approaches. Both authors participated in the selection and framing of the applications chosen for this study. Both authors read and approved the final manuscript.

About the Authors

Theepan Moorthy (S'04) received the B.A.Sc. in Computer Engineering from Queen's University in Kingston, ON, Canada in 2004. After spending two years in industry working on wireless chipset designs he returned to academia to pursue graduate degrees, and earned the M.A.Sc. degree from Ryerson University, Toronto, ON, Canada in 2008.
He later started his doctoral program at the University of British Columbia, Vancouver, Canada and transitioned from previously having worked on FPGA acceleration for video encoding to acceleration of bio-informatics algorithms. During his PhD he has held various internships at PMC-Sierra and Xilinx Research Labs.

Sathish Gopalakrishnan is an Associate Professor of Electrical & Computer Engineering at the University of British Columbia. His research interests center around resource allocation problems in several contexts including real-time, embedded systems and wireless networks. Prior to joining UBC in 2007, he obtained a PhD in Computer Science and an MS in Applied Mathematics from the University of Illinois at Urbana-Champaign. He has received awards for his work from the IEEE Industrial Electronics Society (Best Paper in the IEEE Transactions on Industrial Informatics in 2008) and at the IEEE Real-Time Systems Symposium (in 2004).

Competing interests

The authors declare that they have no competing interests.

References

1. Haidar A, Cao C, Yarkhan A, Luszczek P, Tomov S, Kabir K, Dongarra J (2014) Unified development for mixed multi-gpu and multi-coprocessor environments using a lightweight runtime environment. In: Parallel and Distributed Processing Symposium, 2014 IEEE 28th International. pp 491–500

2. Liu C, Ng HC, So HKH (2015) Quickdough: A rapid fpga loop accelerator design framework using soft cgra overlay. In: Field Programmable Technology (FPT), 2015 International Conference on. pp 56–63

3. Byma S, Steffan JG, Bannazadeh H, Garcia AL, Chow P (2014) Fpgas in the cloud: Booting virtualized hardware accelerators with openstack. In: Field-Programmable Custom Computing Machines (FCCM), 2014 IEEE 22nd Annual International Symposium on. pp 109–116

4. Putnam A, Caulfield AM, Chung ES, Chiou D, Constantinides K, Demme J, Esmaeilzadeh H, Fowers J, Gopal GP, Gray J, Haselman M, Hauck S, Heil S, Hormati A, Kim JY, Lanka S, Larus J, Peterson E, Pope S, Smith A, Thong J, Xiao PY, Burger D (2014) A reconfigurable fabric for accelerating large-scale datacenter services. In: 2014 ACM/IEEE 41st International Symposium on Computer Architecture (ISCA). pp 13–24

5. Lin Z, Chow P (2013) Zcluster: A zynq-based hadoop cluster. In: Field-Programmable Technology (FPT), 2013 International Conference on. pp 450–453

6. Norm Jouppi, Distinguished Hardware Engineer, Google, Google supercharges machine learning tasks with TPU Custom Chip. [Online]. Available: https://cloudplatform.googleblog.com/2016/05/Google-supercharges-machine-learning-tasks-with-custom-chip.html Jouppi, Distinguished Hardware Engineer, Google, Google supercharges machine learning tasks with TPU Custom Chip. [Online]. Available: https://cloudplatform.googleblog.com/2016/05/Google-supercharges-machine-learning-tasks-with-custom-chip.html

7. Cong J, Liu B, Neuendorffer S, Noguera J, Vissers K, Zhang Z (2011) High-level synthesis for fpgas: From prototyping to deployment. IEEE Trans Comput. Aided Des Integr Circ Syst 30(4):473–491

8. Ma S, Andrews D, Gao S, Cummins J (2016) Breeze computing: A just in time (jit) approach for virtualizing fpgas in the cloud. In: 2016 International Conference on, ReConFigurable Computing and FPGAs (ReConFig). pp 1–6

9. Chen F, Lin Y (2015) FPGA accelerator virtualization in OpenPOWER cloud. In: OpenPower Summit

10. Milford M, Mcallister J (2016) Constructive synthesis of memory-intensive accelerators for fpga from nested loop kernels. IEEE Trans Signal Process 99:4152–4165

11. Munshi A (2009) The OpenCL Specification. Khronos OpenCL Working Group

12. Altera ALTERA SDK FOR OPENCL. [Online]. Available: https://www.altera.com/products/design-software/embedded-software-developers/opencl/overview.html

13. Morris GW, Thomas DB, Luk W (2009) Fpga accelerated low-latency market data feed processing. In: 2009 17th IEEE Symposium on, High Performance Interconnects. pp 83–89

14. Chrysos G, Sotiriades E, Rousopoulos C, Pramataris K, Papaefstathiou I, Dollas A, Papadopoulos A, Kirmitzoglou I, Promponas VJ, Theocharides T, Petihakis G, Lagnel J (2014) Reconfiguring the bioinformatics computational spectrum: Challenges and opportunities of fpga-based bioinformatics acceleration platforms. IEEE Design Test 31(1):62–73

15. Lockwood JW, Monga M (2015) Implementing ultra low latency data center services with programmable logic. In: 2015 IEEE 23rd Annual, Symposium on High-Performance Interconnects. pp 68–77

16. Erdmann C, Lowney D, Lynam A, Keady A, McGrath J, Cullen E, Breathnach D, Keane D, Lynch P, Torre MDL, Torre RDL, Lim P, Collins A, Farley B, Madden L (2014) 6.3 a heterogeneous 3d-ic consisting of two 28nm fpga die and 32 reconfigurable high-performance data converters. In: 2014 IEEE International Solid-State, Circuits Conference Digest of Technical Papers (ISSCC). pp 120–121

17. Morgenstern B, Frech K, Dress A, Werner T (1998) DIALIGN: Finding Local Si milarities by Multiple Sequence Alignment. Bioinformatics 14(3):290–294

18. Boukerche A, Correa Jan M, Cristina A, de Melo MA, Ricardo Jacobi P (2010) A Hardware Accelerator for the Fast Retrieval of DIALIGN Bilogical Sequence Alignments in Linear Space. IEEE Trans Comput 59(6):808–821

19. Xilinx Xilinx University Program XUPV5-LX110T Development System. [Online]. Available: http://www.xilinx.com/univ/xupv5-lx110t.htm

20. Moorthy T, Gopalakrishnan S (2014) Gigabyte-scale alignment acceleration of biological sequences via ethernet streaming. In: Field-Programmable Technology (FPT), 2014 International Conference on. pp 227–230

21. Woods L, Eguro K (2012) Groundhog - A Serial ATA Host Bus Adapter (HBA) for FPGAs. IEEE 20th Int. Symp Field-Programmable Cust. Comput. Mach:220–223

22. Xilinx MicroBlaze Soft-Processor IP Protocol Specification. [Online]. Available: http://www.xilinx.com/support/documentation/sw_manuals/xilinx11/mb_ref_guide.pdf

23. Eguro K (2010) SIRC: An Extensible Reconfiguring Computing Communication API. 2010 18th IEEE Annual International Symposium on Field-Programmable Custom Computing Machines:135–138

24. Mendon AA, Huang B, Sass R (2012) A high performance, open source SATA2 core. Field Programmable Logic Appl. (FPL), 2012 22nd Int. Conf. 421–428

25. ARM AMBA AXI Protocol Specification. [Online]. Available: http://www.arm.com/products/system-ip/amba-specifications.php

26. Xilinx Fast Simplex Link IP Protocol Specification. [Online]. Available: http://www.xilinx.com/products/intellectual-property/fsl.html

27. Multi-Port Memory Controller IP Protocol Specification. [Online]. Available: http://www.xilinx.com/products/intellectual-property/mpmc.html

28. Processor Local Bus IP Protocol Specification. [Online]. Available: http://www.xilinx.com/products/intellectual-property/plb_v46.html

29. Summers J, Brecht T, Eager D, Gutarin A (2016) Characterizing the workload of a netflix streaming video server. In: 2016 IEEE International Symposium on, Workload Characterization (IISWC). pp 1–12

30. Delimitrou C, Kozyrakis C (2013) The netflix challenge: Datacenter edition. IEEE Comput. Archit. Letters 12(1):29–32

31. Aaron A, Li Z, Manohara M, Lin JY, Wu ECH, Kuo CCJ (2015) Challenges in cloud based ingest and encoding for high quality streaming media. In: Image Processing (ICIP) 2015 IEEE International Conference on. pp 1732–1736

32. Wiegand T, Sullivan GJ, Bjontegaard G, Luthra A (2003) Overview of the h.264/avc video coding standard. IEEE Trans. Circ. Syst. Video Technol 13(7):560–576

33. ITU Telecom. Standardization Sector of ITU., Advanced video coding for generic audiovisual services. ITU-T Recommendation H.264, May 2003

34. Liu Z, Huang Y, Song Y, Goto S, Ikenaga T (2007) Hardware-Efficient Propagate Partial SAD Architecture for Variable Block Size Motion Estimation in H.264/AVC. Proc 17th Great Lakes Symp. VLSI. 160–163

35. Moorthy T, Ye A (2008) A Scalable Computing and Memory Architecture for Variable Block Size Motion Estimation on Field-Programmable Gate Arrays. Proc. 2008 IEEE conf. Field Programmable Logic Appl:83–88

36. Stone JE, Gohara D, Shi G (2010) OpenCL: A Parallel Programming Standard for Heterogeneous Computing Systems. Comput. Sci. Eng 12(3):66–73

37. Amazon Amazon EC2 F1 Instances. [Online]. Available: https://aws.amazon.com/ec2/instance-types/f1/

38. Microsoft Microsoft Azure. [Online]. Available: https://azure.microsoft.com/en-us/resources/videos/build-2017-inside-the-microsoft-fpga-based-configurable-cloud/

39. Moorthy T (2008) Scalable FPGA Hardware Acceleration for H.264 Motion Estimation. Ryerson University, Theses and Dissertations

13

Optimizing virtual machine placement for energy and SLA in clouds using utility functions

Abdelkhalik Mosa* [iD] and Norman W. Paton

Abstract

Cloud computing provides on-demand access to a shared pool of computing resources, which enables organizations to outsource their IT infrastructure. Cloud providers are building data centers to handle the continuous increase in cloud users' demands. Consequently, these cloud data centers consume, and have the potential to waste, substantial amounts of energy. This energy consumption increases the operational cost and the CO_2 emissions. The goal of this paper is to develop an optimized energy and SLA-aware virtual machine (VM) placement strategy that dynamically assigns VMs to Physical Machines (PMs) in cloud data centers. This placement strategy co-optimizes energy consumption and service level agreement (SLA) violations. The proposed solution adopts *utility functions* to formulate the VM placement problem. A genetic algorithm searches the possible VMs-to-PMs assignments with a view to finding an assignment that maximizes utility. Simulation results using CloudSim show that the proposed utility-based approach reduced the average energy consumption by approximately 6 % and the overall SLA violations by more than 38 %, using fewer VM migrations and PM shutdowns, compared to a well-known heuristics-based approach.

Keywords: Cloud computing, Virtual machine placement, Cloud resource management, Utility functions, Energy-aware, Service level agreement (SLA)

Introduction

Cloud computing delivers application, platform or infrastructure services to large numbers of users with diverse and dynamically changing requirements. To meet the expectations of their users in a cost-effective manner, cloud service providers must make numerous resource management decisions that satisfy different objectives, for example to meet Service Level Agreements (SLAs) while minimizing energy costs [1].

In this paper, we focus on the problem of *adaptively allocating virtual machines (VMs) to physical hosts*, in the context of unpredictable workloads. Specifically, this involves making decisions such as *when to relocate VMs*, *which VMs to relocate, where to place VMs that are to be relocated*, and *which physical machines can be switched off*. These decisions can be made with a view to meeting different objectives; in our case, we seek to maximize the profit of an Infrastructure-as-a-Service (IaaS) service provider by trading off income (which involves meeting SLAs) and expenditure (which involves saving energy by

moving physical machines that are not needed into power saving modes).

We are not the first to address this problem. For example, in a series of papers Beloglazov et al. [2–4] develop heuristic algorithms that make dynamic workload allocation decisions, taking into account energy usage when deciding where to place VMs. In adopting a heuristic approach, these papers focus on identifying criteria that suggest that an adaptation may be beneficial (which tends to involve detecting which hosts are over- or underloaded), and then making reallocation decisions in ways that take into account estimated energy usage. In developing and refining their heuristics, the authors focus on challenges like detecting when the load on a physical node suggests that an adaptation may be beneficial. By systematically refining their heuristics, the authors were able to make proposals that significantly improved on their static counterparts.

We note, however, that such heuristic approaches do not address the objective of the problem directly. Here, the goal is to meet SLAs while conserving energy, but the focus of the heuristics, that determine when adaptations should take place and which VMs should be moved, is on

*Correspondence: amosa@cs.man.ac.uk
School of Computer Science, University of Manchester, Oxford Road, M13 9PL Manchester, UK

the load on physical nodes. Clearly, the load on physical nodes is relevant to this problem, but it is effectively a proxy for the goal. In this paper, we adopt what is referred to as a utility-based approach to adaptive energy-aware virtual machine placement. In the utility-based approach to adaptive systems [5–7], a *utility function* is defined that specifies the goal of the adaptation, and an optimization algorithm explores alternative adaptations, to identify the adaptation that maximizes utility. In this paper, the utility of an assignment a over a time interval t is defined as: $Utility(a, t) = Income(a, t) - EnergyCost(a, t)$.

This utility function captures the objective for the service provider. The *Utility(a,t)* returns the predicted financial return over a period of time t of an assignment a of virtual machines (VMs) to physical machines (PMs). To apply this in practice involves the development of models for estimating the *Income* and *EnergyCost* of an assignment over a time interval t, and the selection of a search function that explores the space of alternative assignments. Thus, the utility based approach captures the goal of the adaptation explicitly and searches for solutions that meet the goal. The utility based approach has been applied to a range of applications, from workflow scheduling on grids [8] to data center cooling [9], and here is applied to adaptive VM placement.

The key contributions of this paper are summarized as follows:

1. An application of the utility-based approach to the VM placement problem.
2. A utility function that estimates the profit from adaptive VM placement taking into account the impact of adaptations, the energy used, and the SLA violations.
3. An empirical evaluation of the proposed solution using the CloudSim simulation framework.

The paper is structured as follows. In "Related work" section, we describe related work on autonomic virtual machine placement and utility-based resource allocation. In "Optimizing virtual machine placement" section, we provide a precise description of the VM placement problem. "Utility-based resource allocation" section indicates how the utility-based approach has been applied to the VM placement problem, and "Experimental evaluation" section empirically evaluates the approach, comparing it to an existing heuristic strategy. Conclusions and future directions are discussed in "Conclusions and further work" section.

Related work

This section discusses work that is related to that described in the paper, considering in turn *virtual machine placement* and *utility based resource allocation*.

We do not re-review less closely related research in cloud computing, of which there is a considerable amount, and for which review articles already exist (e.g. [1, 10, 11]).

Virtual machine placement: In relation to *virtual machine placement*, we review results in terms of *when* placement decisions are made, the *objective* that placement decisions seek to meet, and the *decision-making paradigm* that is used to identify a suitable allocation.

In terms of *when* placement decisions are made, approaches can be considered to be *static* (e.g. [12–14]), in which decisions once made are not reviewed during the lifetime of the VM, or *dynamic* (e.g. [2, 15–18]), in which the VM to PM assignment may change during the execution of the VM. As *dynamic* approaches often make use of information on the actual load that is not available to static approaches, dynamic approaches often use a static approach for initial placement. In the remainder of this section, we will focus on dynamic approaches, as these are the most relevant to this paper.

Virtual machine placement decisions can involve trade-offs, for example between energy usage and risk of SLA violations, so methods implicitly or explicitly seek to meet an *objective*. Dynamic VM placement techniques have been developed that seek to maximize revenue (e.g. [12]), conserve energy (e.g. [17, 19, 20]), and to meet SLAs while saving energy where possible (e.g. [2, 21, 22]). In this paper, we seek to maximize profit, by making allocation decisions that take into account the cost of energy usage and the loss of income that would result from the violation of SLAs.

Researchers have investigated a range of *decision-making paradigms*, which decide when to change the VM to PM assignment, what migrations to carry out, and perhaps also what PMs can be turned off to save energy. Dynamic VM placement proposals have employed heuristics (e.g. [2, 12, 16, 17]), integer linear programming (e.g. [12]) and bespoke algorithms (e.g. [15]). In this paper, we deploy a utility based approach, in which an evolutionary search is used to explore alternative allocations.

We know of no other work that has both addressed the same problem as we address (*dynamic* virtual machine placement with the *objective* of maximizing profit, taking into account both SLAs and energy) using a utility-based *decision-making paradigm*. However, to enable the evaluation of our approach, we compare our results with a proposal that addresses the same problem, but using a different *decision-making paradigm*. Beloglazov et al. [2, 3, 23] proposed a heuristics-based energy-aware resource management system that meets quality of service (QoS) requirements. Their solution follows the divide and conquer concept by dividing the main problem into 4 sub-problems namely, *host overload detection*, *host underload detection*, *VM selection* and *VM placement*. The *host overload detection* problem determines when a host is considered to be overloaded. Once the host is considered overloaded, VMs are selected for migration from this overloaded host to a non-overloaded one. The *host underload detection* problem involves deciding that a host is underloaded. After host underload detection, all VMs in the underloaded host should be migrated to another host if possible, thereby enabling that host to be placed in a power saving mode. The *VM selection* problem involves deciding which VMs should be selected for migration from the overloaded host. Finally, the *VM placement* problem involves choosing the appropriate host for migrating the VMs to. Further details of this approach are provided in "Experimental evaluation" section, where it is compared with our utility-based proposal.

Utility-based resource allocation: In this paper, we use utility functions to compare alternative adaptations, and thereby to select the adaptation that is expected to yield the highest utility. As discussed by Kephart et al. [6], decision-making in computing involves a transition from a current state into one of several alternative future states, by way of candidate adaptations. In this context, it is the role of the utility function to quantify the suitability of each of the alternative future states. In the original proposal for utility-based adaptation [5], a *controller* is responsible for selecting the collection of *control parameters* that maximize the utility function, using a *utility calculator* that implements a model of the environment. Utility functions have been applied in autonomic computing for: configuring the properties of application hosting environments such as web servers [5], for selecting between alternative providers of a service [24], for managing the physical environment within data centres [9], for allocating jobs within a collection of workflows to machines on a grid [8], for optimizing resource utilization for scientific applications [25], and for balancing the load of a collection of database queries over the nodes in a cluster [26]. As the designs of these applications have various features in common, a methodology has been proposed for the development of utility-based applications [27], which we follow in "Utility-based resource allocation" section.

Optimizing virtual machine placement

This section demonstrates the virtual machine placement problem by describing the input, processing, and output model in "Input, processing and output for the VM placement" section. Moreover, "Monitoring, analysis, planning and execution of VM placement" section describes monitoring information that is used for the analysis, planning and the actual execution of the VM placement.

Input, processing and output for the VM placement

Figure 1 illustrates the input, processing, and output of the VM placement problem. The summary of the problem is as follows:

- Input: Given a cloud data center with N heterogeneous physical machines (PMs) with limited resource capabilities, the cloud provider receives VM placement requests consisting of M virtual machines (VMs) which need to be assigned to the PMs. Finally, the cloud user runs application workloads on the VMs. In the conducted experiments, the VMs come in batch mode, however they can be online.

- Processing: The processing of the VM placement problem involves identifying an assignment a that associates each $vm_i \in VM$, with a single $pm_j \in PM$. The processing consists of the *initial placement* controller and *dynamic placement* controller.

  - The *initial placement* controller either accepts or rejects VM placement requests based on the resource constraints in the data center. This is simply a bin packing problem and there are dozens of techniques for solving it in the literature.
  - The *dynamic placement* controller periodically reallocates existing VMs based on resource utilization. The goal of the dynamic placement is to save energy while minimizing SLA violations (SLAVs).

- Output: A VMs-to-PMs assignment.

In this paper, we develop a *utility based* solution for the *dynamic placement* problem. Furthermore, we evaluate the proposed solution and compare it with a *heuristics-based* one proposed in [2, 3]. The dynamic placement based on VM consolidation is a strictly NP-hard problem [28].

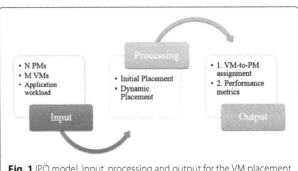

Fig. 1 IPO model. Input, processing and output for the VM placement

Monitoring, analysis, planning and execution of VM placement

Figure 2 shows the loop design model of the proposed utility-based solution in terms of monitoring, analysis, planning and execution (MAPE). The *monitoring (M)* component monitors the CPU utilization of the PMs and the VMs based on the applications' workload in the cloud data center. By the end of each scheduling interval, the *analysis (A)* component searches for alternative VMs-to-PMs assignments based on the collected monitoring data. The search process runs periodically depending on the scheduling interval. The *planning (P)* performs a utility-based assessment of candidate VMs-to-PMs assignments and considers the best one found so far. Moreover, it finds which VMs are going to be migrated, if any, and to where, based on the best found VMs-to-PMs assignment. Finally, the *execution (E)* component performs the migration of the VMs in addition to switching the unused PMs off.

Utility-based resource allocation

Abstracting from several experiences of using the utility based approach, a methodology has been developed for its application [7], which we follow here for applying the approach to VM placement.

Utility property selection

Selecting the properties of the utility function is crucial as they affect the value of the utility function. From [7], utility property selection involves selecting the property that it would be desirable to maximize. Our solution tries to maximize the profit, which is derived from *income*, *energy cost* and *violation costs*. The income represents the money that the cloud provider receives from cloud customers due to hosting their VMs. Energy cost represents the cost of the energy consumed due to placing the VMs

and the running of applications. Finally, the violation costs represent the amount of money that the cloud provider has to pay to cloud customers due to SLA violations (SLAVs).

Utility function definition

The utility function expresses the self-managing policy adopted for creating an autonomic cloud data center. The goal of the utility function is to maximize the profit of VM placement by minimizing energy consumption and SLA violations (SLAVs). Equation (1) provides the high-level definition of the utility function.

$$Utility(a,t) = Income(a,t) - (EstimatedEnergyCost(a,t)$$
$$+ EstimatedViolationCost(a,t) + PDMCost(a,t))$$

$$(1)$$

Here, *a* is a map representing the VMs-to-PMs assignment, and *t* is the assignment time period. *Income(a,t)* is the total income from hosting the customers' VMs; *EstimatedEnergyCost(a,t)* is the expected cost of energy consumption due to the assignment. *EstimatedViolationCost(a,t)* represents the cost of SLA violation due to the over-utilization of the hosting PMs, a cost that is calculated based on the number of VMs in violation. VMs are not available during migration and hence there should be a way to estimate the cost resulting from this violation. *PDMCost(a,t)* represents the violation cost of the *performance degradation due to the migration* (PDM) of VMs among PMs. The utility function requires the development of models for estimating both the *EnergyCost* and the *violation costs* of an assignment over a time interval *t*, which are provided in "Utility model development" section. This is followed by a description of a genetic algorithm that searches the space of VM-to-PM assignments for solutions that maximize the utility.

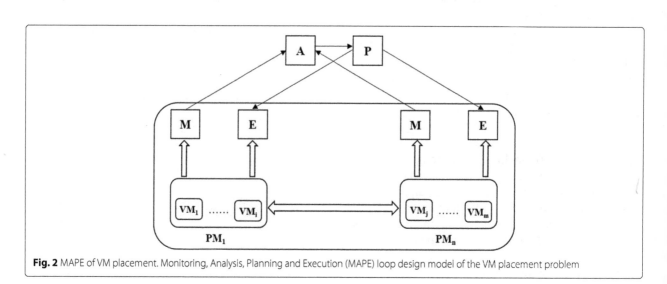

Fig. 2 MAPE of VM placement. Monitoring, Analysis, Planning and Execution (MAPE) loop design model of the VM placement problem

Utility model development

The utility model estimates the *expected energy cost* and the two types of *SLA violations* due to the VMs assignment. The utility model calculations depend on the percentage of *CPU utilization*, which is calculated as shown in the following sub-section.

Calculating PM's CPU utilization based on VM utilization

Algorithm 1 estimates the CPU utilization of the PM based on the candidate assignments. Algorithm 1 uses the captured monitoring information to calculate the CPU utilization of each of the PMs in the candidate assignment. Algorithm 1 depends on two assignments, the *current assignment* and the *candidate assignment*. The current assignment (c), is the currently running VMs-to-PMs assignment. The genetic algorithm produces a number of candidate assignments that need to be compared to the current one. The candidate assignment (a), represents an assignment that might or might not be adopted. If the best candidate assignment is better than (i.e. has a higher fitness value than) the current assignment then the candidate assignment should replace the current one. A new assignment means that some VMs might be removed from a PM while others might be added according to the new VMs-to-PMs mapping. The key idea is passing the candidate assignment a as a parameter to the *EstimatedUtilization(a)* function for computing the expected utilization due to the assignment.

Algorithm 1: The expected CPU utilization of each PM

---

    allPmsUtilizations[] **EstimatedUtilization(a)**
    Result: The CPU utilization of each PM in the cloud data center due to the candidate assignment
    Initialization:
    assignment c ← getCurrentAssignment(pm);
    addedVms ← VMs associated with the PM in a that are not in c;
    removedVms ← VMs associated with the PM in c that are not in a;
    allPmsUtilizations[] ← 0;
    u[pm] ← 0;
    foreach pm in the Assignment a do

        $u[pm]$ ←pm.getUtilization()+
                sum(addedVms.getUtilization())−
                sum(removedVms.getUtilization());
        allPmsUtilizations[].add(u[pm]);
    end
    return allPmsUtilizations[];

In Algorithm 1, *pm* refers to the physical machine; *pm.getUtilization()* returns *pm*'s current CPU utilization in millions of instructions per second (MIPS) and *added.getUtilization()* returns the total CPU utilization of VMs that are in the candidate, *a*, assignment and not in the current, *c*, one. The *removed.getUtilization()* call returns the total CPU utilization of VMs that are in the current assignment *c* and not in the candidate, *a*, one; and *u[pm]* stores the utilization of each PM in MIPS. Finally, *allPmsUtilizations[]* is an array holding the utilization of each single PM in the cloud data center.

Energy cost estimation

Algorithm 2 calculates the expected cost of energy due to the candidate assignment during the time interval *t*. For computing power consumption, a power model should be used. In this work, real power consumption data is used for calculating the power consumption. These real consumption data are provided in the *SPECpower_ssj2008* [3] benchmark. These data are provided with the CloudSim simulator through two different servers, *HP ProLiant ML110 G4* and *HP ProLiant ML110 G5*. Figure 3, from [3], exhibits a table that shows the variation of power consumption of those two servers according to the level of utilization in Watts.

Algorithm 2: Energy Cost Estimation

---

    float **EstimatedEnergyCost(a, t)**
    Result: Total Energy cost of the running PMs
    Initialization:
    powerConsumedPerPm[] = 0;
    totalPowerConsumed = 0;
    totalEnergyCost = 0;
    allPmsUtilizations[] = *EstimatedUtilization(a)*;
    foreach *pm in the Assignment a* **do**
        powerConsumedPerPm[pm] = pm.getPowerModel().getPower (cpuUtilization[pm]);
        totalPowerConsumed += powerConsumedPerPm[pm];
    end
    totalEnergyCost = totalPowerConsumed * energyCostPerSec * t;
    return(totalEnergyCost);

The function *getPower(cpuUtilization[pm])* returns the power according to the power model used and *EstimatedUtilization(a)* is shown in Algorithm 1. The return value from this algorithm is the cost of the total energy consumed due to the assignment in the cloud data center in the specified time period *t*.

Server	0%	10%	20%	30%	40%	50%	60%	70%	80%	90%	100%
HP ProLiant G4	86	89.4	92.6	96	99.5	102	106	108	112	114	117
HP ProLiant G5	93.7	97	101	105	110	116	121	125	129	133	135

Fig. 3 Power consumption at different utilizations, from [3]. Power consumption for *HP ProLiant G4* and *G5* provided by SPECpower benchmark

Violation cost due to PM over-utilization

Many factors might lead to SLA violations in a virtualized environment such as the over-utilization of the PMs, the migration of VMs, performance interference among co-located workloads [29], overheads from co-locating network-intensive or CPU-intensive workloads in isolated VMs, and system failure or outage. However, we only consider the over-utilization of the PMs and the VMs migration, as shown in "Violation cost due to VM migrations" section, for comparison purposes, and as there is no interference between the VMs that constitute the workload used in the experiments in "Experimental evaluation" section. Algorithm 3 calculates the violation cost resulting from the over-utilization of the PMs based on the number of VMs in violation.

VMList represents the list of VMs assigned to each PM, and *demand* represents the total CPU demand of the PM resulting from the currently assigned VMS. The *sort(VMList)* method sorts the VMs in descending order according to the CPU demand. Descending order was used so as to minimize the number of VMs in violation. If the CPU *demand* is greater than the actual PM's CPU

capabilities (*supply*), this means that there is a violation and the number of VMs' in violation will be counted.

Violation cost due to VM migrations

Performance degradation due to migration (PDM) represents the performance degradation due to the overhead resulting from the migration of VMs among PMs. VMs are not available until the end of the migration process, which causes violation to the SLA. Algorithm 4 computes the cost of performance degradation due to VM migration where the *migrationTime* represents the time required until the VM is migrated. The time required to migrate a VM equals the amount of memory used by the VM divided by the available network bandwidth [3].

Algorithm 4: Violation cost due to VM migration

float **PDMCost(a, t)**

Result: Cost of SLA violations (SLAVs) due to migration

Initialization:

migrationTime ← 0; pdmViolationCost ← 0;

foreach *vm in the Assignment a* **do**

  if *the vm is migrated* **then**

    migrationTime ← vm.getAllocatedRam() / pm.getBw();

    pdmViolationCost ← pdmViolationCost + migrationTime * pdmCostSec;

  end

end

return(pdmViolationCost);

Algorithm 3: Violation cost due to PMs' over-utilization

float **EstimatedViolationCost(a, t)**

Result: SLA violation cost due to PMs' over-utilization

Initialization:

numOfVMsInViolation ← 0; violation ← 0;

foreach *pm in the Assignment a* **do**

  VMList ← list of VMs from *a* in *pm* ;

  VMList ← sort(VMList) by demand ;

  demand ← sum of demands in VMList ;

  supply ← pm.getTotalMips();

  while *demand >supply* **do**

    violation++;

    demand ← demand - vmDemand(VMList[violation]);

  end

  numOfVMsInViolation ← numOfVMsInViolation + violation;

end

return(numOfVMsInViolation * slaViolationCostPerSec * t);

Representation design

The solution to the VMs-to-PMs assignment problem is simply represented by a map. This map has *m* elements where each element, key, represents a VM and the value of that element is the PM's ID to which the VM is assigned. Figure 4 displays the representation of the solution.

Optimization algorithm

Finding a good assignment that maximizes the utility, *fitness*, function involves searching candidate assignments. A genetic, evolutionary, algorithm can be used for searching the search space for an appropriate assignment.

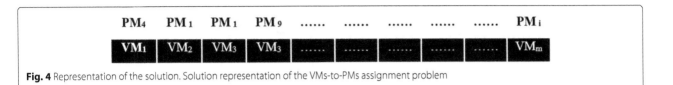

Fig. 4 Representation of the solution. Solution representation of the VMs-to-PMs assignment problem

Genetic algorithms are one of the evolutionary computation methods that are considered as powerful stochastic search and optimization techniques based on the Darwinian principle of natural selection [30, 31]. Genetic algorithms search a population of individuals in parallel; therefore they have the ability to avoid locally optimal solutions. Algorithm 5, adopted from [31, 32], shows a high-level pseudo-code of the genetic algorithm used for finding the VM-to-PM assignment that maximizes the utility. The genetic algorithm goes through the following phases: creation of initial population, fitness evaluation, parents selection, crossover, mutation and new population selection.

Algorithm 5: Genetic Algorithm Pseudo-code, modified version of [31, 32]

Result: Best-found VMs-to-PMs assignment
Initialization:
popSize ← population size; genCount ← number of generations;
$P \leftarrow \{\}$;   ▷ *Population: set of VMs-to-PMs assignments($a_1, a_2, ...a_n$)*
P ← initialVmsToPmsAssignments(popSize);
fitnessEvaluation(P); ▷ *based on the utility function defined in "Utility function definition" section*
while *generation number is less than genCount* **do**
   newPop ← {};   ▷ new population for next generation
   for *popSize times* **do**
      parentAssignment a_i, a_j ← parentsSelection(P);
      childrenAssignment c_i, c_j ← crossover(a_i, a_j);
      newPop ← newPop ∪ {mutate(c_i), mutate(c_j)};
   end
   fitnessEvaluation(P, newPop);
   P ← newPopulation(P, newPop);
end
return(best-found VMs-to-PMs assignment)

Initial population

The initial population consists of a number of individuals where each individual is considered a candidate solution to the problem. In the VM placement problem, each individual is described by a map, where a VM represents the *key* and the *value* of that key is the ID of the PM to which the VM is assigned, as shown in "Representation design" section. The *initial VmsToPmsAssignments(popSize)* in Algorithm 5, generates the initial set of solutions, candidate VMs-to-PMs assignments, by mutating the currently working solution. The current VMs-to-PMs assignment is a member of the initial population so that it can be kept if there is nothing better. The number of individuals in the population depends on the *populationSize* parameter.

Fitness/utility function evaluation

Each individual, *candidate solution*, is evaluated against the fitness, *utility*, function introduced in "Utility function definition and Utility model development" sections. A higher fitness means a better result as the goal is to maximize the income due to the VM placement. The fitness function calculates the utility of each individual.

Parents selection

We need to select individuals from the current population to be parents for the crossover operation. There are many selection methods such as *roulette wheel selection, random selection, tournament selection, rank selection*, and *Boltzmann selection* [33]. We have deployed *random selection* by randomly selecting individuals from the current population for crossover.

Crossover

The crossover operator creates new individuals by combining parts of two individuals. Parents need to be selected from the current population to be crossed over. There are various crossover techniques such as *single point crossover, multi-point crossover, uniform crossover, shuffle crossover* and *ordered crossover* [33]. We have deployed a *single point crossover* where swapping between the two individuals is done beyond the crossover point. The crossover operation creates a new population of the crossed over individuals. Table 1, shows how the new offspring is created by mating two parents using single point crossover. The "‖" symbol represents the crossover point.

Mutation

The mutation function creates new individuals by making changes in one or more values in a single individual. These new individuals are similar to current individuals, with

Table 1 Single point crossover

Parent$_1$	PM$_1$ PM$_2$ PM$_1$ ‖ PM$_3$ PM$_2$ PM$_1$
Parent$_2$	PM$_2$ PM$_1$ PM$_3$ ‖ PM$_1$ PM$_3$ PM$_3$
Offspring$_1$	PM$_1$ PM$_2$ PM$_1$ ‖ PM$_1$ PM$_3$ PM$_3$
Offspring$_2$	PM$_2$ PM$_1$ PM$_3$ ‖ PM$_3$ PM$_2$ PM$_1$

changes occurring based on a pre-defined probability. The mutation is used to make changes to the population from one generation to another. A portion of the current population is randomly selected to be mutated. Each individual, VMs-to-PMs assignment, resulting from the selection is mutated using the *mutation probability*. The mutation process creates a new separate population of the mutated individuals. Table 2 shows an example of how the mutation of the PMs works. The PMs in bold in the original offspring are mutated to new ones in the mutated offspring which means that some VMs are assigned to new PMs.

New population selection
Suppose that population size is N VMs-to-PMs assignments. The population of the next generation is created by selecting best K VMs-to-PMs assignment and copying them to the new population where $K < N$. The remaining $N - K$ solutions are randomly copied to complete the population size. This approach ensures that individuals, VMs-to-PMs assignments, with the highest utility are retained, while also maintaining diversity in the population.

The resulting assignment
The genetic algorithm goes into a loop, the number of iterations of this loop is defined by the number of generations. After the end of the specified number of generations, the algorithm selects the individual with the highest fitness from the current population to represent the solution of the problem.

Experimental evaluation
Baseline heuristic method
We compared our utility-based solution against the heuristics-based one proposed by Beloglazov et al. [2, 3]. Beloglazov et al. [2, 3] have carried out a comprehensive investigation of heuristic techniques for energy-aware dynamic VM placement in cloud data centers. They divided the dynamic VM consolidation problem into four sub-problems and proposed different algorithms for solving each of these sub-problems.

Table 2 Mutating the PMs

Original Offspring	PM$_1$ **PM$_2$** PM$_1$ ... **PM$_1$ PM$_3$** PM$_3$
Mutated Offspring	PM$_1$ PM$_4$ PM$_1$ ... PM$_2$ PM$_2$ PM$_3$

The first sub-problem is *host overload detection* and involves deciding when a specific host PM is considered to be overloaded. Host overload detection requires migrating one or more VMs from the overloaded host to a non-overloaded one. They developed three main solutions for solving the host overload detection problem. These solutions are using a *static CPU utilization threshold*, an *adaptive threshold* using median absolute deviation (MAD) and interquartile range (IQR), and *local regression-based* using local regression (LR) and robust local regression (LRR). They found that the LRR algorithm was the best for solving the host overload detection problem. The second sub-problem was host under-load detection, which involves identifying when to decide that a host PM is under-loaded. They migrate all VMs from an under-loaded host to other hosts, if possible, and then switch that machine into power saving mode. The third sub-problem was VM selection and it involves identifying which VMs should be selected from an overloaded host for migration. They proposed 3 VM selection policies, namely minimum migration time (MMT), random selection (RS) and maximum correlation (MC). They found that *MMT* was the best for VM selection. The final sub-problem was the VM placement problem, and it involves identifying which hosts should be used for placing the migrated VMs. They deployed a power aware best fit decreasing (PABFD) algorithm, which is a modified version of the best fit decreasing (BFD) that considers CPU utilization during the allocation.

According to their evaluations, *LRR* and *MMT* were the best solutions for host overload detection and VM selection problems respectively. Therefore, we compare our proposed solution against the heuristics-based one that uses LRR and MMT.

Performance metrics
Four performance metrics are used for evaluating the effectiveness of the proposed VM placement approach and comparing it with the baseline heuristic method. These performance metrics are energy consumption, overall SLA violations, the number of migrations and the number of PM shutdowns.

- Energy Consumption: represents the total amount of energy consumed by all running PMs in the cloud data center. Lower values of energy consumption help reduce expenditure. This means that the lower the amount of energy consumed, the better the assignment.
- Overall SLA Violations: The SLA violations occur either due to the over-utilization of the PM or due to the migration of VMs among PMs. The lower the overall SLA violations, the better the assignment. The overall SLA violations are represented as a

percentage and calculated as follows:

$$overallSlaViolations = \frac{totalRequestedMips - totalAllocatedMips}{totalRequestedMips}$$

where *totalRquestedMips* is the totals MIPS requested by all VMs and *totalAllocatedMips* is the actual total MIPS allocated to the VMs based on the resource demand.

- Number of Migrations: This metric shows how often the VMs are migrated among PMs. Too many migrations degrade the performance and increase the SLA violations, and too few migrations might lead to an inappropriate assignment, and hence a balance is required to consider this trade-off.
- Number of PM Shutdowns: This metric indicates how many times the PMs are shut down. The frequent switching of a PM on and off might lead to PM failure on the long run [34].
- Profit: The profit metric calculates the average profit per day. The profit is calculated using: *profit = incomeFromVMs − (eneryCost + overallViolationCost)*. It ignores the PMs' cost, and the profit is highly dependent on factors such as the specifics of SLA violations and energy costs.

Simulation environment

The CloudSim simulation toolkit is used for simulating and evaluating the proposed utility-based approach [35, 36]. One cloud data center is simulated using two different types of PM, namely, *HP ProLiant ML110 G4* (Intel Xeon 3040, 2 cores x 1860 MHz, 4096 MB RAM and 1 Gbps BW) and *HP ProLiant ML110 G5* (Intel Xeon 3075, 2 cores x 2660 MHz, 4096 MB RAM and 1 Gbps BW). The cloud data center hosts four different VM types namely large, medium, small and extra small. The four types of the VMs are *large instance* (1 core x 2500 MHz, 870 MB RAM and 100 Mbps BW), *medium instance* (1 core x 2000 MHz, 1740 MB RAM and 100 Mbps BW), *small instance* (1 core x 1000 MHz, 1740 MB RAM and 100 Mbps BW) and *extra-small instance* (1 core x 500 MHz, 613 MB RAM and 100 Mbps BW).

Every VM runs an application with a different workload. The Applications' workloads are represented by CloudSim Cloudlets [36]. The Cloudlets randomly generate utilization data every 5 minutes based on a stochastic model [3]. The average percentage of utilization is approximately 50 %. All the following experiments have been run on an HP Pavilion g6 laptop(Core i7, 6 GB RAM).

Experiment setup

The simulation lasts for one day of simulation time which is the same time used in the heuristics-based solution. The algorithm runs every 5 minutes, 300 seconds, which is the same interval used in VMware's distributed resource scheduler (DRS) [37]. We have used a *population* of 20 individuals, the *number of generations* was 40, the *crossover ratio* was 0.8 and the *mutation probability* was 0.7. The total number of physical machines used in the conducted experiments is 50 and 100 PMs. Moreover, the total number of VMs used range from 50 to 200 VMs.

Two experiments with three different configurations for each were conducted to evaluate the proposed solution. The goal of the first experiment is to test the effectiveness of the solution on lightly loaded data centers while the second experiment tests the solution in more loaded cloud data centers. These scenarios are considered relevant because we need to be confident that: (i) the opportunities that exist to save energy are exploited in lightly loaded settings, and (ii) adaptation costs and attempts at energy saving do not lead to more SLAs being missed in a heavily loaded setting. Eventually, an experiment has been conducted to measure the execution time and compare the profit gained from applying both the utility-based and the heuristics-based solutions.

Experiments descriptions and results
Experiment 1: lightly loaded cloud data centres
Experiment 1 aims to appraise the effectiveness of the proposed utility based solution in a lightly loaded data center. In this experiment, the number of VMs is the same as the number of PMs that they will be allocated to. Three different configurations have been chosen for testing lightly loaded data centers:

1. Configuration 1.1: 50 VMs allocated to 50 PMs.
2. Configuration 1.2: 100 VMs allocated to 100 PMs.
3. Configuration 1.3: 150 VMs allocated to 150 PMs.

Figure 5 shows a scatter plot that presents the results of running *Configuration 1.1*. Each point in the scatter plot shows the results for a run of a workload; the vertical axis reports the energy consumed by the run and the horizontal axis shows the percentage of time when SLAs are not met. Thus a position in the bottom left of the chart is best. The blue triangles are results for the utility-based approach and the orange dots for the heuristic approach. The utility-based solution reduced energy consumption on average by about 10 % and reduced the time in which SLAs were being violated by around 29 %.

Figure 6 demonstrates the results of running *Configuration 1.2*. The utility based solution reduced average energy consumption by about 5 % and the time in which SLAs were being violated on average by around 38 %.

Figure 7 exhibits the results of running *Configuration 1.3*. The utility based solution improved energy consumption by about 5 % and reduced the time in which SLAs were being violated on average by about 40 % compared to the results of the heuristics based solution.

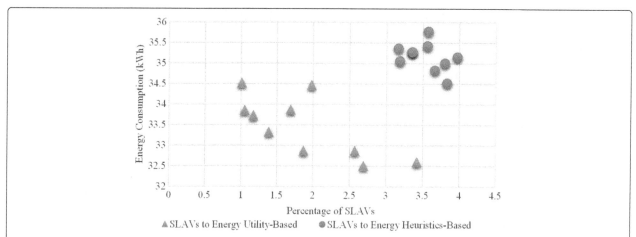

Fig. 5 Overall SLA violations to energy consumption from running *Configuration 1.1*, 10 times. The *blue triangles* represent results from the utility-based solution while *orange circles* represent the heuristics-based one

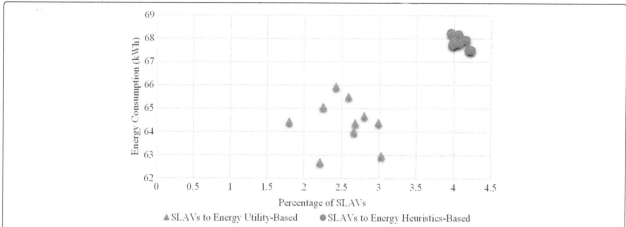

Fig. 6 Overall SLA violations to energy consumption after running *Configuration 1.2*, 10 times. The *blue triangles* depict results from the utility-based approach while *orange circles* represent the heuristics-based one

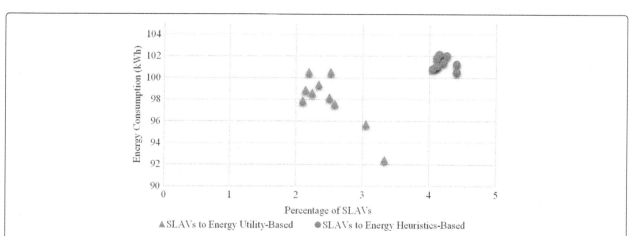

Fig. 7 Overall SLA violations to energy consumption after running *Configuration 1.3*, 10 times. The *blue triangles* represent results from the utility-based approach while *orange circles* represent the heuristics-based one

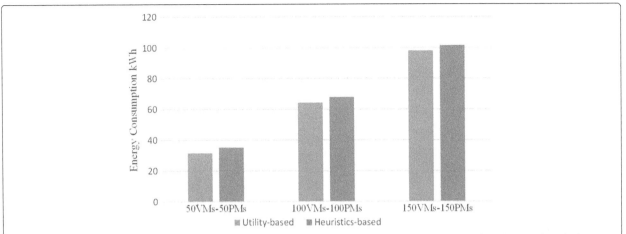

Fig. 8 Average energy consumption, from *Experiment 1*. The *blue* columns represent average energy consumption from the utility-based solution while the *orange* ones from the heuristics-based

For lightly-loaded data centers, the proposed utility-based solution outperforms the heuristics-based one in terms of energy savings and reduction of SLA violations, as summarized in the average values of *Experiment 1* in Figs. 8 and 9. Furthermore, the average values of *Experiment 1*, shown in Figs. 10 and 11, demonstrate that the utility-based solution saves energy consumption and reduces the overall SLAVs using a smaller number of VMs migrations and PMs shutdowns. Experiment 1 shows an average saving in energy consumption in lightly loaded data centers of approximately 5 % and an average reduction in SLA violations of around 36 %. Finally, the average number of VMs migrations and PMs shutdowns in the utility-based solution represent only around 16 and 5 % respectively, of the migrations and PMs shutdowns in the heuristics-based one.

These reductions in the number of VM migrations and PM shutdowns result from the fact that the utility-based approach only migrates when it finds a VM-to-PM assignment for which an adaptation is expected to be beneficial. In contrast, the heuristics based approach migrates whenever there is a problem (i.e. host/PM overload or host under-load); however, a problem may be detected without there being a solution to which it is worthwhile to adapt, and hence the heuristic approach tends to over-adapt.

Experiment 2: more loaded cloud data centres
Experiment 2 aims to assess the impact of increasing the number of VMs per PM on the specified performance metrics. The three configurations used for testing the more loaded data centers are as follows:

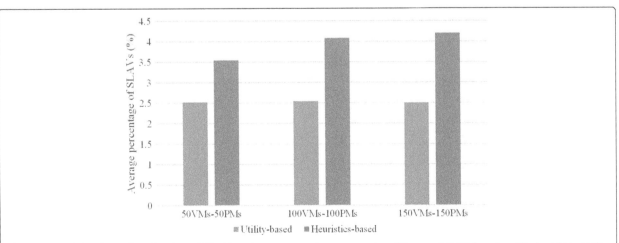

Fig. 9 Average SLA violations from *Experiment 1*. The *blue* columns represent average number of the overall SLAVs from the utility-based approach while the *orange* ones from the heuristics-based

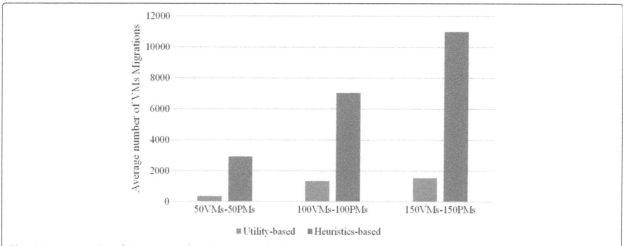

Fig. 10 Average number of VM migrations from *Experiment 1*. The *blue* columns represent the average number of VM migrations from the utility-based approach while the *orange* ones from the heuristics-based

1. Configuration 2.1: 100 VMs allocated to 100 PMs.
2. Configuration 2.2: 150 VMs allocated to 100 PMs.
3. Configuration 2.3: 200 VMs allocated to 100 PMs.

The results of running *Configuration 2.1* are the same as those for *Configuration 1.2* in "Experiment 1: lightly loaded cloud data centres" section, as they have the same configurations. Figure 12 shows a comparison between energy consumption and overall SLAVs after running *Configuration 2.2*. The utility-based solution reduced the average energy consumption and SLA violations by around 6 and 42 %, respectively compared to the heuristics based one. Comparing the results from *Configuration 2.1* and *Configuration 2.2*, we can conclude that increasing the number of VMs by 50 % using the utility based

approach resulted in nearly the same percentage of overall SLA violations, while the energy consumption is increased by about 50 %. However, the same increase in the number of VMs using the heuristics based approach also results in an increase in the percentage of the time spent in violations by about 6 % while the energy consumption is also increased by about 50 %. This means that the utility-based approach is more consistent in terms of SLAVs in more loaded data centers. However, there is slightly more performance degradation in the case of the heuristics based approach.

The scatter plot in Fig. 13 shows the values of energy consumption and overall SLAVs using both solutions after running *Configuration 2.3*. The utility based solution reduced energy consumption by about 6 %. Moreover, the

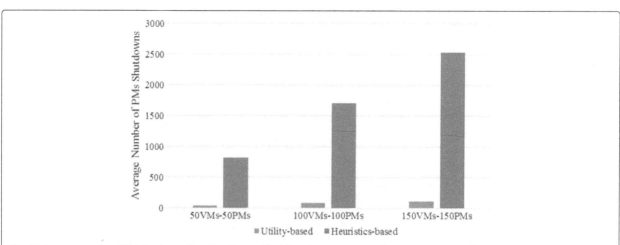

Fig. 11 Average number of PM shutdowns from *Experiment 1*. The *blue* columns represent the average number of PM shutdowns from the utility-based approach while the *orange* ones from the heuristics-based

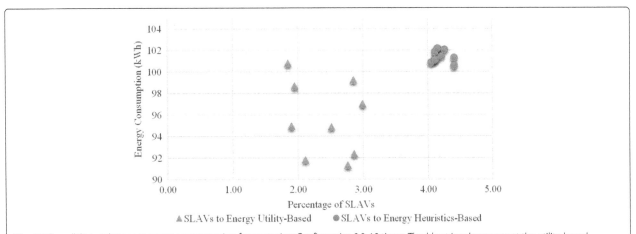

Fig. 12 Overall SLA violations to energy consumption from running *Configuration 2.2*, 10 times. The *blue triangles* represent the utility-based approach while the *orange circles* represent the heuristics-based one

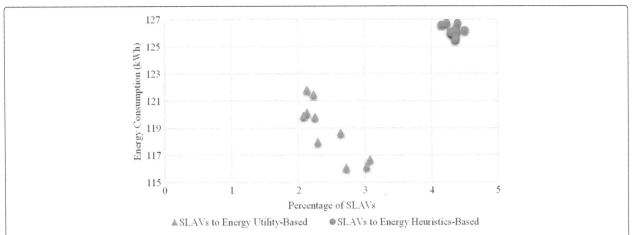

Fig. 13 Overall SLA violations to energy consumption from running *Configuration 2.3*, 10 times. The *blue triangles* represent the proposed utility-based solution while the *orange circles* represent the heuristics-based one

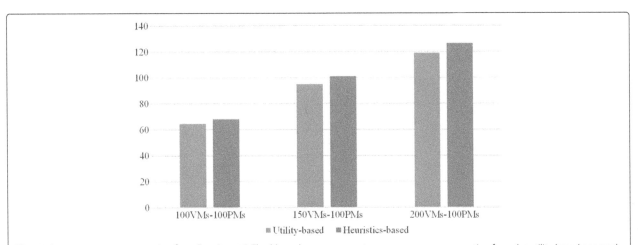

Fig. 14 Average energy consumption from *Experiment 2*. The *blue* columns represent average energy consumption from the utility-based approach while the *orange* ones from the heuristics-based

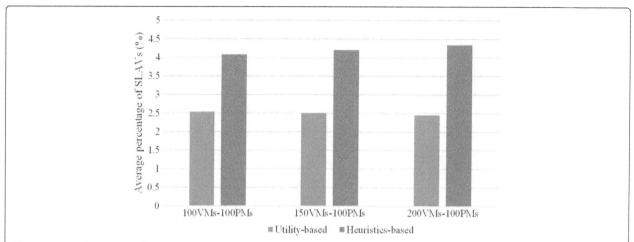

Fig. 15 Average SLA violations from *Experiment 2*. The *blue* columns represent average number of the overall SLAVs from the utility-based approach while the *orange* ones from the heuristics-based

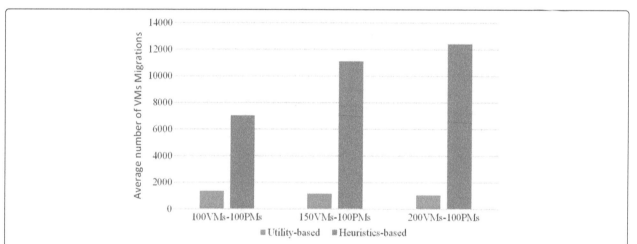

Fig. 16 Average number of VM migrations from *Experiment 2*. The *blue* columns represent the average number of VM migrations from the utility-based approach while the *orange* ones from the heuristics-based

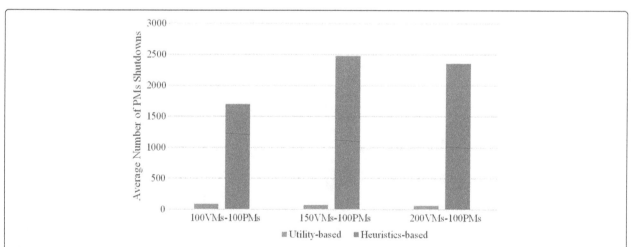

Fig. 17 Average number of PM shutdowns from *Experiment 2*. The *blue* columns represent the average number of PM shutdowns from the utility-based approach while the *orange* ones from the heuristics-based

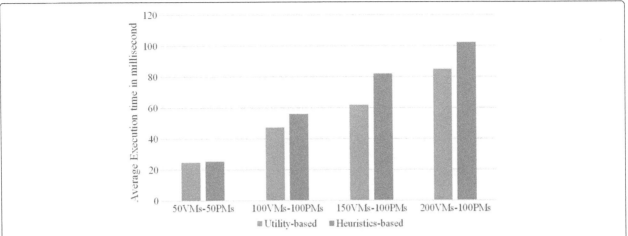

Fig. 18 Average execution time. Each column represents the average execution time; *blue* columns represent the utility-based approach, while the *orange* ones from the heuristics-based

utility based solution reduced time spent in SLA violations by about 43 %.

Figures 14, 15, 16 and 17 confirm that the proposed utility-based solution is also better than the heuristics-based one as it can save more energy and reduces the overall SLAVs using a smaller number of migrations and PM shutdowns. Experiment 2 shows that the utility-based solution reduces the amount of energy consumed in more-loaded data centers by around 6 % and also reduces the average SLA violations by nearly 41 %. Moreover, the average number of VMs migrations and PMs shutdowns in the utility-based solution represent approximately 12 and 3 % respectively, of the migrations and PMs shutdowns in the heuristics-based one.

Results conclude that the proposed utility-based solution saves more energy and reduces SLA violations more effectively than the heuristics-based one both in heavily and lightly loaded data center settings.

Experiment 3: average execution time and profit
Experiment 3 measures the average execution time and the average profit per day for both solutions. The time complexity of the genetic algorithm is O(gnm) + the complexity of the fitness (utility) function; where g is the number of generations, n is the population size and m is the solution size (number of VMs). Figure 18 exhibits the average execution time of both approaches. It demonstrates that the proposed utility-based approach can make a better VMs-to-PMs assignment in less execution time.

The profit is calculated based on the profit metric defined in "Performance metrics" section and the parameters used as shown in Table 3; based on the VM pricing offered by Amazon EC2 pricing[1]. Figure 19 confirms that the average profit per day from the utility-based approach

outperforms the average profit from the heuristics-based approach.

Conclusions and further work
Conclusion
This paper presented an approach based on utility functions for creating a self-managing VM placement solution in cloud data centers that dynamically assigns VMs-to-hosts according to resource utilization. The main goal of the approach is to increase the profit of an IaaS provider by minimizing the cost of energy consumption and the cost of different sources of SLAVs. Experiments have been conducted for comparing the effectiveness of the proposed utility based solution with an existing heuristic-based solution. The heuristic method against which the comparison took place was subjected by its proposers to a systematic evaluation in comparison with alternative heuristics, and shown to perform well [2, 3]. The empirical evaluation uses the original authors' implementation of the heuristic approach.

Evaluation showed that the proposed utility based solution outperformed the existing heuristic based approach in terms of energy savings and minimizing SLAVs in both lightly loaded and more heavily loaded cloud data centers. Perhaps the key factor that differentiates the approaches is that the heuristics based approach adapts whenever there is a problem (*PM overload, or PM under-load*). On the contrary, the utility based approach adapts only if it can identify an adaptation that is expected to improve on the current allocation.

Table 3 Profit parameters

VM_{large}	VM_{medium}	VM_{small}	VM_{XSmall}	Energy	Overall SLAVs
0.293 \$/h	0.146 \$/h	0.073 \$/h	0.028 \$/h	0.11 \$/h	0.4 \$/h

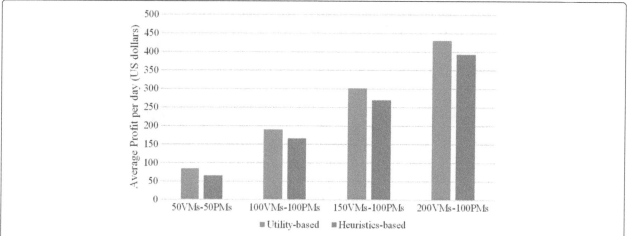

Fig. 19 Average profit per day. The *blue* columns depict the average profit/day from the utility-based approach, while the *orange* ones from the heuristics-based

Future directions

Although the proposal as described has shown considerable promise in empirical evaluations, the following points represent some areas that may benefit from further research:

1. Improving the utility model:
   More work is required to refine the utility model. For example, the calculations of the SLA violations could be improved by implementing a proactive calculation of the expected CPU utilization instead of the reactive one deployed in the paper.
2. Considering memory and network I/O during VM placement:
   In this paper, we only considered CPU during VM placement. Although the CPU consumes most of the server's power, all other host and network resources should be involved in the adaptive VM-to-PM assignment. For example, memory and network I/O should be considered during VM placement as they have a significant effect in memory and network intensive applications.
3. Revisiting the search algorithm:
   We have used a genetic algorithm for exploring the search space to find an efficient assignment that maximizes the utility. However, alternative approaches could be explored, such as the use of multi-dimensional optimization techniques that optimize for SLA violations and energy as distinct dimensions.
4. Scalability with real workload traces:
   Building a scalable VM placement strategy still requires further research for finding the most suitable scaling technique. Moreover, we need to conduct experiments with different workloads and different sizes of Cloud data centres.

5. Considering multi-tenancy constraints:
   The VM placement solution should consider multi-tenancy constraints such as security, anti-colocation and reducing network latency between VMs belonging to the same user.
6. Considering other sources of violations in virtualized environments:
   In our proposed solution, we only considered two sources of violations, namely performance degradation due to migration and the over-utilization of PMs. However, there are many other sources of violations such as violations resulting from the interference among collocated workloads, system outage, and late-time failure.

Endnote

[1] https://aws.amazon.com/ec2/pricing.

Authors' contributions
AM carried out the detailed design, implementation and evaluation of the work. NP conceived the study, and participated in its design and coordination. Both authors read and approved the final manuscript.

Competing interests
The authors declare that they have no competing interests.

References
1. Jennings B, Stadler R (2015) Resource management in clouds: Survey and research challenges. J Network Syst Manage 23(3):567–619. doi:10.1007/s10922-014-9307-7
2. Beloglazov A, Abawajy JH, Buyya R (2012) Energy-aware resource allocation heuristics for efficient management of data centers for cloud computing. Futur Gener Comput Syst 28(5):755–768. doi:10.1016/j.future.2011.04.017
3. Beloglazov A, Buyya R (2012) Optimal online deterministic algorithms and adaptive heuristics for energy and performance efficient dynamic consolidation of virtual machines in cloud data centers. Concurr Comput Pract Experience 24(13):1397–1420. doi:10.1002/cpe.1867

4. Beloglazov A, Buyya R (2013) Managing overloaded hosts for dynamic consolidation of virtual machines in cloud data centers under quality of service constraints. IEEE Trans Parallel Distrib Syst 24(7):1366–1379. doi:10.1109/TPDS.2012.240

5. Walsh WE, Tesauro G, Kephart JO, Das R (2004) Utility functions in autonomic systems. In: Autonomic Computing, 2004. Proceedings. International Conference On. IEEE. pp 70–77

6. Kephart JO, Das R (2007) Achieving self-management via utility functions. IEEE Internet Comput 11(1):40–48

7. Paton NW, Buenabad-Chavez J, Chen M, Raman V, Swart G, Narang I, Yellin DM, Fernandes AAA (2009) Autonomic query parallelization using non-dedicated computers: an evaluation of adaptivity options. VLDB J 18:119–140

8. Lee K, Paton NW, Sakellariou R, Fernandes AAA (2011) Utility functions for adaptively executing concurrent workflows. Concurr Comput Pract Experience 23(6):646–666. doi:10.1002/cpe.1673

9. Das R, Kephart JO, Lenchner J, Hamann HF (2010) Utility-function-driven energy-efficient cooling in data centers. In: Proceedings of the 7th International Conference on Autonomic Computing, ICAC 2010, Washington, DC, USA, June 7-11, 2010. pp 61–70. doi:10.1145/1809049.1809058. http://doi.acm.org/10.1145/1809049.1809058

10. Beloglazov A, Buyya R, Lee YC, Zomaya AY (2011) A taxonomy and survey of energy-efficient data centers and cloud computing systems. Adv Comput 82:47–111. doi:10.1016/B978-0-12-385512-1.00003-7

11. Lorido-Botran T, Miguel-Alonso J, Lozano JA (2014) A review of auto-scaling techniques for elastic applications in cloud environments. J Grid Comput 12(4):559–592. doi:10.1007/s10723-014-9314-7

12. Shi L, Butler B, Botvich D, Jennings B (2013) Provisioning of requests for virtual machine sets with placement constraints in iaas clouds. In: 2013 IFIP/IEEE International Symposium on Integrated Network Management (IM 2013), Ghent, Belgium, May 27-31, 2013. pp 499–505

13. Rabbani MG, Pereira Esteves R, Podlesny M, Simon G, Zambenedetti Granville L, Boutaba R (2013) On tackling virtual data center embedding problem. In: Integrated Network Management (IM 2013), 2013 IFIP/IEEE International Symposium On. IEEE. pp 177–184

14. Wolke A, Tsend-Ayush B, Pfeiffer C, Bichler M (2015) More than bin packing: Dynamic resource allocation strategies in cloud data centers. Inf Syst 52:83–95

15. Borgetto D, Stolf P (2014) An energy efficient approach to virtual machines management in cloud computing. In: Cloud Networking (CloudNet), 2014 IEEE 3rd International Conference On. IEEE. pp 229–235

16. Monil MAH, Qasim R, Rahman RM (2014) Energy-aware VM consolidation approach using combination of heuristics and migration control. In: Ninth International Conference on Digital Information Management, ICDIM. pp 74–79. doi:10.1109/ICDIM.2014.6991413. http://dx.doi.org/10.1109/ICDIM.2014.6991413

17. More D, Metha S, Walase L, Abraham J (2014) Achieving energy efficiency by optimal resource utilisation in cloud environment. In: IEEE Intl. Conf. on Cloud Computing in Emerging Markets (CCEM). pp 1–8

18. Xiao Z, Song W, Chen Q (2013) Dynamic resource allocation using virtual machines for cloud computing environment. IEEE Trans Parallel Distrib Syst 24(6):1107–1117

19. Xu J, Fortes J (2011) A multi-objective approach to virtual machine management in datacenters. In: Proceedings of the 8th ACM International Conference on Autonomic Computing. ACM. pp 225–234

20. Setzer T, Wolke A (2012) Virtual machine re-assignment considering migration overhead. In: Network Operations and Management Symposium (NOMS), 2012 IEEE. IEEE. pp 631–634

21. Monil MAH, Rahman RM (2016) Vm consolidation approach based on heuristics fuzzy logic, and migration control. J Cloud Comput 5(1):1–18

22. Chowdhury MR, Mahmud MR, Rahman RM (2015) Implementation and performance analysis of various vm placement strategies in cloudsim. J Cloud Comput 4(1):1

23. Beloglazov A, Buyya R (2010) Energy efficient resource management in virtualized cloud data centers. In: Proceedings of the 2010 10th IEEE/ACM International Conference on Cluster, Cloud and Grid Computing. IEEE Computer Society. pp 826–831

24. Bennani MN, Menasce D, et al (2005) Resource allocation for autonomic data centers using analytic performance models. In: Autonomic

Computing, 2005. ICAC 2005. Proceedings. Second International Conference On. IEEE. pp 229–240

25. Koehler M (2014) An adaptive framework for utility-based optimization of scientific applications in the cloud. J Cloud Comput 3(1):1–12

26. Paton NW, Aragão MAT, Fernandes AAA (2012) Utility-driven adaptive query workload execution. Futur Gener Comp Syst 28(7):1070–1079. doi:10.1016/j.future.2011.08.014

27. Paton N, De Aragão MA, Lee K, Fernandes AA, Sakellariou R (2009) Optimizing utility in cloud computing through autonomic workload execution. Bull Tech Comm Data Eng 32(1):51–58

28. Ferdaus MH, Murshed M, Calheiros RN, Buyya R (2014) Virtual machine consolidation in cloud data centers using aco metaheuristic. In: European Conference on Parallel Processing. Springer. pp 306–317

29. Moreno IS, Yang R, Xu J, Wo T (2013) Improved energy-efficiency in cloud datacenters with interference-aware virtual machine placement. In: Autonomous Decentralized Systems (ISADS), 2013 IEEE Eleventh International Symposium On. IEEE. pp 1–8

30. Whitley D (1994) A genetic algorithm tutorial. Stat Comput 4(2):65–85

31. Luke S (2013) Essentials of metaheuristics. http://cs.gmu.edu/~sean/book/metaheuristics/Essentials.pdf. Accessed 1 Aug 2016

32. Alcaraz J, Maroto C (2001) A robust genetic algorithm for resource allocation in project scheduling. Ann Oper Res 102(1-4):83–109

33. Sivanandam S, Deepa S (2007) Introduction to Genetic Algorithms. Springer Science & Business Media

34. Monil MAH, Qasim R, Rahman RM (2014) Energy-aware vm consolidation approach using combination of heuristics and migration control. In: Digital Information Management (ICDIM), 2014 Ninth International Conference On. IEEE. pp 74–79

35. Calheiros RN, Ranjan R, De Rose CA, Buyya R (2009) Cloudsim: A novel framework for modeling and simulation of cloud computing infrastructures and services. arXiv preprint arXiv:0903.2525. cloudbus.cis.unimelb.edu.au/reports/CloudSim-ICPP2009.pdf. Accessed 21 Oct 2016

36. Calheiros RN, Ranjan R, Beloglazov A, De Rose CA, Buyya R (2011) Cloudsim: a toolkit for modeling and simulation of cloud computing environments and evaluation of resource provisioning algorithms. Softw Pract Experience 41(1):23–50

37. Gulati A, Shanmuganathan G, Holler A, Ahmad I (2011) Cloud-scale resource management: challenges and techniques. In: Proceedings of the 3rd USENIX Conference on Hot Topics in Cloud Computing. USENIX Association. pp 3–3

14

Research on dynamic time warping multivariate time series similarity matching based on shape feature and inclination angle

Danyang Cao[*] and Jie Liu

Abstract

Different sets of research mainly focus on one variable time series now, while researches involving multivariate time series have been insufficient. In this paper, combined linear segments and fitting error for multivariate time series, we present a new method to reduce the time complexity of DTW distance metric algorithm. Based on the shape feature and the tilt angle, we propose a new approach for similarity matching of DTW multivariate time series. Experimental results demonstrate that this method is helpful for ensuring accuracy and for reducing the time complexity of similarity matching.

Keywords: Similarity matching, Dynamic time warping, Multivariate time series, Shape feature

Introduction

Currently, time series are widely used in economics, management, computers, mathematics, electronics and many other interdisciplinary researches [1]. The study about time series has been developed rapidly since 1990. Time series similarity search is used to research clustering, classification, pattern matching, rule discovery, content anomaly detection and many other aspects etc. Time series similarity is a fundamental problem of time series data mining [2], and its research mainly covers: how to judge the similarity of different time series, how to measure the degree of similarity, and how to find the most-like time sequences.

Time series is a series of recorded values in chronological order. This kind of data is quite common in our life, such as transactions data in stock industry, the vehicles' running state data produced during driving, statistics data of clicking times on webpages, the description data of human body posture matching the postural action, and measurement data of planetary motion trajectory in astronomy industry [1].

Time series analysis is mainly used to extract meaningful statistics and other characteristics of the data, or in other words, to extract the potentially useful information from time series [3]. For example, timing data of power system loading contains plentiful information about characteristics of the power load, and stock timing data contains laws of stock price fluctuation etc. Time series mining is of significant value. It can help people understand the information implied in time series and support people to make the right decision. However, current studies are mostly limited to one variable time series and the results sometimes may have deviation from the real situation. There are many studies on one variable time series, and mature theories and methods in this area have gradually formed. Multivariate time series are composed of several different data vectors [4], and its structure is more complex than one variable. Up to now, the theories and methods to study the multivariate time series are not well developed. However, the study of multivariate time series is more meaningful for many practical applications. For example, when we evaluate the weather conditions of a place, we need to considerate the temperature, pressure, humidity, and other factors to get more reliable results.

In recent years, with growth of massive information and data, more and more multivariate time series were produced. How to extract potential information from these multivariate time series has gradually attracted the

* Correspondence: danyangcaojcc@163.com

College of Computer Science and Technology, North China University of Technology, Shijingshan, Beijing 100144, China

attention of scholars. There are various variables in multivariate time series and they normally work together. If we only consider one variable at a time, we may loss valid information. In addition, for the same time period, multivariate time series data sets tend to occupy a larger space than one variable data set. Even after some dimension reduction process, they still take up very large storage space. Thus, data processing of multivariate time series needs an efficient data representation method. This method should focus on two aspects: pattern representation and similarity matching.

Related work

Pattern representation indicates some kind of changing features, which can summarize and represent the time series. Pattern representation may be the slope after time series is segmented, the mean or variance of the sampling points during a period of time, the symbol representation after discretization, or some function representation [5]. Compared with the original time series, the time series through pattern extraction can be manifested in a more concise form, which can effectively avoid the phenomena of "Curse of Dimensionality". Currently, the typical pattern representation is Discrete Wavelet Transform (DWT) [6], Singular Value Decomposition (SVD) [7], Piecewise Aggregate Approximation (PAA) [8, 9], and Symbolic Aggregate Approximation (SAX) [10] etc. Among them, PAA can approximate the time series best, and it is simple, intuitive, and efficient [11]. Time series pattern representation is the basis of time series similarity matching research, while similarity matching is the core of their research. The similarity of two time series refers to: two time series are transformed, then calculated the values with similarity function, if the values satisfy stipulated error threshold, we think that

the two time series under the condition of this kind of transformation are similar to each other. Although similarity matching has been studied as a key object, there still exist many unsolved difficult problems. For many current algorithms, the experimental results showed that they made a great improvement in operation efficiency. However, these improvements still have many limitations, if the parameters of the experiments are modified slightly, the results will be changed greatly. Currently, the common methods of multivariate time series similarity matching are Minkowski Distance [12], Dynamic Time Warping (DTW) distance [13, 14], Edit Distance [15–17], and Longest Common Subseries (LCS) etc. [17–19].

In similarity matching, DTW distance was first introduced by Berndt and Clifford to time series mining [20]. It could match the time series of equal or unequal length at the same time, support their stretching and bending on the time axis, and identify matching sequence effectively. In the traditional research, people usually changed multivariate time series into the one variable time series, and then calculated DTW distance of each variable directly and independently by making use of the methods achieved in the one variable time series studies. This had been used in many studies of multivariate time series. However, there are different relevant relationships among multivariate time series [21], which can provide more information for multivariate time series similarity matching and help us to improve the accuracy of similarity matching.

In [22], the authors use the Trend Distance (TD) approach based on DTW distance to measure time series. The method was proposed to fit time series by the first-order polynomial of Chebyshev and used TD method to measure the similarity simultaneously. A first order polynomial of Chebyshev is more suitable for one variable time

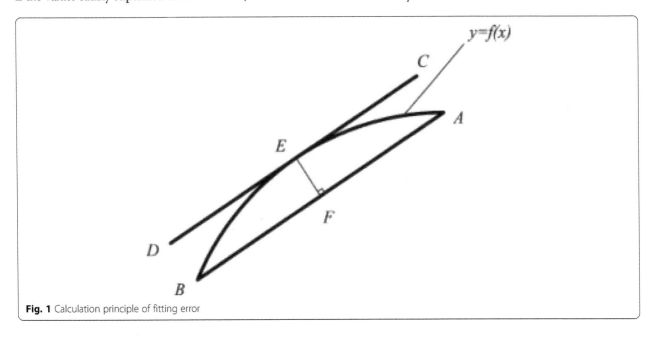

Fig. 1 Calculation principle of fitting error

series, but for multivariate time series, it is much more complex to fit. Moreover, since TD method selected different parameters, the accuracy rate is also quite different in their similarity. In view of this situation, we use a more simple method which combines PAA piecewise linear representation and fitting errors methods to extract pattern features (Piecewise Aggregate Approximation and Error, PAA_ERR), and then select the "tilt angle" and "shape feature value" of each segment which is produced by PAA_ERR method in a variable as the feature representation of the segment, finally, we propose a new similar measure method based on shape feature and inclination angle (Shape and Angle Dynamic Time Warping, SA_DTW) to measure the DTW distance between two time series to match their similarity.

Related concepts and theories

Definition 1 (time series) A time series, in a statistical perspective, refers to different samples values of certain index in the timeline. In a mathematics perspective, it is a series of record values by measuring a certain variable X (t) according to the time sequence. In a broad sense, it means the attribute values during a period of time. Similarly, multivariate time series means time series with multiple variables, based on the previous concept. For Multivariate time series $X_1, X_2,..., X_M$, Where $X_i = (\chi_{i,1}, \chi_{i,2}, \cdots, \chi_{i,N})$, i = 1,2,...,N, especially if M = 1, the given series is a univariate time series (UTS) and if M > 1, it's a multivariate time series(MTS).

We assume that there is a multivariate time series A which contains m variables, and the length of the time series is n, then it can be expressed as a matrix form of m × n:

$$A = \begin{bmatrix} a_{11}, a_{12}, a_{13}, \cdots, a_{1n} \\ a_{21}, a_{22}, a_{23}, \cdots, a_{2n} \\ \vdots \\ a_{m1}, a_{m2}, a_{m3}, \cdots, a_{mn} \end{bmatrix}$$

(1)

Definition 2 (MTS' piecewise line representation) Suppose that there is a multivariate time series A in formula 1, then its piecewise linear representation can be defined as follows:

$$X_i(t) = \begin{cases} f_i(t, w_{i1}) + e_i(t), t \in [1, t_1] \\ f_i(t, w_{i2}) + e_i(t), t \in [t_1, t_2] \\ ... \\ f_i(t, w_{in}) + e_i(t), t \in [t_{n-1}, t_n] \end{cases}, i \in [1, m]$$

(2)

Where W_{ij} denotes the coordinate of two endpoints of the i-th variable from t_{k-1} to t_k, the j-th segment. $f_i(t)$ denotes the W_{ij} linear function linking the starting and ending point of the i-th variable from t_{k-1} to t_k. $e_i(t)$ denotes the fitting error between the original time series and the new fitting segment from t_{k-1} to t_k.

Definition 3 (the fitting error of MTS' piecewise line representation), We assume that there is an MTS A in the formula (1) and let $d_1, d_2,..., d_j$ denotes the vertical

Table 1 The calculation of the cumulative distance of time series

5	22	16	16	16	*17*
8	19	14	14	*14*	15
4	13	9	*9*	9	10
3	11	*8*	8	8	9
9	10	*8*	8	8	9
4	3	*2*	2	2	3
3	*1*	1	1	1	2
A/B	2	3	3	3	2

The first column represent the data of series A{3,4,9,3,4,8,5}. The last row represent the data of series B{2,3,3,3,2}. Other cells represent the DTW distances. The underlined data represent the minimum distance, they make up warping path

distance from j observations in the original time series to fitting line segment. Then the fitting error of the segments for variable i can be represented by the following formula:

$$e_i = \max(d_k) = \max\left(\left|\frac{A\chi_k + By_k + C}{\sqrt{A^2 + B^2}}\right|\right), \quad k \in [1, j]$$

(3)

Where i = 1, 2, ..., m, and it indicates a total of m variables. The calculation principle of fitting error is shown in Fig. 1.

Where | EF | is the length of the line fitting error of each segment. For a segment of all variables, the sum of the fitting error on all variables of multivariate time series is as follow: $e_{total} = \sum_{i=1}^{m} e_i$, where e_{total} denotes a total fitting error of all the variables in a segment.

Definition 4 (Dynamic time warping distance [23]) It is also called DTW distance. Assuming two time series A = $(a_1, a_2,..., a_m)$, B = $(b_1, b_2,..., b_n)$, then the DTW distance formula of the two time series is as follows:

$$D_{dtw} = \begin{cases} 0 & m = n = 0 \\ \infty & m = 0 \text{ or } n = 0 \\ D_{base}(a_1, b_1) + \min \begin{cases} D_{dtw}(A, B[2, -]) \\ D_{dtw}(A[2, -], B) & others \\ D_{dtw}(A[2, -], B[2, -]) \end{cases} \end{cases}$$

(4)

DTW algorithm is to use the classic dynamic programming to find an optimal path with a minimum cost of bending, and the time complexity is O(|A| · |B|). In brief, it is to find the shortest path by constructing an adjacency matrix. The cumulative distance calculated by DTW distance method is shown in Table 1:

In the above table, the DTW distance between time series A and B [1:i] ($D_{dtw}(A, B[1:i])$) is stored in the cell of the top of the i-th column in Table 1. Similarly, D_{dtw} (A [1: i], B) is stored in the cell of the right of the i-th row in Table 1. The same principle can be used to calculate multivariate time series, but in multivariate time series, a_i, b_j indicate the corresponding column vectors.

Multivariate time series model representation

From the TD method of Lee et al., we can see that when the weight values corresponding to the appropriate tilt angle and the time maintaining length were changed, the accuracy rate would be changed significantly. Particularly when the value of tilt angle was 0, the value of time maintaining length was 1, then the accuracy rate was only 0.27, which indicated the time maintaining length might not distinguish differences and similarities of the time series very well. Therefore, in order to reduce the time complexity, to make the measurement more accurate and to make the calculation more efficient, we combined PAA with fitting error to divide the multivariate time series into several segments. Then, on the basis of each tilt angle, we extracted the value of tilt angle and shape feature as pattern representations of the segments.

PAA method is a classic representation of time series, which is able to extract the relatively independent pattern based on morphological changes. The more segments, the higher segmentation accuracy will be. On the contrary, the less segments, the lower segmentation accuracy. In addition, PAA method is capable of data abstraction and noise filtering. Meanwhile, after the combination of PAA and fitting error, it can further screen segments of larger deviation, getting more detailed segmentation. And more importantly, fitting error can combine all the variables of time series, considering the overall situation, which can effectively prevent the loss of information, and further filter noise data.

PAA_ERR: the segmentation method to multivariate time series

When we use the PAA_ERR method on the multivariate time series, we take all the variables as a whole into consideration, that is, we use PAA to divide all variables into segments, if the value of overall fitting error e_{total} of a segment is greater than the threshold value on all the variables, then reprocess the segment, until the e_{total} is less than threshold value.

The steps of this algorithm are as follows:

Assume that time series MTS processed by PAA_ERR can be divided into s segments, then the linear representation of these multivariate time series after processing can be denoted as L(MTS) = {L(x_{i1}, x_{i2}), L(x_{i2}, x_{i3}), ..., L(x_{ik-1},x_{ik}),i∈[1,m],k∈[1,s]}, where i represents a variable of the segmentation, where x_{ik} represents the record value of the time series, L(x_{ik-1},x_{ik}) represents a straight line connecting two points.

The shape feature representation of multivariate time series

In similarity query process, there are two situations needed to be carefully considered: the first is that if there exist "zooming in" or "zooming out" modes similar to the given mode when checking the time series, namely, similar to "zooming in" or "zooming out" mode, then it is an approximate proportional scaling of the length and magnitude to the given mode. For instance, the trend of the stock price change with different time durations could be similar, but this cannot be found with the general equal length pattern queries method. Another case is that in an enlarged similar model, there are some small "vibrating" intervals, and they do not affect the overall trends. In this case, we should focus on the main trend and ignore these small intervals.

An important feature of time series is the changes of growing or declining sequence rate. If the growth or decline rate becomes bigger, it indicates the sequence morphological changes tend to increase; if the growth rate becomes smaller, it indicates that the sequence curves tend to be flat and its morphological changes start to decrease. Hence, these turning points can be found through the changes of line segment slopes.

In the [24] literature, according to the changes of slope, the authors described the shape characteristics of time series as a collection of seven variables {declining rapidly, keeping down, declining slowly, horizontal, rising slowly, keeping rising, rising rapidly}, and they were denoted as M = {-3, -2, -1, 0, 1, 2, 3} corresponding to the above-

Algorithm 1: the PAA_ERR method

Input: multivariate time-series data set: MTS; the initial number of segments: k and the threshold of fitting error: threshold.

Output: the representation of time series A using PAA_ERR segmented method.

Step 1:

MTS=(MTS-min(MTS))/(max(MTS)-min(MTS))
                        // Normalize MTS

Step 2:

seg_err(i)=Calculate_Seg_Err(MTS) //the fitting error of segmented overall after PAA treatment

Step 3:

while seg_err(i)>threshold   // the value of fitting error is greater than the threshold value on all the variables

Step 4:

Divide_Seg(i)   // refragmenting

Step 5:

end

described mode. The specific numbers was shown in Table 2. This method could reflect the degree of dynamic changing trends. However, in literature [23], the authors used the time series which was completely represented by this model, and this method led to the problem that time series was not sensitive to its stretching. It can be seen clearly in Fig. 2, where the representation modes of these two time series would be identical (calculated by Table 2).

Based on the above cases, this paper combined the representation method of "shape mode" with the tilt angle of time-series. Meanwhile, we extracted various segments of its tilt angle and the shape mode as the segment feature representation from time series which was calculated by PAA_ERR calculation method. The inclination angle had a clear physical meaning, which could reflect the local changing trend of time series, and it reduced much calculation. The value of shape mode could show the trends of time series during a period of time. The combination of "shape mode" and the tilt angle reflected the extent of dynamic changing trends more effectively.

We assume that A [m × n] is a multivariate time series of m-variable n-sections after being segmented, the deformation intensity of each segment is denoted as T_i (i = 1, 2,...,n), T_i = max(y_i) - min(y_i) representing the different value between the maximum sample value of each segment and the minimum sample value. $\sum_{j=1}^{n} T_j$ represents the sum of all deformation strength in a variable. Then, the weight of each shape mode segment can be represented by the following formula:

$$\mathfrak{I}_i = \frac{T_i}{\sum_{j=1}^{n} T_j} \tag{5}$$

Where K (i, j) represents the slope of the j-th variable of the i-th segment.

Then multivariate time-series A_{m*n} can be denoted as:

$$\begin{bmatrix} (\alpha_{11}, & \mathfrak{I}_{11}\ p_{11}), & (\alpha_{12}, & \mathfrak{I}_{12}\ p_{12}),..., & (\alpha_{1n}, & \mathfrak{I}_{1n}\ p_{1n}) \\ (\alpha_{21}, & \mathfrak{I}_{21}\ p_{21}), & (\alpha_{22}, & \mathfrak{I}_{22}\ p_{22}),..., & (\alpha_{2n}, & \mathfrak{I}_{2n}\ p_{2n}) \\ & & \vdots & & & \\ (\alpha_{m1}, & \mathfrak{I}_{m1}\ p_{m1}), & (\alpha_{m2}, & \mathfrak{I}_{m2}\ p_{m2}),..., & (\alpha_{mn}, & \mathfrak{I}_{mn}\ p_{mn}) \end{bmatrix} \tag{6}$$

Which α represents the inclination angle of each segment, $\mathfrak{I}$ is the weight of segmented form, p is the value of segmented shape pattern. And in each variable, the sum weight of the shape characteristics is 1.

The similarity matching of SA_DTW method

Suppose the shape characteristics representation of two time series A, A ` can be expressed as follows:

$$A = \begin{bmatrix} (\alpha_{11}, & \mathfrak{I}_{11}\ p_{11}), & (\alpha_{12}, & \mathfrak{I}_{12}\ p_{12}),..., & (\alpha_{1n}, & \mathfrak{I}_{1n}\ p_{1n}) \\ (\alpha_{21}, & \mathfrak{I}_{21}\ p_{21}), & (\alpha_{22}, & \mathfrak{I}_{22}\ p_{22}),..., & (\alpha_{2n}, & \mathfrak{I}_{2n}\ p_{2n}) \\ & & \vdots & & & \\ (\alpha_{m1}, & \mathfrak{I}_{m1}\ p_{m1}), & (\alpha_{m2}, & \mathfrak{I}_{m2}\ p_{m2}),..., & (\alpha_{mn}, & \mathfrak{I}_{mn}\ p_{mn}) \end{bmatrix}$$

$$= [a_1, a_2, \cdots, a_n] \tag{7}$$

$$A^{'} = \begin{bmatrix} \left(\alpha_{11}^{'}, & \mathfrak{I}_{11}^{'}\ p_{11}^{'}\right), & \left(\alpha_{12}^{'}, & \mathfrak{I}_{12}^{'}\ p_{12}^{'}\right),..., & \left(\alpha_{1n}^{'}, & \mathfrak{I}_{1n}^{'}\ p_{1n}^{'}\right) \\ \left(\alpha_{21}^{'}, & \mathfrak{I}_{21}^{'}\ p_{21}^{'}\right), & \left(\alpha_{22}^{'}, & \mathfrak{I}_{22}^{'}\ p_{22}^{'}\right),..., & \left(\alpha_{2n}^{'}, & \mathfrak{I}_{2n}^{'}\ p_{2n}^{'}\right) \\ & & \vdots & & & \\ \left(\alpha_{m1}^{'}, & \mathfrak{I}_{m1}^{'}\ p_{m1}^{'}\right), & \left(\alpha_{m2}^{'}, & \mathfrak{I}_{m2}^{'}\ p_{m2}^{'}\right),..., & \left(\alpha_{mn}^{'}, & \mathfrak{I}_{mn}^{'}\ p_{mn}^{'}\right) \end{bmatrix}$$

$$= [a_1^{'}, a_2^{'}, \cdots, a_n^{'}] \tag{8}$$

The steps of this algorithm are as follows:

    Algorithm 2: the algorithm of multivariate time series pattern

    Input: (1) time series MTS' (m × v) that dealt by PAA_ERR method, where m is the number of variable of time series and v represents the number of sub-time series. (2) the threshold of morphological patterns distinguish : th

    Output: the angle of each segment of multivariate time series: angles, the value of keeping length: pre_length_weights, shape mode value: shape.

    (1) for i=1 to m

    (2) for j=1 to v

    (3) angles[i,j]=calculate_slope(MTS'$_i$)

           //the angle of each segmen

    (4)pre_length_weights[i,j]=calculate_pre_weight(MTSi) // the value of keeping length

    (5)if (K(i-1,j)<−th or −th<K(i-1,j)<th) & K(i,j)<K(i-1,j) then shape(i,j)= −3; end

    (6)if K(i-1,j)<−th & K(i,j)= K(i-1,j) then shape(i,j)=−2; end

    (7)if K(i-1,j)<−th & K(i-1,j)<K(i,j)<−th then shape(i,j)=−1; end

    (8)if K(i-1,j)>th & 0<K(i,j)< K(i-1,j) then shape(i,j)=1; end

    (9)if K(i-1,j)>th& K(i,j)= K(i-1,j) then shape(i,j)=2; end

    (10)if (K(i-1,j)>th or −th<K(i-1,j)<th) & K(i,j)>K(i-1,j) then shape(i,j)=3; else shape(i,j)=0; end

    (11)end

    (12)end

Table 2 Shape mode list of values

	k(i + 1) < −th			−th < k(i + 1) < th	k(i + 1) > th		
	Δk < 0	Δk = 0	Δk > 0				
ki < −th	−3	−2	−1	0	3		
−th < ki < th	−3			0	3		
ki > th	−3			0	Δk < 0	Δk = 0	Δk > 0
					1	2	3

Where a_i, $a_i{}^{\grave{}}$ $(i = 1, 2, ..., n)$ are the column vector of the two time series A, A`. From definition 4, the shape characteristics distance of A, A` is defined as follows:

$$D_{dtw}(A, A') = D_{base}(a_1, a_1') + min \begin{cases} D_{dtw}(A, A'[2, -]) \\ D_{dtw}(A[2, -], A') \\ D_{dtw}(A[2, -], A'[2, -]) \end{cases}$$

(9)

And the base distance is defined as follows:

$$D_{dtw}(a_i, a_j') = \begin{cases} \sum_{k=1}^{m} \left[\lambda_k \left| \Im_{ki} p_{ki} - \Im_{kj} p_{kj}' \right| + \beta_k \left| \alpha_{ki} - \alpha_{ki}' \right| \right] , if |i-j| \le q \\ \infty , \qquad\qquad\qquad\qquad if |i-j| > q \end{cases}$$

(10)

Where, q takes 10 % of the time series' length. In the k-th variable, λ_k, β_k indicate difference between shape mode and the tilt angle weight values, and

$$\lambda_k + \beta_k = 1 \quad (k = 1, 2, ..., m).$$ (11)

Result and analysis

The experiments were performed on Intel (R) Core (TM) i7 CPU, with 2.98 GB memory. The operation system is Windows 7 Ultimate, and the software was MATLAB7.11.0. We tested our implementation with two data sets from http://kdd.ics.uci.edu/databases/: Vicon Physical Action Data Set (VPA) and EEG. The VPA data set was collected from seven male and three female, which reflected human action in both normal conditions and violent scenes; while the EEG data set came from the populations of two distinct: Alcoholic Subjects and Control Subjects. This paper contained two experiments: PAA_ERR and SA_DTW. The PAA_ERR method divided the multivariate time series into several segments, taking compression ratio of multivariate time-series as the main indicator to compare, while SA_DTW method compared time complexity and accuracy of similarity in the algorithm.

PAA_ERR method

For the above two data sets, PAA_ERR algorithm could maintain the original features of multivariate time series and greatly reduced the amount of data. For example, Fig. 3 showed the waveform of the Headering data by using PAA_ERR algorithm. Since PAA_ERR is based on PAA algorithm, for the compression algorithm of time series, we chose PAA algorithm as control.

In Table 3, initSegNum represented the number of initial segments after PAA_ERR algorithm, and finalSegNum indicated the number of final segments. PAA_ERR used the initial segmentation generated by using PAA, and then, further processed the time series by using fitting error. Therefore, in Table 3, the initSegNum' value and finalSegNum' value for the PAA were always equal. The maxSegErr represented the largest fitting error after

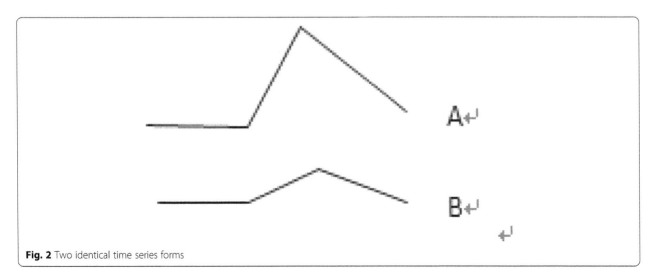

Fig. 2 Two identical time series forms

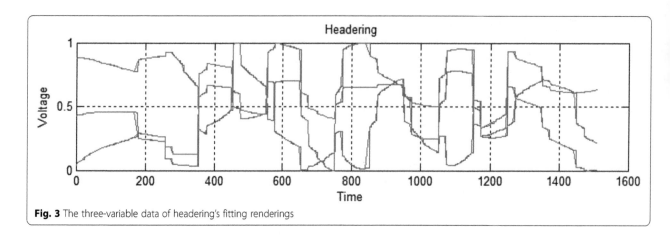

Fig. 3 The three-variable data of headering's fitting renderings

the segmentation. According to previous algorithm, we knew that fitting error of each segment divided from PAA_ERR algorithm was smaller than the threshold; hence the maxSegErr value was basically equal. The timeSeqErr represented the overall fitting error value of the time series which is the sum of all fitting error value of all segments and variables. Compression ratio is the ratio of the number of time series segments calculated by PAA_ERR algorithm to the length of the original time series.

(1) As can be seen from the above table, multivariate time series calculated by PAA_ERR algorithm could guarantee that every fitting error was far smaller than the PAA algorithm, and the overall fitting error of the time series was also significantly smaller than the PAA direct segments. More importantly, the PAA_ERR algorithm could guarantee small fitting error. It also enabled time series compression rate to

reach 90 % and above. So it indicated that PAA_ERR algorithm in multivariate time series piecewise linear representation could get better results by reducing the fitting error.

(2) Figure 3 showed the direct effect from PAA_ERR calculation for the first three-variable data of Headering data when the fitting error threshold was 0.01.

The horizontal axis was a time axis, and the vertical axis was the recorded values after standardization. Blue lines were the original time series and the red ones were the time series after processing algorithms.

Through the above experiment, when the error threshold was set to 0.05, the compression ratio of the original time series could reach 90 %, and the algorithm could effectively preserve the local characteristics and the overall shape trends of the original sequence under the premise of ensuring high compression ratio.

Table 3 Experimental results between PAA and PAA_ERR method

	initSegNum	finalSegNum	maxSegErr	timeSeqErr	Compression ratio
PAA algorithm	50	50	0.7556	20.1941	98.6 %
	100	100	0.7511	19.2898	97.3 %
	150	150	0.5517	17.6011	96.0 %
	200	200	0.4393	16.7043	94.7 %
	250	250	0.4182	15.8199	93.3 %
	300	300	0.3456	15.5139	92.0 %
	350	350	0.2931	15.6895	90.7 %
PAA_ERR algorithm	50	219	0.05	11.5020	94.2 %
	100	252	0.05	11.5370	93.3 %
	150	284	0.05	11.6466	92.4 %
	200	312	0.05	11.3508	91.6 %
	250	345	0.05	11.3428	90.8 %
	300	401	0.05	11.2568	89.3 %
	350	453	0.05	11.4785	87.9 %

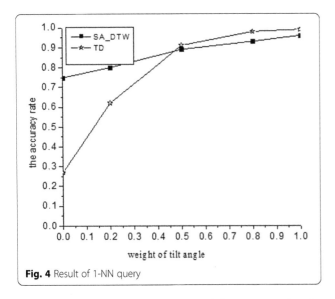

Fig. 4 Result of 1-NN query

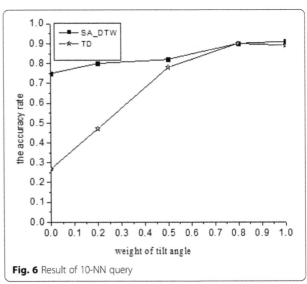

Fig. 6 Result of 10-NN query

PAA_ERR method used the overall fitting error for the final segment. For those time series of small time span but large sequence trend changes, time segment calculated by PAA_ERR would get very close to the original sequence, and resulted in poor final segment results. Therefore, in the next experiment, we also used a time series with smaller trend change sequence as a test object.

SA_DTW method

In the experiment, we adopted multivariate time series, Australian Sign Language signs (High Quality) dataset provided by UCI public databases. It used a total of 22 attributes to depict the bending degrees of every finger in right and left hand. And the two hands were depicted with 11 attributes respectively, in which six attributes described the information of hand position and the other five variables used to describe the bending degrees

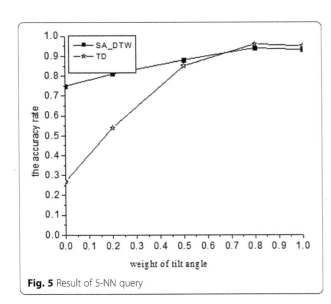

Fig. 5 Result of 5-NN query

of the thumb, forefinger, middle finger, ring finger and the little finger. The data set contained 95 categories (a category represented a gesture), each category had 27 groups of data, and the sampling rate was 0.01 s, namely each frame data was collected by every 0.01 s. In order to facilitate the comparison of our experiment, we used the TD method, which was also adopted by Li Zhengxin and others in their experiment, as the object of experimental comparison. The entire experiment could be divided into two steps. Step 1: to choose one sequence randomly from the experiment data set as an input instance. Step 2: for the chosen one and remaining sequences, using TD method and SA_DTW method to implement the distance calculation. Then, select the closest one, five, or ten sequences, record the sequence numbers different from the input instance of different categories, and then use the 4 to 7 formula to calculate its accuracy. Repeating the experiment was repeated for 50 times to calculate its accuracy.

As was shown in Figs. 4, 5 and 6, when the weight of slope angle was changed, the accuracy of TD method and SA_DTW method would be also changed. In the diagram, when the slope angle weight value was 0, the weight of TD method's time span and SA_DTW's shape mode value were 1 respectively, the accuracy of TD method decreased to 20 %, while SA_DTW still had high accuracy. It indicated that the shape weight we proposed in this paper was more suitable for the representation of multivariate time series model. It also can be seen through Table 4 that

Table 4 Comparison of computation time between SA_DTW and DTW

Dataset	T_{SA_DTW}/T_{TD}
VPA	0.6
EEG	0.75

SA_DTW method is better than TD methods on reducing the time complexity.

Conclusion

This paper presented a new method of similarity search: SA_DTW. It adopted shape mode and tilt angle to represent the feature of each segment. SA_DTW carried out a whole segment on all variables, and reflected the correlation among various variables to some extent. In addition, it supported time series' stretching and bending on the time line. Through the experiments we could see SA_DTW could effectively reduce the time complexity compared with the DTW method. The method that combined shape feature and tilt angle could greatly improve the accuracy of similarity matching.

Acknowledgments
This paper is supported by Beijing Natural Science Foundation (NO.4144073), supported by Research Fund of North China University of Technology, supported by National Natural Science Foundation of China (NO. 41471303), supported by training project for outstanding young teachers of North China University of Technology.

Authors' contributions
DC provided the idea of the paper, carefully designed the algorithm in the manuscript, reviewed and edited the manuscript. JL performed the experiments and presented performance analysis. Both authors read and approved the final manuscript.

Competing interests
The authors declare that they have no competing interests.

References
1. Qian-yun MO, Cheng Z (2008) Parallel computing dynamic warping distances for time sequences on the cluster computing systems. Microelectron Comput 25:155–158
2. Khan Z, Anjum A, Soomro K, Tahir MA (2015) Towards cloud based big data analytics for smart future cities. J Cloud Comput 4(1):1
3. Prema V, Uma Rao K (2015) Time series decomposition model for accurate wind speed forecast. Renewables Wind Water Solar 2–18:2015
4. Hai-lin LI (2015) Feature representation of multivariate time series based on correlation among variables. Control Decis 30:441–446
5. Yan-yan Z, Rong-cong X, Xiao-yun C (2006) Time series piecewise linear representation based on slope extract edge point. Comput Sci 33:139–142
6. Chan K, Fu AW (1999) Efficient time series matching by wavelets. In: Richard ST (ed) Proceedings of 15th IEEE International Conference on Data Engineering (ICDE). IEEE Computer Society, Sydney, pp 126–133
7. Korn F, Jagadish H, Faloutsos C (1997) Efficiently supporting ad hoc queries in large datasets of time sequences. In: Joan P (ed) Proceedings of ACM SIGMOD international conference on management of data. Morgan Kaufmann Publisher, Tuescon, pp 289–300
8. Keogh E, Pazzani M (2000) A simple dimensionality reduction technique for fast similarity search in large time series databases. In: Terano T, Liu H, Chen AL (eds) Proceedings of 4th Pacific-Asia conference on knowledge discovery and data mining. Springer-Verlag, Kyoto, pp 122–133
9. Yi B, Faloutsos C (2000) Fast time sequence indexing for arbitrary Lp norms. In: Abbadi AE, Brodie ML, Chakravarthy S et al (eds) Proceedings of the 26th International Conference on Very Large Databases (VLDB). Morgan Kaufmann Publishers, Cairo, pp 385–394
10. Lin J, Keogh E, Londardi S et al (2003) A symbolic representation of time series, with implications for streaming algorithms. In: Mohammed JZ, Charueds AC (eds) Proceedings of the 8th ACM SIGMOD workshop on research (DMKD). ACM Press, San Diego, pp 55–68
11. Bin M, Jin-lai Y (2009) Efficient time series lower bounding technique. Comput Eng Appl 45(11):168–171
12. Agrawal R, Faloutsos C, Swami A (1993) Efficient similarity search in sequence databases. //Proc of the 4th International Conference on Foundations of Data Organization and Algorithms. Chicago, p 69-84.
13. Keogh E (2005) Exact indexing of dynamic time warping[J]. Knowl Inf Syst 7(3):358–386
14. Yi B, Jagadish H, Faloutsos C (1998) Efficient retrieval of similar time sequences under time warping. In: Sipple RS (ed) Proceedings of International Conference of Data Engineering (ICDE). IEEE Computer Society, Orlando, pp 201–208
15. Ristad ES, Yianilos PN (1997) Learning string edit distance. In: Douglas FH (ed) Proceedings of 14th International Conference on Machine Learning (ICML). Morgan Kaufmann Press, Nashville, pp 287–295
16. Chen L, Ng R (2004) On the marriage of Lp-norm and edit distance. In: Nascimento MA, Zsu MT, Kossmann D et al (eds) Proceedings of 30th International Conference on Very Large Databases (VLDB). Morgan Kaufmann Publishers, Toronto, pp 792–801
17. Das G, Gunopulos D, Mannila H (1997) Finding similar time series. In: Komorowski J, Zytkow J (eds) Proceeding of 1st European Symposium on Principles of Data Mining and Knowledge Discovery (PKDD). Springer-Verlag, Bergen, pp 88–100
18. Vlachos M, Kollios G, Gunopulos D (2002) Discovering similar multidimensional trajectories. In: Agrawal R, Dittrich K, Ngu AH (eds) Proceedings of 18th International Conference on Data Engineering (ICDE). IEEE Computer Society, San Jose, pp 673–684
19. Vlachos M, Hadjieleftheriou M, Gunopulos D et al (2003) Indexing multi-dimensional time-series with support for multiple distance measures. In: Getoor L, Senator TE (eds) Proceedings of ACM SIGKDD International Conference on knowledge discovery and data mining. ACM Press, Washington DC, pp 216–225
20. Berndt DJ, Clifford J (1994) Using dynamic time warping to find patterns in time series. Working Notes of the Knowledge Discovery in Databases Workshop, Seatle
21. Zhen-xing W, Lai-wan C (2012) Learning causal relations in multivariate time series data[J]. ACM Trans Int Syst Technol 3(4):71–76
22. Zheng-xin L, Feng-ming Z, Ke-wu L (2011) DTW based pattern matching method for multivariate time series. Pattern Recognit Artif Intell 24(3):425–430
23. Hui X, Yun-fa H (2005) Data mining based on segmented time warping distance in time series database. J Comput Res Dev 42(1):72–78
24. Xiao-li D, Cheng-kui G, Zheng-ou W (2007) Research on shape-based time series similarity matching. J Electron Inf Technol 29(5):1228–1231

15

A resource management technique for processing deadline-constrained multi-stage workflows

Norman Lim[1][*] [iD], Shikharesh Majumdar[1] and Peter Ashwood-Smith[2]

Abstract

The use of cloud computing that provides resources on demand to various types of users, including enterprises as well as engineering and scientific institutions, is growing rapidly. An effective resource management middleware is necessary to harness the power of the underlying distributed hardware in a cloud. Two of the key operations provided by a resource manager are resource allocation (matchmaking) and scheduling. This paper concerns the problem of matchmaking and scheduling an open stream of *multi-stage jobs* (or *workflows*) with Service Level Agreements (SLAs) on a cloud or cluster. Multi-stage jobs require service from multiple system resources and are characterized by multiple phases of execution. This paper presents a resource allocation and scheduling technique called RM-DCWF: Resource Management Technique for Deadline-constrained Workflows that can efficiently matchmake and schedule an open stream of multi-stage jobs with SLAs, where each SLA is characterized by an earliest start time, an execution time, and a deadline. A rigorous simulation-based performance evaluation of RM-DCWF is conducted using synthetic workloads derived from real scientific workflows. In addition, the impact of various system and workload parameters on system performance is investigated. The results of this performance evaluation demonstrate the effectiveness of RM-DCWF as captured in a low number of jobs missing their deadlines.

Keywords: Resource allocation and scheduling on clouds, Multi-stage jobs with SLAs, Workflows with SLAs, Jobs with deadlines

Introduction

Over the past few years, distributed computing paradigms such as cluster computing and cloud computing have been generating a lot of interest among consumers and service providers as well as researchers and system builders. For example, a number of reputable financial institutions and market research organizations have predicted a multi-billion-dollar market for the cloud computing industry [1, 2]. An important feature of cloud computing is that it allows users to acquire resources on demand and pay only for the time the resources are used. Investigating and devising effective *resource management techniques* for clouds and clusters is necessary to harness the power of the underlying distributed hardware and to achieve the performance objectives of a system [3], which can include generating high job throughput and low job response times, meeting the quality of service (QoS) requirements of jobs that are often captured by a service level agreement (SLA), and maintaining a high resource utilization to generate adequate revenue for the cloud service provider. As in the case of grids, a predecessor of cloud computing that also supported resources on demand, QoS and satisfying SLAs remain an important issue for cloud computing [3, 4]. Handling of jobs with a SLA often leads to an advance reservation request [5] that is characterized by an *earliest start time*, a required *execution time*, and a *deadline* for completion. This is of critical importance for latency-sensitive business and scientific applications that can include live business intelligence and sensor-based applications which rely on a timely processing of the collected data. Two of the key operations that a resource manager needs to provide are *resource allocation* (*matchmaking*) and *scheduling*. Note that the matchmaking and scheduling operations are jointly referred to as

* Correspondence: nlim@sce.carleton.ca
[1]Department of Systems and Computer Engineering, Carleton University, Ottawa, ON, Canada
Full list of author information is available at the end of the article

mapping operation [6]. Given a pool of resources, the matchmaking algorithm chooses the resource(s) to be allocated to an incoming job. Once a number of jobs are allocated to a specific resource, a scheduling algorithm determines the order in which jobs allocated to the resource should be executed for achieving the desired system objectives. Performing effective matchmaking and scheduling is difficult because the SLA of the jobs need to be satisfied, while also considering system objectives, which can include minimizing the number of jobs that miss their deadlines as well as generating adequate revenue for the service provider.

Due to cloud computing becoming more prevalent, a variety of applications are being run on clouds, including those that are characterized by multiple phases of execution and require processing from multiple system resources (referred to as *multi-stage jobs*). Scientific applications and workflows that are used in various fields of study, such as physics and biology, are examples of multi-stage jobs that are run on clouds. Moreover, another example of a popular multi-stage application that is typically run on clouds is MapReduce [7], which is a programming model (proposed by Google) for simplifying the processing of very large and complex data sets in a parallel manner. MapReduce is used by many companies and institutions, typically in conjunction with cloud or cluster computing, for facilitating *Big Data analytics* [8–10]. The focus of this paper is to devise an efficient matchmaking and scheduling technique for processing an *open stream* of *multi-stage jobs* (*workflows*) with SLAs on a distributed computing environment with a fixed number of resources (e.g. a private cluster or a set of resources acquired a priori from a public cloud). Most existing research focuses on meeting the SLA for jobs that require processing from only a single resource or handling of a fixed number of multi-stage jobs executing on the system. There is comparatively less work available in the literature focusing on resource management for a workload comprising and open stream of multi-stage jobs with SLAs. Handling of an open stream of multi-stage jobs increases the complexity of the resource allocation and scheduling problem due to a continuous stream of jobs arriving on the system. Thus, the novel matchmaking and scheduling techniques described in this paper are expected to make a significant contribution to the state of the art.

This paper presents a novel resource allocation and scheduling technique, referred to as RM-DCWF: Resource Management Technique for Deadline-constrained Workflows, that can effectively perform matchmaking and scheduling for an open stream of multi-stage jobs with SLAs, where each SLA comprises an earliest start time, an execution time, and an end-to-end deadline. RM-DCWF decomposes the end-to-end deadline of a job into components

(i.e. sub-deadlines), each of which is associated with a task in the job. The individual tasks of the job are then mapped on to the resources where the objective is to satisfy the job's SLA and minimize the number of jobs that miss their deadlines. In our preliminary work [11], a resource allocation and scheduling technique for processing deadline-constrained MapReduce [7] jobs (comprising of only two phases of execution) is described. The algorithm described in [11] can only handle MapReduce jobs. The algorithm presented in this paper is new as it focuses on a more complex resource management problem that considers jobs and workflows characterized by multiple (two or more) phases of execution as present in scientific workflows, for example. Furthermore, the jobs handled by the algorithm introduced in this paper can have various structures characterized by different precedence relationships among the respective constituent tasks that are not considered in [11]. To the best of our knowledge, none of the existing work focuses on all aspects of the resource management problem that this paper focuses on: devising a resource allocation and scheduling algorithm for multi-stage jobs with SLAs on a system subjected to an open stream of job arrivals. The main contributions of this paper include:

- A novel resource allocation and scheduling technique, RM-DCWF, for handling an open stream of multi-stage jobs with SLAs. Two task scheduling policies are devised.
- Two algorithms devised to decompose the end-to-end deadline of a multi-stage job to assign each task of the job a sub-deadline.
- Insights gained into system behavior and performance from a rigorous simulation-based performance evaluation of RM-DCWF using a variety of system and workload parameters. The synthetic workloads used in the experiments are based on real scientific workflows described in the literature.
- A comparison of the performance of the proposed technique with that of a conventional first-in-first-out (FIFO) scheduler as well as a technique from the literature [29] that has objectives similar to RM-DCWF is presented.

The rest of the paper is organized as follows. Section "Related work" summarizes related work, and Section "Problem description and resource management model" provides a description of how the resource allocation and scheduling problem is modelled. The algorithms devised to decompose the end-to-end deadline for multi-stage jobs are described in Section "Deadline budgeting algorithm for workflows". In Section "RM-DCWF's matchmaking and scheduling algorithm", RM-DCWF and its matchmaking and scheduling algorithms are presented. The results of the performance evaluation of RM-DCWF and the insights gained into system behavior are discussed in Section "Performance Evaluation of RM-DCWF". Lastly, Section "Conclusions and Future Work" presents the conclusions and offers directions for future work.

Related work

The use of distributed computing environments for processing multi-stage jobs (workflows) has received significant attention from researchers in the past few years. A representative set of existing work related to resource management on distributed systems for processing multi-stage jobs, including workflows (see Section "Resource management on distributed systems for processing workflows") and MapReduce jobs (see Section "Resource management techniques on distributed systems for processing MapReduce jobs"), is presented next.

Resource management on distributed systems for processing workflows

A representative set of existing work related to resource management on clouds for processing workflows is presented next. A workflow is usually modelled using a directed acyclic graph (DAG) where each node in the graph represents a task in the workflow and the edges of the graph represent the precedence relationships among the tasks.

The focus of [12, 13] is on describing workflow scheduling algorithms for grids. More specifically, in [12], the authors propose a workflow scheduling algorithm using a Markov decision process based approach that aims to optimally schedule the tasks of the workflows such that the number of workflows that miss their deadlines is minimized. The authors of [13] present a heuristic-based workflow scheduling algorithm, called Partial Critical Paths (PCP), whose objective is to generate a schedule that satisfies a workflow's deadline, while minimizing the financial cost of executing the workflow on a service-oriented grid.

The following papers present various techniques to schedule workflows on a cloud environment. In [14], a heuristic scheduling algorithm for clouds to process workflows where users can specify QoS requirements, such as a deadline or financial budget constraint, is presented. The objective is to ensure that the workflow meets its deadline, while the financial budget constraint is not violated. The technique described in [15] uses a particle swarm optimization (PSO) methodology to develop a heuristic-based scheduling algorithm to minimize the total financial cost of executing a workflow in the cloud. PSO is a stochastic optimization technique that is frequently used in computational intelligence. The authors of [16] also present a PSO-based technique (set-based PSO) for scheduling workflows with QoS requirements, including deadlines, on clouds. In [17], a Cat Swarm Optimization (CSO)-based

workflow scheduling algorithm for a cloud computing environment is presented. The proposed algorithm considers both data transmission cost and execution cost of the workflow, and its objective is to minimize the total cost for executing the workflow.

The research described in [18] devises a resource management technique for workflows with deadlines executing on hybrid clouds. Initially, the algorithm attempts to only use the resources of the private cloud to execute the workflow. However, if the deadline of the workflow cannot be met, the algorithm decides the type and number of resources to allocate from a public cloud so as to satisfy the deadline of the workflow. The framework presented in [19] focuses on the virtual machine (VM) provisioning problem. It uses an extensible cost model and heuristic algorithms to determine the number of VMs that should be provisioned in order to execute a workflow, while considering requirements such as the completion time of the workflow. The framework uses both single and multi-objective evolutionary algorithms to perform resource allocation and scheduling for the workflows. In [20], the authors present an evolutionary multi-objective optimization-based workflow scheduling algorithm, specifically designed for an infrastructure-as-a-service platform, that optimizes both the workflow completion time and cost of executing the workflow.

In [21], the authors present a resource allocation technique based on force-directed search for processing multi-tier Web applications where each tier provides a service to the next tier and uses services from the previous tier. The focus of [22] is on scheduling multiple workflows, each one with their own QoS requirements. The authors present a scheduling strategy that considers the overall performance of the system and not just the completion time of a single workflow. In [23], the authors describe a workflow scheduling technique for clouds that considers workflows with deadlines and the availability of cloud resources at various time intervals (time slots). The motivation is that public cloud service providers do not have unlimited resources and their resources must be shared among multiple users. Thus, the scheduling algorithm has to consider the available time slots for executing the user's requests and not assume that resources are unlimited and can be used at any time.

Resource management techniques on distributed systems for processing MapReduce jobs

This section presents a representative set of work that focuses on describing resource management techniques for platforms processing MapReduce jobs with deadlines, which have become important for latency-sensitive business or scientific applications, such as live business intelligence and real-time analysis of event logs [24].

In [24], the authors present a technique called Minimum Resource Quota Earliest Deadline First with Work-

Conserving Scheduling (MinEDF-WC) for processing MapReduce jobs characterized by deadlines. MinEDF-WC allocates the minimum number of task slots required for completing a job before its deadline and has the ability to dynamically allocate and deallocate resources (task slots) from active jobs when required.

A policy for dynamic provisioning of public cloud resources to schedule MapReduce jobs with deadlines is described in [25]. Initially, jobs are executed on a local cluster and if required, resources from a public cloud are dynamically provisioned to meet the job's deadline. The authors of [26] devise algorithms for minimizing the cost of allocating virtual machines to execute MapReduce jobs with deadlines. For example, the authors present a Deadline-aware Tasks Packing (DTP) approach where the idea is to assign the map tasks and reduce tasks of jobs to execute on existing VMs as much as possible until a job cannot meet its deadline, in which case a new VM is provisioned to execute the job.

In [27], the authors focus on the joint considerations of workload balancing and meeting deadlines for MapReduce jobs. Scheduling algorithms are proposed that are based on integer linear programming and solved with a linear programming solver using a rounding approach. A new MapReduce scheduler for processing MapReduce jobs with deadlines based on bipartite graph modelling, called the Bipartite Graph Modeling MapReduce Scheduler (BGMRS), is presented in [28]. BGMRS considers nodes with varying performance (e.g., those present in a heterogeneous cloud computing environment) and is able to obtain the optimal solution of the scheduling problem for a batch workload by transforming the problem into a well-known graph problem: minimum weighted bipartite matching.

In [29], a MapReduce Constraint Programming based Resource Management technique (MRCP-RM) is presented for processing an open stream of MapReduce jobs with SLAs, where each SLA comprises an earliest start time, an execution time, and a deadline. The objective of MRCP-RM is to minimize the number of jobs that miss their deadlines. Furthermore in [30], the authors adapt the MRCP-RM algorithm and implement it on Hadoop [31], which is a popular open-source framework that implements the MapReduce programming model. Experiments are conducted on a Hadoop cluster deployed on Amazon EC2 that demonstrate the effectiveness of the resource management technique.

Comparison with related work

The related works described in this section consider multi-stage jobs (workflows) with deadlines; however, most of the works focus on scheduling a single workflow or a fixed number of workflows (i.e. a batch workload on a closed system). To the best of our knowledge, none of the existing work focuses on all aspects of the resource management problem that this paper focuses on: matchmaking and scheduling an *open stream* of multi-stage jobs (that includes both scientific workflows and MapReduce jobs) with SLAs, where each SLA is characterized by an earliest start time, an execution time and an end-to-end deadline, on a distributed computing environment, such as a set of resources acquired a priori from a public cloud.

Problem description and resource management model

This section describes how the problem of matchmaking and scheduling an open stream of multi-stage jobs with SLAs on a distributed computing environment is modelled (see Fig. 1). Such an environment can correspond to a private cluster or a set of nodes acquired a priori from a cloud (e.g., Amazon EC2) for processing the jobs. The distributed environment is modelled as a set of resources, $R = \{r_1, r_2, ..., r_m\}$ where m is the number of resources in the system. Each resource r in R has a capacity (c_r), which specifies the number of tasks that resource r can execute in parallel at any point in time. Note that other researchers have modelled resources in a similar manner (see [12, 14, 16, 18], for example).

The system is subject to an open stream of multi-stage jobs. Each multi-stage job j that arrives on the system is characterized by an earliest start time (s_j) and an end-to-end deadline (d_j) by which the job j should complete executing. In addition, each job j also comprises a set of tasks, where each task t has an execution time (e_t) and can have one or more precedence relationships. The multi-stage job and the precedence relationships between its tasks can be modelled using a directed acyclic graph (DAG) (see Fig. 2, for example). The nodes (vertices) of the DAG represent the tasks of the job, and the edges of the DAG show the precedence relationships between the tasks of the job.

The example multi-stage job shown in Fig. 2 is characterized by two phases of execution where the number i in the small circle indicates the ith execution phase. An *execution phase* in a multi-stage job is a collection of tasks that perform a specific function in the job. Note that the execution phase that a constituent task belongs to is specified by the user when the job is submitted to the system. In the sample job shown in Fig. 2, the first phase of execution comprises three tasks: t1, t2, and t3, and the function of these three tasks is to read and parse the input data. These three tasks do not have any *direct preceding* tasks (referred to as *parent tasks*) that need to be completed before they start executing. This implies that these tasks can start executing at the job's earliest start time specified by the user. The tasks t4 and t5, which analyze and perform computation on the parsed data, are part of the second phase of execution. Each of these tasks has a parent task t0, as well as *indirect preceding tasks* t1, t2, and t3. The tasks t4 and t5 cannot

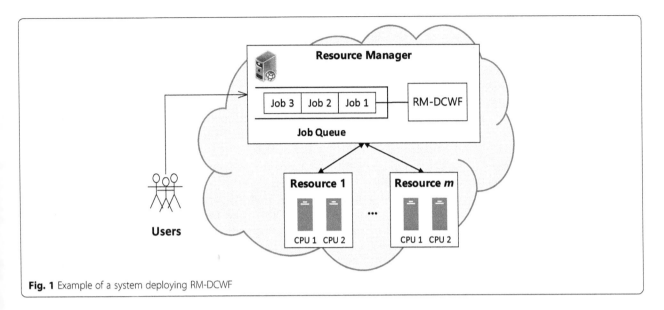

Fig. 1 Example of a system deploying RM-DCWF

start executing until task t0 finishes, which in turn cannot start executing until tasks t1, t2, and t3 finish executing. Note that some workflows are modelled using a DAG with special tasks, referred to as *dummy tasks*, whose only purpose is to enforce precedence relationships between tasks in the DAG, and thus, dummy tasks have an execution time equal to 0. For example, in Fig. 2, task t0 is a dummy task that ensures tasks in the second phase of execution start to execute only after all the tasks in the first phase have completed.

As shown in Fig. 1, jobs that arrive on the system are placed in a job queue, where jobs are sorted by non-decreasing order of their deadlines (i.e., jobs that have earlier deadlines are placed in front of jobs with later deadlines). The resource manager uses RM-DCWF, presented in this paper, to perform matchmaking and scheduling. More specifically, when the resource manager is available (i.e., not busy mapping another job) and the job queue is not empty, it removes the first job in the job queue to map onto the resources of the system, R. The requirements for mapping the jobs on to R are described

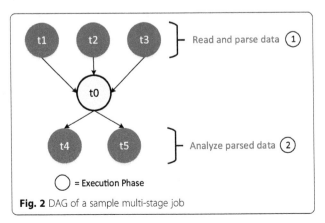

Fig. 2 DAG of a sample multi-stage job

next. The tasks of each job j can only execute after s_j and after their parent tasks have completed executing. In addition, each task of job j should complete its execution before the deadline of the job (d_j); otherwise, job j will miss its deadline. Note that d_j is a soft deadline, meaning that although jobs are permitted to miss their deadlines, the desired system objective is to minimize the number of late jobs. At any point in time, the number of tasks that a resource r in R can execute in parallel must be less than or equal to its capacity, c_r. A resource will execute the tasks it has been assigned in the order generated by RM-DCWF. However, a task that has been scheduled but has not started executing can be rescheduled or assigned to another resource, if required.

Deadline budgeting algorithm for workflows

Algorithm 1 presents the *Deadline Budgeting Algorithm for Workflows* (DBW algorithm), which is used by RM-DCWF to decompose the end-to-end deadline of a multi-stage job into components and to assign each task of the job a sub-deadline. The input required by the DBW algorithm is a multi-stage job j and two integer arguments: setOpt to indicate the approach used to calculate the *sample execution time* of the job j (SET_j) and laxDistOpt to specify how the *laxity* (or *slack time*) of the job j (L_j) is to be distributed among its constituent tasks. SET_j is an estimate of the execution time of job j that is calculated by the DBW algorithm and L_j is the extra time that job j has for meeting its deadline, if it starts executing at its earliest start time. L_j is calculated as follows:

$$L_j = d_j - s_j - SET_j \tag{1}$$

The first step of the DBW algorithm is to calculate SET_j (line 1). SET_j is calculated using the user-estimated task execution times of the job and can be calculated in one of two ways, depending on the supplied `setOpt` argument. The first approach (`setOpt = 1`) is to calculate the execution time of job j when it executes at its maximum degree of parallelism on the set of resources R with m resources, while not considering any contention for resources (denoted SET_j^R). Recall from the previous section, the definition of R, which is a set of resources that models the distributed system job j will execute on. The approach used by the algorithm for matchmaking and scheduling the tasks of job j onto the m resources and computing SET_j^R is briefly described. The tasks of job j are allocated in non-increasing order of their execution times: the *ready* task with the highest required task execution time is allocated first; the task with the next highest execution time is considered next and so on. Tasks are considered *ready* when all of their parent tasks, as captured in the precedence graph that characterizes the workflow, have completed executing. A best-fit technique is used for allocating the tasks of the job to the resources. Each task of the job is allocated on that resource that can execute the task at its earliest possible time. Thus, the algorithm attempts to complete each task and the job at its earliest possible finish time. The second approach (`setOpt = 2`) is to calculate the execution time of the job when it executes on R, while considering the current *processing load* of the resources (i.e., considering the other jobs already executing or scheduled on R) (denoted $SET_j^{R\_PL}$). This is accomplished by scheduling the job on the system's resources to retrieve its expected completion time and then removing the job from the system. Next, the algorithm calculates the laxity of the job (L_j) using Eq. 1 (line 2). Note that when L_j is calculated using SET_j equal to SET_j^R, the laxity of the job is referred to as the *sample laxity* (SL) because the job execution time is calculated on R without considering the current processing load of the resources in R. When L_j is calculated using SET_j equal to $SET_j^{R\_PL}$, the laxity of the job is referred to as the *true laxity* (TL) because the job execution time is calculated on R while considering the current processing load of the resources in R. The final steps of the algorithm are to distribute the laxity of the job to each of its constituent tasks and to calculate a sub-deadline for each of the tasks (line 3) by invoking one of two algorithms devised: (1) the *Proportional Distribution of Job Laxity (PD) Algorithm*, which is described in Section "Proportional Distribution of Job Laxity Algorithm", and (2) the *Even Distribution of Job Laxity (ED) Algorithm*, which is discussed in Section "Even Distribution of Job Laxity Algorithm". The algorithm that is used depends on the supplied laxDistOpt input argument.

Algorithm 1: Deadline Budgeting Algorithm for Workflows

Input: job j, integer *setOpt*, integer *laxDistOpt*

Output: none

1: Depending on *setOpt*, calculate the sample execution time of job j (SET_j).
2: *jobLaxity* $\leftarrow d_j - s_j - SET_j$
3: According to *laxDistOpt*, invoke the PD algorithm or the ED algorithm.

Proportional distribution of job laxity algorithm

The PD algorithm (shown in Algorithm 2) distributes the laxity of the job to its constituent tasks according to the length of the task's execution time. This means that a task with a longer execution time is assigned a larger portion of the job's laxity, resulting in the task having a higher sub-deadline. The input required by the algorithm includes a job j to process and an integer argument, `setOpt`, to indicate how SET_j is calculated. Recall from the discussion earlier that SET_j can be calculated in one of two ways: `setOpt = 1` corresponds to SET_j^R and `setOpt = 2` corresponds to $SET_j^{R\_PL}$. A walkthrough of the algorithm is provided next.

The first step of Algorithm 2 is to calculate the sample completion time of job j (denoted SCT_j) as:

$$SCT_j = s_j + SET_j$$

where s_j is the earliest start time of job j (line 1). The second and third steps involve retrieving s_j and L_j, respectively, of the supplied job j and saving them in local variables (lines 2–3). Next, the PD algorithm performs the following operations on each task t in the job j (line 4). The first operation is to calculate the *cumulative laxity* of the task t (denoted CL_t) (line 5) as:

$$CL_t = \frac{SCT_t - s_j}{SCT_j - s_j} \times L_j$$

where SCT_t is the sample completion time of task t. Note that the sample completion time of each task is determined during the calculation of SET_j (line 1 in Algorithm 1) as follows:

$$SCT_t = s_t + e_t$$

where s_t is the scheduled start time of task t (determined by the scheduling algorithm) and e_t is the execution time of task t. The cumulative laxity of a task t is the maximum laxity that task t can have (i.e. the laxity that task t has given that none of t's preceding tasks, direct or indirect, use any of their laxities). After calculating CL_t, the sub-deadline of the task t (sd_t) is then calculated (line 6) as follows:

$$sd_t = SCT_t + CL_t \tag{2}$$

The sub-deadline of the task t is then set as shown in line 7. If the task t does not have more than one parent task, the processing of task t is complete and the algorithm moves on to process the next task; otherwise, the algorithm invokes the task's setParentTasksSubDeadlines()

method (lines 8–10). The objective of this method is to set the sub-deadline of all of t's parent tasks to the sub-deadline of the task among all of t's parent tasks that has the highest sub-deadline. The reason for performing this operation is that a task t cannot start executing until all of its parent tasks finish executing, and thus, all the parent tasks of task t should have the same sub-deadline. Note that after adjusting the sub-deadlines of the parents of task t, the sub-deadlines of the grandparents of task t are not altered as they do not need to be adjusted. The PD algorithm ends after processing all the tasks in the job j.

Algorithm 2: Proportional Distribution of Job Laxity Algorithm

Input: job j, integer *setOpt*
Output: none

```
1:   Depending on setOpt, calculate SCTⱼ and store the value in sct.
2:   est ← j.getEarliestStartTime()
3:   jobLaxity ← j.getLaxity()
4:   for each task t in job j do
5:       cumulativeLaxity ← [(t.getSCT() - est) / (sct- est)] * jobLaxity
6:       subdeadline ← t.getSCT() + cumulativeLaxity
7:       t.setSubDeadline(subdeadline)
8:       if t has more than one parent task then
9:           call setParentTasksSubDeadline(t)
10:      end if
11:  end for
```

Even distribution of job laxity algorithm

The ED algorithm (see Algorithm 3) does not consider the length of the task's execution time and instead distributes the laxity of the job evenly among the execution phases of the job. Recall from Section "Problem Description and Resource Management Model" that an execution phase in a multi-stage job is a collection of tasks that perform a specific function in the job. The ED algorithm requires each task in a job to have an *execution phase* attribute, which is an integer (1, 2, 3, ...) that indicates the phase of execution that the task belongs to. A walk-through of the ED algorithm is provided next.

Algorithm 3: Even Distribution of Job Laxity Algorithm

Input: job j
Output: none

```
1:   jobLaxity ← j.getLaxity()
2:   executionPhases ← Get the number of execution phases in job j.
3:   laxPerEP ← jobLaxity / executionPhases
4:   Create an empty map, cumulativeLaxities <execution phase, cumulative laxity>.
5:   for i = 1 to executionPhases do
6:       cl ← i * laxPerEP
7:       cumulativeLaxitites.put(i, cl)
8:   end for
9:   for each task t in job j do
10:      ep ← t.getExecutionPhase()
11:      cumulativeLaxity ← cumulativeLaxities.get(ep)
12:      subDL ← t.getSCT() + cumulativeLaxity
13:      t.setSubDeadline(subDL)
14:      if t has more than one parent task then
15:          call setParentTasksSubDeadline (t)
16:      end if
17:  end for
```

The input required by the algorithm is a job j to process. The first step is to retrieve the laxity of the job and save the value in a local variable (line 1). Next, the algorithm

retrieves the number of execution phases in job j and stores the value in a variable named executionPhases (line 2). This is accomplished by checking the execution phase attribute of each task t in job j. The laxity that each execution phase should be assigned is then calculated as follows:

$$L_j^{ep} = L_j / n_j^{ep}$$

where n_j^{ep} is the number of execution phases in job j (line 3). The cumulative laxity for each execution phase, which is the maximum amount of laxity that an execution phase can have, is then calculated as shown in lines 4–8. More specifically, the cumulative laxity of each execution phase ph for a job j is calculated as:

$$CL_j^{ph} = ph \times L_j^{ep}$$

where ph is an integer in the set $\{1, 2, 3, ..., n_j^{ep}\}$ that represents the execution phase. A map data structure named cumulativeLaxities is used to store the cumulative laxity for each execution phase, where the *key* is the execution phase and the *value* is the cumulative laxity. The last phase of the algorithm (lines 9–17) uses the cumulative laxity values to calculate and assign a sub-deadline for each of job j's tasks. The following operations are performed on each task t of job j. First, the execution phase of the task t is retrieved as shown in line 10. The cumulative laxity of the task is then retrieved from the cumulativeLaxities map using the value of the execution phase as the key (line 11). Next, the sub-deadline of the task is calculated using Eq. 2 and assigned to the task (lines 12–13). Similar to the PD algorithm, the ED algorithm invokes setParentTasksSubDeadlines() if the task t has more than 1 parent task. After all the tasks of job j are processed the algorithm ends.

RM-DCWF's matchmaking and scheduling algorithm

This section describes RM-DCWF's matchmaking and scheduling algorithm (also referred to as the *mapping* algorithm), which is composed of two sub-algorithms: (1) the *Job Mapping algorithm* (discussed in Section "Job Mapping Algorithm") and (2) the *Job Remapping algorithm* (described in Section "Job Remapping Algorithm"). When there is a job j available to be mapped, the Job Mapping algorithm is invoked. If the Job Mapping algorithm is unable to schedule job j to meet its deadline, the Job Remapping algorithm is invoked to remap job j and a set of jobs that may have caused job j to miss its deadline.

Job mapping algorithm

The Job Mapping algorithm is comprised of two methods: (1) mapJob() presented in Algorithm 4 and (2) mapJob-Helper() described in Algorithm 5. Note that the variables shown in the algorithms that are underlined indicate that the variables are fields belonging to RM-DCWF instead of being local variables. A walkthrough of map-Job() is provided first, followed by a description of map-JobHelper(). The input required by mapJob() comprises the following: a job to map j, an integer setOpt, an integer laxDistOpt, and an integer tsp. Note that except for the argument tsp, which specifies the *task scheduling policy*, these are the same input arguments used by the DBW algorithm. The method returns true if the job j is scheduled to meet its deadline; otherwise, false is returned.

The first step of mapJob() is to invoke the DBW algorithm to decompose the end-to-end deadline of the job j and assign each of job j's tasks a sub-deadline (line 1). Next, RM-DCWF's rootJob field is set to j (line 2). The root-Job field stores the current job that is being mapped by RM-DCWF. The third step is to clear RM-DCWF's prevRemapAttempts list (line 3), which stores the various sets of jobs that a job remapping attempt has previously processed. RM-DCWF's jobComparator field, which specifies how jobs that need to be remapped are sorted, is then set to the *Job Deadline Comparator* (line 4) to sort jobs by non-decreasing order of their respective deadlines. A more detailed discussion of the purpose of these fields, which are used by the Job Remapping algorithm, is provided in the next section. In line 5, RM-DCWF's taskSchedulingPolicy field, which specifies how tasks are scheduled, is initialized. Two task scheduling policies are devised. *TSP1* schedules tasks to execute at their earliest possible times, and *TSP2* schedules tasks to execute at their latest possible times such that the tasks meet their respective sub-deadlines. The last step is to invoke Algorithm 5: mapJobHelper() (line 6).

Algorithm 4: RM-DCWF algorithm's *mapJob()*

Input: job *j*, integer *setOpt*, integer *laxDistOpt*, integer *tsp*

Output: a Boolean: true if the job *j* is scheduled to meet its deadline; false, otherwise.

1: **call** DBW(*j*, *setOpt*, *laxDistOpt*)
2: *rootJob* ← *j*
3: Clear the *prevRemapAttempts* list.
4: Set *jobComparator* to the Job Deadline Comparator.
5: Set *taskSchedulingPolicy* ← *tsp*
6: **return** *mapJobHelper(j*, true, true)

A walkthrough of mapJobHelper(), which performs the allocation and scheduling of job j onto the set of resources in the system, is provided next. The input required by mapJobHelper() includes the following: a job j to map, a Boolean isRootJob, which is set to true if this is the first time job j is being mapped; otherwise, it is set to false, and a Boolean checkDeadline, which is set to true if the method should try to map job j to meet its deadline; otherwise, it is set to false and the method has to map job j on the system, but it does not have to schedule job j to meet its deadline. The map-JobHelper() method starts by initializing the local variable isJobMapped to true (line 1). Next, all of job j's tasks that need to be mapped are sorted in non-

increasing order of their respective execution times (line 2), where ties are broken in favour of the task with the earlier sub-deadline. If the tasks also have the same sub-deadline, the task with the smaller task id (a unique value) is placed ahead of the task with the larger id. The method then attempts to map each of job j's tasks (lines 3–4) by performing the following operations for each task t in job j. First, the startTime variable is initialized by invoking the task t's getEarliestStartTime() method (line 5), which returns the time that task t can start to execute while considering any precedence relationships that t has. If getEarliestStartTime() returns –1, it means that an earliest start time for task t cannot be determined as yet because not all of task t's parent tasks have been scheduled. In this case, mapJobHelper() stops processing task t for the moment and attempts to map the next task in job j (line 6). On the other hand, if startTime is not –1, the processing of task t continues. If RM-DCWF's taskSchedulingPolicy field is set to TSP2 (line 7), the expected start time of the task is updated and set as shown in line 8. The expected completion time of the task is then calculated using the expected start time of the task (line 9).

After calculating the expected start time and completion time of task t, the method checks whether t has an execution time equal to 0 (i.e., checks if task t is a dummy task, defined in Section "Problem Description and Resource Management Model") (line 10). If task t is a dummy task, it does not need to be scheduled on a resource because it has an execution time equal to 0 and only the task's scheduled start time and completion time need to be set (line 11). The task t is also added to the RM-DCWF's mapped-Tasks list (line 12), which stores all the tasks that have been successfully mapped for job j. On the other hand, if task t has an execution time greater than 0 (line 13), the method attempts to find a resource r in R that can execute t at its expected start time. If t cannot be scheduled to execute at its expected start time, the task is scheduled at the next best time depending on the value of the taskSchedulingPolicy field (line 14). If taskSchedulingPolicy is set to TSP1, the method schedules task t at its next earliest possible time. On the other hand, if taskSchedulingPolicy is set to TSP2, the method schedules the task at its next latest possible time, while ensuring the task's sub-deadline is satisfied.

If a resource r cannot be found to complete executing task t before job j's deadline, it means job j cannot be mapped to meet its deadline in the current iteration. Thus, if the supplied input argument checkDeadline is set to true (line 15), mapJobHelper() attempts to remap job j and a set of jobs that may have caused j to miss its deadline by performing the following operations (lines 16–18). First, the removePartiallyMappedJob() method is invoked to remove each of the tasks stored in the mappedTasks list from the system (line 16). Algorithm 7: remapJob()

(described in more detail in the next section) is then invoked and the return value is saved in a variable called isJob-Mapped (line 17). The next step (line 18) is then to go to line 27 to check the value of isJobMapped. If isJob-Mapped is set to true, meaning the job has been successfully scheduled to meet its deadline, the mappedTasks list is cleared, job j is added to RM-DCWF's mappedJobs list (line 28), and true is returned (line 29). Otherwise, isJob-Mapped is set to false, meaning job j cannot be scheduled to meet its deadline (line 30). This leads to mapJobHelper() being re-invoked, but this time with the checkDeadline argument set to false, which will map job j even if it misses its deadline (line 31). False is then returned (line 32) to indicate job j will not meet its deadline.

Algorithm 5: RM-DCWF algorithm's *mapJobHelper()*

Input: job j, Boolean *isRootJob*, Boolean *checkDeadline*
Output: a Boolean: true if the job j is scheduled to meet its deadline; false, otherwise.

1:   *isJobMapped* ← true
2:   Sort job j's *tasksToMap* list in non-increasing order of the execution time of the task.
3:   **while** the *tasksToMap* list is not empty **do**
4:     **for** each task t in job j's *tasksToMap* list **do**
5:       *startTime* ← t.getEarliestStartTime()
6:       **if** *startTime* = -1 **then continue**
7:       **if** *taskSchedulingPolicy* = TSP2 **then**
8:         *startTime* ← t.getSubDeadline() – t.getExecutionTime()
9:       *endTime* ← startTime + t.getExecTime()
10:       **if** *startTime* = *endTime* **then**
11:         t.setScheduledTime(*startTime*, *endTime*)
12:         *mappedTasks*.add(t)
13:       **else**
14:         Find a resource r in R that can execute t at its requested time or the next best time depending on *taskSchedulingPolicy*.
15:         **if** t cannot be mapped to meet j's deadline **and** *checkDeadline* = true **then**
16:           **call** removePartiallyMappedJob()
17:           *isJobMapped*←remapJob(job, isRootJob)
18:           **goto** line 27
19:         **else**
20:           Map t on r.
21:           *mappedTasks*.add(t)
22:         **end if**
23:       **end if**
24:     **end for**
25:     *tasksToMap*.removeAll(*mappedTasks*)
26: **end while**
27: **if** *isJobMapped* = true **then**
28:   *mappedTasks*.clear(); *mappedJobs*.add(j)
29:   **return** true
30: **else**
31:   **call** mapJobHelper(job, true, false)
32:   **return** false
33: **end if**

If either of the conditions shown in line 15 are not true (i.e., a resource is found that can complete executing task t before job j's deadline or the input argument checkDead-line is false), it means that task t can be scheduled to execute on resource r (line 20) and t is then added to the mappedTasks list (line 21). The next task of job j is then processed by repeating lines 3–26. This sequence of operations continues until all of job j's tasks are mapped on the system. After all of job j's tasks have been mapped, lines 27–29 are executed (as described earlier), and then the method returns.

Job remapping algorithm

The Job Remapping algorithm is comprised of two methods: (1) remapJob() presented in Algorithm 6 and (2) remapJobHelper() outlined in Algorithm 7. A discussion of remapJob() is provided first, followed by a discussion on remapJobHelper(). The input arguments required by remapJob() include a job j to remap and a Boolean isRootJob. The isRootJob argument is set to true if it is the first invocation of remapJob() for attempting to remap job j in this iteration; otherwise, isRootJob is set to false. If job j and the set of jobs that may have prevented job j from meeting its deadline are remapped and scheduled to meet their deadlines, the method returns true; otherwise, false is returned.

Algorithm 6: RM-DCWF algorithm's *remapJob()*

Input: job j, Boolean *isRootJob*
Output: a Boolean: true if job j and the set of jobs to remap all are scheduled to meet their deadlines; otherwise, false.

1:   *taskSchedulingPolicy* ← TSP1
2:   **if** calling remapJobHelper(j, *isRootJob*) **returns** true **then**
3:     **return** true
4:   **else**
5:     **if** *isRootJob* = false **then return** false
6:     Change *jobComparator* to the *Job Laxity Comparator*.
7:     **return** remapJobHelper(j, *isRootJob*)
8: **end if**

The first step of remapJob() is to set RM-DCWF's taskSchedulingPolicy field to TSP1 so the tasks that are remapped are scheduled to execute at their earliest possible times (line 1). The second step is to invoke Algorithm 7: remapJobHelper() (line 2). Recall from line 4 of Algorithm 4 ((mapJob()) that the jobComparator field, which specifies how the jobs that need to be remapped are sorted, is initially set to the *Job Deadline Comparator*. The Job Deadline Comparator sorts jobs in non-decreasing order of their respective deadlines with ties broken in favour of the job with the smaller laxity (i.e., tighter deadline). If remapJobHelper() returns true, remapJob() also returns true (line 3). On the other hand, if remapJobHelper() returns false, remap-Job() continues by checking the supplied isRootJob argument (line 4). If isRootJob is false (line 5), meaning that this invocation of remapJob() is not for the original attempt for mapping job j, the method returns false to stop this particular remapping attempt from continuing (line 5). Otherwise, the method continues and RM-DCWF's jobComparator field is changed to the *Job Laxity Comparator* (line 6) and remapJobHelper() is invoked again to check if remapping the jobs in a different order can generate a schedule in which all the jobs to remap can meet their deadlines (line 7).

The Job Laxity Comparator sorts jobs by non-decreasing order of their respective *normalized laxity* with ties going in favour of the job with an earlier deadline. If the jobs have the same deadline, the job with the earlier arrival time (which is unique for each job) is given priority. The normalized laxity of a job j (denoted NL_j) is calculated as follows:

$$NL_j = \frac{L_j}{SET_j} \tag{3}$$

where L_j is the laxity of job j and SET_j is the sample execution time of job j (recall Section "Deadline Budgeting Algorithm for Workflows"). The reason for using NL_j instead of L_j for sorting the jobs is because L_j is not always a good indicator of how stringent the deadline of a job is. A job can have a large laxity value, but still have a very tight deadline if the job has a high execution time. For example, given two jobs: (1) job $j1$ has s_{j1} equal to 0, d_{j1} equal to 6000, and SET_{j1} equal to 5000, and (2) job $j2$ has s_{j2} equal to 5500, d_{j2} equal to 6000, and SET_{j2} equal to 100. Using this information along with Eq. 1 and Eq. 3, the following values can be calculated: L_{j1} is equal to 1000, L_{j2} is equal to 400, NL_{j1} is equal to 0.2, and NL_{j2} is equal to 4. As can be observed, job $j1$ has a higher laxity compared to job $j2$ (i.e., $L_{j1} > L_{j2}$); however, $j1$'s normalized laxity is much smaller compared to $j2$'s normalized laxity ($NL_{j1} < NL_{j2}$), meaning job $j1$ has a more stringent deadline.

A walkthrough of `remapJobHelper()` (shown in Algorithm 7) is provided next. The input arguments and output value returned by `remapJobHelper()` are the same as those described for `remapJob()`. The first step of the method is to retrieve a subset of the jobs already scheduled on the system that may have caused job j to miss its deadline and store these jobs in the `jobsToRemap` list (line 1). This includes all the jobs in RM-DCWF's `mappedJobs` list that execute within the interval $[s_j, d_j]$. Next, the supplied job j is added to the `jobsToRemap` list (line 2) and then the `jobsToRemap` list is sorted using RM-DCWF's `jobComparator` (line 3). Since it is possible to have multiple (nested) invocations of `remapJobHelper()`, lines 4–6 determine when an invocation of `remapJobHelper()` (referred to as a *remapping attempt*) should be rejected. More specifically, before a remapping attempt is started, the method checks if RM-DCWF's `prevRemapAttempts` list, which stores the various sets of jobs that previous invocations of `remapJobHelper()` have processed, contains the same jobs (in the same order) as the `jobsToRemap` list (line 4). If this is true, the method returns false to stop the remapping attempt (line 5). On the other hand, if the remapping attempt is allowed to continue, the `jobsToRemap` list is added to RM-DCWF's `prevRemapAttempts` list (line 7). Next, the method checks if the supplied argument `isRootJob` is true (line 8), and if so, the current state of the system is saved to a set of variables (line 9). This involves saving the scheduled tasks of each resource in the system and making a copy of RM-DCWF's `mappedJobs` list. Furthermore, the scheduled start time and assigned resource for each task currently mapped on the system is

saved. The reason for saving this information is because it may be changed during the job remapping attempt, and if the remapping attempt is not successful, the original state of the system has to be restored.

The next step is to remove all the jobs in `jobsToRemap` from the system (line 11), which involves removing the jobs from RM-DCWF's `mappedJobs` list and removing each task of each job from its assigned resource's `scheduledTasks` list. This needs to be done so that the jobs in `jobsToRemap` can be remapped on the system. All the jobs in `jobsToRemap` that have already missed their deadlines are then moved to a new list called `lateJobs` (line 12) so that the jobs that have not missed their deadlines can be remapped first. The jobs in `jobsToRemap` (line 13) are then remapped in the specific order as determined by the `jobComparator` (recall line 3). This is accomplished by invoking Algorithm 5: `mapJobHelper()` as shown in line 14. If mapJobHelper() returns true, the method maps the next job in `jobsToRemap`. If at any point `mapJobHelper()` returns false (line 14), it means that one of the jobs in `jobsToRemap` cannot be scheduled to meet its deadline and the job remapping attempt has failed. The method then checks if `isRootJob` is true (line 15), and if so, the state of the system that is saved in line 9 is restored (line 16). False is then returned to indicate that the remapping attempt has failed (line 18). On the other hand, if all the jobs in `jobsToRemap` are successfully remapped to meet their deadlines, the next step is to perform mapping for the jobs in `lateJobs` (i.e., the jobs that have missed their deadlines). This is accomplished by invoking `mapJobHelper()` (Algorithm 5) with the `checkDeadline` input argument set to false for each of the jobs in `lateJobs` (line 21). Lastly, a value of true is returned by the method to indicate the remapping attempt is successful (line 22).

Algorithm 7: RM-DCWF algorithm's *remapJobHelper()*

Input: job j, Boolean *isRootJob*

Output: a Boolean: true if job j and the set of jobs to remap all are scheduled to meet their deadlines; otherwise, false.

1:   *jobsToRemap* ← Get subset of mapped jobs that can cause j to miss its deadline.

2:   *jobsToRemap*.add(j)

3:   Sort *jobsToRemap* using the *jobComparator*.

4:   **if** *prevRemapAttempts* list contains the same jobs in the same order as the *jobsToRemap* list **then**

5:      **return** false

6:   **end if**

7:   Add *jobsToRemap* to *prevRemapAttempts* list.

8:   **if** *isRootJob* = true **then**

9:      Save current state of the system.

10: **end if**

11: Remove jobs in *jobsToRemap* from the system.

12: Move jobs in *jobsToRemap* that have missed their deadlines to the *lateJobs* list.

13: **for** each job *j1* in *jobsToRemap* **do**

14:     **if** calling mapJobHelper(*j1*, false, true) **returns** false **then**

15:        **if** *isRootJob* = true **then**

16:          Restore state of the system saved in line 9.

17:        **end if**

18:        **return** false

19:     **end if**

20: **end for**

21: Remap each job *j2* in *lateJobs* by calling mapJobHelper(*j2*, false, false).

22: **return** true

Time complexity analysis of the RM-DCWF matchmaking and scheduling algorithm

As discussed in this section, the worst-case time complexity of the RM-DCWF matchmaking and scheduling algorithm is $O(n^2)$ where n is the number of jobs (or workflows) that arrive on the system. In the worst-case scenario, the algorithm will have to reschedule all the jobs in the system each time a new job arrives. For example, given $n = 100$, we have the following scenario. First, a job $j1$ arrives on the system and is scheduled. Sometime later, a new job $j2$ (with a deadline that is earlier than $j1$'s deadline) arrives before job $j1$ is completed and the algorithm schedules $j2$ and reschedules $j1$. Before jobs $j1$ and $j2$ complete, a new job $j3$ with a deadline that is earlier than the deadlines of $j1$ and $j2$ arrives. The algorithm schedules $j3$ and then reschedules $j1$ and $j2$. This process continues for the remaining 97 jobs that arrive on the system. The total number of jobs that the algorithm schedules in this worst case is then equal to:

$$1 + 2 + 3 + \dots + n = \frac{n^*(n+1)}{2} = \frac{n^2 + n}{2}$$

Thus, the worst-case time complexity of the algorithm is $O(n^2)$. Note that in practice, the time complexity of the algorithm will be lower because not all jobs will need to be rescheduled when a new job arrives on the system. For example, some jobs will have completed executing and other jobs will not need to be rescheduled because they do not contend with the same time slots as the newly arriving job. Moreover, if scheduling a job is deemed to take too long because of the large number of jobs that need to be rescheduled, it is possible to limit the number of jobs to reschedule. For example, this can be accomplished by modifying line 1 of Algorithm 7 to restrict the size of the `jobsToRemap` list. Such a modification will limit the number of jobs that can be added to the list, thus limiting the number of jobs that can be rescheduled at a given point in time.

Furthermore, an in-depth and rigorous empirical performance evaluation of the algorithms using various workloads and workload and system parameters is presented in Section "Performance Evaluation of RM-DCWF". The results of the performance evaluation (discussed in more detail in Section "Results of the Factor-at-a-Time Experiments") demonstrate that the algorithm leads to a reasonably small system overhead. For example, in experiments with a very high contention for resources, leading to an average resource utilization of 0.9, the average matchmaking and scheduling time of the algorithm was measured to be less than 0.05 s.

Performance evaluation of RM-DCWF

This section describes the two types of simulation experiments conducted to evaluate the performance of RM-DCWF. The first type of experiments (presented in Section "Results of the Factor-at-a-Time Experiments" and Section "Investigation of Using a Small Number of Resources") investigate the effect of various system and workload parameters on the performance of RM-DCWF. More specifically, *factor-at-a-time* experiments are conducted where one parameter is varied and the other parameters are kept at their default values. The second type of experiments (presented in Section "Comparison with a First-in-first-out (FIFO) Scheduler" and Section "Comparison with MCRP-RM") compare the performance of RM-DCWF with that of a FIFO Scheduler and the MapReduce Constraint Programming based Resource Management technique (MRCP-RM) described in [29], respectively. MRCP-RM has objectives that are similar to that of RM-DCWF: perform matchmaking and scheduling for an open stream of multi-stage jobs with SLAs, where each job's SLA is characterized by an earliest start time, an execution time, and an end-to-end deadline.

The rest of this section is organized as follows. The experimental setup and the metrics used in the performance evaluation are described in Section "Experimental Setup". Following this, a description of the system and workload parameters used in the factor-at-a-time experiments is provided in Section "System and Workload Parameters for the Factor-at-a-Time Experiments". The results of the experiments are then presented and discussed.

Experimental setup

The experiments are executed on a PC running Windows 10 (64-bit) with an Intel Core i5–4670 CPU (3.40 GHz) and 16 GB of RAM. Note that in the experiments, only the execution of the workload on the system is simulated. RM-DCWF and its associated algorithms are executed on the PC that was described at the beginning of this section. RM-DCWF is evaluated in terms of the following performance metrics in each simulation run:

- *Proportion of Late Jobs* $(P) = N/n$ where N is the number of late jobs in a simulation run and n is the total number of jobs processed during the simulation.
- *Average Job Turnaround Time* (T). The turnaround time of a job j (tat_j) is $CT_j - s_j$ where CT_j is job j's completion time and s_j is j's earliest start time, respectively. Thus, $T = \sum_{j \in J}(tat_j)/n$.
- *Average Job Matchmaking and Scheduling Time* (O) is the average processing time required by RM-DCWF to partition a job's deadline among its tasks and matchmake and schedule a job. $O = \sum_{j \in J}(o_j)/n$ where o_j is the processing time required for mapping job j on the system.

Note that O is a value that is measured using Java's System.nanoTime() [32] method, whereas P and T are values produced as outputs of the simulation. The *O*-by-*T* ratio (denoted *O/T*) is used as an indicator of the processing overhead of RM-DCWF. This is an appropriate indication of the processing overhead because it puts the measured values of the algorithm runtimes (*O*) into context by considering the value of *O* relative to the mean job turnaround time (*T*).

System and workload parameters for the factor-at-a-time experiments

The workloads used in the factor-at-a-time experiments are based on real scientific applications (workflows) that have been described in the literature. More specifically, the three scientific applications that are used in the experiments are named *CyberShake*, *LIGO*, and *Epigenomics*. A brief discussion of each application that includes presenting the DAG of the workflow is provided next. A more detailed description of all three applications can be found in [33].

CyberShake is a seismology application that is created by the Southern California Earthquake Center to predict earthquake hazards in a region. The DAG of a sample CyberShake workflow is presented in Fig. 3. As shown, the workflow has five phases of execution. Recall from Section "Problem Description and Resource Management Model" that the number *i* in the small circle indicates the *i*th execution phase. The first, second, and fourth execution phases each contain multiple tasks to execute whereas the third and fifth execution phase each only have one task to execute.

The Laser Interferometer Gravitational Wave Observatory (LIGO) Inspiral Analysis workflow is used to search for and analyze gravitational waveforms in data collected by large-scale interferometers. The input data is partitioned into multiple blocks so that the data can be analyzed in parallel. Fig. 4 shows the DAG of a sample LIGO workflow, which has 6 phases of execution. In this

sample LIGO workflow there are two blocks of data being processed in parallel, where each block of data has multiple waveform data (i.e. TmptlBank tasks) to process.

The Epigenomics (Genome) workflow is used for automating several commonly used operations in genome sequence processing. Fig. 5 shows a DAG of a sample Genome workflow, which is characterized by one or more *lanes*, each of which starts with the execution of a fastQSplit task. If there is more than one lane in the workflow, as shown in the example in Fig. 5, there are two mapMerge stages. The first mapMerge stage is for merging the results within a particular lane (execution phase 6), and the second mapMerge stage (referred to as the global mapMerge stage) is for merging the results of all the lanes in the workflow (execution phase 7).

Table 1 outlines the system and workload parameters used in the factor-at-a-time experiments. These experiments investigate the effect of the following parameters on system performance: job arrival rate, earliest start time of jobs, job deadlines, and the number of resources. A walkthrough of Table 1 is provided next. Note that the distributions used to generate the parameters of the workload, including the job arrival rate, earliest start time of jobs, and job deadlines are adopted from [11, 29]. The first component of the table describes the workload. For a given workflow type (CyberShake, LIGO, or Genome), there are three job sizes, each of which has an equal probability of being submitted to the system: *small*, *medium*, and *large*, comprising 30 tasks, 50 tasks, and 100 tasks, respectively. The distributions used for generating the execution times of the tasks for each workload are described in [33]. The open stream of job arrivals is generated using a Poisson process. The arrival rates used in the experiments of a given workload type are different since each of the workloads is characterized by jobs with different execution times. The average execution time of a CyberShake

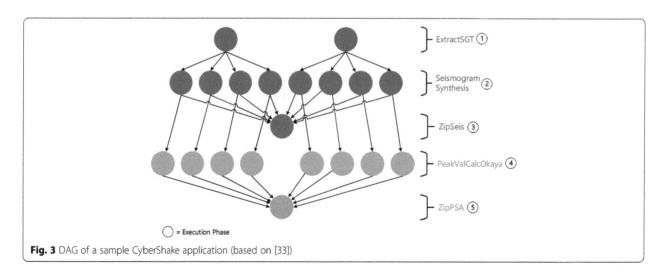

Fig. 3 DAG of a sample CyberShake application (based on [33])

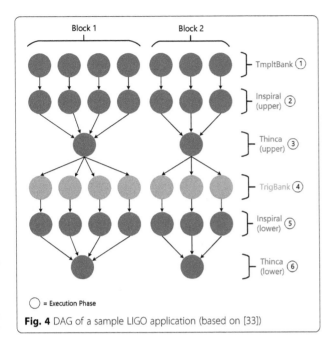

Fig. 4 DAG of a sample LIGO application (based on [33])

job, LIGO job, and Genome job on a single resource is equal to 1551 s, 13,300 s, and 160,213 s, respectively. The parameters λ_{CS}, λ_{LG}, and λ_{GN} specify the job arrival rates used for the CyberShake, LIGO, and Genome workloads, respectively. The arrival rates for each workflow are chosen such that resource utilization ranging from moderate (~50%) to moderately-high (~70%) to high (~90%) is generated on the system when using the default number

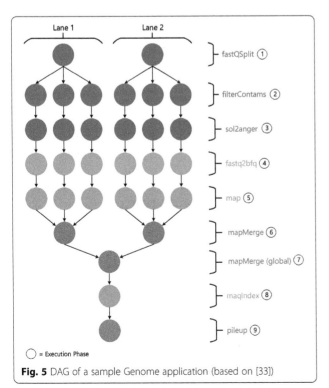

Fig. 5 DAG of a sample Genome application (based on [33])

of resources (50 resources, where each resource has a capacity equal to 2). The earliest start time of a job j (s_j) can be its arrival time (at_j) or at a time in the future after at_j. A random variable x, which follows a Bernoulli distribution with parameter p, is defined. The parameter p is the probability that a job j has s_j greater than at_j. If x is 0, s_j equals at_j; otherwise, s_j equals the sum of at_j and a value generated from a discrete uniform (DU) distribution with a lower-bound equal to 1 and an upper-bound equal to a parameter s_{max}. The deadlines of the jobs are generated by multiplying SET_j^R (recall Section "Deadline Budgeting Algorithm for Workflows") with an *execution time multiplier* (*em*) and adding the resulting value to s_j. The parameter *em* is used to determine the laxity (or slack time) of a job and is generated using a uniform distribution (U) where 1 is the lower-bound and em_{max} is the upper-bound of the distribution.

The remaining components of Table 1 describe the system used to execute the jobs and the configuration of RM-DCWF. The number of resources (m), which represents the number of nodes in the distributed system for processing the jobs, is varied from 40 to 50 to 60, where each resource has a capacity (c_r) equal to 2. Recall from Section "Problem Description and Resource Management Model", c_r specifies the number of tasks that a resource r can execute in parallel at any given point in time. RM-DCWF's Job Mapping algorithm can handle resources with different values of c_r as the algorithm performs resource allocation and scheduling by considering the set of all the resource slots provided by all the resources in R. Note that how the capacity of the resources, as reflected by their number of resource slots, is distributed among the individual resources in the system does not affect performance because matchmaking and scheduling are performed on the resource slots, each of which has an equal speed of execution. As a result, system performance does not change if c_r is different for the different resources in R as long as the sum of the number of resource slots in all the resources in R remains the same. Thus, the *total resource capacity* of the system, the sum of the number of resource slots for all the resources in R, is an important parameter that can affect system performance. This parameter is varied by varying the value of m in the experiments described in Section "Effect of the Number of Resources".

The configuration of RM-DCWF is defined as *x-y-z* where x specifies the laxity distribution algorithm (i.e., PD or ED, described in Section "Deadline Budgeting Algorithm for Workflows"), y specifies the approach to calculate the laxity of the job (i.e., SL or TL, described in Section "Deadline Budgeting Algorithm for Workflows"), and z specifies the task scheduling policy (i.e., TSP1 or TSP2, described in Section "Job Mapping Algorithm"). In total, there are 8 different RM-DCWF

Table 1 System and Workload Parameters for the Factor-at-a-Time Experiments

Parameter	Values	Default Value
Workload		
Type	{CyberShake, LIGO, Genome}	–
Job arrival rate (job/s)	$\lambda_{CS} = \{1/18,\ 1/22,\ 1/30\}$ $\lambda_{LG} = \{1/150,\ 1/180,\ 1/265\}$ $\lambda_{GN} = \{1/1800,\ 1/2290,\ 1/3205\}$	$\lambda_{CS} = 1/22$ $\lambda_{LG} = 1/180$ $\lambda_{GN} = 1/2290$
Earliest start time of jobs, s_j (sec)	$s_j = \begin{cases} at_j, & x = 0 \\ at_j + DU(1, s_{max}) & x = 1 \end{cases}$ where at_j is the arrival time of job j, $x \sim$ Bernoulli(0.5), and $s_{max} = \{1, 5, 25\} * 10^4$	$s_{max} = 50{,}000$
Job Deadline, d_j (sec)	$d_j = s_j + SET_j^R * em$ where $em \sim U(1, em_{max})$ and $em_{max} = \{2, 5, 10\}$	$em_{max} = 5$
System		
Number of Resources, m	$m = \{40, 50, 60\}$	$m = 50$
Resource Capacity	$c_r = 2$	–
Configuration of RM-DCWF		
Laxity Distribution Algorithm	{PD, ED}	–
Approach to calculate the job laxity	{SL, TL}	–
Task Scheduling Policy	{TSP1, TSP2}	–

configurations, and thus, for each workload type, the factor-at-a-time experiments are conducted 8 times. This is performed to determine which configuration provides the best performance for a given workload.

Results of the factor-at-a-time experiments

The results of the factor-at-a-time experiments are presented in this section. Each simulation run was executed long enough to ensure that the system was operating at a steady state. Furthermore, each factor-at-a-time experiment is repeated a sufficient number of times such that the desired trade-off between simulation run length and accuracy of results was achieved. The confidence intervals for T and O at a confidence level of 95% are observed to remain less than ±5% of the respective average values in most cases. For P, the confidence intervals are observed to be in most cases less than ±10% of the average value. Such an accuracy of the simulation results is deemed adequate for the nature of the investigation: the focus of which is investigating the trend in the variation of a given performance metric in response to changes in the system and workload parameters and to compare the performance of the various RM-DCWF configurations. The values averaged over the simulation runs and the confidence intervals are shown in the figures and tables presented in this section. In the figures, the confidence intervals are shown as bars originating from the mean values; however, some of the bars are difficult to see since the confidence intervals are small. Note that the confidence intervals are considered while deriving a conclusion regarding the relative performance of the respective RM-DCWF configurations.

To conserve space and provide clarity of presentation, only the results of the two RM-DCWF configurations, one using PD and the other one using ED, that demonstrated the best overall performance in terms of P are presented in the following sub-sections. A more detailed discussion of the results of the performance evaluation can be found in [34]. More specifically, the two RM-DCWF configurations that are compared for each workload type are summarized:

- PD-SL-TSP1 vs ED-SL-TSP2 for the CyberShake workload
- PD-SL-TSP1 vs ED-SL-TSP1 for the LIGO workload
- PD-SL-TSP1 vs ED-SL-TSP1 for the Genome workload

Note that in the following sub-sections, the results of the experiments using the CyberShake workload are shown in figures, where P is displayed in its own figure and T and O are graphed in the same figure with T being displayed as a bar graph that uses the scale on the left Y-axis and O being displayed as a sequence of points that uses the scale on the right Y-axis. To maintain a reasonable number of figures, the results of each of the experiments using the LIGO and Genome workloads are shown in their own tables where the values of P, T, and O can be presented concisely.

Effect of job arrival rate

The impact of the job arrival rate on system performance is discussed in this section. The results of the experiments using the CyberShake workload are presented in Fig. 6 and Fig. 7. The figures show that for PD-SL-TSP1, P, T, and O increase with λ_{CS}. When λ_{CS} is high, jobs arrive on the system at a faster rate, which leads to more jobs being present in the system at a given point in time and an increased contention for resources. This in turn prevents some jobs from executing at their earliest start times, resulting in T increasing and some jobs to miss their deadlines (which increases P). The increased contention for resources also causes O to increase because RM-DCWF takes more time to find a resource to map the tasks of the job such that the job does not miss its deadline. Furthermore, since jobs are more prone to miss their deadlines at high values of λ_{CS}, RM-DCWF's Job Remapping algorithm, which is a source of overhead, is invoked more often, contributing to the increase in O.

It is observed that for ED-SL-TSP2, P and O increase with λ_{CS}, and T tends to remain relatively stable. In addition, when λ_{CS} is 1/22 jobs per sec or lower, both systems achieve comparable values of P; however, when λ_{CS} is 1/18 jobs per sec, ED-SL-TSP2 is observed to achieve a lower P. This can be attributed to ED-SL-TSP2 efficiently using the laxity of jobs to delay the execution of jobs with a later deadline to execute jobs with an earlier deadline, which in turn reduces the contention for resources at certain points in time and leads to a lower P. Although, as shown in Fig. 7, by delaying the execution of jobs, ED-SL-TSP2 achieves a higher T compared to PD-SL-TSP1. The O of ED-SL-TSP2 is higher compared to that of PD-SL-TSP1 when λ_{CS} is 1/22 jobs per sec or smaller. This is because more time is required by TSP2 to search for a resource that can execute a task at its latest possible time such that its sub-deadline is satisfied, compared to the time required by TSP1 to find a resource to execute tasks at their earliest possible times. However, when λ_{CS} is 1/18 jobs per sec,

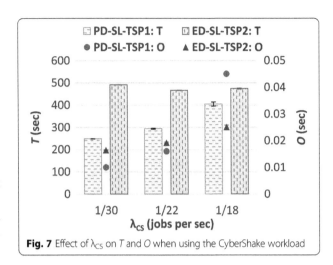

Fig. 7 Effect of λ_{CS} on T and O when using the CyberShake workload

PD-SL-TSP1 has a higher O, which can be attributed to the Job Remapping algorithm being invoked more often when using PD-SL-TSP1 compared to when using ED-SL-TSP2.

Table 2 and Table 3 present the results of the experiments when using the LIGO workload and the Genome workload, respectively. Unlike the CyberShake workload, when using the LIGO and Genome workloads, configuring RM-DCWF to use ED with TSP2 did not produce a better performance in comparison to using ED with TSP1. This demonstrates that TSP2 is only effective for certain workflows and the average job execution time and the structure of the job (e.g., precedence relationships between the tasks of the job) can affect the performance of TSP2. As shown in the tables, the trend in performance of P, T, and O are identical to that of the CyberShake workload when using PD-SL-TSP1. Furthermore, the results also show that both PD-SL-TSP1 and ED-SL-TSP1 achieve very similar results because TSP1 schedules tasks to start executing at their earliest possible times, regardless of their respective sub-deadlines. Over all the experiments performed to investigate the effect of the job arrival rate, the results demonstrate that RM-DCWF can achieve low values of P (less than 2% even at high arrival rates) and has a low

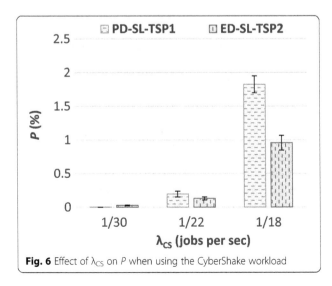

Fig. 6 Effect of λ_{CS} on P when using the CyberShake workload

Table 2 LIGO workload: effect of λ_{LG} on P, T, and O

λ_{LG} (jobs/s)	P (%)		T (sec)		O (sec)	
	PD-SL-TSP1	ED-SL-TSP1	PD-SL-TSP1	ED-SL-TSP1	PD-SL-TSP1	ED-SL-TSP1
1/265	0.02	0.02	1346	1346	0.008	0.008
	±0.01	±0.01	±0.6	±0.6	±0.00	±0.00
1/180	0.11	0.11	1466	1466	0.009	0.009
	±0.01	±0.01	±4.6	±4.6	±0.00	±0.00
1/150	1.03	1.06	2005	2006	0.017	0.016
	±0.12	±0.12	±29	±28	±0.001	±0.001

Table 3 Genome workload: effect of λ_{GN} on P, T, and O

λ_{GN} (jobs/s)	P (%)		T (sec)		O (sec)	
	PD-SL-TSP1	ED-SL-TSP1	PD-SL-TSP1	ED-SL-TSP1	PD-SL-TSP1	ED-SL-TSP1
1/3205	0.01	0.01	17,544	17,544	0.008	0.008
	±0.00	±0.00	±927	±927	±0.000	±0.000
1/2290	0.07	0.07	17,963	17,963	0.008	0.008
	±0.01	±0.01	±1007	±1007	±0.000	±0.000
1/1800	1.43	1.40	52,312	52,472	0.048	0.051
	±0.45	±0.44	±12,915	±13,003	±0.015	±0.016

processing overhead as indicated by the small O (less than 0.025 s) and small O/T (less than 0.005%).

Effect of earliest start time of jobs

The impact of the earliest start time of jobs on system performance is described in this section. Fig. 8 and Fig. 9 present the results when using the CyberShake workload. It is observed that for PD-SL-TSP1, P, T, and O decrease with an increase in s_{max}. When s_{max} is large, jobs have a wider range of earliest start times with some jobs having an earliest start time near their arrival times, while other jobs have their earliest start times further in the future. This leads to less contention for resources and allows more jobs to execute at or closer to their earliest start times, resulting in a lower P, T, and O. Similar to PD-SL-TSP1, it is observed that for ED-SL-TSP2, P and O decrease as s_{max} increases. However, T is observed to increase with s_{max}. This is due to ED-SL-TSP2 scheduling tasks to execute at their latest possible times, while ensuring the respective sub-deadlines of the tasks are met. When the contention for resources is low (e.g., when s_{max} is large), ED-SL-TSP2 can more readily schedule tasks to start executing at their latest possible start times since jobs are less prone to miss their deadlines and the Job Remapping algorithm does not need to

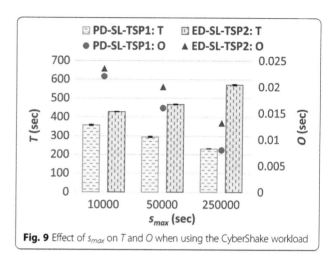

Fig. 9 Effect of s_{max} on T and O when using the CyberShake workload

be invoked as often. Overall, it is observed that similar to the results presented in the previous section, ED-SL-TSP2 tends to achieve a lower P (35% lower on average), but this is accompanied by a higher T (75% higher on average) and higher O (32% higher on average) compared to PD-SL-TSP1.

The results of the experiments using the LIGO workload are presented in Table 4. It is observed that for both systems, P, T, and O seem to be insensitive to s_{max}, which is different from the results of PD-SL-TSP1 shown in Fig. 8 and Fig. 9, where P, T, and O are observed to decrease as s_{max} increases. The reason for this can be attributed to the LIGO workload comprising jobs with higher average execution times compared to those of the CyberShake workload, as well as the values of s_{max} used not significantly reducing the amount of jobs that have overlapping execution times (i.e., not reducing the contention for resources). The average job execution time (on a single resource) of the CyberShake workload (equal to 1551 s) is much smaller compared to that of the LIGO workload (13,300 s).

Table 5 presents the results of the experiments using the Genome workload. It is observed that P and T tend to increase and O remains stable as s_{max} increases. The increase in P could be attributed to the values of s_{max} experimented with (e.g., 50,000 and 250,000 s) causing more jobs to have overlapping execution times and thus increasing the contention for resources. This did not happen when using the other two workloads because the Genome workload comprises jobs with very high average execution times (~160,213 s on a single resource), which is significantly higher compared to those of the Cyber-Shake and LIGO workloads. Increasing the values of s_{max} experimented with when using the Genome workload is expected to generate a similar trend in performance to the results of the CyberShake workload. This is because there will be less chance for the execution of jobs to overlap with one another.

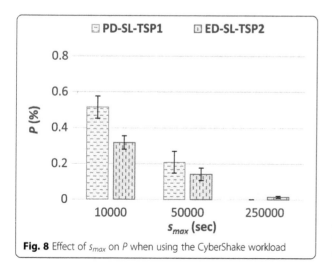

Fig. 8 Effect of s_{max} on P when using the CyberShake workload

Table 4 LIGO workload: effect of s_{max} on P, T, and O

s_{max} (sec)	P (%)		T (sec)		O (sec)	
	PD-SL-TSP1	ED-SL-TSP1	PD-SL-TSP1	ED-SL-TSP1	PD-SL-TSP1	ED-SL-TSP1
10,000	0.10	0.10	1450	1450	0.009	0.009
	±0.01	±0.01	±3.3	±3.3	±0.000	±0.000
50,000	0.11	0.11	1466	1466	0.009	0.009
	±0.01	±0.01	±4.6	±4.6	±0.000	±0.000
250,000	0.09	0.08	1441	1427	0.009	0.009
	±0.01	±0.01	±4.7	±4.1	±0.000	±0.000

Effect of job deadlines

The impact of job deadlines on system performance is presented in this section. The results of the experiments using the CyberShake workload, as depicted in Fig. 10 and Fig. 11, show that for both systems, P decreases as em_{max} increases. This is because at a higher em_{max} jobs have more laxity and are thus less susceptible to miss their deadlines. Moreover, for ED-SL-TSP2, T is observed to increase as em_{max} increases. This can be attributed to jobs not having to execute at or close to their s_j to meet their deadlines when they have more slack time and the Job Remapping algorithm having to be executed less often. In addition, RM-DCWF may delay the execution of some jobs to allow a job with an earlier deadline to execute first. On the other hand, when em_{max} is small, jobs need to execute closer to their earliest start times and the Job Remapping algorithm is invoked when a job cannot be scheduled to meet its deadline. O is thus observed to increase for both systems, as em_{max} decreases because it leads to multiple invocations of the Job Remapping algorithm.

When comparing PD-SL-TSP1 and ED-SL-TSP2, it is observed that both systems perform comparably in terms of P when em_{max} is 5 or 10. However, when em_{max} is 2, it is observed that PD-SL-TSP1 achieves a smaller P compared to ED-SL-TSP2. This is because when the deadlines of the jobs are more stringent, jobs need to execute closer to their earliest start times to meet their deadlines, which agrees with the objective of TSP1 and not with the objective of TSP2, which schedules jobs to

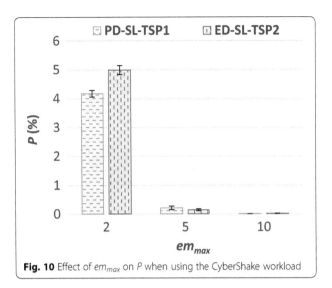

Fig. 10 Effect of em_{max} on P when using the CyberShake workload

execute at their latest possible times. Similar to the results described in the previous sections, PD-SL-TSP1 also achieves a lower T and a lower or similar O compared to ED-SL-TSP2.

The results of the experiments using the LIGO workload and Genome workload are presented in Table 6 and Table 7, respectively. It is observed that the trend in performance observed for both systems when using the LIGO and Genome workloads are identical to that of the CyberShake workload when using PD-SL-TSP1: P decreases, O decreases, and T remains approximately at the same level as em_{max} increases. Overall, it is observed that RM-DCWF can achieve a low P (less than 4.2%) even when jobs have tight deadlines (i.e., em_{max} is 2). In addition, O is small (less than 0.03 s), and the processing overhead, as indicated by O/T, is less than 0.01% for all the experiments described in this sub-section.

Table 5 Genome workload: effect of s_{max} on P, T, and O

s_{max} (sec)	P (%)		T (sec)		O (sec)	
	PD-SL-TSP1	ED-SL-TSP1	PD-SL-TSP1	ED-SL-TSP1	PD-SL-TSP1	ED-SL-TSP1
10,000	0.04	0.04	17,693	17,693	0.008	0.008
	±0.01	±0.01	±959	±959	±0.000	±0.000
50,000	0.07	0.07	17,963	17,963	0.008	0.008
	±0.01	±0.01	±1007	±1007	±0.000	±0.000
250,000	0.08	0.08	18,171	18,171	0.008	0.008
	±0.01	±0.02	±1049	±1049	±0.000	±0.000

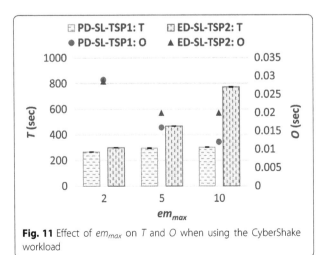

Fig. 11 Effect of em_{max} on T and O when using the CyberShake workload

Effect of the number of resources

In this section, the impact of m, the number of resources, on system performance is discussed. From the results of the experiments using the CyberShake workload (refer to Fig. 12 and Fig. 13), it is observed that for PD-SL-TSP1, P, T, and O decrease as m increases. This is because as m increases, there are more resources in the system to execute the jobs, leading to a lower contention for resources. The reason for the higher O when m is small can be attributed to the Job Mapping algorithm requiring more time to find a resource to map a task. When there are fewer resources in the system (small m), there are more tasks scheduled on each resource, leading to more time being required to find the ideal resource to execute a task. In addition, the high contention for resources makes jobs susceptible to miss their deadlines and leads to RM-DCWF's Job Remapping algorithm being invoked more often.

For ED-SL-TSP2, P, T, and O follow a similar trend in performance as observed for PD-TL-TSP1, except when m is 60. When m is 60, T is slightly higher compared to the case when m is 50. This can be attributed to the availability of ten additional resources, resulting in a lower contention for resources and a smaller P, and thus leading to a lower number of invocations of the Job Remapping Algorithm, which remaps jobs to start executing at their earliest possible times. This in turn allows TSP2 to schedule more tasks to execute at their latest possible times, while satisfying their respective sub-deadlines.

When comparing the performance of PD-SL-TSP1 and ED-SL-TSP2 for the CyberShake workload, it is observed that ED-SL-TSP2 achieves a smaller P and the most significant reduction in P is observed when m is 40 (refer to Fig. 12). Similar to the results presented in the previous sections (see Fig. 6, for example), scheduling tasks to execute at their latest possible time, while satisfying their respective sub-deadlines (i.e., using TSP2) tends to give rise to a lower P but a higher T when processing the CyberShake workload. The lower P can be attributed to ED-SL-TSP2 efficiently using the laxity of jobs to delay the execution of jobs with a later

deadline to execute those with an earlier deadline. However, as shown in Fig. 13, it is observed that when m is 40, PD-SL-TSP1 achieves a higher T compared to ED-SL-TSP2. This can be attributed to PD-SL-TSP1 delaying the execution of multiple jobs that miss their deadlines for a long period of time for executing jobs that have not missed their deadlines. In the case of ED-SL-TSP2, fewer jobs need to be delayed because when m is 40, ED-SL-TSP2 achieves a smaller P compared to PD-SL-TSP1 (refer to Fig. 12).

The results of the experiments using the LIGO workload (see Table 8) and the Genome workload (see Table 9) follow a similar trend in system performance to that of the CyberShake workload when using PD-SL-TSP1: P decreases, T decreases, and O tends to decrease as m increases. It is observed once again that both PD-SL-TSP1 and ED-SL-TSP1 achieve similar results for both workloads. When m is 60, O is observed to be slightly higher compared to when m is 50. Even though, there is less contention for resources when m is 60, the Job Mapping algorithm may need to search through more resources to find the resource to schedule a task to start at its earliest possible time. This in turn leads to a slight increase in O.

Table 7 Genome workload: effect of em_{max} on P, T, and O

em_{max}	P (%)		T (sec)		O (sec)	
	PD-SL-TSP1	ED-SL-TSP1	PD-SL-TSP1	ED-SL-TSP1	PD-SL-TSP1	ED-SL-TSP1
2	0.49	0.49	17,933	17,933	0.009	0.009
	±0.12	±0.12	±1001	±1001	±0.000	±0.000
5	0.07	0.07	17,963	17,963	0.008	0.008
	±0.01	±0.01	±1007	±1007	±0.000	±0.000
10	0.03	0.03	17,963	17,963	0.007	0.007
	±0.01	±0.01	±1007	±1007	±0.000	±0.000

Table 6 LIGO workload: effect of em_{max} on P, T, and O

em_{max}	P (%)		T (sec)		O (sec)	
	PD-S-TSP1	ED-SL-TSP1	PD-SL-TSP1	ED-SL-TSP1	PD-SL-TSP1	ED-SL-TSP1
2	2.44	2.43	1458	1457	0.012	0.011
	±0.14	±0.14	±4.4	±4.4	±0.000	±0.000
5	0.11	0.11	1466	1466	0.009	0.009
	±0.01	±0.01	±4.6	±4.6	±0.000	±0.000
10	0.04	0.04	1458	1463	0.009	0.008
	±0.01	±0.01	±6.2	±4.6	±0.000	±0.000

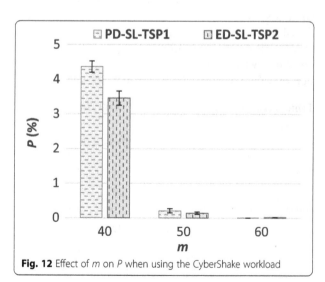

Fig. 12 Effect of m on P when using the CyberShake workload

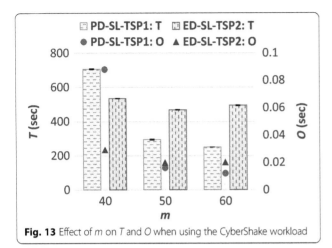

Fig. 13 Effect of *m* on *T* and *O* when using the CyberShake workload

Table 9 Genome workload: effect of *m* on *P*, *T*, and *O*

m	P (%)		T (sec)		O (sec)	
	PD-SL-TSP1	ED-SL-TSP1	PD-SL-TSP1	ED-SL-TSP1	PD-SL-TSP1	ED-SL-TSP1
40	1.29	1.30	52,320	52,106	0.032	0.035
	±0.40	±0.42	±13,743	±13,597	±0.011	±0.012
50	0.07	0.07	17,963	17,963	0.008	0.008
	±0.01	±0.01	±1007	±1007	±0.000	±0.000
60	0.02	0.02	17,583	17,583	0.009	0.009
	±0.00	±0.00	±935	±935	±0.000	±0.000

Figures 14 and 15 show the effect of λ_{cs} on *P*, *T*, and *O* when processing the CyberShake workload on a system where *m* is 20. It is observed from Fig. 14 that PD-SL-TSP1 outperforms ED-SL-TSP2 in terms of *P*. This means that when the number of resources is small, it is more effective to schedule tasks to start executing at their earliest possible times (i.e., using TSP1) as opposed to scheduling tasks to execute at their latest possible times (using TSP2). In other words, when there are limited resources, the system should try to execute and complete jobs as soon as possible to lower the contention for resources when other jobs arrive on the system. Fig. 15 also shows that when λ_{cs} is 1/75 or 1/55 jobs per sec, PD-SL-TSP1 achieves a lower *T* and similar *O* compared to ED-SL-TSP2, once again demonstrating that for a small number of resources and low to moderate job arrival rates it is more effective to schedule tasks to execute at their earliest possible times. When λ_{cs} is 1/45 jobs per sec, PD-SL-TSP1 still achieves a lower *P* in comparison to ED-SL-TSP2. However, it is interesting to note that for this arrival rate that leads to a high contention for resources, PD-SL-TSP1 achieves a higher *T* and *O* in comparison to ED-SL-TSP2.

Investigation of using a small number of resources

In the experiments described in Section "Effect of the Number of Resources", the number of resources, *m*, was varied from 40 to 60. This section describes the results of a set of experiments conducted to investigate the effect of using a small number of resources (20 resources, each with 2 resource slots). In this system, not all jobs will be able to execute at their maximum degree of parallelism. The fixed factors in this set of experiments include *m*, the workload, CyberShake, and all the other workload and system parameters described in Table 1 that are held at their default values. CyberShake is chosen because it is the workload that produced the most interesting set of results in the previous experiments in which the various configurations of RM-DCWF (captured in the last three rows of Table 1) exhibited different levels of performance. Since the number of resources is small, the default arrival rates for the CyberShake workload that are listed in Table 1 could not be used because it would lead to an unstable system (that is characterized by a job arrival rate exceeding the job service rate). Instead λ_{cs} is set to 1/45, 1/55, and 1/75 jobs per sec., corresponding to a resource utilization of approximately 0.9, 0.7, and 0.5. This is in line with the system utilizations achieved in the experiments described in Section "Results of the Factor-at-a-Time Experiments".

Table 8 LIGO workload: effect of *m* on *P*, *T*, and *O*

m	P (%)		T (sec)		O (sec)	
	PD-SL-TSP1	ED-SL-TSP1	PD-SL-TSP1	ED-SL-TSP1	PD-SL-TSP1	ED-SL-TSP1
40	4.11	4.14	3210	3218	0.034	0.032
	±0.27	±0.27	±125	±126	±0.003	±0.003
50	0.11	0.11	1466	1466	0.009	0.009
	±0.01	±0.01	±4.6	±4.6	±0.000	±0.000
60	0.03	0.03	1360	1360	0.010	0.010
	±0.01	±0.01	±1.1	±1.1	±0.000	±0.000

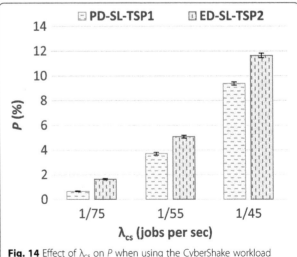

Fig. 14 Effect of λ_{cs} on *P* when using the CyberShake workload with *m* = 20

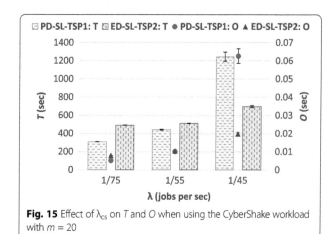

Fig. 15 Effect of λ_{cs} on T and O when using the CyberShake workload with $m = 20$

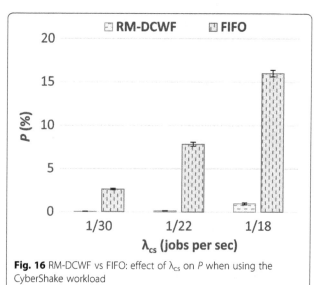

Fig. 16 RM-DCWF vs FIFO: effect of λ_{cs} on P when using the CyberShake workload

Comparison with a first-in-first-out (FIFO) scheduler

To the best of our knowledge there are no existing algorithms in the literature for matchmaking and scheduling on a cloud/cluster subjected to an open stream of workflows, each of which is characterized by general precedence relationships among its constituent tasks and a deadline for completion. In order to investigate the effectiveness of the various optimization techniques used in RM-DCWF, a comparison with a simple, conventional technique that does not use such optimization techniques is conducted. A first-in-first-out (FIFO) scheduling algorithm that can handle multi-phase workflows with general precedence relationships among its constituent tasks is devised for the purpose.

In this section, the results of experiments conducted to compare the performance of RM-DCWF with that of the conventional FIFO technique are presented. The FIFO technique devised is a simple scheduling strategy that stores jobs that arrive on the system in a FIFO queue. Thus, the jobs are scheduled in the same order in which they arrive on the system. As in the case with RM-DCWF, a best-fit strategy (as described in Section "Deadline Budgeting Algorithm for Workflows") is used allocate the tasks of a job to resources. For reasons similar to those discussed in Section "Investigation of Using a Small Number of Resources", the CyberShake workload is chosen as a fixed parameter and the job arrival rate, λ_{cs}, is varied. The remaining system and workload parameters (described in Section "System and Workload Parameters for the Factor-at-a-Time Experiments") are once again held at their default values. RM-DCWF is configured to use ED-SL-TSP2, which as described in Section "Effect of Job Arrival Rate", is observed to achieve the best performance when processing the CyberShake workload.

As shown in Fig. 16, RM-DCWF achieves a significantly lower P (99% to 94% smaller as λ_{cs} varies from 1/30 to 1/18 jobs per sec) in comparison to FIFO. This

can be attributed to RM-DCWF prioritizing the execution of jobs with earlier deadlines, and FIFO executing jobs in the order they arrive on the system. Achieving a low P is the main objective for resource management performed by RM-DCWF. As far as the secondary performance metric T is concerned, FIFO achieves a lower T in comparison to RM-DCWF (see Fig. 17). This is expected because FIFO prioritizes executing jobs that have earlier arrival times and schedules each job to execute at its earliest possible time. This in turn allows jobs to finish executing earlier and results in jobs having a smaller turnaround time. Another reason for FIFO achieving a lower T is because RM-DCWF is configured to use TSP2, which schedules tasks to complete executing at their latest possible times, while not missing their sub-deadlines. Fig. 17 also displays that RM-WCDF achieves a slightly smaller O compared to FIFO. The higher O achieved by FIFO can be attributed to FIFO attempting to schedule all the arriving jobs, which

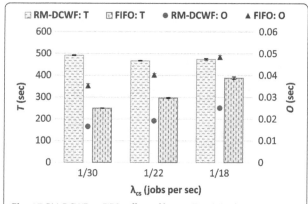

Fig. 17 RM-DCWF vs FIFO: effect of λ_{cs} on T and O when using the CyberShake workload

arrive relatively close to each other due to the high arrival rate, to execute at their earliest start times causing a high contention for resources. RM-WCDF makes use of the slack time of jobs to delay their execution, which in turn results in less contention for resources at certain points in time. The experimental results demonstrate the effectiveness of RM-DCWF that uses a number of techniques for optimizing system performance. This is demonstrated by the achieving of a lower P and O by RM-DCWF in comparison to a simple scheduling technique such as FIFO.

Comparison with MCRP-RM

This section discusses the results of the experiments conducted to compare the performance of RM-DCWF with that of MRCP-RM [29] (described in Section "Related Work"). Note that MRCP-RM is only applicable to jobs with two phases of execution, such as MapReduce [7] jobs, whereas in addition to MapReduce jobs, RM-DCWF can also handle jobs with different structures and more than two execution phases. Thus, the workload that is used in this comparison is a synthetic MapReduce workload that is used and described in [29]. RM-DCWF is configured to use PD-SL-TSP1, which is observed to have the best performance when processing this MapReduce workload. Factor-at-a-time experiments are performed to investigate the effect of various system and workload parameters on the performance of RM-DCWF and MRCP-RM.

Figure 18 and Table 10 present the performance of RM-DCWF and MRCP-RM in terms of P, T, and O as the job arrival rate (λ) is varied. As shown in Fig. 18, when λ is 0.0175 jobs per sec or smaller, the resource contention levels are low-to-moderate (e.g., average resource utilization is approximately less than 0.7), and it is observed that both RM-DCWF and MRCP-RM achieve comparable values of P. However, when λ is

Table 10 RM-DCWF vs MRCP-RM: effect of λ on T and O

λ (jobs/s)	T (sec)		O (sec)	
	RM-DCWF	MRCP-RM	RM-DCWF	MRCP-RM
0.001	383 ± 2	383 ± 2	0.010 ± 0	0.018 ± 0
0.01	395 ± 2	394 ± 2	0.010 ± 0	0.043 ± 0
0.015	413 ± 2	417 ± 2	0.010 ± 0	0.074 ± 0
0.175	429 ± 2	435 ± 2.5	0.012 ± 0	0.10 ± 0
0.1875	444 ± 3	450 ± 3	0.013 ± 0	0.12 ± 0
0.02	465 ± 4	471 ± 3	0.012 ± 0	0.18 ± 0.01
0.02125	502 ± 6	508 ± 6	0.016 ± 0	0.25 ± 0.02
0.0225	564 ± 12	566 ± 10	0.019 ± 0	0.43 ± 0.04
0.025	1332 ± 76	1788 ± 118	0.110 ± 0	2.9 ± 0.48

between 0.01875 to 0.0225 jobs per sec, generating a moderate-to-high contention for resources (e.g., average resource utilization is approximately between 0.7 and 0.85), MRCP-RM is observed to achieve up to a 22% lower P (on average 11% lower) compared to that achieved by RM-DCWF. At very high values of λ (e.g., 0.025 jobs per sec or higher), it is observed that the performance of MRCP-RM starts to deteriorate and RM-DCWF starts to outperform MRCP-RM (RM-DCWF has a 37% reduction in P). This can be attributed to the very high contention for resources (average resource utilization is greater than 0.9) causing jobs to queue up on the system and MRCP-RM having to solve complex constraint programs comprising a large number of decision variables and constraints. MRCP-RM requires more time to solve these complex constraint programs, which results in O increasing. The high O causes a delay in the execution of jobs and leads to jobs missing their deadlines. For all the values of λ experimented with, it is observed that RM-DCWF achieves a significantly lower O compared to MRCP-RM (on average 85% lower) (see Table 10). This can be attributed to RM-DCWF using a heuristic-based matchmaking and scheduling algorithm that is less computationally-intensive compared to MRCP-RM's matchmaking and scheduling algorithm, which is based on constraint programming.

The results of the other factor-at-a-time experiments performed to compare RM-DCWF and MRCP-RM, which can be found in [34], demonstrate a relative performance achieved by RM-DCWF and MRCP-RM that is similar to the results described in this section. When the contention for resources is reasonable, MRCP-RM and RM-DCWF achieve comparable values of P and T. On the other hand, when the contention for resources is high, such as when λ is 0.025 job per sec, RM-DCWF is observed to achieve a lower P compared to MRCP-RM. At these higher system loads, RM-DCWF achieves a

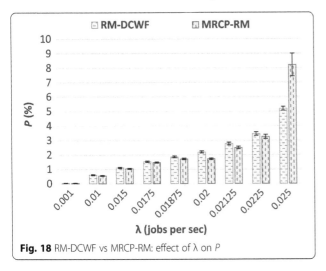

Fig. 18 RM-DCWF vs MRCP-RM: effect of λ on P

superior performance and thus demonstrates a higher scalability when system load is high.

Conclusions and future work

This paper describes a resource allocation and scheduling technique called RM-DCWF that can efficiently perform matchmaking and scheduling for an open stream of multi-stage jobs (workflows) with SLAs on a computing environment such as a private cluster or a set of resources acquired a priori from a public cloud. Each job arriving on the system is characterized by a SLA comprising an earliest start time, an execution time, and an end-to-end deadline. The RM-DCWF algorithm decomposes the end-to-end deadline of a job into sub-deadlines, each of which is associated with a task in the job. The individual tasks of the job are then mapped on to the resources where the objective is to satisfy the job's deadline and minimize the number of late jobs in the system. An in-depth simulation-based performance evaluation is conducted to investigate the effectiveness of RM-DCWF. The workloads used in the experiments are based on real scientific workflows from various fields of study, including biology and physics. A number of insights into system behaviour and performance are gained by analyzing the experimental results and are summarized next.

- *Effect of system and workload parameters*: An increase in the job arrival rate, λ, or a decrease in the earliest start time of jobs, s_j, or a decrease in the deadline of jobs, d_j, or a decrease in the number of resources, m, tends to lead to an increase in the proportion of late jobs, P, due to the increased contention for resources.
- *RM-DCWF configuration using the Proportional Distribution of Job Laxity Algorithm (PD)*: Overall, it is observed that using Task Scheduling Policy 1 (TSP1) generates lower or similar values for the proportion of late jobs, P, average job turnaround time, T, and average job matchmaking and scheduling time, O, than those achieved with Task Scheduling Policy 2 (TSP2). Furthermore, the two approaches used to calculate the laxity of the job (Sample Laxity, SL and True Laxity, TL) achieve similar performance with the SL approach achieving a slightly smaller P in most cases. When using PD, the results of the experiments showed that the highest performing RM-DCWF configuration (in terms of P) for all three workloads experimented with is *PD-SL-TSP1*.
- *RM-DCWF configuration using the Even Distribution of Job Laxity Algorithm (ED)*: The results demonstrate that for the CyberShake workload

using ED-SL-TSP2 achieves the lowest P in most cases. However, when using the LIGO and Genome workloads, the best performance in terms of P is achieved by ED-SL-TSP1. When using ED, the results of the experiments showed that the two approaches used to calculate the laxity of the jobs (SL and TL) achieve comparable performance.
- *PD-based configuration vs ED-based configuration*: For the CyberShake workload, it is observed that overall ED-SL-TSP2 outperforms PD-SL-TSP1 in terms of P but it has a slightly higher T because TSP2 schedules tasks to execute at their latest possible times while meeting their respective sub-deadlines. In the case of the LIGO and Genome workloads, both PD-SL-TSP1 and ED-SL-TSP1 achieve similar values of P, T, and O. This can be attributed to TSP1 scheduling tasks to execute at their earliest possible times, regardless of their sub-deadlines.
- *Effectiveness of RM-DCWF*: For the system and workload parameters experimented with in Section "Results of the Factor-at-a-Time Experiments", it is observed that RM-DCWF can achieve low values of P (on average 0.62%). Even when the contention for resources is high and jobs are more susceptible to miss their deadlines (e.g., when λ is high, or d_j is small, or m is small), P is less than 5% and on average 2.2% for all the experiments conducted.
- *Efficiency of RM-DCWF*: Over all the experiments described in Section "Results of the Factor-at-a-Time Experiments", RM-DCWF achieved low values of O (less than 0.05 s and on average 0.02 s). Furthermore, O/T, an indication of the matchmaking and scheduling overhead, is also very small (less than 0.01%) for all the experiments conducted.
- *Effect of using a small number of resources*: When executing the CyberShake workload on a system with $m = 20$, which prevented some jobs from executing at their maximum degree of parallelism, it was observed that PD-SL-TSP1 outperforms ED-SL-TSP2 in terms of P. When there are a limited number of resources, better performance can be achieved if the system schedules jobs to complete executing as soon as possible to lower the contention for resources when other jobs arrive later on the system.
- *Comparison with the FIFO Scheduler*: The results of experiments comparing RM-DCWF with a FIFO Scheduler demonstrated that RM-DCWF achieves a significantly lower P and a lower O compared to the FIFO Scheduler. However, as expected the FIFO Scheduler did achieve a lower T because it prioritizes executing jobs that have earlier arrival times and schedules each job to execute at its earliest possible time.

- *MapReduce Workload and Comparison with MRCP-RM*: A summary of observations resulting from the performance evaluation to compare RM-DCWF and MRCP-RM when using a MapReduce workload is provided. At low-to-moderate contention for resources (e.g., $\lambda \leq 0.0175$ jobs per sec), RM-DCWF and MRCP-RM achieve comparable performance in terms of P. When the contention for resources is moderately high (e.g., average resource utilization is approximately 0.8), for a λ of 0.02 jobs per sec, for example, MRCP-RM outperforms RM-DCWF. At very high contention for resources (e.g., $\lambda \geq 0.025$ jobs per sec), RM-DCWF outperforms MRCP-RM. For all the values of λ experimented with, RM-DCWF achieves on average an O that is 85% lower compared to that achieved by MRCP-RM.

- These observations indicate that MRCP-RM's constraint programming-based resource management algorithm led to its superior performance over the heuristic-based RM-DCWF at medium system load, but because of its lower overhead RM-DCWF demonstrated higher scalability and superior performance at higher system loads.

Overall, the results of the experiments demonstrate that the objective of the paper that concerns the devising of an effective resource allocation and scheduling technique for processing an open stream of multi-stage jobs with SLAs on a cluster or a cloud with a fixed number of resources has been realized. RM-DCWF demonstrated that it can generate a schedule leading to a small P and T with a small O and O/T over a wide range of workload and system parameters experimented with. The choice of which RM-DCWF configuration (laxity distribution algorithm and task scheduling policy) to use is dependent on the workload to process; however, a good starting point is to use PD-SL-TSP1. If the system does not exhibit satisfactory performance, RM-DCWF can be reconfigured to use ED-SL-TSP2 when the next job arrives on the system or the next time this the same type of workload needs to be processed. When using TSP1, the choice of whether to use PD or ED, and SL or TL is not crucial as all the configurations using TSP1 achieve similar performance. However, if TSP2 is used, it is observed that using ED-SL-TSP2 typically achieves better performance compared to the other configurations that include TSP2.

A direction for future work is to adapt the resource management techniques to work in a computing environment where the number of resources in the system can be dynamically changed. Moreover, the resource management techniques can also be adapted to distributed computing environments with heterogeneous resources and multi-datacentre environments. This can involve devising more advanced techniques for supporting data locality when processing multi-stage jobs, which includes techniques for estimating the data transmission time and processing time for tasks based on the input data size and networking/processing capacities of the resources. Supporting data locality for multi-stage jobs that are characterized by multiple phases of execution may need to consider the possibility of one phase of execution sharing data with another phase of execution. If data needs to be shared among these two phases of execution, the tasks in these two phases of execution should be assigned to execute on nodes that are as close to each other as possible to minimize the data transmission overhead. Lastly, validating the results of the experiments for additional cases by conducting experiments using different combinations of workload and system parameters is also a part of the plan for future research.

Abbreviations

DAG: Directed Acyclic Graph; DBW: Deadline Budgeting Algorithm for Workflows; ED: Even Distribution of Job Laxity Algorithm; MRCP-RM: MapReduce Constraint Programming based Resource Management technique; PD: Proportional Distribution of Job Laxity Algorithm; RM-DCWF: Resource Management Technique for Deadline-constrained Workflows; SL: Sample Laxity; SLA: Service Level Agreement; TL: True Laxity; TSP1: Task Scheduling Policy 1; TSP2: Task Scheduling Policy 2

Acknowledgments

We are grateful to Huawei Technologies Canada and the Natural Sciences and Engineering Research Council of Canada (NSERC) for supporting this research.

Authors' contributions

The work presented in this paper is based on NL's Ph.D. research and thesis, which is supervised by SM. PAS is a collaborator and industrial partner for this research. NL devised and implemented the algorithms and conducted the simulation experiments. SM and PAS provided guidance and participated in system design. All the authors read and approved the final manuscript.

Competing interests

The authors declare that they have no competing interests.

Author details

[1]Department of Systems and Computer Engineering, Carleton University, Ottawa, ON, Canada. [2]Huawei Technologies Canada, Kanata, ON, Canada.

References

1. Columbus L (2015) Roundup Of Cloud Computing Forecasts And Market Estimates, 2015. http://www.forbes.com/sites/louiscolumbus/2015/01/24/roundup-of-cloud-computing-forecasts-and-market-estimates-2015/. Accessed 14 Nov 2016
2. Gartner (2015) Gartner Says Worldwide Cloud Infrastructure-as-a-Service Spending to Grow 32.8 Percent in 2015. http://www.gartner.com/newsroom/id/3055225. Accessed 14 Nov 2016
3. Manvi SS, Shyam GK (2013) Resource management for infrastructure as a service (IaaS) in cloud computing: a survey. Journal of Network and Computing Applications 41:424–440
4. Buyya R, Garg SK, Calheiros RN (2011) SLA-oriented resource provisioning for cloud computing: challenges, architecture, and solutions. In: proceedings

of the international conference on cloud and service computing, Hong Kong, China, 12-14 Dec 2011, p 1-10

5. Foster I, Kesselman C, Lee C, Lindell B, Nahrstedt K, Roy (1999) a distributed resource management architecture that supports advance reservations and co-allocation. In: Proceedings of the International Workshop on Quality of Service, London, UK, 1-4 June 1999, p 27–36

6. Maheswaran M, Siegel HJ (1998) A dynamic matching and scheduling algorithm for heterogeneous computing systems. In: proceedings of the heterogeneous computing workshop, Orlando, USA, 30 march 1998, p 57-69

7. Dean J, Ghemawat S (2004) MapReduce: simplified data processing on large clusters. In: proceedings of the international symposium on operating system design and implementation, San Francisco, USA, 6-8 Dec 2004, p 137-150

8. Dittrich J, Quiane-Ruiz J-A (2012) Efficient Big Data Processing in HadoopMapReduce. VLDB 2012/PVLDB, 5:12:2014–2015

9. Collins M (2011) Hadoop and MapReduce: big data analytics. Gartner. Available: https://www.gartner.com/doc/1521016/hadoop-mapreduce-big-data-analytics. Accessed 13 Jan 2017

10. Gift N (2010) Solve cloud-related big data problems with MapReduce. IBM. Available: http://www.ibm.com/developerworks/cloud/library/cl-bigdata/. Accessed 13 Jan 2017

11. Lim N, Majumdar S, Ashwood-Smith P (2014) Resource management techniques for handling requests with service level agreements. In: proceedings of the international symposium on performance evaluation of computer and telecommunication systems, Monterey, USA, 6-10 July 2014, p 618-625

12. Yu J, Buyya R, Tham CK (2005) Cost-based scheduling of scientific workflow applications on utility grids. In: proceedings of the international conference on e-science and grid computing, Melbourne, Australia, 5-8 Dec 2005, p 140-147

13. Abrishami S, Naghibzadeh M, Epema DHJ (2012) Cost-driven scheduling of grid workflows using partial critical paths. IEEE Transactions on Parallel Distributed Systems 23(8):1400–1414

14. Wan C, Wang C, Pei J (2012) A QoS-aware scientific workflow scheduling schema in cloud computing. In: proceedings of the international conference on information science and technology, Wuhan, China, 23-25 march 2012, p 634-639

15. Pandey S, Wu L, Guru S, Buyya R (2010) A particle swarm optimization-based heuristic for scheduling workflow applications in cloud computing environments. In: proceedings of the international conference on advanced information networking and applications, Perth, Australia, 20-23 April 2010, p 400-407

16. Chen WN, Zhang J (2012) A set-based discrete PSO for cloud workflow scheduling with user-defined QoS constraints. In: proceedings of the international conference on systems, man, and cybernetics, Seoul, South Korea, 14-17 Oct 2012, p 773-778

17. Bilgaiyan S, Sagnika S, Das M (2014) Workflow scheduling in cloud computing environment using cat swarm optimization. In: proceedings of the international advance computing conference, Gurgaon, India, 21-22 Feb 2014, p 680-685

18. Bittencourt LF, Senna CR, Madeira ERM (2010) Scheduling service workflows for cost optimization in hybrid clouds. In: proceedings of the international conference on network and service management, Niagara Falls, Canada, 25-29 Oct 2010, p 394-397

19. Szabo C, Kroeger T (2012) Evolving multi-objective strategies for task allocation of scientific workflows on public clouds. In: proceedings of the IEEE congress on evolutionary computation, Brisbane, Australia, 10-15 June 2012, p 1-8

20. Zhu Z, Zhang G, Li M, Liu X (2016) Evolutionary multi-objective workflow scheduling in cloud. IEEE Transactions on Parallel and Distributed Systems 27(5):1344–1357

21. Goudarzi H, Pedram M (2011) Multi-dimensional SLA-based resource allocation for multi-tier cloud computing systems. In: proceedings of the international conference on cloud computing, Washington, USA, 4-9 July 2011, p 324-331

22. Meng X, Lizhen C, Haiyang W, Yanbing B (2009) A multiple QoS constrained scheduling strategy of multiple workflows for cloud computing. In: proceedings of the international symposium on parallel and distributed processing with applications, Chengdu and Jiuzhai Valley, China, 10-12 Aug 2009, p 629-634

23. Li X, Qian L, Ruiz R (2016) Cloud workflow scheduling with deadlines and time slot availability. IEEE Transactions on Services Computing, Preprint available: http://ieeexplore.ieee.org/document/7383307/

24. Verma A, Cherkasova L, Kumar VS, Campbell RH (2012) Deadline-based workload management for MapReduce environments: pieces of the performance puzzle. In: proceedings of the network operations and management symposium, Maui, Hawaii, USA, 16-20 April 2012, p 900-905

25. Mattess M, Calheiros RN, Buyya R (2013) Scaling MapReduce applications across hybrid clouds to meet soft deadlines. In: proceedings of the international conference on advanced information networking and applications, Barcelona, Spain, 25-28 march 2013, p 629-636

26. Hwang E, Kim KH (2012) Minimizing cost of virtual Machines for Deadline-Constrained MapReduce applications in the cloud. In: proceedings of the international conference on grid computing, Beijing, China, 20-23 sept 2012, p 130-138

27. Lai ZR, Chang CW, Liu X, Kuo TW, Hsiu PC (2014) Deadline-aware load balancing for MapReduce. In: proceedings of the international conference on embedded and real-time computing systems and applications, Chongqing, China, 20-22 Aug 2014, p 1-10

28. Chen C, Lin J, Kuo S (2015) MapReduce scheduling for deadline-constrained jobs in heterogeneous cloud computing systems. IEEE Transactions on Cloud Computing, Preprint available: http://ieeexplore.ieee.org/document/7229311/

29. Lim N, Majumdar S, Ashwood-Smith P (2014) A Constraint Programming-Based Resource Management Technique for Processing MapReduce Jobs with SLAs on Clouds," In: Proceedings of the International Conference on Parallel Processing, Minneapolis, USA, 9-12 Sept 2014, p 411–421

30. Lim N, Majumdar S, Ashwood-Smith P (2017) MRCP-RM: a technique for resource allocation and scheduling of MapReduce jobs with deadlines. IEEE Transactions on Parallel and Distributed Systems 28(5):1375–1389

31. The Apache Software Foundation. Hadoop. http://hadoop.apache.org. Accessed 16 Jan 2016

32. Oracle Corporation. System.nanoTime(). https://docs.oracle.com/javase/7/docs/api/java/lang/System.html#nanoTime(). Accessed 14 Nov 2016

33. Bharathi S, Chervenak A, Deelman E, Mehta G, Su MH, Vahi K (2008) Characterization of scientific workflows. In: proceedings of the workshop on workflows in support of large scale science, Austin, USA, 17 Nov 2008, p 1-10

34. Lim N (2016) Resource management techniques for multi-stage jobs with deadlines running on clouds. Dissertation, Carleton University, Ottawa, ON, Canada, Ph.D

Permissions

All chapters in this book were first published in JoCCASA, by Springer International Publishing AG.; hereby published with permission under the Creative Commons Attribution License or equivalent. Every chapter published in this book has been scrutinized by our experts. Their significance has been extensively debated. The topics covered herein carry significant findings which will fuel the growth of the discipline. They may even be implemented as practical applications or may be referred to as a beginning point for another development.

The contributors of this book come from diverse backgrounds, making this book a truly international effort. This book will bring forth new frontiers with its revolutionizing research information and detailed analysis of the nascent developments around the world.

We would like to thank all the contributing authors for lending their expertise to make the book truly unique. They have played a crucial role in the development of this book. Without their invaluable contributions this book wouldn't have been possible. They have made vital efforts to compile up to date information on the varied aspects of this subject to make this book a valuable addition to the collection of many professionals and students.

This book was conceptualized with the vision of imparting up-to-date information and advanced data in this field. To ensure the same, a matchless editorial board was set up. Every individual on the board went through rigorous rounds of assessment to prove their worth. After which they invested a large part of their time researching and compiling the most relevant data for our readers.

The editorial board has been involved in producing this book since its inception. They have spent rigorous hours researching and exploring the diverse topics which have resulted in the successful publishing of this book. They have passed on their knowledge of decades through this book. To expedite this challenging task, the publisher supported the team at every step. A small team of assistant editors was also appointed to further simplify the editing procedure and attain best results for the readers.

Apart from the editorial board, the designing team has also invested a significant amount of their time in understanding the subject and creating the most relevant covers. They scrutinized every image to scout for the most suitable representation of the subject and create an appropriate cover for the book.

The publishing team has been an ardent support to the editorial, designing and production team. Their endless efforts to recruit the best for this project, has resulted in the accomplishment of this book. They are a veteran in the field of academics and their pool of knowledge is as vast as their experience in printing. Their expertise and guidance has proved useful at every step. Their uncompromising quality standards have made this book an exceptional effort. Their encouragement from time to time has been an inspiration for everyone.

The publisher and the editorial board hope that this book will prove to be a valuable piece of knowledge for researchers, students, practitioners and scholars across the globe.

List of Contributors

Rui Lu
National Computer Network Emergency Response Technical Team Coordination Center of China, Beijing, China

Neil Caithness, Michel Drescher and David Wallom
Oxford e-Research Centre, University of Oxford, 7 Keble Road, OX1 3QG Oxford, UK

Erdal Cayirci
Electrical and Computer Engineering Department, University of Stavanger, Stavanger, Norway

Anderson Santana de Oliveira
SAP Labs France, Mougins, France

Alexandr Garaga
SAP Labs France, Mougins, France
Network Security Team, Eurecom, Biot, France

Yves Roudier
Network Security Team, Eurecom, Biot, France

Saurabh Dey and Srinivas Sampalli
Dalhousie University, Halifax, Canada

Qiang Ye
University of Prince Edward Island, Charlottetown, Canada

Django Armstrong, Karim Djemame and Richard Kavanagh
School of Computing, University of Leeds, Leeds, UK

Mohammad Alaul Haque Monil
Department of Computer and Information Science, University of Oregon, Eugene, OR, USA

Rashedur M. Rahman
Department of Electrical and Computer Engineering, North South University, Dhaka, Bangladesh

Samir Elmougy, Shahenda Sarhan
Department of Computer Science, Faculty of Computers and Information, Mansoura University, Mansoura 35516, Egypt

Manar Joundy
Department of Computer Science, Faculty of Computers and Information, Mansoura University, Mansoura 35516, Egypt
University of Al-Qadisiyah, Al-Qadisiyah, Iraq

Caspar Ryan and Zahir Tari
School of Computer Science and Information Technology, GPO, RMIT University, Box 2476, Melbourne, Australia

Harald Mueller and Spyridon V. Gogouvitis
Corporate Technology, CT RDA ITP, Siemens AG, Otto-Hahn-Ring 6, 81739 Munich, Germany

Philip Church and Andrzej Goscinski
School of Computer Science and Information Technology, GPO, RMIT University, Box 2476, Melbourne, Australia
School of Information Technology, Deakin University, Geelong, Australia

Mahdi Mollamotalebi and Shahnaz Hajireza
Department of Computer, Buinzahra Branch, Islamic Azad University, Buinzahra, Iran

Patricia T. Endo
University of Pernambuco (UPE), BR 104 S/N, Caruaru, Brazil
Federal University of Pernambuco, GPRT, Recife, Brazil

Moisés Rodrigues, Judith Kelner and Djamel H. Sadok
Federal University of Pernambuco, GPRT, Recife, Brazil

Glauco E. Gonçalves
Federal University of Pernambuco, GPRT, Recife, Brazil
Rural Federal University of Pernambuco, Recife, Brazil

Calin Curescu
Ericsson Research, Kista, Sweden

Xiaolin Li, Chung-Horng Lung and Shikharesh Majumdar
Department of Systems and Computer Engineering, Carleton University, Ottawa, Canada

Theepan Moorthy and Sathish Gopalakrishnan
The Department of Electrical and Computer Engineering, The University of British Columbia, Vancouver, BC, Canada

Abdelkhalik Mosa and Norman W. Paton
School of Computer Science, University of Manchester, Oxford Road, M13 9PL Manchester, UK

Danyang Cao and Jie Liu
College of Computer Science and Technology, North China University of Technology, Shijingshan, Beijing 100144, China

Norman Lim and Shikharesh Majumdar
Department of Systems and Computer Engineering, Carleton University, Ottawa, ON, Canada

Peter Ashwood-Smith
Huawei Technologies Canada, Kanata, ON, Canada

Index

Printed in the USA
CPSIA information can be obtained
at www.ICGtesting.com
JSHW051416221024
72173JS00006B/1368

9 781682 855966